Strikes in the United States 1881–1974

Warwick Studies in Industrial Relations

General Editors: G. S. Bain and H. A. Clegg

Also in this series

Strikes in the
United States 1881–1974

P. K. EDWARDS

BASIL BLACKWELL · OXFORD

© Social Science Research Council 1981

First published in 1981 by
Basil Blackwell Publisher
5 Alfred Street
Oxford OX1 4HB
England

British Library Cataloguing in Publication Data

Edwards, P K
   Strikes in the United States 1881–1974. – (Warwick
   studies in industrial relations).
   1. Strikes and lockouts – United States –
   History
   I. Title   II. Series
   331.89'2973   HD5324

   ISBN 0-631-12518-3

Typeset by Freeman Graphic, Tonbridge
Printed in Great Britain by the Blackwell Press Ltd,
Guildford, London, Oxford, Worcester

Contents

List of Tables

List of Figures

List of Abbreviations and Symbols

Strike Indices
N   Number of Strikes
ST   Number of *Strikers*
W   Number of *Workers Involved* in Strikes
D   Number of *Days Lost* in Strikes

Other Variables
A   Average *Annual* Earnings
B   Number of Employees in a Plant *Before* a Strike
C   Total *Civilian* Employment
E   Total Non-Agricultural *Employment*
H   Average *Hourly* Earnings
P   *Price* Level
P.P.   Political *Party of the President*
% Dem.   Per cent of Congress *Democrat*
Q   *Quarterly* Dummy
T   Number of *Trade Union* Members
U   Number *Unemployed*
(Hence the number of workers involved in strikes per head is given by
W/E, the unemployment rate by U/E, the level of real hourly wages by
H/P, and so on.)

Other Abbreviations
Ch   Proportionate Change in a Variable (i.e. Ch. H/P is the rate of
         change of real hourly wages)
D–W   Durbin–Waton Statistic
R^2 Coefficient of Determination, Corrected for Degrees of
         Freedom
—   In tables, signifies between zero and half last significant digit

Editor's Foreword

Warwick University's first undergraduates were admitted in 1965. The teaching of industrial relations began a year later, and in 1967 a one-year graduate course leading to an MA in Industrial Relations was introduced. Research in industrial relations also commenced in 1967 with a grant from the Clarkson Trustees, and received a major impetus in 1970 when the Social Science Research Council established its Industrial Relations Research Unit at the University.

The series of Warwick Studies in Industrial Relations was launched in 1972 as the main vehicle for the publication of the results of the Unit's projects. It is also intended to disseminate the research carried out by staff teaching industrial relations in the University. The first six titles in the series were published by Heinemann Educational Books of London, and subsequent volumes have been published by Basil Blackwell of Oxford.

Strikes are inevitably a central topic in industrial relations but detailed studies of long-term trends of strike activity are surprisingly rare. This absence is particularly notable in the United States where the rate of strike activity has always been high compared with that in other countries and where strikes have at times involved massive, bitter, and violent struggles between workers and employers. This study, begun by Paul Edwards at Oxford and substantially revised since he has been a research fellow in the Unit, repairs this omission. It analyses trends in strike activity over a period of almost a century and provides detailed estimates of the distribution of strikes between industries and of how this distribution has altered. It brings together in a coherent fashion a wide range of information about American strike patterns.

In explaining these patterns it asks two main questions: what do strikes show about the effect of industrialization on worker protest, and why has America's strike record been so different from that of other countries? On the first question it shows, contrary to many popular assumptions, that industrialization did not exert automatic or uniform effects but that industrial change affected the fortunes of key groups of workers in ways which had very different implications for their strike activity. It also shows that variations in strike activity between one year and the next have consistently reflected economic factors such as unemployment and price changes and not wider political influences. The overall pattern of strike activity, as measured by the frequency, size, and duration of strikes, has remained remarkably constant despite enormous industrial and institutional changes. This leads to the answer to the second question. America's high strike rate can be explained by a constant and unremitting struggle between employers and workers for control of the workplace. This struggle has been brought under institutional control by the establishment of collective bargaining on a wide scale but never eliminated.

George Bain
Hugh Clegg

Preface

It is now a hundred years since the first serious attempt to count strikes was made in the United States, as part of the population census of 1880. This book attempts to put strike experience during the intervening period in perspective. The exigencies of data collection mean that analysis stops with 1974 but events since then do not require that the interpretation of American strikes be fundamentally altered. My argument is that strikes have been longer, and often more violent, than those in other countries because they reflect an unremitting struggle between employers and workers for control of the workplace. In other countries the struggle has been politicized or brought under institutional control. In the United States similar tendencies have been weak because employers have been persistently hostile to trade unions and because unions have, as a result, been unable to establish a permanent and stable position. Developments since 1974 such as the continuing decline in levels of union membership and the flight of industry from the comparatively well-organized traditional industrial areas strengthens the view that unions have always had to fight for their existence. Prominent stoppages such as that in the coal industry in 1977–78 show workers' continued willingness to strike.

In arguing that strikes have reflected persistent struggles for control of the workplace, I direct considerable critical attention to the work of Edward Shorter and Charles Tilly, who are the major exponents of the view that strikes in most European countries reflected wider political forces. Although their work has serious problems of theory and method, it remains of fundamental importance in demonstrating the importance of worker strategy in strikes and in disposing of the myth that strikes reflected a blind and irrational response to the 'shock' of industrialization. My criticisms are to be seen as attempts to build upon these and other insights, for example in exploring in detail different patterns of response to industrialization, and not as an attack on the basic change in direction in studies of strikes which Shorter and Tilly's work represents.

My interest in patterns of strike activity began when I was a graduate student. I am deeply indebted to Alan Fox, John Goldthorpe and Anthony Heath for guiding this interest as well as for the broader sociological education which they provided. The present research was carried out under the supervision of Roderick Martin, to whom I owe my greatest debt for his sympathetic guidance in organizing a mass of statistical and historical material around a unified theme. John Goldthorpe and Anthony Heath also read all or part of the manuscript and made many useful comments. In preparing the present volume I have been greatly assisted by George Bain and Hugh Clegg who have gone through successive drafts with patience and good humour and whose comments have been of enormous benefit. I am also grateful to Connie Bussman and Norma Griffiths for typing the manuscript with great care and to Janet Godden for her meticulous editorial work.

Parts of Chapter 3 first appeared, in a different form, in the *British Journal of Industrial Relations* for November 1978. I am grateful to the editor of the Journal for permission to use this material here.

Thanks are due to the Social Science Research Council for funding the research through a post-graduate grant and, since the Council is responsible for the Industrial Relations Research Unit, for providing the opportunity of preparing the work in its present form. Between these two periods of a studentship from and employment by the SSRC I relied on my wife for financial, as well as the more usually-acknowledged moral, support. I am especially grateful to her for her continued belief in the research and for encouraging me to persist with it.

The help of all these people was invaluable. The lapses and limitations which doubtless remain are due not to a lack of effort on their part but to shortcomings in the original material or to my obstinacy in not accepting suggestions for improvement, for which I alone am responsible.

Paul Edwards

1

Introduction

This study describes and tries to explain the pattern of strike activity in the United States over a period of almost a century. Detailed reasons for the analysis of American strike patterns will be given below, but it is first necessary to indicate why the strike as such should be the object of attention.

Every strike is the product of a specific context of labour-management relations. Therefore, it might be suggested, to look at strikes alone is to bring together under one heading an extremely diverse set of phenomena. All strikes, however, involve the collective refusal to work under existing conditions of employment,[1] and represent a state of overt conflict between workers and their employers. It is true that there are many different types of strike: some strikes have a great and lasting impact whereas others have only a limited effect and are rapidly forgotten. But the purpose of concentrating on strikes is to see how often the strike weapon is used, where and when it is employed and with what effect, and so on. In other words, to examine strikes is not to assume that they constitute a homogeneous group. Indeed, the aim of this study is to show how the characteristics of American strikes have changed. The only assumption required in this is that the strike can be distinguished from other actions.

As argued at more length below,[2] strikes are collective and complete cessations of work. They are thus marked off, to a greater or lesser extent, from other forms of industrial action. Although conflict can be expressed in many ways, strikes can be seen as distinct phenomena which can be analysed in their own right. A study of strike patterns is not a substitute for the detailed examination of the various ways in

---

1. See F. Peterson, *Strikes in the United States, 1880–1936* (Washington, D.C.: U.S. Department of Labor Bulletin no. 651, 1938), p. 3.

2. See below, Appendix B, pp. 297–9.

1

which conflict is expressed, but it has the advantage of concentrating on behaviour which is undoubtedly 'conflict' and which is conceptually distinct from other actions.

Thus, the strike is treated here as an important form of collective action but is not used as an index of all aspects of such action. Trends in the characteristics of strikes can be used to assess various arguments about changes in the nature of worker protest, but the amount of strike activity cannot be used as a straightforward index of the amount of protest, since protest can be expressed in many different ways. Similarly, data on strikes cannot in themselves be used to argue that the amount of class conflict is increasing or decreasing. Brecher, for example, takes it for granted that an upsurge in strike activity indicates the presence of 'mass insurgence' and rank and file rebellion.[3] A strike may well be associated with intense class conflict, but there is no necessary link between the two things. In this study, patterns of strike activity are examined to consider the significance of particular episodes; for example, the nature and extent of the 'rank and file revolt' of the 1960s will be examined. But no assumptions are made about the implications of such episodes for wider social conflicts.

The main interest, then, is in patterns of strike activity. This implies a strong statistical focus. As will be seen in Chapter 3, the analysis of strike statistics, particularly from an econometric point of view, has become extremely popular recently. The usual procedure is to derive a theoretical model and use some measure of strike activity as the dependent variable. The dominant statistical technique is regression analysis. This study uses regression analysis and other techniques where appropriate, but its overall aim is wider than the testing of specific economic hypotheses. Instead of using strike trends as a convenient dependent variable, strikes themselves are the main interest: the aim is not to test particular models, but to examine what has been happening to strikes and why. This interest implies a longer-term focus than that which is common in econometric studies. Data on a limited period may be suitable for testing specific models, although, as will be seen in later chapters, this assumption has itself been questioned; but to analyse strike patterns the longest possible time span is needed.

The starting date of 1881 has been chosen since that is the first year for which adequate statistical information is available. Details of American strike statistics, together with a consideration of the problems of the use of such data, will be found in Appendix B. It is suf-

3. J. Brecher, *Strike: The True History of Mass Insurgence in America from 1877 to the Present* (San Francisco: Straight Arrow, 1972).

ficient to note here that, despite well-known problems with official statistics in general and strike statistics in particular, the American data are adequate for the analysis of broad trends of strike activity. For many purposes, particularly the analysis of responses to early industrialization, it would be desirable to go back before 1881. But this study is concerned with patterns of activity, and nothing systematic can be said on events before that date.

The pattern of strikes in the United States is of interest for several reasons. In simple quantitative terms, the country accounts for an important part of the world strike picture: in the period 1948–53, for example, over half the recorded days lost in strikes, and nearly a quarter of the workers involved, were in the United States.[4] No adequate treatment of American strike patterns has been made since the publication of Griffin's work in 1939.[5] The time is therefore ripe for a re-examination of strike trends.

The United States is important for other, more sociologically interesting, reasons. As will be shown below, its strike rate has been very high compared with that of other countries, but its labour movement has been among the least radical in political terms, and the absence of a permanent socialist movement has long puzzled scholars. The examination of strike trends can throw some light on this paradox of militancy combined with conservatism.[6] In particular, by revealing the nature of strike activity, it can contribute to an understanding of the militancy side of the paradox.

Apart from these general questions, some particular aspects of American strikes have attracted attention. For Ross and Hartman, writing in 1960, it was the failure of American strikes to 'wither away' which distinguished them from the general trend in industrialized countries.[7] For Shorter and Tilly in 1974 it was not the overall level of strike activity but its 'shape' which was important: in Europe the shape of strikes (as measured by their frequency, size, and duration) altered dramatically after the second world war, whereas in America it re-

---

4. 'Industrial Disputes, 1937–54', *International Labour Review*, LXXII, pp. 78–91 (1955) at pp. 88–9.
5. J. I. Griffin, *Strikes: a Study in Quantitative Economics* (New York: Columbia University Press, 1939).
6. On this paradox see, for example, S, Aronowitz, *False Promises: The Shaping of American Working Class Consciousness* (New York: McGraw-Hill, 1973), p. 259; S. Lens, *The Crisis of American Labor* (New York: Sagamore Press, 1959), p. 19.
7. A. M. Ross and P. T. Hartman, *Changing Patterns of Industrial Conflict* (New York: Wiley, 1960), esp. pp. 162–8.

mained unaltered.[8] Both groups of writers attempted to explain these findings but, although both research teams were based in America and staffed by Americans, neither study was based on a detailed examination of American strikes. This made their accounts of 'American exceptionalism' partial and superficial. The present study seeks to avoid these deficiencies by basing its explanation of the comparative position of American strikes on a detailed study of those strikes.

However, this is a case study, not a comparative analysis. Although international comparisons point to some interesting features of American strikes which warrant further investigation, the main interest lies elsewhere. In a period of almost a century, there have been dramatic changes in the nature and extent of American industry; the impact of industrialization on strikes is the main theme of later chapters. The United States makes a particularly useful example in that it is generally seen as a country in which industrial capitalism developed in an extreme form. The impact of industrialization should thus be seen in a clear light, without the obscuring effect of pre-industrial traditions.[9]

Studies of the effect of industrial change on social structures have a long history, and this is not the place to review them in detail. But it will be useful briefly to distinguish the main approaches to the problem of the link between industrialization and patterns of worker protest in general and strikes in particular. In a well-known statement, Kerr and his associates argue that:[10]

worker protest in the course of industrialization tends to peak relatively early and to decline in intensity thereafter . . . At the early stages the break with the traditional society is sharpest; the labour force is making the more basic and difficult adjustments to the discipline and pace of industry . . . The amount of latent protest at the early stages is related directly to the pace of industrial growth . . . [and] to the extent to which the new industrial order adapts or destroys the institutions of the traditional society.

8. E. Shorter and C. Tilly, *Strikes in France, 1830–1968* (Cambridge: Cambridge University Press, 1974), esp. pp. 306–30.
9. This is not to suggest that the United States lacked 'pre-industrial' values. As Chapter 4 will show, such values were often important. But the extent of their significance in restraining capitalist development seems to have been less than in Europe.
10. C. Kerr *et al.*, *Industrialism and Industrial Man* (British 2nd edn; Harmondsworth: Penguin, 1973), pp. 218–19. The view that the extent of conflict is greatest during early industrialization has a long history. It was, for example, explicitly stated by Engels in one of his more deterministic moments, with particular reference to the United States: see letter of Engels to Sorge, 31

Similarly, Siegel argues that the character of conflict changes.[11] In early industrialization it is amorphous and volatile, with large demonstrations which flare up and rapidly subside, but as time goes on expressions of protest become 'rational, predictable, and stylized' and their size and revolutionary potential decline. For Dunlop, the 'rule-making process ... becomes more explicit and formally constituted in the course of industrialization.'[12]

These arguments refer to industrial conflict in general and to the whole process of industrialization. Thus it might appear that they cannot properly be assessed against data on one form of conflict (strikes) over a limited period (the years since 1881). It is true that trends in the overall level of strike activity cannot measure trends in industrial conflict more generally. But the character of strike action should reflect the effects of industrialization. Strikes should stop being spontaneous and volatile, and become planned and organized actions.[13] And the overall level of strike activity should not be ignored. When worker protest is the focus, as it is for Kerr *et al.*, the strike must be given primary attention. In the United States in particular, it has dominated other expressions of protest. Such actions have of course been significant at various times, notably during the Civil Rights movements, but their relevance for the analysis of specifically work-oriented protest is unclear. If long-term trends of protest are to be examined, the strike must be the major topic of concern.

The period since 1881 is not ideal for an examination of 'early' protest. But the writers under consideration are themselves vague about the timing of the peak of discontent which should accompany early industrialization. And 'the break with the traditional society' must be a lengthy process. Changes in American industry during the 1880s, such as the growth of large-scale industry, the breakdown of 'craft' forms of the division of labour, and the emergence of 'trusts', certainly marked a

---

December 1892, reprinted in K. Marx and F. Engels, *Letters to Americans, 1848–1895: A Selection*, ed. A. Trachtenberg (New York: International Publishers, 1953), p. 244.

11. A. J. Siegel, 'Method and Substance in Theorizing about Worker Protest', *Aspects of Labor Economics*, National Bureau of Economic Research (Princeton: Princeton University Press, 1962), pp. 21–52, following quotation from p. 44. See also C. Kerr, 'Changing Industrial Structures', *Labor Commitment and Social Change in Developing Areas*, ed. W. E. Moore and A. S. Feldman (New York: Social Science Research Council, 1960), pp. 348–59.
12. J. T. Dunlop, *Industrial Relations Systems* (Carbondale: Southern Illinois University Press, 1970), p. 343.
13. More detailed predictions about strikes will be taken up in Chapter 4.

break with the past,[14] and should have affected the character of strike action. Moreover, a contrast should be evident between industries which were undergoing a break with the past and sectors which had not yet reached this stage or had already passed through it.

An alternative approach to that of Kerr must be briefly outlined. The general arguments of the 'logic of industrialism' school have come in for widespread criticism.[15] But the specific arguments on strikes have recently been subjected to sustained attack by Shorter and Tilly. At the general level Shorter and Tilly point out that, although 'breakdown' may lead to discontent, there will be a concomitant fall in workers' capacity for collective organization. As a result, the amount of strike activity need not peak during the early stages of industrialization.[16] And, at the empirical level, they note that there are several aspects of strike activity which conventional theories cannot explain. For example, the tendency for strikes to occur in waves cannot be explained by industrialization (nor, according to Shorter and Tilly, by interpretations stressing economic conditions or feelings of 'anger' and 'alienation' among workers).[17]

Shorter and Tilly's own view is that two key factors have been ignored in conventional accounts of industrialization. The first is organization: collective action is possible on a large scale only when workers are well-organized, and organization is the crucial variable intervening between the structural changes induced by industrialization and expressions of protest. The second factor is politics: strike activity need not decline as industrialization advances, because strikes come to serve new ends as means of exerting pressure in the political arena to be used whenever the interests of the working class are threatened. Strike

14. For arguments that these changes marked a distinctly 'early' stage, see, for example, S. D. Hays, *The Response to Industrialism, 1885–1914* (Chicago: University of Chicago Press, 1957), p. 1; H. L. Wilensky and C. N. Lebeaux, *Industrial Society and Social Welfare* (New York: Russell Sage, 1958), pp. 87–8.

15. See, for example, J. H. Goldthorpe, 'Social Stratification in Industrial Societies', *Class, Status and Power,* ed. R. Bendix and S. M. Lipset (2nd edn; London: Routledge, 1967) pp. 648–59.

16. Shorter and Tilly, op. cit., p. 8. Shorter and Tilly attribute to Kerr the view that early industrialization leads to material deprivations, in contrast to the view attributed to Smelser that the breakdown of pre-existing cultural values is the key. But, from the passage quoted above, it is clear that Kerr *et al.* produce 'breakdown' as well as 'deprivation' arguments. Cf. N. J. Smelser, *Social Change in the Industrial Revolution* (Chicago: University of Chicago Press, 1959).

17. Shorter and Tilly, op. cit., pp. 344–5.

activity may even be increased, because the concentration of workers in large cities and factories improves worker organization, and because increasing politicization provides a more important focus for strikes than sectional economic interests.[18]

The 'organizational-political' model as employed by Shorter and Tilly and other writers[19] has highlighted several important weaknesses with earlier theories and provides a more generally satisfactory approach to early industrial protest. But it is also specifically concerned with the modern pattern of strikes, whereas earlier writers, in line with Ross and Hartman's views on the withering away of the strike, gave it little attention. In this study the development of the modern strike pattern is as important as the initial response to industrialization. Industrial change did not cease after the first use of factory methods, and the later developments of mass production and automated methods carried equally important implications for the amount and character of worker protest. An understanding of 'modern' strikes can be developed only when such developments are given explicit attention.

A second advantage of the organizational-political approach is that it focuses attention on the interaction between technical change and institutional factors. It replaces the assumption that industrialization had certain inevitable effects on worker protest with the view that these effects were mediated by institutional factors. It follows that institutional developments in the 'modern' period must also be given attention. For writers in this tradition, the key turning-point for strike trends was not the end of early and rapid industrialization but a dramatic institutional change. During the 1930s Social Democratic governments in several countries began to take over many functions which had previously been left to market forces. Many key battles were thus moved from the economic to the political arena, and the nature of strike activity changed as a result. Strikes were no longer struggles with individual employers but symbolic means of putting pressure on the political centre. As demonstrations, they became shorter and larger than previous 'economic' strikes.

As Shorter and Tilly recognize, the view that the strike was transformed during the 1930s does not apply to the United States. Thus subsequent chapters will not attempt to apply the organizational-political model to the United States or to test it against American data,

18. Ibid., pp. 234–5.
19. D. A. Hibbs, 'Industrial Conflict in Advanced Industrial Societies', *American Political Science Review*, LXX, pp. 1033–58 (1976); W. Korpi and M. Shalev, 'Strikes, Industrial Relations and Class Conflict in Capitalist Societies', *British Journal of Sociology*, XXX, pp. 164–87 (1979).

since it is apparent from the outset that it cannot be used as it stands. However, the model provides the most convenient framework for examining the links between structural changes and institutional factors: although the political side may not be directly applicable, the organizational aspects can be tested more directly. And, by assessing the nature of modern strike patterns, the model gives a useful starting-point for the analysis of long-term trends of strike activity.

Although users of the organizational-political model seek to explain 'American exceptionalism', this issue is not discussed here until the final chapter. There is a fundamental problem of the link between theory and evidence in this area, which makes it more satisfactory to put forward an account of international differences at the end of the analysis than to advance a new account at the outset and proceed to 'test' it against the data. The problem may be considered in relation to the work of Shorter and Tilly, where the attempt to provide a rigorous and well-specified theory raises it in particularly acute form.

Shorter and Tilly outline their political account and claim that, 'by laying out great slabs of data',[20] they are able to test it. In fact, they provide remarkably little raw data and these data have, of course, been selected and combined in various ways. It has become a commonplace that the presentation of certain data involves the suppression of other information and that all processes of selection are 'theory-impregnated'.[21] But there are degrees of severity in this problem, and the study of strike trends falls at the 'severe' end of the spectrum. At the most general level, an account of French strikes which stresses the political involvement of trade unions is bound to turn out to be broadly consistent with the data. The characteristics of French unions are so well-known that a theory about them cannot be seen as logically prior to relevant evidence.

It is true that Shorter and Tilly derive specific hypotheses from their general theory and that several of these can be directly tested. For example, the writers are able to demonstrate a concentration of strikes in the Paris region, which is consistent with their view that strikes are used to put pressure on the political centre.[22] But such evidence is of only limited value in testing the writers' more general theories. For example, the fact that strike waves tend to coincide with indices of political crisis says nothing about the causal relationship between the two.

20. Shorter and Tilly, op. cit., p. 9.
21. K. R. Popper, *Objective Knowledge: An Evolutionary Approach* (Oxford: Clarendon Press, 1973), esp. pp. 71–72.
22. Shorter and Tilly, op. cit., p. 283.

Other examples of the failure of specific pieces of evidence to support more general claims could be given,[23] but most significant here is Shorter and Tilly's attempt to show that union organization was a necessary factor intervening between structural conditions and strikes. On general grounds, some form of organization may well be necessary for strikes to occur. But at this level any theory stressing organization is virtually axiomatic. At a more specific level, Shorter and Tilly can show a tendency for strike activity and levels of union organization to be associated, but this cannot establish the necessity of the latter for the former. Indeed, on the basis of one case study it is impossible to show whether certain changes in union organization were necessary or merely contingent.

Shorter and Tilly have followed the common practice of claiming to have applied hard, 'scientific' tests to a clearly-specified theory. Their data are consistent with their theory, but it is hard to imagine how that theory could be made strictly scientific, that is how it could be made refutable. This point applies in particular to international comparisons of strike activity, and is the reason why the account to be advanced here will be reserved until the final chapter. There is only one set of advanced industrialized countries on which a theory of the effect of industrialization can be tested. Once an account of international differences has been produced which is broadly consistent with the data, there are no new data which can be called on to refute it. However, a new account may explain features of strikes which have remained puzzling in other accounts or may provide a more generally illuminating interpretation. In the present case, a general account of American strikes will be produced which, it is hoped, avoids the weaknesses which are identified in other interpretations. But this account grew out of the data and of reflections on previous analyses, and it would be wrong to pretend otherwise.

This study is concerned, then, with patterns of strike activity within the context of industrial change. It attempts to assess various theories of the impact of industrialization, but without assuming that a specific interpretation can be rigorously tested. The United States provides a particularly useful basis for the study, given the country's position in

23. For example, they say of union members who struck in the period 1880–1910 that 'not all these unionists were "revolutionary", but the bulk of their strikes were nonetheless fundamentally political' (Shorter and Tilly, op. cit., p. 75). No data on stated strike issues support this assertion and in any case it has already been said that 'the poorest way of knowing what workers want in strikes is to go by what they say they want' (op. cit., p. 66).

the world strike picture and its history of industrial growth relatively unfettered by 'extraneous' influences.

Within this general approach, particular issues naturally require attention. The most important of these is the view that industrial conflict has become 'institutionalized': as unions have established themselves and become acceptable to management, conflict has been channeled into institutions such as grievance procedures and has ceased to be expressed in strikes.[24] The significance of this view will be taken up in later chapters, but is mentioned here for three reasons. Firstly, Shorter and Tilly's approach clearly has close affinities with a more general theory of institutionalization in that both stress the key role of trade unions in the amount and nature of industrial conflict; moreover, both argue for a change in the pattern of strikes once unions become established. In concentrating on Shorter and Tilly, later chapters will not treat them in isolation but will attempt to relate their arguments to a wider body of literature. Secondly, if unions are crucial in the mediation of structural factors, some consideration is required of how this process occurs. The institutionalization thesis provides a convenient means to consider this process and will be used as a focus for the discussion of the detailed impact of the 'institutionalization' of unions on strikes. Thirdly, most American versions of the thesis stress collective bargaining as the key factor in the alteration of strike patterns. Since the arrival of collective bargaining on a wide scale came well after the main period of industrial growth, it is possible to compare the effects on strikes of industrialization as such with those of the growth of bargaining.

In discussing such matters as the institutionalization of unions and the impact of industrialization, some key examples will be given, but the aim is not to produce a narrative account of American strikes; the use of qualitative material will be selective. The focus is on general trends, with strike statistics forming the core of the analysis. Such an approach is not an alternative to more detailed investigations but is complementary to them. As argued above, the success of an interpretation of strikes at the macro level can be measured by the extent to which aspects of the strike picture are illuminated; one test of this is the interpretation's consistency with more detailed studies. Considerable use will therefore be made of secondary materials, but only in so

---

24. For the 'classic' arguments on this, see R. A. Lester, *As Unions Mature* (Princeton: Princeton University Press, 1958); R. Dubin, 'Constructive Aspects of Industrial Conflict', *Industrial Conflict,* ed. A. Kornhauser, R. Dubin and A. M. Ross (New York: McGraw-Hill, 1954), pp. 37–47.

far as they affect the general argument. The main contribution of this study lies in the use of statistical methods to unravel and explain strike patterns in one important country. It tries to answer one large question: how and why has the American strike picture altered during the enormous industrial and institutional changes of the past century?

2

The Trend of Strikes, 1881–1974

Overall Strike-proneness

Throughout this study, the symbols N, W, and D represent, respectively, the numbers of strikes, workers involved, and 'days lost'. Thus, W/N indicates the mean size of strikes, D/N the number of days lost per strike, and so on. Since the number of strikes means little in itself, the index of strike frequency is the number of strikes per non-agricultural employee; writing E for employment, this may be represented as N/E. Similarly, the indices W/E and D/E give the relative measures for worker involvement and days lost. Ross and Hartman have suggested that trade union membership, which is represented here by the symbol T, is a more useful deflator than is total employment because union members are the group most likely to strike; and indices using T will measure workers' ability to *organize and strike*.[1] The following discussion therefore includes the measures W/T and D/T.

The indices mentioned above are given in Table 2.1 for ten year periods from 1881 to 1970, plus the period 1971–74. A more detailed breakdown is given in Table A.1 in Appendix A, while Table A.2 puts the information in relative form, with the indices for 1927–29 set at 100. The sources for these tables, and for all other tables where a source is not specifically mentioned, are given in Appendix D. The data are generally comparable, but in estimating employment for the years up to 1920 several different series have had to be used, so that the figures are far from being totally reliable, although they are adequate for the estimation of trends.

If trade unions are the key factor in the level of industrial conflict, one would expect their arrival on a major scale in the 1930s to exert an important effect on the amount of strike activity. The precise nature of

---

1. A. M. Ross and P. T. Hartman, *Changing Patterns of Industrial Conflict* (New York: Wiley, 1960), pp. 11–12.

TABLE 2.1

STRIKE INDICES BY DECADES, 1881–1974

	W/N no.	D/N 000s	D/W no.	W/T × 1000	D/T no.	N/E × 1m.	W/E × 1000	D/E no.
1881–90	282			737		99.1	28.0	
1891–1900	274			860		113	31.0	
1901–10	179			282		162	29.0	
1911–20	397			434		143	56.7	
1921–30	521			163		40.6	21.1	
1931–40	432	6.60	15.3	182	2.78	79.6	34.4	0.525
1941–50	604	8.76	14.5	186	2.69	98.9	59.8	0.866
1951–60	510	7.88	15.5	124	1.91	80.2	40.9	0.632
1961–70	462	7.44	16.1	106	1.71	69.5	32.1	0.517
1971–74	465	6.98	15.0			72.0	33.5	0.503

NOTE
The units in which the indices are expressed will be clear from the following examples:

no.: simple number; e.g. in 1971–74 the mean size of strike (W/N) was 465 workers.

000s: thousands; e.g. in 1971–74 the average strike involved the loss of 6,980 days.

× 1m.: index multiplied by one million; in 1971–74 there were 72 strikes per million non-agricultural workers.

SOURCE
See Appendix D, which contains information on the sources of all tables where a source is not mentioned.

the effect is unclear, since it could be argued that unions allow protest which was previously hidden to become overt (so that strike activity increases), or that they provide means to channel protest in peaceful directions (with the result that the level of activity falls). But one effect or the other should operate. The standard theory of the institutionalization of conflict, referred to briefly in the previous chapter, takes the latter view, but a variant, associated particularly with the work of Kerr, argues that conflict will peak in the early years of industrialization and then decline.[2] This variant thus expects the level of strike activity to fall to a low level once the 'early' stage of industrial growth has been passed. Various versions of the institutionalization theory expect strike

2. C. Kerr *et al.*, *Industrialism and Industrial Man* (Harmondsworth: Penguin, 1973), pp. 218–19. Note the difficulty of deciding what exactly constitutes 'early' industrialization.

activity to decline at one time or another; Shorter and Tilly's argument, discussed in Chapter 1, does not say whether activity will increase or decrease with the arrival of mass unionism, but some change in the strike pattern should be apparent.[3]

The evidence fits none of these hypotheses closely since the watershed between periods of high and low strike activity came at around 1920, after the United States had become heavily industrialized and before widespread 'union implantation' and collective bargaining.[4] This is borne out further in Figure 2.1, which gives a five-year moving average of strike frequency; the advantage of this method is that it reduces the impact of 'exceptional' years while showing the year-to-year trends of activity. Strike frequency rose during the 1880s, fell in the 1890s and then rose to peak levels in the early years of the present century. It remained high until the 1920s, when a dramatic decline occurred. The militancy of the 1930s was not sufficient to raise the index to pre-1920 levels. Since 1940, there has been a historically low number of strikes per head, with a decline in the 1950s and some recovery subsequently.

It could be argued that this pattern reflects the processes described by institutionalization theorists. Those stressing industrialization might suggest that there is a time-lag between the shift to an industrial economy and the decline in strike activity, while a supporter of the role of bargaining could suggest that the system introduced in the 1930s has contained conflict at low levels. The former argument is hard to assess since there is no prediction in the theory about the length of the time-lag, but on the whole it is not plausible. The first two decades of the present century cannot be equated with the period of 'early' protest identified in the theory and the rapid decline of activity in the 1920s cannot be seen as a case of the workers coming to terms with industry. The economy had been industrialized for far too long for this to be plausible, and specific reasons for the marked fall in strike frequency in the twenties can be adduced.[5] Moreover, the arguments from industrialization see the strike as an immediate and spontaneous protest

---

3. E. Shorter and C. Tilly, *Strikes in France, 1830–1968* (Cambridge: Cambridge University Press, 1974).

4. The contrast between the years before and after 1920 would be even more marked if, as Appendix B suggests, estimates of strike frequency for 1906–15 under-estimate the level of activity, compared with data for previous and subsequent periods. No official data exist for 1906–15, and indirect estimates may be unsatisfactory: see below, pp. 303–5, especially Table B.1.

5. Four reasons are suggested by H. M. Douty, 'The Trend of Industrial Disputes, 1922–1930', *Journal of the American Statistical Association*, XXVII,

FIGURE 2.1
**FIVE YEAR MOVING AVERAGE OF NUMBER OF STRIKES PER MILLION
NON-AGRICULTURAL EMPLOYEES, 1883–1973**

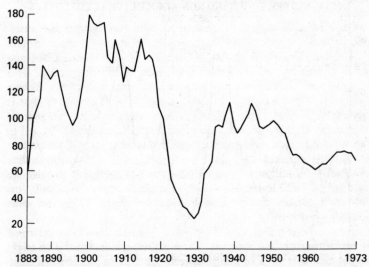

against new conditions: there should be a very close link between industrial growth and strike activity. In other words, the time-lag hypothesis is not consistent with the rest of the theory.

The argument that the growth of collective bargaining was crucial has a greater plausibility: after a period of conflict in the 1930s, when unions were struggling for recognition, and the 1940s, when the conflict turned on the scope of collective bargaining, strike frequency declined to very low levels. This theory would not pretend to give a complete account of the movements of strike activity, but would merely suggest that it can explain what has happened since the thirties. However, the data for the period from 1881 as a whole show that the decline in activity since 1950 is relatively insignificant. Although a fall can be observed, the period since 1940 looks on Figure 2.1 more like a plateau than a downward slope. The plateau is certainly lower than that

pp. 168–72 (1932) at pp. 171–72: a relatively stable price level and a rise in money wages; the growth of company unions and welfare plans; a lack of aggression by the labour movement; and the effect of increased industrial concentration on corporations' power. Cf. I. Bernstein, *The Lean Years* (Cambridge, Mass.: Houghton-Mifflin, 1960), pp. 84–103; G. Soule, *Prosperity Decade* (London: Pilot Press, 1947), pp. 198–227.

FIGURE 2.2

**FIVE-YEAR MOVING AVERAGE OF NUMBER OF WORKERS INVOLVED
IN STRIKES PER THOUSAND NON-AGRICULTURAL EMPLOYEES,
1883–1973**

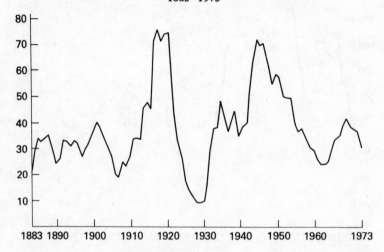

for the early years of the century, but the explanation of the shift to a low level of strike frequency need not lie in the institutionalization theory. The experience of the 1920s might have led to an alteration in workers' militancy which the subsequent depression did not reverse.[6]

These points also apply to Shorter and Tilly, who similarly expect a change in strike activity during the 1930s. 'Union implantation' seems to have increased strike frequency in the short-term, but there are no very marked differences between the periods before and after the 1930s.

As Appendix B shows in detail, there are weaknesses with the index of strike frequency: in particular, any trend towards the centralization of bargaining or an increase in the size of establishments will exert a downward influence on the number of separate disputes recorded. Thus the evidence on worker involvement must be considered. The data in the tables and the graphical presentation in Figure 2.2 indicate that the

6. It might be argued that the institutionalization theory is still *consistent* with the data, and cannot be rejected. However, an alternative account, based on specific historical factors, is more parsimonious than one which postulates a general process towards harmony.

level of worker involvement has been remarkably constant in the long-term. Although there was a marked fall during the 1950s, the level reached at the bottom of the trough in the early 1960s was very similar to that prevailing at the end of the nineteenth century: the moving average of worker involvement has fluctuated around the level of thirty workers involved in strikes per thousand non-agricultural employees and has shown no long-term tendency to rise or fall.[7] The two great peaks in the series indicate the strike waves which occurred after each of the world wars.

Data on days lost are available only since 1927 and are thus less valuable than those on worker involvement in assessing long-term trends, but they are useful as far as they go. Tables 2.1 and A.1, and Figure 2.3, show that there has been no overall tendency for strike volume (D/E) to decline. The year-to-year changes parallel those in worker involvement, although the amplitude of the fluctuations is greater; in particular, the rise in activity during the 1960s is very marked. A corollary of this parallel movement with worker involvement is a fairly constant number of days lost per striker (D/W). Since the 'average striker' has consistently lost about fifteen days, it does not seem that what might be called the intensity of conflict has changed.

Strike Duration
As noted in Appendix C, the D/W index is not an unbiased estimate of the average duration of strikes. The direct evidence on average duration is therefore given in Table 2.2, which shows the mean and median duration of stoppages, and Table A.3, which gives a more detailed breakdown by categories of duration.

The mean strike has consistently lasted about twenty days, and the median strike about ten days. The meaning of the information on duration by worker involvement and striker-days is less straightforward,

---

7. Note that any tendency towards the increased size of plants and the interdependence of operations is likely to increase the number of workers recorded as 'involved' in strikes, because indirect as well as direct involvement is included. But the extent of this tendency is limited since workers indirectly involved are included only when they are employed in the same plants as workers directly involved. And the upward bias in worker involvement is unlikely to be very great; we are concerned with changes over time and not absolute levels, and there has probably always been some interdependence of operations (see below, Table 4.4, for a comparison of direct and indirect involvement in the period 1881–1905). There are counter-trends; for example, employers are less prone than they were in the past to lock out their entire work forces, so that total worker involvement tends to be more closely related to direct involvement.

FIGURE 2.3

**FIVE-YEAR MOVING AVERAGE OF NUMBER OF STRIKER-DAYS PER
THOUSAND NON-AGRICULTURAL EMPLOYEES, 1929–73**

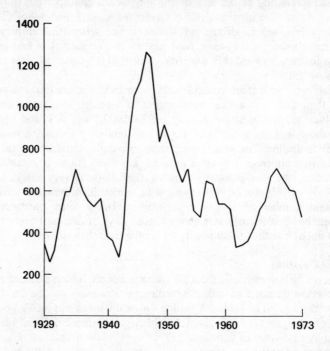

since the term 'mean striker-day', for example, does not immediately
signify very much. What it shows is the length of the strike in which the
'average' day was lost; since this is much greater than the length of the
average strike, most days are lost in long stoppages. Not only have the
mean and median strikes remained much the same length, but there has
also been a marked constancy in the proportion of stoppages of a given
length. For example, as Table A.3 shows, strikes lasting one day but less
than two days account for just over 10 per cent of the total, while
those of seven to fourteen days' duration account for about 20 per
cent. This table also shows the extent of the concentration of workers
involved and days lost in the longest strikes. Well over 40 per cent of all

TABLE 2.2

MEAN AND MEDIAN DURATION OF STRIKES IN DAYS, 1881–1974

	Estimates of Mean By Number of Strikes			Median
	(1)	(2)	(3)	
1881–85	27.3	26.0	24.5	11.8
1886–89	19.8	24.9	25.2	9.13
1890–93	17.2	28.8	28.2	7.44
1894–97		26.1	26.4	
1898–1901		25.8	35.1	
1902–05		31.1	34.3	
1906–08		16.1		
1909–11		14.3		
1912–13		15.6		

	By Number of Strikes		By Workers Involved		By Days Lost	
	Mean	Median	Mean	Median	Mean	Median
1916–18	19.1	8.78				
1919–22	36.6	9.52				
1923–25	24.5	11.8				
1927–29	24.8	12.3	43.2	22.5	103	112
1930–33	20.2	10.7	27.7	16.9	60.6	50.5
1934–37	22.6	11.9	24.8	13.8	54.9	45.7
1938–41	21.8	11.0	21.9	12.6	49.5	53.6
1942–45	8.69	4.00	10.4	5.33	27.1	20.5
1946–49	23.7	11.4	31.1	17.4	67.7	54.4
1950–53	19.8	8.69	25.5	11.7	63.7	53.4
1954–57	20.1	9.53	22.2	10.7	58.7	49.7
1958–61	22.6	10.4	31.7	16.1	79.2	90.9
1962–65	23.0	10.3	24.4	12.9	60.3	50.9
1966–69	22.9	10.7	26.9	12.8	66.1	57.7
1970–72	25.3	11.3	25.9	11.5	77.8	82.7
1973–74	25.1	12.0	24.1	13.1	58.8	39.2

NOTE

For 1881–1913, the median and estimate (1) for the mean are from part (a) of Table A.3, relating to the detailed evidence on 'cessations'. Estimate (2) for the mean is from J. I. Griffin, *Strikes: A Study in Quantitative Economics* (New York: Columbia University Press, 1939), p. 87. Estimate (3) is from Commissioner of Labor data on mean duration per establishment involved.

For 1916–74, B.L.S. data are used (cf. Griffin, loc. cit., where it is stated that the B.L.S. did not compute strike data for 1916–26; the data are reported in the various annual articles on strikes and lockouts in the *Monthly Labor Review,* usually the May or June issue each year). Estimates assume that the mid-point of the '90 days and over' category of duration is 120 days.

striker-days occur in stoppages lasting for over sixty days, whereas only 5 per cent or less occur in disputes that last for less than a week.[8]

The only major deviation from the pattern of a constant strike length occurred in the period 1942–45 when the mean and the median duration fell markedly. The reason for this was, of course, the efforts by the government and most union leaders to prevent strikes from breaking out during the war years. It is interesting that, on the limited evidence available, a similar pattern does not seem to have occurred in the first world war, despite the fact that 'no-strike' pledges were made in both wars. Many reasons may be suggested for this, but most interesting here is what may be called the 'radical' view, that between the wars unions became more effectively 'incorporated'; the argument would be that in the second world war the unions were prepared to work with the Administration in discouraging strikes that were seen as threats to national security, whereas in the first they were less willing and able to do this.

Since strike frequency during the second world war was greater than in previous and subsequent periods, and worker involvement remained at high levels, it seems that there was a problem of rank and file dissatisfaction facing the union leaders; although it was possible to impose quick settlements, and although the leaders could cite the low volume of strikes as evidence for labour's commitment to the war, the presence of large, frequent, and short stoppages suggests that strikes were being used as rank and file protests. The available evidence does not show any such marked change in strike patterns during the first world war. There is evidence that in the so-called 'Defense' period, as well as during the second war itself, union leaders were prepared to help the government in restraining strikes wherever possible.[9] Between 1916 and 1918 the labour movement was much more divided in its attitude to the war and some of the most significant strikes were carried out by the Industrial Workers of the World (I.W.W.) or were without formal union involvement.[10]

8. This bears out the view that series on worker involvement and days lost are highly reliable: their heavy concentration in long strikes means that the missing of short stoppages biases the figures very little. See below, Appendix B, pp. 295–6.

9. J. Seidman, *American Labor from Defense to Reconstruction* (Chicago: University of Chicago Press, 1953), pp. 24, 48, 132; A. Preis, *Labor's Giant Step* (New York: Pathfinder Press, 1972), pp. 99–131, 184–86, 212; M. Josephson, *Sidney Hillman* (New York: Doubleday, 1952), chaps 21 and 22. See also Chapter 5, below.

10. A. M. Bing, *Wartime Strikes and Their Adjustment* (New York: E. P. Dutton, 1921); J. S. Gambs, *The Decline of the I.W.W.* (New York: Russell and

Strikes between 1942 and 1945 cannot be seen as revolutionary or even as being directed specifically against the war: the main focus was the level of wages, since wage increases were controlled but prices were still rising. The strikes can, to some extent, be seen as protests against the government and union leaders and the 'radical' view thus receives some support. But it must also be said that the general level of support for the second war was greater than that for the first;[11] in other words, the shift in strike patterns was not due solely to union collaboration with the government. This question cannot be considered further here, but it is important to note that the 1942—45 period was the only one in which American strikes fitted the pattern of being short demonstrations of protest. The significance of this will be considered further in the following section.

The lack of any trend in the duration of strikes is remarkable in view of the marked changes which have been observed in other countries.[12] The reasons for the distinctive pattern of American strikes will be considered at length in the final chapter, but the implications of the evidence on strike duration for various theories must be noted briefly. A standard expectation is that collective bargaining will make strikes shorter, because means are provided for the settlement of disputes short of waiting for the exhaustion of one of the parties; and bargaining is also said to mean that conflicts are no longer over fundamental matters, so that there is less reason for strikes to be lengthy battles.[13] Whatever

---

Russell, 1966), pp. 36—52; M. Dubofsky, *We Shall Be All* (Chicago: Quadrangle Books, 1969), pp. 349—448; D. Montgomery, 'The "New Unionism" and the Transformation of Workers' Consciousness in America, 1909—22', *Journal of Social History*, VII, pp. 509—29 (1974).

11. Seidman, op. cit., p. 275. See also G. W. Taylor, 'Labor's No-strike Pledge: A Statistical View', *War Labor Policies*, Vol. 1 of *Yearbook of American Labor*, ed. C. E. Warne *et al.* (New York: Philosophical Library, 1945), pp. 137—42.

12. See Shorter and Tilly, op. cit., pp. 306—30; Ross and Hartman, op. cit., esp. pp. 70—81.

13. See, for example, P. Taft, 'The Philosophy of the American Labor Movement', *Labor in a Changing America*, ed. W. Haber (New York: Basic Books, 1966), pp. 133—42. The view that the duration of strikes will fall is not often stated explicitly, but is implicit in a large body of literature: see, for example, J. T. Dunlop, 'The Function of the Strike', *The Frontiers of Collective Bargaining*, ed. J. T. Dunlop and N. W. Chamberlain (New York: Harper and Row, 1967), pp. 103—21. The implications of such analyses for strike trends are analysed at length in P. K. Edwards, 'Strikes in the United States, 1881—1972: a Critical Examination of the Theory of the Institutionalization of Industrial Conflict' (D. Phil. thesis, University of Oxford, 1977), pp. 79—90.

the validity of these arguments in general, the evidence on strike duration does not support them. Similarly, little support is given to Shorter
and Tilly's theory: if the coming of collective bargaining altered the
nature of worker mobilization, there is no evidence that this had any
effect on the length of strikes. Strikes have not become brief demonstrations of protest.

The Incidence of Large Strikes

Although some writers argue that collective bargaining will make strikes
less frequent and shorter, others suggest that those stoppages which
still occur will be large battles, because both sides are able to mobilize
massive resources.[14] This view may be assessed by examining Table 2.3,
which shows the incidence of large strikes from 1927 to 1974, combining periods of three or four years to avoid the problem of 'exceptional'
years. The expectation that large strikes will become more significant is
not borne out: such strikes have not accounted for a rising proportion
of stoppages, workers involved or days lost. There is no overall trend in
any of the three indices despite the changes in industrial relations which
have occurred since the 1930s. Even during the second world war large
strikes were important, which contrasts with the decline in the duration
of strikes during the war years. There was a fall in the incidence of large
strikes in the 1950s but an increase in the 1960s which, as Chapter 6
suggests in more detail, can be related to pressures such as inflation.
Thus the trend of large strikes supports neither the view that large-scale
conflicts will become more important nor the alternative hypothesis
that the growth of moderation will make national stoppages less likely.

The Shape of Strikes

Shorter and Tilly have measured the shape of strike activity by drawing
a box the sides of which indicate the mean size (W/N), the frequency
(N/E), and the duration of strikes.[15] They prefer the median to the
mean as the measure of duration so that extreme values will not be
given disproportionate weight. The median also has the advantage,
when one is calculating from a frequency distribution, of being relatively unambiguous, whereas the estimate for the mean will depend on

14. For an interesting early statement of such a view, see J. Mitchell, *Organized
     Labor* (Philadelphia: American Book and Bible House, 1903), pp. 299, 347,
     354. See also E. T. Hiller, *The Strike* (Chicago: University of Chicago Press,
     1928), p. 65; S. and B. Webb, *Industrial Democracy* (2nd edn; London:
     Longmans, Green & Co., 1914), p. 221.
15. Shorter and Tilly, op. cit., pp. 46–56.

TABLE 2.3

INCIDENCE OF LARGE STRIKES, 1927–74

	Percentage of Strike Measures Accounted for by Strikes Each Involving at least 10,000 Workers		
	N	W	D
1927–29	0.3	34.0	45.3
1930–33	0.8	35.7	34.0
1934–37	0.6	37.0	31.0
1938–41	0.4	36.2	27.5
1942–45	0.5	29.9	46.9
1946–49	0.5	57.3	58.6
1950–53	0.5	33.4	48.0
1954–57	0.5	36.0	42.3
1958–61	0.5	39.5	57.3
1962–65	0.4	26.4	27.7
1966–69	0.6	36.2	42.1
1970–72	0.5	47.5	46.9
1973–74	0.5	30.8	25.0

assumptions about how strikes are distributed over the final open-ended category (in America, strikes with a duration of '90 days and over'). However, neither measure of duration gives an unambiguous meaning to the volume of the box which is created. To obtain a measure of the volume of strikes, D/E, the measure of average duration would have to be replaced by the number of days lost per worker involved, D/W. As a comparison of the relevant columns of Tables 2.2 and A.1 will show, D/W is not the same as the average duration of strikes. For any one strike, D/W is equivalent to the duration, but the relationship does not hold in the aggregate because one is dealing with averages. This is explained more fully in Appendix C. Despite this limitation of the figures for average duration, they provide an indication of how long strikes lasted, and are thus of more interest here than the D/W measure. To obtain a comprehensive view of changes in strike shapes, both the mean and the median will be used.

Shorter and Tilly argue that in France strikes have been growing larger, shorter, and more frequent; that is, the W/N and N/E dimensions of the box have increased, while the duration has declined. Figures 2.4 and 2.5 show the shapes of American strikes for selected periods, by mean and median duration respectively. The dramatic change of shape which occurred in other countries has been absent. When the median is considered, the shape in 1881–85 is not very different from that in the 1920s and early thirties. Although more recently there has been an

FIGURE 2.4

STRIKE SHAPES, BY MEAN DURATION

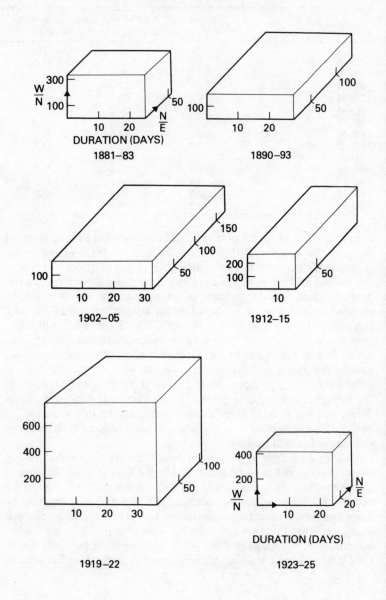

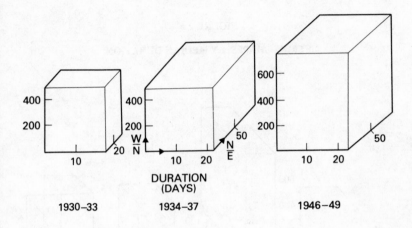

1930–33   1934–37   1946–49

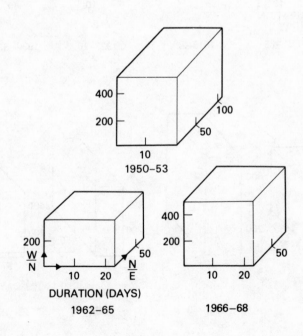

FIGURE 2.5

STRIKE SHAPES, BY MEDIAN DURATION

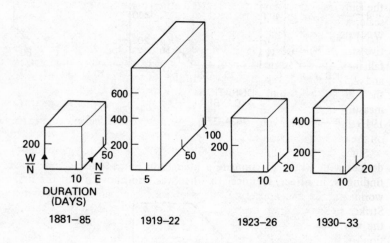

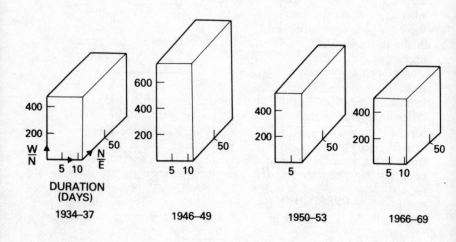

increase on the N/E dimension, this has not been accompanied by any fall in the median duration. For the mean duration, the boxes for the periods after the first world war are of a very similar shape, but before the war there is a tendency for them to be 'flat' in that the strikes are relatively small, but frequent, and with quite a high duration.

It is important to be clear what these boxes signify. Their shape shows only the relationship between the three dimensions and, since the scale on which each dimension is measured is a matter of choice, the only relevant comparison is with other boxes drawn to the same scale; a 'flat' box could represent strikes with a greater size (a higher W/N) than a 'tall' one. Further, there could be an increase in the relative size of one of the dimensions while in absolute terms there was a fall in the index in question. With the dimensions used in Figures 2.4 and 2.5, the remarkable thing about the shape of American strikes is the continuing resemblance to a cube, particularly when the mean is the measure of duration. Any contrast is between the 'flat' strikes before 1916 and the larger ones since then; it is unfortunate that no data exist on the median duration of strikes for the period 1894–1916.

Since the boxes showing the shape of strikes are merely convenient devices with which to compare a number of dimensions at once, this finding is, in effect, identical to what was said above about the first world war as the apparent watershed for American strike activity. Strikes since then have been less frequent and larger than those before the war. But this contrast is not sufficient to represent a 'transformation' of the strike and in particular it does not conform to the Shorter–Tilly model for the differences between 'early' and 'modern' strike shapes. Early strikes, it will be recalled, are long, infrequent and small, whereas modern ones are shorter, more frequent and larger. Although there has been some increase in size in America, frequency has moved in the opposite direction to that predicted and duration has remained unchanged.

Although the volume of the boxes in Figure 2.4 does not measure strike volume, it is possible to use the overall size of the boxes in order to make a rough comparison of the total amount of strike activity in different periods. In the long-term there has certainly been no tendency for the volume of the boxes to decline. If anything, there has been an increase, suggesting that arguments that there will be a tendency for strike activity to fall as industrialization advances are incorrect. The other notable point about the volume of the boxes is the size of that for 1919–22 compared with that for 1946–49. As noted above, these two periods marked the two great peaks in worker involvement but not only was the size of strikes greater after the first world war than after the second, but the duration of stoppages was also larger. In other words, the unrest after the first war seems to have marked the overall peak of industrial conflict in America.

Strike Waves

Shorter and Tilly introduced the concept of strike waves to indicate periods of high levels of conflict: a wave occurs 'when both the number of strikes and the number of strikers in a given year exceed the means of the previous five years by more than 50 per cent'.[16] Thus, a wave is defined in terms of previous rates of activity, which means that there are problems with coping with cases where activity increases gradually; there may be a large number of strikes in a year but, because previous years have also had a high rate of activity, the year may not be counted as having a wave of strikes. Nevertheless, the use of Shorter and Tilly's technique will be of use in seeing whether the incidence of 'strike waves' has changed and whether the character of waves has altered: the latter will help in the assessment of the aspect of the institutionalization theory concerned with the character of industrial relations.

A list of all years in which either the number of strikes or the number of workers involved exceeded the mean of the previous five years by the required amount is given in Table A.4. There were twenty such years, but only seven qualified for inclusion as 'wave years' under the Shorter–Tilly definition. These seven were: 1886, 1887, 1903, 1933, 1934, 1937, and 1944. It appears, therefore, that the incidence of strike waves has declined markedly since the second world war. However, as will be shown in detail in Chapter 4, the variability of strike indices has declined. That is, strike activity in one year has become more closely related to activity in adjoining years and, as a result, fewer 'wave' years have been recorded. Similarly, the occurrence of three wave years in the 1930s might suggest that this decade was particularly prone to conflict; but, when the very low level of activity in the 1920s is considered, it is apparent that any increase in the 1930s would be particularly likely to be counted as a strike wave.

Shorter and Tilly argue that wave years had particular significance in France because of their association with times of political upheaval. It will be recalled that, for Shorter and Tilly, the strike has become a means of putting pressure on the political centre, with the result that peaks of strike activity can be related to political factors. Despite the failure of American strikes to change shape, the writers incorporate an interpretation of these strikes into their political theory. The details of

16.   Ibid., pp. 106–07.

this are not important here, except to note that Shorter and Tilly see strikes before and during the New Deal as having a political focus. It is true that the New Deal can be seen as a time of considerable political change, but strike waves other than those in the 1960s cannot be related to political factors. Even in the 1930s, there is no evidence that strikes were overtly political in the sense that strikers consciously sought to put pressure on the political centre. There may have been common influences which affected both the level of strike activity and political matters, but, as Chapter 5 will show in more detail, the upsurge in strikes during the 1930s cannot be represented as part of a politically-motivated movement.

The Union and Strikes

Several writers assume that the union is a necessary mediating influence between workers' dissatisfactions and overt protests. But the union movement has grown in such a way that it is hard to demonstrate that this is the case. Unions in America have grown most rapidly in times of 'general social unrest' and these times have also been characterized by a high rate of strike activity.[17] There is, therefore, no reason to treat union growth as a variable logically prior to strike activity. It might be suggested that workers will first join unions and will then strike so that unionization can be seen as an influence mediating the effects of 'unrest', but there is a large body of writing which suggests that, in many cases, strikes break out before unions are organized and that it is this evidence of worker protest which stimulates the unions into starting an organizing drive.[18] In other words, strikes can lead to union growth.

17. J. T. Dunlop, 'The Development of Labor Organization: A Theoretical Framework', *Insights into Labor Issues*, ed. R. A. Lester and J. Shister (New York: Macmillan, 1948), pp. 163–96; I. Bernstein, 'Union Growth and Structural Cycles', *Labor and Trade Unionism*, ed. W. Galenson and S. M. Lipset (New York: Wiley, 1960), pp. 73–89; I. Bernstein, 'The Growth of American Unions', *American Economic Review*, XLIV, pp. 301–18 (1954). Cf. A. A. Blum, 'Why Unions Grow', *Labor History*, IX, pp. 39–72 (1968). For criticism of the 'unrest' theory see O. Ashenfelter and J. H. Pencavel, 'American Trade Union Growth: 1900–60', *Quarterly Journal of Economics*, LXXXIII, pp. 434–48 (1969). I do not necessarily want to support the unrest theory; all I want to suggest is that union growth and strike activity may both depend on some other variable, and that unionization cannot be seen as logically prior to strike activity.

18. This is most obvious in the case of the early New Deal Period. See S. Fine, *The Automobile under the Blue Eagle* (Ann Arbor: University of Michigan

Moreover, there are many cases where the failure of a strike has had disastrous and long-lasting effects on the union.[19] It is true that the defeat of the union might have come anyway, but the strike can be seen as an influence mediating the more basic causes of the defeat just as much as the union mediates the impact of unrest on strikes.

It is obvious that unions are in one sense important influences on strikes. They provide experienced leadership, organization and discipline, a focus of loyalty and, not least, finance to strikers who may be very uncertain of themselves and who may be awestruck by the power of the employers. The central role of unions in enhancing the position of the working class cannot be denied, but accepting the importance of the union does not require us to treat it as a necessary factor in explaining strike activity. The link between unions and strikes is a complex one which should be considered without making assumptions as to its character.

For Ross and Irwin, strikes must be understood in relation to the 'institutional strivings' of unions: 'the modern strike is not a spontaneous outburst and cannot be understood solely by reference to the grievances of the rank and file'.[20] Strikes, for Ross and Irwin, come to serve the needs of the union and its leaders and are fought to strengthen the union's institutional position. There are obvious problems with determining the impact of unions on labour relations. As MacDonald has argued, the fact that unionism is part of general social changes makes it hard to assess how management practices would have developed in the long term in the absence of unions.[21] The hypothetical non-union standard may not be a valid base for comparison with what has actually occurred. Certain results might have occurred even in the absence of the union as a particular form of organisation: the 'union is, after all, a device or vehicle that owes its origin to the existence of certain strongly felt needs'. One may add that, since 'institutional strivings'

Press, 1963), pp. 142–208; C. R. Daugherty, M. G. de Chazeau and S. S. Stratton, *The Economics of the Iron and Steel Industry* (New York: McGraw-Hill, 1937), pp. 932–77; R. McKenney, *Industrial Valley* (New York: Harcourt, Brace and Co., 1939), pp. 93–188.

19. See, for example, L. Wolff, *Lockout* (New York: Harper and Row, 1965); D. Brody, *Steelworkers in America* (Cambridge, Mass.: Harvard University Press, 1960), e.g. pp. 50–112; Soule, op. cit., p. 202.

20. A. M. Ross and D. Irwin, 'Strike Experience in Five Countries, 1927–47', *Industrial and Labor Relations Review*, IV, pp. 323–42 (1951), at p. 336.

21. R. M. MacDonald, *Collective Bargaining in the Automobile Industry* (New Haven: Yale University Press, 1963), pp. 49–53; following quote from p. 52.

and rank and file needs and desires interact, it is hard in practice to separate them.

The evidence on union involvement in strikes may now be considered. Official agencies have always attempted to record the association of a strike with a union, but the methods employed have differed. The Commissioner of Labor recorded whether or not a strike was 'ordered' by a union, either by direct vote or by a business agent. The Bureau of Labor Statistics has recorded whether a union was called in during a strike or whether the strikers were union members. Thus an 'unofficial' action by unionists would not be counted by the Commissioner as 'ordered' but it would be seen by the Bureau as 'connected' with a union.[22] With this in mind, the trend of union involvement in strikes may be considered (Table 2.4). Since the 1930s, nearly every strike has had 'union involvement' but even during the first world war only 15 per cent of those strikes whose connection with a union was reported were without a union presence. It would be dangerous to compare these figures directly with those of the Commissioner, but it is clear that there was a strong upward trend in the proportion of strikes 'ordered' during the period he covered. The union has attained 'proprietorship' of the strike, but one must question the assertion by Ross that it was not achieved until after the first world war;[23] by 1902—05 three-quarters of all strikes were ordered by unions.

This finding does not, however, deal with the question of the relative strike-proneness of unionists and non-unionists. For this, indirect methods have to be used. The first serious attempt to derive a satisfactory measure was made by Douglas in 1923; with a little manipulation, the measure can be shown to be the ratio of the number of strikes called by a union to the number not called by a union, multiplied by the ratio of non-unionists to unionists in the work force.[24] Douglas also calculated a similar measure based on worker involvement instead of the number of strikes. He found that union strike liability was over twenty times that of non-unionists and that for worker involvement the disparity was even greater. From this, and from the rise in his index

22. U.S. Commissioner of Labor, *Twenty-first Annual Report, 1906* (Washington, D.C.: Government Printing Office, 1907), p. 109; F. Peterson, *Strikes in the United States, 1880—1936* (Washington, D.C.: U.S. Department of Labor Bulletin no. 651, 1938), p. 166; J. I. Griffin, *Strikes: A Study in Quantitative Economics* (New York: Columbia University Press, 1939), p. 99.

23. A. M. Ross, 'The Natural History of the Strike', *Industrial Conflict*, ed. A. Kornhauser, R. Dubin and A. M. Ross (New York: McGraw-Hill, 1954), pp. 23—36, at p. 24.

24. P. H. Douglas, 'An Analysis of Strike Statistics', *Journal of the American*

between 1881 and 1921, he concluded that the union is a permissive factor in strikes, making possible the expression of what is on the minds of all workers.[25]

Table A.5 reports Douglas's findings and also brings them up to date. In addition, it contains calculations based on an index invented by Griffin. In the terms used here, the index is the ratio of workers involved in strikes ordered by unions, L, to the number of unionists in the work force.[26] As Griffin observes, the use of the index rests on two assumptions: that all the workers involved in strikes ordered by unions were union members and that no workers struck more than once in a year. The first assumption is probably the stronger since, in the early years of union activity, it is likely that many strikers will not be members, with the result that the involvement of unionists will be overstated.[27]

Table A.5 shows great increases in the two measures used by Douglas and a decline in Griffin's index. The reason for the latter trend is clear:

Statistical Association, XVIII, pp. 866−77 (1923). Douglas's definition can be written as:

$$\frac{\dfrac{S}{N} \times \dfrac{E-T}{E}}{\dfrac{T}{E} \times \dfrac{N-S}{N}}$$

where S is the number of strikes called by a union. This is identical to:

$$\frac{S(E-T)}{T(N-S)}$$

which can be expressed as:

$$\frac{S}{N-S} \times \frac{E-T}{T}$$

which is the definition given in the text. The index for worker involvement is obtained by replacing N by W and S by L, the number of workers involved in strikes ordered by unions.

25. Douglas, op. cit., p. 876.
26. Griffin, op. cit., pp. 106−08. Griffin defines his index as:

$$\frac{W}{T} \times \% \text{ of workers involved in strikes ordered by unions.}$$

In the present terminology, the second term becomes $(L/W) \times 100$, and the whole expression therefore equals $(L/T) \times 100$.

27. For example, in the anthracite strike of 1900 union membership was about 9,000, but 112,000 workers went out: M. Coleman, *Men and Coal* (New York: Farrar and Rinehart, 1943), pp. 64, 68.

TABLE 2.4

TRADE UNION INVOLVEMENT IN STRIKES, 1881–1974

	% of Strikes	% of Workers Involved in Strikes
	Ordered by T.U.	
1881–85	52.7	63.3
1886–89	62.9	75.0
1890–93	71.7	76.4
1894–97	59.3	77.0
1898–1901	68.0	77.5
1902–05	78.6	85.1
	Connected with T.U.	
1916–18	85.5 (58.4)	n.a.
1919–22	94.5 (70.4)	n.a.
1923–26	88.1 (81.3)	n.a.
	With Union Involvement	
1927–29	87.7	93.9
1930–33	82.1	92.7
1934–36	92.2	97.2
1937–41	96.4	98.7
1942–45	95.5	99.0
1946–49	98.3	99.7
1950–55	98.7	99.7
1959–60	99.1	99.8
1961–63	99.0	99.9
1964–66	98.8	99.7
1967–69	98.3	99.6
1970–72	98.1	99.5
1973–74	99.0	99.9

NOTE

For 1916–26, figures in brackets are for the % of all strikes, figures without brackets for strikes where the association with a union was reported. For changes of definition, see text.

the number of workers involved in union-led strikes L, has increased little, but the number of union members, T, has risen very fast. Thus we need to add to Griffin's conclusion that 'whatever decline is noted must be ascribed to external forces rather than to a natural tendency within the union itself toward a more sparing use of the strike'[28] the observation that the major external force is a statistical artefact. The

28. Griffin, op. cit., p. 116.

rise in Douglas's indices reflects the way in which they were constructed. Thus the first component is the ratio of ordered to non-ordered strikes. A slight increase in the proportion of union-led strikes can lead to a very large rise in the ratio.[29] Despite the very large numbers involved in Douglas's calculations (the implication of the index is that in 1961–63 unionists were over two thousand times as likely as non-unionists to be involved in strikes) they avoid the problems of Griffin's index and show in a very notable way that the common arguments that unions will reduce strike activity are unfounded.[30] This gives more detailed support to the finding of the first section of this chapter that worker involvement in strikes has not declined despite the great increase in union density that has occurred since 1881 (see Table A.6 for illustrative figures on union density).

Brief mention must be made of the index using the ratio of workers involved in strikes to union membership (W/T). As noted at the beginning of this chapter, Ross and Hartman regard this as a measure of strike patterns in general and not specifically of union involvement: it has therefore been included in the general Tables 2.1 and A.1. These tables show that the index fell consistently from very high levels at the end of the nineteenth century to a present level which is about one-sixth of that at the turn of the century. According to Ross and Hartman, this is strong evidence that the strike has been withering away, but all it shows is that union membership has increased much more rapidly than has the number of workers involved in strikes. In other words, the W/T measure is even more imperfect as an indirect index of union involvement in strikes than is L/T.

A final feature of union involvement is the strike activity of unions with differing national affiliations. Parts (a), (b), and (c) of Table A.7 show the dominance over strikes of the major national federations, a

---

29. Thus if the proportion of strikes called by a union rose from 98.5 per cent to 99.5 per cent the first term, $S/(N-S)$, in the formula in note 24 would increase threefold, from 98.5/1.5 to 99.5/0.5.

30. For the view that unions will reduce strike activity, see, in addition to the writings of the institutionalists, S. Gompers, *Seventy Years of Life and Labour*, Vol. I (London: Hurst and Blackett, 1925), p. 286; and the recommendations of the government report on the Pullman strike of 1894, cited in M. Derber, *The American Idea of Industrial Democracy, 1865–1965* (Urbana: University of Illinois Press, 1970), p. 87. Cf. Griffin's remarkable anticipation of later writing: 'does the establishment and maintenance of a union in a particular industry cause strikes to "wither away" and industrial relations to assume the aspect of peace and tranquility that many authors seem to imagine will be the result of thorough unionization?' (Griffin, op. cit., p. 96).

position which has been maintained since 1927. Not too much should be read into the fluctuations that have occurred, since these are often due to the affiliation or dissaffiliation of various unions.[31] From these three parts of the table, union federations can be compared on the size of, and loss per striker (D/W) in, their strikes. It would be possible to do this by constructing new tables but this is not necessary since a comparison can be made of the proportions of strikes, workers involved and days lost accounted for by each federation. For example, if the A.F.L. had 80 per cent of the strikes and 40 per cent of the strikers, the mean size of its strikes would be half the average.

Using this method, it will be seen that, up to the foundation of the C.I.O., the A.F.L. had strikes that were slightly larger than average and that the loss per striker in its strikes was also greater than average. But after 1936 the C.I.O. had the largest strikes, which on the whole also had the greatest loss per striker. This fact might be attributed to a high degree of militancy of new unions which would then decline as they aged, but even in the 1950–55 period the C.I.O. unions continued to have large strikes, a fact which is explained more by their concentration in the mass-production industries than by their age.

The final part of Table A.7 shows the relative strike-proneness of unions by their affiliation. On all three dimensions the A.F.L. unions were the least strike-prone and they were also the most likely to reduce their strike activity during the second world war. The first fact can be explained by the differing industrial distributions of the A.F.L. and C.I.O. unions, but the second suggests a difference in the internal characteristics of the members of the two federations. The A.F.L. unions were the more prepared to follow the no-strike pledge and can be seen as being the more fully 'incorporated'.

This section has shown that there is no evidence at the aggregate level to suggest that the presence of unions reduced strike activity. Indeed, the evidence from Douglas's index suggests the reverse, but, because of the difficulties with the index itself and because the available data record only union 'involvement', this cannot be taken as a firm conclusion. Nor was the domination of strikes by unions a necessary development; the union has certainly come to play a central role in the planning and execution of strikes, but the nature of its influence on strike activity in general is less certain.

---

31. Thus the increases registered by the 'other union' category in 1942–45 can be attributed to the disaffiliation of the United Mine Workers from the C.I.O. in 1942.

The Issues in Strikes

As is well-known, the difficulties with the statistical descriptions of the issues over which strikes are fought[32] are very great. Problems of principle are compounded by the changes of category which have taken place since 1881. But it is possible to say something about the trends in strike issues if only the broadest categories, between which definitional changes have not been too large, are considered.

The distribution of strikes by class of cause is given in Table 2.5; Table A.8 gives the breakdown by workers involved and days lost. Since the B.L.S. began to record strikes the categories of issue have been reasonably consistent, but the Commissioner of Labor's data are less clear because of the very large number of categories used and because of the failure to identify the 'principal cause' in some cases.[33] Combining the categories into useful aggregates leaves a large group over 'other issues'. This can be reduced by following Millis and Montgomery in their estimation of the number of strikes over work conditions, but the figures in this category are probably not very comparable with those for more recent years.[34]

The most notable feature of Table 2.5 is the continuing predominance of disputes over wages. Although there has been some decline in their importance since the end of the nineteenth century, they still account for over half of all strikes and, as Table A.8 shows, an even greater proportion of workers involved and days lost. The decline since the 1880s may be part of a trend going back even further; the available information on strikes before 1880, presented in Table A.9, shows that wages accounted for 78 per cent of all strikes where the issue was known.[35] Clearly, the data for these years are extremely incomplete,

32. See below, Appendix B, pp. 300–01.
33. See Griffin, op. cit., pp. 73–4.
34. H. A. Millis and R. E. Montgomery, *Organized Labor* (New York: McGraw-Hill, 1945), pp. 700–01.
35. This information is very incomplete; more strikes were recorded for 1880 than for the whole of the period 1741–1879. The data were collected by a search by the Commissioner's staff through the major trade and labour papers. They thus represent a sample of those strikes which were important enough to receive comment in the press. The starting date of 1741 implies acceptance of the view that a bakers' dispute in that year was a true strike. Cf. J. R. Commons *et al., History of Labour in the United States* (New York: Macmillan, 1918), Vol. I, p. 25, where it is argued that the first true strike of wage earners occurred in 1786. The same view is expressed by P. S. Foner, *From Colonial Times to the Foundation of the American Federation*

TABLE 2.5

PERCENTAGE OF STRIKES WITH GIVEN ISSUE, 1881–1974

	Wages and Hours	Wages, Hours and Union Recog.	Union Recog. and Security	Other Work Conditions	Inter/intra Union	Other
1881–85	73.3	1.4	7.8	4.1		13.4
1886–89	60.6	2.1	14.3	4.1		18.8
1890–93	52.7	2.8	15.6	3.2		25.8
1894–97	60.0	3.0	15.9	2.9		18.2
1898–1901	51.8	4.6	22.6	3.4		17.6
1902–05	45.8	6.1	28.8	3.2		16.0
1914–15	55.3	5.8	20.8			18.2
1916–18	63.6	5.4	16.3			14.7
1919–22	63.1	4.7	16.5			15.7
1923–26	47.2	3.2	17.2			32.4
1927–29	39.3	8.2	30.2		3.1	19.2
1930–33	55.8	9.2	19.1		2.8	13.1
1934–37	34.1	28.8	23.5		2.7	10.9
1938–41	30.8	22.0	28.6		6.0	12.5
1942–45	45.5	8.4	11.7	30.0	4.4	
1946–49	47.2	12.9	14.6	20.6	4.8	
1950–53	51.0	4.7	12.7	25.4	6.1	
1954–57	50.5	7.1	12.0	22.7	7.8	
1958–60	50.6	8.4	8.6	23.1	9.3	
1961–65	50.1		15.7	22.9	11.4	
1966–69	56.2		11.7	22.1	10.0	
1970–72	54.8		10.0	26.4	8.7	
1973–74	60.8		7.0	27.5	4.7	

NOTE

The categories of issue are broadly those used by the B.L.S. in the period 1927–60. Before 1942, work conditions strikes were not separated from the 'other' category. For the derivation of strikes over 'other working conditions' in 1881–1905, see text. In 1961, the B.L.S. re-organized its categories; the sub-divisions of the 'wages and hours' group were altered and 'wages, hours and union recognition' dropped. In this table, 'wages and hours' includes all wage and hours and supplementary benefit issues, and also the category 'other contractual matters'. 'Other work conditions' includes job security, plant administration and other working conditions issues.

of Labor, Vol. I of *History of the Labor Movement in the United States* (New York: International Publishers, 1947), p. 70. Cf. R. B. Morris, *Government and Labor in Early America* (New York: Columbia University Press, 1946), p. 201, for the view that several strikes in 1778 and later years take precedence.

but they are consistent with those for the period since 1880. The tendency for the significance of wage issues to decline is contrary to the view that collective bargaining will enable disputes on non-wage matters to be amicably settled; one would expect shopfloor disputes arising from 'misunderstandings' to be prevented from turning into stoppages and that recognition strikes would become less necessary. The lack of any such pattern is clear from Table 2.5.

The major challenge to the dominance of the wages dispute came during the New Deal; from 1934 to 1941 over half the number of strikes involved questions of union recognition and security. This represents, of course, the response to the provisions of the Wagner Act and its predecessor, the National Industrial Recovery Act of 1933.[36] Some measure of the direct stimulus to organizational demands is provided by the contrast with the 1916–18 period, when the government took steps which were then unprecedented in assisting unions, but when recognition strikes showed no increase.[37] The impact of the recognition strikes of the '30s is particularly notable when the series for days lost is examined; the proportion accounted for by wage strikes is usually very high, but in these years it dropped to about half its normal level. Organizational strikes remained important during the second world war, which is somewhat surprising in that one would expect a resurgence of disputes over wages in an inflationary period; it seems that matters of 'union security' (closed shop provisions, the check-off of dues etc.) were particularly significant and that these provided a suitable focus for strikes during the war. In the late 1940s wage demands rose in importance under peacetime conditions.

After the union has achieved a recognized position in the industry, strikes over 'union organization' might be expected to decline in significance. As Spielmans notes, this proposition is hard to test: the strikes which the establishment of bargaining can be expected to reduce are less than the whole 'recognition and security' category; and the reduction will affect only those industries where bargaining has been

36. The N.I.R.A.'s Section 7a contained guarantees on the right to organize, but it lacked means of enforcement. After the whole Act was declared unconstitutional in 1935, it was replaced by the National Labor Relations Act (the Wagner Act). See, for example, I. Bernstein, *The New Deal Collective Bargaining Policy* (Berkeley and Los Angeles: University of California Press, 1950); R. C. Cortner, *The Wagner Act Cases* (Knoxville: University of Tennessee Press, 1964).

37. See Bing, op. cit.; J. S. Smith, 'Organized Labor and Government in the Wilson Era, 1913–21: Some Conclusions', *Labor History*, III, pp. 265–86 (1962); G. D. Nash, 'Franklin D. Roosevelt and Labor: the World War I Origins of Early New Deal Policy', *Labor History*, I, pp. 39–52 (1960).

established.[38] However, in broad terms it does not appear that this expectation is met. Although there has been a fall in the importance of recognition strikes since the '30s, such stoppages have by no means been eliminated and it is hard to equate those that remain with a struggle for recognition in industries where bargaining does not exist. Instead of a pattern of recognition strikes breaking out and then subsiding to very low levels, it appears that the proportion of these strikes in the total has fallen to levels similar to those prevailing before the New Deal.

Strikes over 'other working conditions' are significant from two points of view. On the one hand there are arguments that collective bargaining provides a means to resolve workplace issues, so that strikes on such issues should decline in importance. On the other there is the 'radical' view that shopfloor issues will reflect the protests of the rank and file; an increase in strikes over 'other work conditions' would be expected in the 1960s, when an upsurge in shopfloor protest is said to have taken place.

A consistent series on these strikes is available only since 1942, so that it is difficult to say anything definite about their long-term trends. But there is no marked downward trend in their importance: although they were significant during the second world war, their proportion in the total has remained remarkably stable since then. The lack of a marked rise in the 1960s conflicts with the view that in these years shopfloor protest took on a new significance.

Despite the problems with the data on 'other work issues' strikes in 1881–1905, some comparison with later years is possible if the category of 'other' strikes is included. In other words the focus is on all strikes other than those on wage and union matters. Such strikes accounted for about 20 per cent of the total in 1881–1905, a figure similar to the proportion of 'other work conditions' stoppages in 1942–74. Thus, this type of stoppage has played a small, but significant, part in the strike movement as a whole. Its presence indicates that the pure bargaining strike has never been totally dominant, and has not increased in significance recently.[39]

38. J. V. Spielmans, 'Strikes under the Wagner Act', *Readings in Labor Economics*, ed. F. S. Doody (Cambridge, Mass.: Addison-Wesley Press, 1950), pp. 179–88.
39. Chapter 4 considers work conditions strikes in 1881–1905 in more detail; see below, pp. 93–5. The significance of job control issues in general is taken up in Chapter 7, pp. 233–42. The predominance of wage matters in the stated issues in strikes does not, of course, mean that control problems were unimportant.

From Tables 2.5 and A.8, one can see which issues led to particularly large stoppages or to the loss of a large number of days per strike, following the same strategy as that adopted in the comparison of union federations. Wage strikes have been larger than average for every period except 1934–37, and the loss per striker in them greater than average except for 1934–41. Thus, these strikes seem to be the most strenuously fought battles, although in the 1930s the most intense conflicts occurred on other issues. As one would expect, union recognition strikes in the 1930s had above-average levels of loss per striker, and their relative size also increased. But the increase in size was not very marked; that is, the tendency for recognition strikes to become the largest and 'longest' disputes[40] was not as great as one might expect from the argument that the '30s were the great time for organizing battles. Recognition strikes became relatively more frequent, larger and longer, but the battle seems to have been spread over more fronts than is often suggested.

Apart from the '30s, recognition strikes have not been marked by a great size or loss per striker. This suggests a need to modify Taft's statement that 'the resistance to labor is greatest when it seeks by organization to affect the terms of employment.'[41] In general, it is wage strikes which seem, on the evidence presented so far, to involve the greatest battles. This point also affects arguments about the causes of, and not just issues in, strikes. A common view is that the insecurity of workers and the denial at work of the rights enjoyed outside it are prime causes of unrest.[42] The fact that wage disputes involve the greatest battles is indirect evidence against this, but it could still be said that these battles merely reflect a deeper discontent, which does not find its expression in any particular type of strike. However, the continued dominance of wage strikes, together with the findings noted above concerning the constancy of worker involvement in, and the

40. 'Longest' in the sense of Ross and Hartman (op. cit., p. 12), i.e. having a high D/W ratio.
41. Taft, op. cit., p. 136. Cf. Daugherty *et al.,* op cit., p. 1056; B. M. Selekman, *Labor Relations and Human Relations* (New York: McGraw-Hill, 1947), pp. 14–41.
42. L. D. Brandeis, 'The Fundamental Cause of Industrial Unrest', *Unions, Management and the Public,* ed. E. W. Bakke, C. Kerr and C. W. Anrod (2nd edn; New York: Harcourt, Brace and Co., 1960), pp. 232–4; F. Peterson, 'Causes of Industrial Unrest', *Annals of the American Academy of Political and Social Science,* no. 274, pp. 25–31 (1951); R. W. Johnson, 'An Employer Looks at Labor-management Relations', *Industrial and Labor Relations Review,* I, pp. 486–92 (1948), at p. 486.

duration of, all strikes, suggest that the emphasis on insecurity is unjustified. This is not to say that workers no longer experience insecurity, but the alleviation of particular forms of insecurity through the growth of bargaining rights has not led to the predicted changes in the level or patterns of strike activity.

Finally, 'other work conditions' strikes are about average size but have a relatively low loss per striker, a fact which is consistent with the view of them as quite large but brief job actions. But at the present level of analysis it is not possible to say any more about them.

The Results of Strikes

The interest in the data on the results of strikes lies in the light they throw on the view that early strikes tend to fail, whereas experience and organization increase the rate of success. It is possible to examine not only the results statistics in isolation but also the cross-classification of causes with results and the effect of union involvement on the outcome.

Table 2.6 shows the results of strikes from 1881 to 1945. It will be seen that there is a problem of comparability since the first part of the table refers to establishments while the second deals with strikes. And the status of Griffin's data for 1906–15 is unclear;[43] although he states that his figures are for strikes, the information he gives for 1881–1905 comes directly from the Commissioner of Labor's statistics relating to establishments. It therefore seems advisable to treat Griffin's and the Commissioner's data together.

It is clear from Table 2.6 that there has been no very strong trend towards an increase in the proportion of worker victories and neither has there been a very significant drop in the proportion of outright defeats. In view of the special circumstances operating in particular periods, it is hard to be more definite than this. The increase in the success rate in the late 1930s, for example, may have been only a temporary feature and for the period 1934–45 as a whole the rate was probably not very different from that at the end of the nineteenth century. The figures of strike results put into perspective the various claims that one period was a time of great gains for labour and that another was marked by continuous defeats; even in the period 1938–41, one fifth of all strikes, and one tenth of workers involved and days lost in them, were counted as 'lost'.

43. Griffin, op. cit., p. 91.

The Trend of Strikes

TABLE 2.6

STRIKE RESULTS, 1881–1945

	% of Establishments where strike was		
	Won	Compromised	Lost
1881–85	56.1	8.7	35.2
1886–89	44.2	13.1	42.8
1890–93	43.7	9.8	46.5
1894–97	53.0	15.1	31.9
1898–1901	54.4	15.0	30.6
1902–05	38.5	19.1	42.4
1906–08	30.0	16.3	53.7
1909–11	34.1	17.6	48.4
1912–15	38.2	19.9	41.9

	% of Strikes			% of Workers Involved in Strikes which were			% of Days Lost in Strikes which were		
	Won	Comp.	Lost	Won	Comp.	Lost	Won	Comp.	Lost
1916–18	34.6	37.8	27.7						
1919–22	29.0	29.5	41.5						
1923–26	44.4	19.0	36.4						
1927–29	29.1	27.6	43.4	20.3	32.6	47.1	6.3	18.0	75.7
1930–33	32.8	23.5	43.8	29.4	44.6	26.0	18.8	43.1	38.1
1934–37	45.8	28.8	25.3	41.4	42.5	16.2	35.3	44.0	20.6
1938–41	44.9	36.0	19.1	42.9	45.5	11.5	44.9	43.6	11.5
1942–45	41.2	29.0	29.8	27.7	40.9	31.4	18.7	56.6	24.7

NOTE
For difference between 1906–15 and earlier period, see text.

A marked feature of the table is the growth of compromise solutions. This might suggest that labour relations became more amicable, in that negotiated solutions to problems were found. But problems with the data on results make such a conclusion dangerous. Thus, if there is a tendency to hold strikes on an increasing number of issues, it will be more likely that a 'compromise' will be worked out. And a strike may be seen as a compromise merely because it was ended by negotiations and not the surrender of one of the parties: a negotiated settlement is likely to contain face-saving clauses for the side which has to give way on the key issues and may thus appear to be a compromise when in fact it was a defeat for one side. If anything can be concluded from the growth of compromises, the figures for 1942–45 are interesting. They show that there was no increase in the proportion of strikes compromised but that there was a marked rise for striker-days; although the costly strikes in terms of days lost were settled by mutual concessions, a significant number of stoppages remained to be fought out. This suggests, in line with comments made above, that the war years were not marked by as high a degree of industrial peace as is often thought.

Issues in and Results of Strikes

It is important to know whether particular issues in strikes are associated with a high or low rate of success. Table 2.7 gives the results of strikes on selected issues for 1881–1905 and 1927–36. Although the different statistical bases of the figures for the two periods make comparisons between them dangerous, it is interesting to note that wage strikes have, if anything, tended to become less successful. This is remarkable in view of the claim that business unionism is particularly capable when it comes to winning material gains for the workers. And comparisons within each section indicate that, at one time, wage strikes are no more likely to be won than are stoppages on other broad categories of issue.

The sub-divisions of Table 2.7 show many of the patterns one would expect. Thus strikes for wage increases are notably more successful than those against wage decreases, and sympathy strikes are notably unsuccessful. But there have been notable fluctuations in the rate of success of various types of strikes. This is shown in Table A.10, which gives the results of stoppages over particular issues for a number of sub-periods. Thus the rate of success of wage increase strikes seems to have fallen between 1881 and 1905. Not only was there considerable fluctuation in all categories, but the periods of success did not go together, suggesting that one type of strike may be appropriate for one period and another type for a different one. For 1927–41 there was, as one would expect, an increase in the number of organizational strikes which were won, but the rate of success of wages strikes also rose markedly. Thus, for all issues, the period 1938–41 was remarkably successful, suggesting that, although 1937 may have been the 'turning point' for labour, it was in the years up to the second world war that the advantage was pushed home.[44]

Union Involvement and Results

For the years 1881–1905, information is available on the results of strikes by union involvement; this is summarized in Table 2.8. Strikes

---

44. W. Galenson, '1937: The Turning Point for American Labor', University of California at Berkeley, Institute of Industrial Relations Reprint no. 120 (1959).

TABLE 2.7

RESULTS OF STRIKES BY ISSUE, 1881–1905 AND 1927–36

	% Establishments with Given Result and Issue, 1881–1905		
	Won	Comp.[a]	Lost
All wage strikes	47.9	20.3	31.8
Wage increase	50.0	18.7	31.4
Against wage decrease	34.5	12.7	52.3
Wage increase, and other[b]	46.9	25.2	28.0
Against wage decrease, and other	67.4	6.2	26.4
All hours strikes	52.0	17.5	30.5
Hour decrease	50.7	10.1	39.2
All union recog. and rules	46.8	13.5	39.7
Recog. and rules	55.5	1.6	42.9
Recog. and rules, and other[b]	38.7	24.6	36.8
Docking, fines, work conditions and rules	45.2	17.6	24.6
Sympathy	20.0	3.0	77.0

	% Strikes with Given Result and Issue, 1927–36		
	Won	Comp.	Lost
All wage strikes	35.0	28.1	36.8
Wage increase[c]	40.3	31.5	28.2
Wage decrease[d]	26.5	22.7	50.8
All hours strikes	37.8	23.8	38.5
Hour decrease	43.3	25.8	30.9
All union organization	42.0	21.6	36.4
Recog., wages and hours	44.3	31.9	23.8
Recog., closed shop, discrimination, other	40.5	14.9	44.5
Sympathy	29.2	31.2	39.6

NOTES
a. Comp. = compromised.
b. For 1881–1905, 'and other' indicates that the named issue was combined with other issues; i.e. 'wage increase, and other' includes all strikes in which a wage increase was an issue, even if this was not the principal cause. A strike for a wage increase and union recognition is therefore included in the 'wage increase, and other' and the 'recog. and rules, and other' categories.
c. Includes 'wage increase and hour decrease'.
d. Includes 'wage decrease and hour increase'.

ordered by unions were consistently more successful than those not so ordered; when the data are examined on a year-to-year basis, it can be seen that only in 1886, 1889 and in 1894 was the proportion of victories in union-led strikes lower than the proportion in non-union strikes. And, as Griffin notes, there has been a widening of the gap

TABLE 2.8

RESULTS OF STRIKES BY UNION INVOLVEMENT, 1881–1905

	% of Establishments in which Strikes Ordered by Unions were			% of Establishments in which Strikes not Ordered by Unions were		
	Won	Comp.	Lost	Won	Comp.	Lost
1881–85	61.5	9.8	28.7	36.1	6.4	57.5
1886–89	42.8	14.6	42.6	37.6	8.0	54.4
1890–93	46.4	9.4	44.2	36.5	8.7	54.8
1894–97	53.9	16.2	29.9	33.6	12.0	54.4
1898–1901	60.1	16.3	23.5	32.7	11.9	55.4
1902–05	42.3	20.3	37.4	26.1	11.9	62.1
1881–1905	49.5	15.9	34.7	33.8	9.9	56.3

between union and non-union rates of success, although this is not very pronounced.[45] It is hard to assess whether the size of the gap is smaller or larger than would be expected from arguments about the advantages of union organization to strikers. But it is clear that organization was no guarantee of success and, conversely, that it was quite possible to win strikes without the presence of the union; extreme arguments about the efficacy of union involvement must be rejected.

It would be possible to deal with this question more adequately if data were available on union involvement by issues; one could see whether, for example, high rates of success in union-led strikes were associated with their being concentrated on those issues where success was particularly likely. Some progress can be made, however. Since Table 2.7 showed that the rates of success did not vary much between classes of issue, it is unlikely that a concentration on particular issues can explain much of the advantage of union-led strikes. Moreover, the trends in the success rates of strikes on various issues shown in Table A.10 are not strongly associated with the fluctuations in the rate of success of strikes ordered by unions. Data reported in Chapter 4 on the results of strikes by industry do not suggest that there was a strong concentration of union involvement in sectors where the rate of success was very high.[46] Thus the difference between strikes ordered and those not ordered seems to be a 'genuine' one.

45. Griffin, op. cit., p. 114.
46. See below, Table 4.8, p. 101.

Duration and Result

It is commonly held that the rate of success will decline with the length of stoppages, because workers' resources will be exhausted more rapidly than those of the employer. The official tabulations provide relevant information only for the years 1927—41, but data relating to 'cessations' for the period 1881—94 have also been employed.[47] The results are presented in Table 2.9, which shows a very marked tendency for the proportion of successes to decline, and of failures to rise, as the length of stoppages increases. For cessations, the decline was continuous, but for strikes between 1927 and 1941 a different pattern emerges. For the first seven years, there was a marked break around the 30 days' duration mark, with shorter strikes having about the same rate of success; in addition the overall rate of decline in the success rate was quite shallow. By contrast, during the years 1934—41, a continuous and more rapid decline occurred. In view of the fact that the overall rate of success was rising from 1927 to 1941, this suggests that long strikes have a more or less constant success rate and that the variation in the overall rate is due to fluctuations within the shorter categories. However, the evidence on which this conclusion is based is limited and it may not have general applicability. But it does accord with commonsense to argue that employers will either give way to workers' demands quickly or will hold out as long as they can, and that in the latter case the balance of resources will be more or less constant so that one can expect a constant rate of success in long strikes.[48]

Trends in Selected Industries

Trends of worker involvement for nine industries are shown in Figure A.1. The difficulties of establishing consistent series for the period since

---

47. The term 'cessation' refers to a line of data in the first two of the Commissioner of Labor's reports devoted to strikes: see below, Appendix B, pp. 308—9.

48. This is, of course, a short-term prediction, in the long term the balance of resources may change as union strike funds grow or as strikers come to make more systematic use of social security payments. On the former, see G. M. Janes, *The Control of Strikes in American Trade Unions* (Baltimore: John Hopkins University Press, 1916), pp. 88—113. On the latter, see A. J. Thieblot and R. M. Cowin, *Welfare and Strikes* (Philadelphia: University of Pennsylvania Press, 1972); for a sceptical view see J. W. Durcan and W. E. J. McCarthy, 'The State Subsidy Theory of Strikes: An Examination of Statistical Data for the Period 1956—70', *British Journal of Industrial Relations*, XII, pp. 26—47 (1974).

TABLE 2.9

RESULTS OF STRIKES, BY DURATION, 1881–94 AND 1927–41

		% of Establishments in which 'Cessations' of Given Length were Won or Lost					
		1–6 days	7–14 days	15–29 days	30–59 days	60–89 days	90 days and over
1881–85	Won	55.8	47.2	42.3	33.7	32.4	28.5
	Lost	39.1	45.9	48.8	57.1	61.1	63.4
1886–89	Won	49.3	35.0	32.2	26.6	23.2	25.3
	Lost	43.6	54.2	57.9	63.5	68.2	68.7
1890–94	Won	57.5	41.4	35.9	28.0	20.4	21.8
	Lost	36.6	50.3	54.1	61.4	69.6	67.3
		% of Strikes with Given Length which were Won or Lost					
		1–6 days	7–14 days	15–29 days	30–59 days	60–89 days	90 days and over
1927–29	Won	31.4	32.6	31.1	22.3	18.2	20.5
	Lost	43.6	36.2	41.6	44.4	55.5	64.1
1930–33	Won	34.6	37.2	34.2	23.4	24.2	21.7
	Lost	47.1	35.0	39.1	54.4	41.4	44.6
1934–37	Won	51.1	42.1	43.0	32.8	30.0	24.4
	Lost	28.5	29.4	27.1	40.9	37.4	45.5
1938–41	Won	51.6	46.5	41.0	38.4	28.0	26.8
	Lost	17.4	17.0	18.2	21.8	27.3	37.9

the 1880s are considerable (see Appendix D) but the data are reasonably comparable; in particular, definitions of industry groups do not seem to have altered so much that comparison would be impossible. However, given the problems with the reliability of figures on the number of strikes in individual industries,[49] discussion here is limited to worker involvement. There is also the practical problem that, except for coal and clothing, no data are available for the period 1906–26, but this is not too serious since in most industries collective bargaining was not firmly established until the 1930s.

Three industries show the pattern expected by the institutionalization theory, namely a peak of activity followed by a marked decline. These are clothing, textiles, and tobacco (parts c, d, and h of Figure A.1). The clothing industry provides the ideal example for the institu-

---

49. See below, Appendix B, pp. 294–5.

tionalists.[50] After a period of frequent and 'spontaneous' strikes run by ephemeral unions during the 1880s and 1890s, established unions appeared at the start of the twentieth century and conducted an organized campaign for recognition. This culminated in the great strikes of 1909–10, after which recognition was achieved and the unions settled into a pattern of mutual accommodation with the employers which often developed into the final 'stage' of full co-operation between the two sides. Although there were challenges to this system, it has survived largely intact and, as the graph of worker involvement shows, strike activity has been at very low levels since the second world war. The figure also shows that the industry was not immune from the increase of activity in the 1930s, but the theory would explain this in terms of the need to re-establish bargaining after the problems of the 1920s.

Although the textile industry shows the predicted trends, it is not a case which fits the theory. The C.I.O.'s Textile Workers Union has established itself more firmly than previous organizations, but the industry is still not marked by a pattern of accommodation with the employers. Union density and the coverage of workers by collective agreements remain low.[51] The decline in strike activity is associated with union weakness rather than strength and the industry remains one in which the workers make irregular challenges to the domination of management.

Developments in the tobacco industry are usually related to the mechanization of production and the growth of cigarette production at the expense of the cigar trade. At the end of the nineteenth century the method of making cigars entirely by hand was replaced by a number of processes which reduced the need for skilled craftsmen;[52] the challenge

50. See L. Levine, *The Women's Garment Workers* (New York: B. W. Huebsch, 1924); J. Seidman, *The Needle Trades* (New York: Farrar and Rinehart, 1942); M. Dubofsky, *When Workers Organize* (Amherst: University of Massachusetts Press, 1968); R. J. Myers and J. W. Bloch, 'Men's Clothing', *How Collective Bargaining Works* (New York: Twentieth Century Fund, 1942); S. H. Slichter, *Union Policies and Industrial Management* (Washington, D.C.: Brookings Institute, 1941), pp. 504–28.
51. H. J. Lahne, *The Cotton Mill Worker in the Twentieth Century* (New York: Farrar and Rinehart, 1944); G. S. Mitchell, *Textile Unionism in the South* (Chapel Hill: University of North Carolina Press, 1931); W. Galenson, *The C.I.O. Challenge to the A.F.L.* (Cambridge, Mass.: Harvard University Press, 1960), pp. 325–48; *The Trade Union Situation in the United States* (Geneva: International Labour Office, 1960), pp. 105–12.
52. W. D. Evans, 'Effects of Mechanization in Cigar Manufacturing', *Monthly Labor Review*, XLVI, pp. 1100–20 (1938); E. F. Baker, *Technology and Woman's Work* (New York: Columbia University Press, 1964), pp. 31–5.

to the position of the Cigar Makers' Union may be seen as a central cause of the high rate of strike activity in the 1880s, a matter which will be taken up again in Chapter 4. The growing importance of cigarettes made possible the introduction of mass production methods in the twentieth century; the industry thus seems to fit the expectation of a high rate of protest against the changes associated with industrialization, followed by a period of accommodation. But the marked increases in activity in the 1940s and 1960s suggest that the process of accommodation has been far from complete.

The remaining six industries fail in various ways to match the expectations of the theory. Later chapters will consider particular cases in more detail, but the salient points may be noted here. In the primary metals industries (part a of Figure A.1) there was a very high level of worker involvement throughout the 1940s and 1950s, and even in the sixties the level was greater than that in the organizing period of the thirties. This, combined with the very low levels at the end of the 1920s, suggests that the recognition of the union has given the workers the opportunity to strike which the previous system of 'industrial absolutism' denied them.[53] Strike activity declined at the end of the nineteenth century as the system was being established and has since recovered to levels similar to those of the 1880s. The coal industry (part B of Figure A.1) has been characterized by very marked fluctuations of activity with no clear trend being apparent. Although it has one of the longest histories of bargaining and union recognition, it has never achieved lasting industrial peace.[54] The notable fall in worker involvement in the 1950s was seen by some observers as marking a great change from the past since the union seemed to have achieved important breakthroughs on pension rights and other fringe benefits, but the sharp rise of activity in the sixties showed these hopes to be premature.

The vehicle and machinery industries (parts E and G of Figure A.1) have a pattern similar to that of steel, with levels of activity being high, by historical standards, since the second world war. Although worker involvement in vehicles has been declining, its overall level remains high, even in comparison with the 1930s, which is remarkable when it is remembered that this industry is widely seen as the leader of militancy

53. Preis, op. cit., pp. 419–21. See also Galenson, *The C.I.O. Challenge*, op. cit., pp. 75–119; R. R. R. Brooks, *As Steel Goes* (New Haven: Yale University Press, 1940).
54. W. Fisher, 'Bituminous Coal' and 'Anthracite', *How Collective Bargaining Works*, op. cit., pp. 229–79 and 280–312; Coleman, op. cit.; M. Baratz, *The Union and the Coal Industry* (New Haven: Yale University Press, 1955).

in the New Deal period.[55] Here, and in machinery, current levels of activity are greater than those at the end of the nineteenth century, which suggests that the shift to mass production has increased the 'proneness to conflict'. The contrast between the modern and early vehicle industries is particularly notable.

One might expect that the printing and publishing industry would have a stable and low level of activity in view of the tradition of the control of work by the craftsmen and the central role of the union in the industry's affairs. But part F of Figure A.1 shows that, although the level of worker involvement was lower than that elsewhere, there has been a strong upward trend since the end of the 1920s. Although explanations of the increase in activity in the paper-milling industry might be advanced which are consistent with the institutionalization theory,[56] the parallel rise in printing and publishing goes counter to the theory's predictions. The final part of the figure shows the trend of activity in the contract construction industry. Again, no pattern of the withering away of the strike is apparent; on the contrary, the long-term trend is strongly upward. Particular reasons might be adduced as to why the industry has high levels of activity but the rising trend cannot be explained by the institutionalization theory.[57]

This brief review suggests, then, that the institutionalization theory is on weak ground when trends within industries need to be explained. More generally, trends in selected industries do not reveal any very marked discontinuities. Thus, it seems unlikely that there has been a change in the shape of strikes at the industry level, a conclusion which will be examined in more detail in following chapters. Moreover, it seems that industrialization had different effects in different industries, with mass production being associated with rising activity in some industries and reductions in others. The reasons for this will be taken up again in Chapter 4.

55. Fine, op. cit.; S. Fine, *Sit-down: The General Motors Strike of 1936–37* (Ann Arbor: University of Michigan Press, 1969); I. Howe and B. J. Widick, *The U.A.W. and Walter Reuther* (New York: Random House, 1949).

56. See P. Eliel, 'Industrial Peace and Conflict: a Study of Two Pacific Coast Industries', *Industrial and Labor Relations Review*, II, pp. 477–501 (1949); P. L. Kleinsorge and W. C. Kerby, 'The Pulp and Paper Rebellion: A New Pacific Coast Union', *Industrial Relations*, VI, pp. 1–20 (1966).

57. Disputes between craft unions and the power of workers to halt production at critical points are often mentioned. See W. Haber and H. M. Levinson, *Labor Relations and Productivity in the Building Trades* (Ann Arbor: Bureau of Industrial Relations, University of Michigan, 1956).

Conclusions

There was no natural tendency for strike activity to decline: the outstanding feature of American strike patterns is their long-term constancy, with measures of worker involvement and duration showing no general upward or downward trend. More interestingly, the contrast between 'early' and 'modern' types of protest is largely inapplicable; although there is some evidence for the 'transformation' of the strike immediately after the first world war, this is not very strong. The brief consideration of 'strike waves', together with the examination of strikes during the second world war, suggested that strikes cannot, in general, be seen as politically-oriented actions. This point will be considered at greater length in the following chapter.

Although the broadest expectations of the institutionalization theory are unfounded, a weaker argument might be advanced. This is that institutionalization is contingent on economic circumstances and that, although the overall level of strike activity may not have changed, trends in activity are related to economic circumstances. It may be asked whether the trends identified above can be related to some external cause such as the business cycle, and Chapter 3 will answer some of these questions. Similarly, the evidence of the present chapter is not sufficient to assess Shorter and Tilly's explanation of the failure of American strikes to change 'shape'. Although the coming of mass unionism has not altered strike patterns, it is possible that the association between levels of unionization and strike activity has altered. Hence, analysis of year-to-year changes in strike rates, and of the correlates of these changes, is required. Chapter 3 turns to a detailed analysis of the broad changes which have been described and analysed here.

3

The Economic, Organizational, and Political Determinants of Strike Activity

Introduction

The central issue of this chapter is two-fold: how is strike activity related to economic, organizational, and political factors; and has the nature of the relationship changed? Snyder has recently extended Shorter and Tilly's thesis that in France organizational and political factors exerted a dominating influence on strike activity to cover the United States.[1] He argues that a concentration on economic variables is insufficient: although several studies have obtained impressive results when such variables are used to predict strike frequency, this is because only a limited number of countries and time periods have been considered. Economists, according to Snyder, ignore the 'institutional settings' within which economic variables operate; for a fuller understanding of the processes involved these settings must be made the centre of the analysis. Two ideal types of institutional setting are identified. In the first, collective bargaining is well institutionalized, unions are large and have a stable membership, and labour has an established political position. In the second, there is a low level of institutionalization, unions are small, and there is no participation in political activities.

Snyder applies this model to three countries, using strike activity as the dependent variable. He argues that in France and Italy the second type of setting has been a persistent feature of industrial relations but

1. D. Snyder, 'Institutional Setting and Industrial Conflict: Comparative Analyses of France, Italy and the United States', *American Sociological Review*, XL, pp. 259–78 (1975). See also idem, 'Early North American Strikes: A Reinterpretation', *Industrial and Labor Relations Review*, XXX, pp. 325–41 (1977).

that in the United States there has, since the second world war, been a shift from the second to the first. He tests this view by running regression equations for the periods 1900–48 and 1948–70. The argument is that, in France and Italy during both periods and in the United States during the first, political and organizational factors exerted most influence on strike activity; but in the United States in the second period economic influences were more significant. On the basis of the regression results Snyder argues that a change in the institutional setting of industrial conflict in the United States has altered the 'parameters' of conflict.

Although useful in moving away from the narrow confines of economists' models, this argument has difficulties of its own. At the most general level, there is a disjuncture between it and Shorter and Tilly's thesis from which it is derived. For Shorter and Tilly European strike shapes have altered because strikes have become demonstrations aimed at the political centre; in other words, political factors have become more important. But for Snyder the institutional setting of conflict has not changed. In the United States, on the other hand, the setting is said to have changed but, as was seen in Chapter 2, the shape of strikes has not altered. This problem could be solved by arguing that in France political factors have always been important and that it is only within this side of the model that changes have occurred. But there remains the difficulty of explaining why the shape of American strikes has not altered in response to a change of setting, and also why the overall level of activity has altered little.

There are also difficulties at a more detailed level, namely the application of the model to the evidence. These have been considered elsewhere[2] and the argument will not be repeated in detail. But it is obviously very difficult to obtain adequate measures of political factors. For the United States Snyder uses the political party of the President and the percentage of seats in Congress held by Democrats to measure the characteristics of the political centre. Not only are these indices different from those used in France and Italy, so that any direct comparison of the results of the three countries is suspect, but there is no obvious mechanism whereby the composition of the political centre affects strike rates. Economists have provided plausible accounts of the influence of such factors as the level of unemployment on strikes, but no similar arguments have been provided for the very crude political

2. P. K. Edwards, 'Time Series Regression Models of Strike Activity: A Reconsideration with American Data', *British Journal of Industrial Relations*, XVI, pp. 320–34 (1978).

indices which are available. There are also difficulties with using trade union density, which is Snyder's measure of organizational factors, to explain strike activity; these will be taken up further below.

Although Snyder's results are interesting, substantial problems of interpretation mean that the argument for a change in institutional setting requires further investigation. Moreover, as Snyder would presumably admit, his identification of two types of setting does not exhaust all possibilities; at best the idea that a once-for-all shift from one setting to another occurred is a first approximation to a more detailed picture. Thus, in the following analysis three periods and not two will be used. The precise coverage varies slightly according to the availability of data, the periods being approximately 1881—1910, 1900—39, and 1946—72.[3] These represent, respectively, the 'early' period of rapid industrialization and the breakdown of craft methods of production, the years in which Snyder's non-institutionalized setting was dominant, and the period during which an institutionalized system has been in operation. The distinction between the three periods is certainly not rigid or clear-cut, but the differences are sufficient for present purposes.

Before Snyder's model is assessed certain general aspects of strike activity must be considered. Thus the following section examines the interrelationships between aspects of the 'strike movement'. This is followed by an examination of the broad links between the business cycle and strikes; although Snyder is critical of economists, his own results rest on a limited number of regression equations and do not dispose of the possibility that a broader pattern of association may be present. It is then possible to turn to regression models of the kind used by Snyder.

Changes in the Character of the Strike Movement

Interrelations among Strike Indices

The contrasts between 'early' and 'modern' and between 'non-institutionalized' and 'institutionalized' forms of conflict refer to secular changes in strike activity, but they also contain implications for the way in which strike indices co-vary. Thus, from the argument that early strikes are mass upheavals, one would expect indices of frequency,

3. The overlap of the first two periods is needed to obtain a period long enough for statistical analysis to give significant results. The terminal date of 1972 is merely one of convenience, reflecting the availability of data when the analysis was first carried out. It seems very unlikely that the addition of two or three years at the end would materially affect the results.

worker involvement, and duration to move together; but, as strikes become more planned and predictable, a pattern of frequent and short strikes during prosperous periods, with large and long stoppages during depressions, may develop, with the result that frequency and duration become inversely related. Similarly, the frequency and size of strikes may be directly related in the 'early' period, whereas they will be expected to be inversely related subsequently. In the 'modern' period, strikes over 'aggressive' demands will be concentrated in prosperous periods, and will therefore be related to strike frequency, whereas in the 'early' period outbursts of activity may not be associated with aggressive demands.

With these expectations in mind, we can turn to Table 3.1, which reports the zero-order correlation coefficients between selected strike measures for the three periods under consideration. The indices for strike frequency (N/E), worker involvement (W/E), size (W/N) and duration are already familiar, but some comment on the other measures is required. The 'per cent wage and hour' variable measures the proportion of strikes called on wage and hours issues; it may be taken as an index of the tendency to call strikes over economic matters rather than union organization and the like. Similarly, 'per cent wage increase' means the proportion of strikes in which the issue was a demand for a wage increase; it is a rough indicator of the proportion of strikes over 'aggressive' demands. It is only rough since other forms of demand may be equally aggressive and since, in a period of rising prices, a demand for increases in wages to restore real incomes need not indicate militancy. However, there is a difference between trying to change the economic terms of the labour contract and seeking to preserve the *status quo*, and thus between making wage demands and attempting to alter the way in which the contract is negotiated. And, although strikes over other demands may be equally aggressive, stoppages for wage increases indicate a particular type of aggression which it is worth examining. The 'per cent won' and 'per cent lost' measures refer simply to the proportions of strikes which were won or lost.

One other preliminary point must be mentioned. It is well known that correlations between indices which contain common terms may be 'spurious'; the fact that both indices contain the common term means that they are not fully independent.[4] If the common term is in the

---

4. K. Pearson, 'Mathematical Contributions to the Theory of Evolution: On a Form of Spurious Correlation which may Arise when Indices are used in the Measurement of Organs', *Proceedings of the Royal Society*, LX, pp. 489–502 (1897). The point has been re-stated with reference to strike statistics by D. Britt and O. R. Galle, 'Structural Antecedents of the Shape of Strikes:

Determinants of Strike Activity

TABLE 3.1

ZERO ORDER CORRELATIONS BETWEEN STRIKE INDICES

	N/E	W/E	W/N	% Wage and Hour	Duration	% Wage Increase	% Won
1881–1915							
W/E	0.55						
W/N	−0.39	0.52					
% wage and hour	−0.50	−0.08	0.52				
Duration	0.07	0.25	0.28	−0.32			
% wage increase	−0.07	0.04	0.17	0.67	−0.60		
% won	−0.53	−0.18	0.36	0.34	0.07	0.07	
% lost	0.30	−0.03	−0.38	−0.25	0.04	−0.17	−0.86
1916–39							
W/E	0.66						
W/N	−0.02	0.63					
% wage and hour	0.13	0.26	0.21				
Duration	0.01	0.26	0.37	0.28			
% wage increase	0.64	0.53	0.05	0.22	−0.27		
% won	0.09	0.01	0.07	0.59	−0.25	0.04	
% lost	−0.56	−0.27	0.09	−0.55	0.43	−0.43	−0.65
1940–72							
W/E	0.81						
W/N	0.51	0.90					
% wage and hour	−0.36	−0.16	0.09				
Duration	−0.51	−0.20	0.04	0.33			

NOTE

Series on %s won and lost not available for 1940–72; series on wage increase strikes available only up to 1960.

Significant levels are not indicated in the body of the table since it is unclear whether a one- or two-tailed test should be employed. To be significantly different from zero, coefficients must exceed the levels given below:

		1881–1915	1916–39	1940–72
Two-tailed test	5% signif. level	0.335	0.404	0.345
	1% signif. level	0.432	0.515	0.443
One-tailed test	5% signif. level	0.283	0.344	0.284
	1% signif. level	0.393	0.472	0.404

numerator of the indices, the correlation will tend to be positive, whereas if it is in the numerator of one and the denominator of the other the correlation will tend to be negative. For example, one would expect W/N to be associated positively with W/E and negatively with

A Comparative Analysis', *American Sociological Review*, XXXIX, pp. 642–51 (1974), at p. 646.

N/E. As Table 3.1 shows, these expectations were met in the period 1881–1915, but in 1916–39 the association between size and frequency was not significant and in 1940–72 it was positive. This suggests that 'spurious' correlations between variables do not necessarily outweigh 'genuine' ones, a point which is borne out when other associations are considered, for example that between the proportion of strikes lost and strike frequency in 1881–1915.

The expectations outlined at the start of this section are not completely fulfilled. For 1881–1915, the relationship between frequency and the success rate was in the predicted direction, but that between size and frequency was not. Moreover, there were insignificant relationships between duration and frequency and the proportion of 'aggressive' strikes and frequency, whereas positive and negative correlations, respectively, were expected. Predictions concerning the 'modern' pattern of activity are more difficult to assess since data on the rate of success of strikes and the proportion with aggressive demands are not available for 1940–72. For this period, the duration-frequency link was in the expected direction, but the relationship between size and frequency was not. For 1916–39, only the association between frequency and aggressive strikes was significant. If this period is seen as a 'modern' one, this finding is in line with expectations, but, if it is seen as a time when relations were not institutionalized, the finding is contrary to expectations. In any event, the absence of significant relationships on the other three dimensions under consideration suggests that the period fits neither characterization closely.

There is some evidence to suggest, then, that the 1916–39 period was transitional between 'early' and 'modern' patterns of activity; the size-frequency association, for example, was not significant in this period whereas it was negative previously and positive subsequently. However, as has been seen, the direction of relationships in the 'early' and 'modern' periods was not always the same as that predicted on the basis of this contrast. In other words, there may be a distinction between two types of strike pattern, but the distinction does not fit the early-modern contrast.

Several other important features of Table 3.1 must be noted. The link between frequency and worker involvement became increasingly strong, a fact which is consistent with that part of the institutionalization theory which suggests that the strike movement will become more 'concentrated'. In other words, frequency and worker involvement will vary together because they both reflect institutional decisions and not more 'random' influences. In 1881–1915, these two variables were inversely associated with the proportion of strikes on wage and hours matters, whereas in 1916—39 the association was direct. Since the institutionalization theory argues that strikes will become increasingly orientated to economic issues, this finding apparently gives it some support; in contrast to earlier periods, high levels of strike activity in 1916—39 were associated with a large proportion of disputes on economic matters. However, the timing of this change weakens this interpretation, since 1916—39 can be seen as a period when relations were not institutionalized.

A common view about the effect of the business cycle on strikes is that in booms stoppages will be frequent, concentrated on economic demands and short; whereas in depressions they will be long and large battles, and less concerned with economic matters, particularly wage increases. One would thus expect the patterns of Table 3.1 (p. 56) to reflect this effect. As already noted, frequency and duration were not related in 1881—1939, although in 1940—72 the correlation was in the predicted direction. But frequency was generally inversely associated with the proportion of strikes on economic matters, and the proportion for wage increases was not associated with size, although it had the predicted negative relationship with duration in 1881—1915. The direct link between the percentage of strikes lost and duration is consistent with the view that lost strikes will be concentrated in depressions, but at the same time there was an inverse link between the proportion lost and the size of strikes, which goes counter to predictions.

Overall, inter-relationships among aspects of the strike movement do not exhibit the tidy patterns which the institutionalization theory and business cycle arguments might lead one to expect. One relationship is in the predicted direction and another is not; and the direction of the correlation between two variables is not stable from one period to the next. This may be partly due to differences in the degree to which the level of an index in one year is related to its level in the previous year. In other words, if the frequency of strikes fluctuates widely from year to year, the index of frequency may not be strongly related to other indices.

The Variability of Strike Activity

Fluctuations in the strike rate are also important for the view that strike patterns have become 'modernized'. One might expect 'early' protests to occur randomly, with the result that the number of strikes in one year is unrelated to the number in previous and subsequent years. By contrast, there should be a low level of variability in 'modern' strike patterns.

TABLE 3.2

**STRIKE INDICES: VARIABILITY AND CORRELATION WITH TIME
TREND, 1882–1972**

| | Coeff. of Variation (%) | | | Coeff. of Correlation with Time Trend | | |
	N	W	D	N	W	D
1882–93	45.2	47.0		0.75	0.23	
1894–1905	44.8	35.9		0.75	0.24	
1906–15	20.1	45.2		0.06	0.69	
1916–27	56.6	83.3		–0.93	–0.57	
1928–39	66.6	67.4	52.4	0.82	0.69	0.58
1940–51	20.7	46.3	92.3	0.43	0.41	0.38
1952–63	16.2	39.1	59.1	–0.77	–0.79	–0.39
1964–72	19.1	35.6	43.4	0.77	0.51	0.53

NOTE
Coefficient of variation is the standard deviation, divided by the mean, times 100.

As Table 3.2 shows, these expectations are met for the number of
strikes, in that the variability of the number in the years since 1940 was
much lower than that at the end of the nineteenth century. However,
there was no simple downward trend, since variability was greatest in
the period 1928–39; and, for worker involvement, variability at the
end of the nineteenth century was similar to that in the 1960s. More
interestingly, the low coefficient of variation of strike frequency since
1940 can be explained in terms of the character of collective bargaining, and not of the modernity of the strike movement. Since fixed-term
contracts are the norm, strikes in any industry will show a three, four,
or five year cycle depending on the length of contracts typically in
force. When all industries are considered, these cycles will cancel each
other out, so that the number of strikes is more or less constant. However, it so happens that more contracts expire in some years than
others, and thus the cancelling out effect is only approximate. This, and
the fact that not all strikes occur at the expiration of contracts, accounts
for the remaining variability of strike frequency.

Table 3.2 also gives the correlation coefficients between the three
main strike indices and the time variable. As would be expected from
the findings of Chapter 2, there has been no clear tendency for the
strike to 'wither away': in only two of the eight periods was the correlation between time and the strike measures inverse. Moreover, these two
periods, the 1920s and 1950s, were those in which theories about the

'maturation' of industrial relations flourished.[5] The evidence of Table 3.2 shows how limited these theories are, and how dangerous it is to generalize from short-term trends.

Strikes and the Business Cycle

It is a commonplace that economic conditions influence the development of the labour movement. For example, both Commons and Ware argued that business fluctuations influenced not only the rate of growth of the movement but also its character: in recessions the movement would be reformist, backward-looking and keen on co-operative ventures whereas in expansions it would adopt trade unionism and a more forward-looking approach.[6] But the nature of the impact of economic conditions has been in dispute.[7] Before turning to the evidence on strikes and the business cycle, the relationship which earlier work leads one to expect must be briefly examined.

It has often been noted that there is a tendency for the amount of strike activity to be directly associated with the level of business activity.[8] There is also a systematic tendency for the turning points of the two cycles to be close together, with the strike cycle slightly leading that of business. This circumstance led Griffin and other writers to suggest that strikes had a direct effect on levels of business activity by affecting employers' expectations about the future;[9] but Rees casts

5. See, respectively, E. T. Hiller, *The Strike* (Chicago: University of Chicago Press, 1928), pp. 193–4, 223–31; R. A. Lester, *As Unions Mature* (Princeton: Princeton University Press, 1948), p. 32 and *passim*.
6. J. R. Commons *et al.*, *History of Labour in the United States*, Vol. I (New York: Macmillan, 1918), esp. pp. 11, 361–3, 381–9; N. J. Ware, *The Industrial Worker, 1840–60* (Boston; Houghton Mifflin, 1924), pp. 198–232.
7. For criticism of the view of Commons and others that unions stem solely from economic or industrial causes see R. F. Hoxie, *Trade Unionism in the United States* (New York: Russell and Russell, 1966), pp. 62–6. See also I. Bernstein, 'The Growth of American Unions', *American Economic Review*, XLIV, pp. 301–18 (1954).
8. A. H. Hansen, 'Cycles of Strikes', *American Economic Review,* XI, pp. 616–21 (1921); J. I. Griffin, *Strikes: A Study in Quantitative Economics* (New York: Columbia University Press, 1939), pp. 47–51, 62–71; A. Rees, 'Industrial Conflict and Business Fluctuation', *Journal of Political Economy*, LX, pp. 371–82 (1952); P. S. O'Brien, 'Industrial Conflict and Business Fluctuation: A Comment', *Journal of Political Economy*, LXXIII, pp. 650–4 (1965); A. R. Weintraub, 'Prosperity versus Strikes: An Empirical Approach'. *Industrial and Labor Relations Review*, XIV, pp. 231–8 (1966).
9. Griffin, op. cit., pp. 50–51. See also V. W. Lanfear, *Business Fluctuations and the American Labor Movement, 1915–22* (New York: Columbia Univer-

severe doubt on this by pointing out that strike activity is never high enough to be able to influence business confidence in the aggregate. However, Rees's own interpretation of the lead of the strike cycle is also incomplete.[10]

More generally, the reasons for the close link between strikes and economic fluctuations have been spelt out less fully than one would expect. As Levitt points out, the implicit argument goes as follows.[11] The strike is potentially more effective in booms than recessions for two sorts of reason. On the workers' side, resources to last out a strike are relatively great, and the tight condition of the labour market means that the use of strike-breakers need not be feared. On the employers' side, inventories are relatively low (so that customers cannot be supplied from stockpiles or production continued using stocks of raw materials) and the chances for making profits too tempting to miss. It might also be argued that rising prices will reduce workers' real income and will therefore contribute to feelings of discontent, or that the pressures of working at full capacity will make workers restless and will cause petty disputes over breakdowns of machinery and the like to develop into stoppages.

This is clearly not a complete account of why strike activity should be related to economic conditions. No one would deny that workers' bargaining power is influenced by the economic climate, but there is no reason why this should necessarily be reflected in patterns of strike activity. If the employer is anxious to continue production, he will be likely to give way to demands without a strike being necessary. Prosperity may take the edge off workers' discontents, so that the ability to strike may not be matched by a willingness to stop work. And tensions caused by working at high pressure may be reflected in increased absenteeism and sickness instead of strikes. Moreover, a general tendency for strikes to be associated with business conditions does not indicate the strength of the relationship, and it is therefore necessary to

---

sity Press, 1924), p. 60; E. H. and D. B. Jurkat 'Economic Function of Strikes', *Industrial and Labor Relations Review*, II, p. 527–45 (1949).

10. For the incompletness of Rees's account, see O'Brien, op. cit.

11. T. Levitt, 'Prosperity versus Strikes', *Industrial and Labor Relations Review*, VI, pp. 220–26 (1953). On the economic interpretation of strikes in general, see M. R. Fisher, *Measurement of Labour Disputes and their Economic Effects* (Paris: Organization for Economic Co-operation and Development, 1973), pp. 43–53. For the classic statement of the determinants of labour's bargaining power, see A. Marshall, *Elements of the Economics of Industry* (4th edn; London: Macmillan, 1907), pp. 366–7.

examine how great is the dependence of the strike series on business activity.

A further hypothesis to be examined is that the characteristics of the strike movement will vary over the business cycle. One obvious argument is that strikes will be more successful in booms than depressions; another is that demands for wage increases will be concentrated in prosperous periods. Less immediately obvious is the argument that booms will be characterized by short stoppages, which are generally small, whereas strikes in depressions will be large and long.[12] The rationale for this is that bargaining disputes in booms will be settled quickly and will often relate to limited aspects of the employment contract. By contrast, the more fundamental disputes in recessions, over redundancies or managerial attempts to regain some of the control over the work place yielded when business was brisk, will be lengthy battles involving many workers.

Two indices for the business cycle have been used: the unemployment rate and a constructed index measuring the broader impact of economic conditions. The significance of the unemployment rate is obvious.[13] But it might be suggested that the link between business activity and strikes is less direct than the use of the unemployment rate implies: strike activity may reflect only broadly the impact of economic changes, with a small change in unemployment having little effect but with a large change having a disproportionate impact. Thus, in their paper on trade union growth, Ashenfelter and Pencavel argue that the amount of discontent felt by workers will be a function of the depth of the previous depression, with the discontent being dissipated as time goes on.[14] Two measures have therefore been constructed of the depth

---

12. H. A. Turner, G. Clack and G. Roberts, *Labour Relations in the Motor Industry* (London: Allen and Unwin, 1967), pp. 112–13; see also Levitt, loc. cit.

13. Official data exist for the period since 1900; but it has been possible to estimate a series going back to 1881. For details of this, see Appendix D.

14. O. Ashenfelter and J. H. Pencavel, 'American Trade Union Growth: 1900–60', *Quarterly Journal and Economics*, LXXXIII, pp. 434–48 (1969), at p. 437. Bain and Elsheikh have criticized Ashenfelter and Pencavel in terms which also have a bearing on the approach used here. They suggest that it is not clear what the workers' 'stock of grievances' postulated by Ashenfelter and Pencavel is; that the process whereby grievances lead workers to join unions is not specified; and that it is questionable whether the lagged unemployment measures catch any more 'discontent' than indices of increasing prices and falling employment, which are already included in the Ashenfelter-Pencavel model. The first point is not a problem here since the measures used are not represented as indices of 'discontent'; they are merely indices of the broad trend of the business cycle and attempt to abstract from im-

of depressions and the height of booms called, respectively, 'trough' (for the trough of business activity) and 'peak'. Two indices are required in studying strike activity since previous periods of prosperity are as likely as previous depressions to affect workers' feelings of 'discontent'.

'Peak' and 'trough' are more loosely connected with immediate conditions than the Ashenfelter and Pencavel index since no allowance is made in them for the dissipation of the effects of a depression or boom. The measure of unemployment troughs is calculated as follows.[15] The annual series of unemployment was examined and a number of recessions (defined as years in which unemployment was greater than in preceding and subsequent years) identified. For the years between each trough the value of the index is the unemployment rate of the previous trough, unless the rate in the current year exceeds that in the recession year, in which case the current rate is substituted. Thus the index reflects the depth of the last recession to have occurred, unless the present one is deeper than the previous one. The reason for constructing the index in this way is that, if current unemployment is higher than that in the previous recession, the impact of present conditions will be more significant than that of the past situation. It is true that, if unemployment is continuously increasing, the index will measure current and not historical levels of unemployment, with the result that it will not indicate the effects of past recessions. But it is better to amend the meaning of the index slightly than to try to explain strike activity in a period of high unemployment with an index which claims to measure the effects of recessions but which uses previous, and lower, unemployment rates to do so.

Although Ashenfelter and Pencavel use their lagged unemployment measure as an index of 'discontent', the peak and trough indices should not be seen in a similar light. It is obvious that the level of 'discontent' is influenced by many things and that the depth of past recessions is only a very rough proxy for it. More fundamentally, discontent is an individual characteristic whereas Ashenfelter and Pencavel's model of

---

mediate influences. Bain and Elsheikh's second point applies to *any* aggregate analysis, since one cannot specify fully every assumption that is made. Their third criticism does not apply since the constructed indices are not used in the same model as the rate of unemployment, and since results reported below suggest that the constructed indices have an influence on strikes which is separable from that of price changes. See G. S. Bain and F. Elsheikh, *Union Growth and the Business Cycle* (Oxford: Blackwell, 1976), p. 40.

15. The peak measure is calculated analogously.

union growth operates at the aggregate level. Therefore, as several writers have suggested, any number of hypotheses at the individual level can 'fit' aggregate models.[16] Throughout this study, an attempt is made to avoid the danger of interpreting aggregate regression results in an individualistic way. The institutionalization and business cycle theories make statements about the overall nature of industrial relations and patterns of conflict. It is therefore appropriate to test them using aggregate data.

Table 3.3 reports the correlation coefficients between measures of strike activity and the three indices of the business cycle. The strike indices are the same as those used in Table 3.1; that is, worker involvement and the number of strikes are deflated by the level of employment. This is essential when any long run of years is considered; it is remarkable that the early investigations of economists, and indeed many more recent approaches, used uncorrected measures. The overwhelming impression from Table 3.3 is that the association between strikes and the business cycle is very weak. Only in 1940–72 did the unemployment rate achieve a correlation significantly different from zero: with the proportion of strikes over wages and hours. As one would expect, the correlation was inverse, indicating a tendency for strikes over economic demands to be concentrated in periods of expansion. Similarly, the trough measure achieved a number of significant correlations only in 1940–72. The direct link with strike frequency suggests that a deep recession led to a high strike rate subsequently. The strong inverse association with strike duration, which also held less strongly in earlier years, indicates that deep recessions tended to make subsequent protests shorter. The peaks measure was also most significantly linked with strikes in the most recent period; the inverse link with strike activity shows that a period of prosperity tended to reduce the strike rate subsequently.

Despite these generally unsatisfactory results, it is possible that there is a broader pattern of association.[17] Thus Hill and Thurley have

16. E. Evans 'Research Note: On Some Recent Econometric Models of Strike Frequency', *Industrial Relations Journal*, VII, No. 3, pp. 72–6 (1976), at p. 74; J. Shorey, 'Time Series Analysis of Strike Frequency', *British Journal of Industrial Relations*, XV, pp. 63–75 (1977), at p. 73. More general problems with economic models of strike activity and the use of macro data to 'test' micro theories are considered in Edwards, op. cit.

17. Cf. D. Yoder, 'Economic Changes and Industrial Unrest in the United States', *Readings in Labor Economics*, ed. F. S. Doody (Cambridge, Mass.: Addison-Wesley, 1950), pp. 163–78. At p. 175, Yoder writes: 'while business conditions are reflected in strikes, there is no simple pattern of covariation. Strikes appear generally to increase when business is expanding rapidly from un-

TABLE 3.3

ZERO-ORDER CORRELATIONS BETWEEN STRIKE INDICES AND MEASURES OF THE BUSINESS CYCLE

	N/E	W/E	W/N	% Wage and Hour	Duration	% Wage Increase	% Won	% Lost
				1881–1915				
U/E	−0.24	0.04	0.19	−0.07	−0.16	−0.11	−0.19	0.10
Trough	0.03	0.17	0.06	−0.08	−0.40	0.08	−0.22	−0.15
Peak	−0.14	0.14	0.19	−0.09	0.33	0.17	0.04	0.08
				1916–39				
U/E	−0.07	−0.08	0.01	−0.14	−0.29	−0.37	0.17	−0.06
Trough	0.19	0.14	0.08	−0.17	−0.34	−0.13	0.35	−0.28
Peak	0.29	−0.03	−0.28	−0.64	−0.28	−0.18	0.40	−0.63
				1940–72				
U/E	−0.24	−0.31	−0.33	−0.50	0.33			
Trough	0.40	0.06	−0.20	−0.58	−0.75			
Peak	−0.25	−0.42	−0.49	−0.52	0.20			

NOTE
For significance levels, see Table 3.1.
U is the number unemployed; i.e. U/E is the unemployment rate.
For the meaning of Trough and Peak, see text.

argued that the sociological significance of conflict will vary with the business cycle.[18] Conflict will be greatest during the upswing and downswing of the cycle since, in the former, workers will use 'rational' bargaining techniques to obtain concessions from the employer and, in the latter, there will be increasing perceptions of class conflict. By contrast the bottom of the depression will be characterized by depression and withdrawal and the top of the boom by individual rather than collective feelings of anomie.

The results of dividing the business cycle into the four periods indicated are given in Table 3.4. The method is naturally only rough when annual data are used since the turning points of the cycle cannot be very clearly established, but some comparison is possible. There was no

usually low levels. They decrease when business is declining or when it holds on somewhat subnormal levels.'

18. S. Hill and K. Thurley, 'Sociology and Industrial Relations', *British Journal of Industrial Relations*, XII, pp. 147–70 (1974), at pp. 167–9.

TABLE 3.4

STRIKE INDICES FOR PERIODS OF THE BUSINESS CYCLE 1882–1972

	Upswing	Boom	Downswing	Recession
		1882–1905		
N/E	136	101	125	115
W/N	218	314	250	326
Duration	27.6	35.1	31.5	23.3
		1901–28		
N/E	127	105	105	125
W/N	318	281	394	269
Duration	23.7	18.8	23.7	30.9
		1901–38		
N/E	103	115	86.3	110
W/N	363	311	392	313
Duration	23.4	19.2	23.4	29.1
		1947–72		
N/E	78.6	80.8	71.1	71.7
W/N	488	513	467	589
Duration	21.9	21.5	22.8	23.4
		1901–72		
N/E	87.4	97.6	80.3	87.9
W/N	436	412	453	527
Duration	21.3	18.5	22.0	25.7

NOTE
N/E is the number of strikes per million employees. W/N is the number of workers involved per strike. Duration is the mean duration of strikes, in days.

consistent tendency for strike frequency to be greatest in the up and downswings. Neither were the longest and largest strikes concentrated in the downswings, contrary to the prediction that it is here that class conflict will be most apparent. The recession period has generally had the longest and largest stoppages; only in 1882–1905 did the downswing have the longest strikes, and only in 1901–38 the largest.

The view that strikes will be large in recessions and smaller in booms receives some support from the data for the years 1901–72 as a whole; strikes were larger in the downswing than the upswing and were larger still in the recession period. However, this did not hold for the various sub-periods; thus in 1947–72 the size of strikes was greater in boom periods than in the up or downswings and in 1901–38 the size in booms and recessions was nearly identical. Indeed, there is no pattern of relationship between strikes and the level of business activity which held for all the periods considered. Moreover, there was no simple shift from one pattern to another, a point which will have to be given much more attention when the 'institutional parameters of conflict' are considered.

Thus, the view that strike activity will depend on the business cycle has won rather too easy acceptance. Even writers like Levitt who criticize the view that 'prosperity leads to strikes' accept that there is an empirically regular link between economic activity and strikes. But the different forms of analysis in Tables 3.3 and 3.4 have failed to indicate any very clear patterns.

How can this be equated with the findings of the early economists that cycles of strikes and business go together? The answer is that these writers showed only that the turning points of the cycles occur at similar points and that in any one business cycle strike activity is directly associated with the level of business activity. But over a number of cycles the relationship is unstable; different levels of unemployment will be related to different levels of strike activity. Many factors affect the decision to strike, but they may be grouped into two: those which increase strike activity in booms, such as the growth of workers' bargaining power; and those, such as the complacency which comes with prosperity[19] and the willingness of employers to give way without a strike, which reduce activity. The balance between these two sets of forces will vary between cycles and thus the overall effect of the business cycle on strikes will be limited.

The Economic Model

In moving away from a straightforward economic model of strike activity Shorter and Tilly and Snyder provide only a limited range of tests of such a model; it seems preferable to re-assess it in its simple form before adding organizational and political variables. Moreover, Snyder does not deal with the question of whether changes have taken place within the economic and organizational-political models. For example, the unemployment rate may have had an increased impact on strike activity and the level of wages a reduced effect. These changes are as important as changes between models in examining alterations in the 'parameters' of strike activity.

19. On this, see Levitt, loc. cit.

Tests on Annual Data

Two of the variables most frequently used by economists are the unemployment rate and the rate of change of real wages. The significance of the former has been considered above; the latter is usually taken as an index of workers' aspirations or of the gap between aspirations and achievement.[20] The complexities of this view of the index cannot be considered here, and the rate of change of wages will be treated as a rough measure of the speed with which prosperity increases. But the level of wages is also important in long-term analyses since one might expect improvements in the standard of living to take the edge off 'discontents' and thus to reduce strike activity.[21]

The most obvious procedure is to carry out the simple regression of strike frequency on the unemployment rate or the rate of change of real wages for the longest time span for which data are available. In both cases, virtually no association was present; and several other experiments, such as introducing lags into the model, yielded unsatisfactory results.[22]

When the three sub-periods are considered, the position improves substantially. The results of predicting strike frequency (N/E) from several independent variables are given in Table 3.5. This and the following tables concentrate on strike frequency since, as early writers have shown and as will become apparent later, indices of frequency are more closely related to structural factors than are other measures of strike activity.[23] It is desirable to test the economic models where they have the greatest chance of performing well, and, to facilitate comparison of different models, it is convenient to use the same dependent variable throughout. The procedure in reporting the results is to give

20. See, in particular, O. Ashenfelter and G. E. Johnson, 'Bargaining Theory, Trade Unions and Industrial Strike Activity', *American Economic Review*, LIX, pp. 35–49 (1969) at p. 41; see also L. C. Hunter, 'The Economic Determination of Strike Activity: A Reconsideration', University of Glasgow Discussion Papers in Economics, No. 1 (Glasgow: University of Glasgow, Department of Economics, 1973), p. 11.

21. Use of the term 'discontent' does not mean that individualistic hypotheses are being smuggled into a macro analysis. It is obvious that some 'model of man' must be used, even in the most aggregate analysis; and the expectation about the effects of the rate of change of real wages on strikes does not involve a model so complex that the macro analysis is vitiated.

22. For details of this, and other 'failed experiments', see P. K. Edwards, 'Strikes in the United States, 1881–1972' (D. Phil. thesis, University of Oxford, 1977), pp. 169–70 and tables A–11 and A–13.

23. See J. W. Skeels, 'Measures of U.S. Strike Activity', *Industrial and Labor Relations Review*, XXIV, pp. 515–25 (1971).

TABLE 3.5

REGRESSION RESULTS, ECONOMIC VARIABLES: DEPENDENT VARIABLE N/E

	Independent Variables						R^2	D–W
	Trough	Peak	A/P	Ch.A/P	Ch.A	Ch.P		
1890–1910	Neg	Neg	Pos	Pos			0.47	1.50
	1%	NS	1%	NS				
1900–39	Pos	Pos	Neg	Pos			0.69	1.33
	5%	5%	1%	NS				
1946–72	Pos	Neg	Neg	Pos			0.65	1.74
	5%	1%	5%	NS				
1890–1910	Neg	Neg	Pos		Pos	Pos	0.51	1.70
	1%	NS	1%		NS	NS		
1900–39	Pos	Pos	Neg		Pos	Pos	0.78	1.65
	1%	1%	1%		NS	NS		
1946–72	Pos	Neg	Neg		Pos	Neg	0.68	1.53
	5%	1%	1%		5%	5%		

NOTE
R^2 = overall coefficient of determination, corrected for degrees of freedom. 'D–W' is the Durbin-Watson statistic.
Pos and Neg = respectively, that the coefficient of an independent variable is positive or negative.
1% and 5% = level of significance of the coefficient.
NS = not significant.
A = average annual money wage.
P = consumer price index; i.e. A/P is the level of real wages.
Ch. denotes proportional change in; i.e. Ch.A/P, Ch.A and Ch.P are, respectively, the rates of change of real wages, money wages and prices.

the sign of the coefficients of the independent variables and to state whether they achieve one of the two conventional levels of significance or are not significant; this seems preferable to cluttering the table with the actual coefficients and their 't' values. All the equations include a constant term but, again for reasons of clarity, this is not reported. The coefficient of determination (R^2) is given when the correction for degrees of freedom has been carried out; finally, the Durbin–Watson statistic, the measure of autocorrelation, is reported.

The peak and trough measures are used as indices of the business cycle since this generally appears to improve the solution, compared to the use of unemployment rate. In the first three equations of Table 3.5, these measures are used in combination with the level and rate of change of real wages; quite high, and increasing, R^2s were obtained.[24] The rate of change of wages did not contribute significantly to the result in any of the three periods, which is surprising in view of the theoretical importance, as a measure of the 'expectations-achievement gap', which it has been given. The level of wages had a direct effect on strike frequency at first, but since 1900 there has been an inverse relationship. The latter effect is, of course, that predicted by the institutionalization theory, but the theory would be on stronger ground if the shift in direction occurred after the second world war: that is, after institutionalized bargaining had been established. The timing of the shift around the turn of the century is consistent with the argument from industrialization.

In the latter part of Table 3.5, the change in real earnings is broken down into its wage and price components. Neither achieved significance in the first two periods, but, compared with the use of real wage changes, the solutions improve: the R^2s were higher and the Durbin–Watson increased. As one would expect, the coefficient for the change in prices was positive, indicating that rapid inflation encouraged strike activity. But in 1946–72, when the variable attained significance, its coefficient was negative. This is surprising in view of the general expectation that price inflation will encourage strikes, and the fact that such an association has been found to hold in Canada.[25] And a fast rate of increase of money earnings was associated with a rise in N/E whereas

24. There may be problems of multicollinearity (which means that the independent variables are highly correlated with each other, with the result that estimates of their regression coefficients are (when the correlations are very high) extremely unstable). Given below, therefore, are the zero-order correlation coefficients between the independent variables used in Table 3.5, for the period 1946–72:

	Trough	*Peak*	*A/P*	*Ch.A/P*	*Ch.A*	*Ch.P*
Peak	–0.15					
A/P	–0.08	0.55				
Ch.A/P	–0.29	0.20	–0.10			
Ch.A	–0.27	–0.50	–0.27			
Ch.P.	–0.22	–0.47	–0.23		0.79	

   For definition of variables, see note to Table 3.4. On the whole the levels of the coefficients are reasonable, but the lower values for the change of real wages (Ch.A/P) variables than for the changes of wages and prices (Ch.A and Ch.P) suggest that the model using the rate of change of real wages is the more valid.

25. W. D. Walsh, 'Economic Conditions and Strike Activity in Canada', *Industrial Relations*, XIV, pp. 45–54 (1975), at p. 51.

the level of wages tended to reduce strike frequency. Thus it appears that a rising level of real wages reduced 'discontent' whereas a rapid increase in money wages increased it.

The interpretation of the peak and trough variables is rather complex. The negative coefficient for 'trough' in 1890–1910 indicates that a deep recession tended to reduce subsequent strike activity, but in the two later periods the effect was in the opposite direction. In the first two periods, the peak variable operated in the same direction as 'trough'; that is, in 1890–1910 deep recessions and high booms reduced subsequent strike activity, whereas in 1900–39 they tended to increase activity. Other things equal, one might expect the discontent caused by depressions to stimulate protests later, so the early negative coefficient of the trough variable is a puzzle. Expectations for 'peak' are less clear. One might argue, as do Hill and Thurley, that the downswing of the business cycle will be marked by class conscious protests; thus the higher the previous boom, the greater will be the subsequent protest. On the other hand, past prosperity may make workers relatively content, so that they will be prepared to take a passive line in recessions. The evidence from Table 3.5 suggests that the latter view holds for the first and third periods, and the former for the second period. Only in 1946–72 was there a clear situation in which past booms were associated with low strike activity subsequently, and past recessions with high rates of activity later.

These results suggest, in line with the findings noted above, that the relationship between economic variables and strike activity is unstable, a point which has been overlooked by writers who concentrate on relatively short periods of time. An explanation of the patterns revealed in Table 3.5 can be found, however.

When the negative coefficient of the trough variable in 1890–1910 is considered with the positive one for the level of wages, and contrasted with the reverse situation in later years, it appears that early and later protests had a different character. In the early years rising wages seem to have enabled workers to strike: when living standards were very low workers lacked the resources to strike, but when real wages reached a somewhat higher level they were in a position to protest against their conditions. But at the same time a deep recession destroyed much of what they had gained previously and led to a cautious approach during the recovery from the recession. After this early period real wages reached higher levels and prosperity took the edge off discontents; but a recession made workers determined to regain their losses. The evidence from the peak variable can now be fitted into this interpretation. In the early period, a high level of business activity led to complacency, but, in the years after the shift in the effects of the trough and wage variables, booms encouraged workers to strike to defend their gains. But this was not a permanent position since, as prosperity increased further, the need to defend the gains declined. Or, as the institutionalization theorists would put it, bargaining had become established by this final period and employers no longer tried to destroy unions after a boom and therefore there was less need to strike. This interpretation clearly cannot stand on the basis of the regression results alone; the next three chapters will bring evidence of a different kind to bear on it.

These changes within the economic model are consistent with the view that the economic 'parameters' of strike activity have changed. However, one cannot conclude that there are three distinct 'stages' involved, since more detailed analysis might suggest that there are more aspects to be considered. And, despite the changes, the model as a whole works reasonably well for all three periods, in contrast to the implications of the organizational-political model.

Quarterly Data

Annual data can measure only the most general relationships between strikes and business conditions. Quarterly data have therefore been used to provide a more detailed analysis. As argued above, the association between strikes and economic conditions may not be stable, and the most useful procedure is therefore to take Ashenfelter and Johnson's model, which was originally tested against data for 1952–67, and apply it to the period 1962–72.[26]

The first equation in Table 3.6, which applies Ashenfelter and Johnson's preferred equation to 1962–72, shows two important differences from the results for 1952–67. The coefficient of the time variable became positive, indicating a strong upward trend in strike frequency, in addition to that which can be explained by the other variables in the equation. More importantly, the measure of the change in real wages (defined, following Ashenfelter and Johnson, as the difference between the rates of change of wages and prices) failed to attain significance. This suggests that the great weight which was placed on the negative coefficient for 1952–67 was misplaced. The failure of this relationship to continue in 1962–72 suggests that the influence of real wage changes on strikes was not consistent; and the implication is that

26. Ashenfelter and Johnson, op. cit. The model used here has various detailed differences from Ashenfelter and Johnson's; for example, the real wage variable is simply the difference between the rates of change of wages and prices, whereas Ashenfelter and Johnson used a distributed lag form. But the similarities are close enough for the two to be comparable.

Ashenfelter and Johnson's theoretical arguments may be mis-specified.

In the second equation, Ashenfelter and Johnson's seasonal dummies are replaced by an index of the number of contract expirations. The dummies were used as proxies for contract expiration, on the grounds that the probability of a strike will be affected by the number of labour-management contracts expiring. But data on contract expirations are available and can be used directly; the data are taken from B.L.S. reports on contracts filed with them. It is true that this is only a sample of all the contracts in existence, and that it is non-random since it relates only to contracts covering at least one thousand workers. But the use of seasonal dummies has the obvious disadvantage that strikes have always been related to seasonal variations,[27] with the result that the dummies may reflect a general seasonal impact on strike activity, and not the specific effect of contract expirations. The coefficient of determination fell from 0.85, in the first equation, to 0.56 in the second, even though the new variable was significant at the 1 per cent level; as one would expect, the number of contracts expiring exerted a direct effect on strike frequency. Thus it seems that the seasonal dummies cannot be taken as proxies for contract expirations. Moreover, a considerable amount of the variance explained in the Ashenfelter–Johnson model is due to general seasonal factors, which do not have any particular economic significance.

The remaining equations in Table 3.6 repeat the above exercise for the number of workers involved in strikes and the logarithm of the number of striker-days. Although, as noted above, it has been suggested that worker involvement should be predicted in a manner different from that applied to strike frequency, it seems reasonable to apply the economic model to variables other than strike frequency.[28] Economists have been criticized for concentrating on frequency, and the perspec-

27. Griffin, op. cit. pp. 51–6; F. Peterson, *Strikes in the United States, 1880– 1936* (Washington, D.C.: U.S. Department of Labor Bulletin No. 651, 1938), pp. 43–5. Note also the obvious limitations of a model which assumes that strikes occur only at the end of bargaining contracts. As will be seen in Chapter 6, strikes which were not at the end of existing contracts accounted for up to 54 per cent of the total in the period 1961–74; see below, pp. 181–2.

28. For studies which apply the same model to different strike measures, see Skeels, op. cit. and Snyder, op. cit. Although it may prove to be the case that different estimating equations and, indeed, different theoretical models are required to predict various aspects of strikes, it is far from clear at present precisely what these differences are. It thus seems useful to explore the role of the same model in explaining different features of strikes, while bearing in mind that strike frequency and worker involvement may be influenced by different factors.

TABLE 3.6

REGRESSION RESULTS, QUARTERLY DATA, 1962–72

Dependent Variable	Independent Variables								R^2	D–W
	U/E	(Ch.H–Ch.P)	Number of Workers in C.E.s	C.E.s	Time	O_1	O_2	O_3		
N	Neg 1%	Neg NS			Pos 1%	Pos NS	Pos 1%	Pos 1%	0.85	1.44
N	Neg 1%	Neg NS	Pos 1%		Pos 1%	NS	Pos 1%	Pos 1%	0.56	2.02
W	Neg NS	Neg NS			Pos 1%	Neg NS	Pos 1%	Pos NS	0.54	0.92
W	Neg NS	Neg NS		Pos 1%	Pos 1%		Pos 1%		0.42	1.58
Log D	Neg 5%	Neg NS			Pos 1%	Neg NS	Pos NS	Pos 5%	0.52	0.97
Log D	Neg 5%	Neg 5%		Pos NS	Pos 1%				0.46	1.47

NOTE

C.E. denotes contract expiration; thus the two variables are the number of contracts expiring in a quarter and the number of workers covered by contracts that expire. O_1, O_2, and O_3 are dummy variables for each of the first three quarters of the year.

tive must therefore be widened. Moreover, the series on the number of workers involved in contract expirations may be more reliable than those on the number of such expirations; although the number of expirations relates only to contracts covering at least one thousand workers, the number of workers covered by these large contracts is likely to approximate more closely to worker involvement in strikes, than is the number of expirations to strike frequency.

In none of these equations did the Ashenfelter—Johnson model explain a high proportion of the variance of the dependent variable; and the Durbin—Watson statistic was not within the acceptable region. When the seasonal dummies were replaced by the number of workers covered by expiring expirations, the D—W statistic improved and, although the R² declined, the fall was not so marked as in the case of the number of strikes. The pattern for striker-days was similar, although here both measures of contract expiration were used.

In all six equations, the coefficient for the change in real wages was negative, following the predictions of Ashenfelter and Johnson, but in only one did it achieve significant levels. This, together with the findings concerning the seasonal dummies, casts considerable doubt on the empirical side of their model; its wider theoretical significance is not of prime importance here. More generally the strong negative association between the unemployment rate and all measures of strike activity is in line with previous findings. Thus, indices of the severity and volume of activity were linked to business activity in the same way as the measure of strike frequency; that is, the overall amount of activity did not increase in recessions, expectations to the contrary notwithstanding. But we should be cautious about extending these findings for 1962—72 more widely, since the relationship between strikes and economic indices is far from stable.

Unionization and Strikes

The pattern of association between union density and eight measures of the strike movement is given in Table 3.7. The pattern is mixed, with the correlation coefficients being quite large in the first and third periods but with little significant association in the intervening years. In line with the argument that the organizing power of unions will enable workers to strike, the correlations with N/E and W/E were positive; and the negative association with strike duration suggests that unions avoided long stoppages. But other features of the table are more ambiguous. Thus, one might expect union density to be directly associated

TABLE 3.7

**ZERO-ORDER CORRELATION COEFFICIENTS BETWEEN UNION
DENSITY AND STRIKE INDICES**

	Union Density (T/E)		
	1881–1915	1916–39	1940–72
N/E	0.62	0.35	0.46
W/E	0.25	0.19	0.53
W/N	–0.43	–0.04	0.47
% wage and hour	–0.44	–0.37	–0.18
Duration	–0.30	0.23	–0.29
% wage increase	0.05	–0.20	
% won	–0.73	0.19	
% lost	0.46	–0.40	

NOTE
For significance levels, see note to Table 3.1.

with the proportion of strikes on economic issues, whereas the relationship was in fact inverse. Similarly, there was no significant link with the
proportion of strikes for wage increases, although a direct link might be
expected.

Perhaps the most remarkable feature of Table 3.7 is the strong inverse association between union density and the proportion of strikes
won in 1881–1915. This goes against all assertions that unions will
make striking more successful. The explanation may lie in the pattern
of association with the strike movement as a whole. In this period,
union density was associated with small strikes over non-economic
matters, and these strikes tended to be short and to be lost. Since
unions were concentrated among skilled craftsmen, this suggests that
union growth encouraged these workers to protest at the erosion of
their traditional position with the coming of large-scale industry.
Strikes with the characteristics mentioned were typically those associated with skilled men's protests, a point which is developed at more
length in Chapter 4. Thus, in the period 1881–1915, the union seems
to have been used to support craftsmen's struggles, and only later to
have been associated with planned 'economic' actions. The change in
the direction of association between union density and the size of
strikes also supports this view.

The importance of unionization, in comparison with economic variables, in explaining strike activity can now be considered. Since the
organizational power of workers is of interest, the most appropriate

TABLE 3.8

REGRESSION RESULTS, ECONOMIC AND UNION DENSITY VARIABLES: DEPENDENT VARIABLE N/E

	Independent Variables						R^2	D–W
	T/E	Trough	Peak	A/P	Ch.A	Ch.P		
1890–1970	Neg	Neg	Neg	Pos	Neg	Pos	0.48	1.67
	NS	1%	NS	NS	NS	NS		
1900–39	Pos	Pos	Pos	Neg	Pos	Pos	0.78	1.71
	NS	1%	1%	1%	NS	NS		
1946–72	Neg	Pos	Neg	Neg	Pos	Neg	0.70	1.64
	NS	5%	1%	1%	5%	5%		

NOTE
T is number of trade union members; i.e. T/E is union density.

measure is the level of union density, and not its rate of change. Several models were considered, the results of the most 'successful' being reported in Table 3.8.[29] Although satisfactory results were obtained for the model as a whole for the last two periods, of the six variables in the equation only the measure of union density (T/E) failed to attain significance throughout. Similar results for T/E emerged from the other models considered. Moreover, a comparison with the R^2s reported in Table 3.5 indicates that the addition of union density to the economic model did not raise its overall explanatory power.

The failure of union density to operate significantly in combination with the more general economic variables casts very great doubt on the view that organizational factors must be given an independent role in the determination of strike activity. The contrast between the results of Table 3.8 and those for the zero-order correlations between density and strike activity also suggests that reliance on correlational analysis alone can be highly misleading.

It may be wondered why union organization seems to be relatively unimportant in America when Shorter and Tilly attached so much significance to it in France. One answer, of course, is that the countries are different. But a more mundane explanation is possible. Economic variables have been used here to predict union density as well as strike activity. The details of this experiment are not important at present, but the more significant findings may be noted. Thus, predicting the

29. For other results, see Edwards, 'Time Series Regression Models', op. cit., table 2 and Edwards, 'Strikes in the United States', op. cit., pp. 186–7 and table 4–12.

number of union members in 1890—1910 from the peak and trough variables and the level and rate of change of real wages resulted in an R^2 of 0.96. Similarly the peak and trough variables and the level of wages explained 94 per cent of the variance in the number of union members in 1930—41. The level of union density thus depended strongly on economic conditions and Shorter and Tilly's findings may simply reflect this. In other words, union density may merely mediate part of the effect of economic variables, without adding any explanatory power of its own.

Union organization may be crucial to the expression of protest in strikes. But, if it is crucial, the approach of Shorter and Tilly has not demonstrated it. Indeed, such an approach cannot do so because it does not begin with economic variables and then examine the independent influence of union density. On the logical level, as noted above, the path analysis model used by these writers merely tests a set of theoretical arguments against the data and does not compare their validity with that of other arguments; it is one of many models which may fit the evidence. On the technical level, Shorter and Tilly insert union organization as a variable intervening between economic conditions and strike activity; but, since union density is strongly associated with these conditions, it is bound to appear to be an important factor in its own right, whereas in fact it may be merely passing on part of the direct influence of the economic variables on strike activity.

The failure of union organization to exert a significant influence in the regression models does not mean that unionization can be dismissed as an important factor in strike activity. Regression models explain the variance in the dependent variable in terms of the variance of the independent ones. Those things which exert a constant influence on the dependent variable, and which may be necessary for any activity to occur, will not appear to be important within a regression model.[30] The inclusion of union density in the regression models used here neither taps the whole of the influence of unions on strike activity nor takes into account their effect on the character of this activity. But the failure of union density to operate as a significant influence in the years before the second world war is important. For the years after the war,

---

30. That is, factors which exert a constant influence on strikes do not co-vary with strike activity and their influence is not reflected in regression models. For example, such things as the 'frustrations of work under capitalism' may be necessary for strikes to occur, but will not appear to be significant unless the strength of their impact on strikes varies. In the present case, union density can be significant only when its fluctuations are large enough to be associated with the wide fluctuations in strike activity.

when union density was relatively constant, it is not surprising that it cannot account for variations in strike activity, but for the earlier years it was fluctuating considerably and could have been expected to have been important.

The conclusion must be that changes in the coverage of unions, even at a time when they were growing fast, did not affect strike activity, as compared with the influence of economic variables. Later chapters will investigate whether the character of strikes has been changed by unions and whether differences in the strike-proneness of different industries at one time are associated with the density of union organization.

The Institutional Parameters of Industrial Conflict

The two measures of the political position of labour used by Snyder are the proportion of seats in Congress held by Democrats and the political party of the President. As reported elsewhere, using these two variables plus a time variable to explain strike frequency yielded moderately satisfactory overall results.[31] From Snyder's arguments, one would expect a fall in the explanatory power of the model in the period since 1945, compared with earlier years. There was in fact no marked change, and for worker involvement in strikes there was an increase: there is thus no evidence that the political model performed better in the 'non-institutionalized' than in the 'institutionalized' period.

Other experiments with a combination of economic and political and organizational variables similarly suggested that there was no clear-cut distinction between two periods, with one set important in the early period and the other in the late. Finally, a model similar to that used by Snyder was employed; its results are given in Table 3.9. The proportions of total variance explained are somewhat lower than those achieved by Snyder: 76 per cent in 1900–39 and 64 per cent in 1946–72, as against 83 per cent and 70 per cent. This can be explained by four influences: the absence of a time variable in the model used here; the fact that Snyder predicted to the logarithm of the number of strikes; the possibility that his R^2 was not corrected for degrees of freedom; and the fact that the periods covered differ slightly. The two models are thus similar in their overall explanatory power, but the present one does not indicate any marked shift in the parameters of conflict. Certainly the 'party of the President' variable lost significance and the trough variable gained it, but the 'per cent Democrat', peak,

31. Edwards, 'Time Series Regression Models', op. cit., table 3.

TABLE 3.9

**REGRESSION RESULTS, POLITICAL, ECONOMIC AND UNION DENSITY
VARIABLES: DEPENDENT VARIABLE N/E**

	Independent Variables						R^2	D–W
	P.P.	% Dem.	Trough	Peak	A/P	T/E		
1900–39	Neg	Pos	Pos	Pos	Neg	Pos	0.76	1.71
	5%	NS	NS	NS	1%	NS		
1946–72	Pos	Pos	Pos	Neg	Neg	Neg	0.64	1.76
	NS	NS	NS	1%	5%	NS		

and union density measures were not significant in either period. Hence, a rigid division between these two periods is not possible. Moreover, the levels of R^2 reported in Table 3.9 are rather lower than those for the economic variables alone given in Table 3.5. One cannot reject the hypothesis that levels of economic activity are adequate predictors of the rate of strike activity.

The broader questions raised by Snyder's approach must now be considered. The 'per cent of Congress Democrat' variable consistently failed to have a significant effect on strike activity. Similarly, Skeels found that a dummy variable representing presidential election years did not add to the explanatory power of his model.[32] This suggests that the choice of indicators of 'political' factors is far from straightforward. More importantly, Snyder has not shown that his approach is the most appropriate for the study of political influences on strikes. Indices of strike frequency and worker involvement are not necessarily the most relevant dependent variables since political influences may affect the character and aims of a strike movement more than the total amount of protest.

Although it is reasonable to suppose that strikes which are seen as threats to the health and welfare of the country will be subject to political influences,[33] this need not hold for strikes in general. Economic factors are common to all strikes, but political ones are likely to have an impact which is limited to a small range of strikes. It has not

32. Skeels, op. cit., p. 521.
33. On various aspects of public involvement in labour disputes see E. E. Witte, *The Government in Labor Disputes* (New York: McGraw-Hill, 1932); J. L. Blackman, *Presidential Seizure in Labor Disputes* (Cambridge, Mass.: Harvard University Press, 1967); I. Bernstein, H. L. Enarson and R. W. Fleming (eds), *Emergency Disputes and National Policy* (New York: Harper and Bros, 1955).

been demonstrated that political matters affect strikes as a whole.

The limitations of using simple 'political attitude' variables are readily apparent. Strike activity declined during Republican administrations, but this was largely due to the influence of the 1920s and the 1950s; it is unlikely that strike activity in these years would have been very different if a Democrat had been in the White House. The 1930s may appear to be a contrasting case, for the encouragement of the New Deal Democrats to unionization cannot be denied. But the massive changes that occurred in the thirties may have had a common origin, in that the shift to the Democrats and the growth of working class militancy cannot be separated.[34] More generally, the meaning of the contrast between Democrat and Republican has surely altered; the Democrats of the 1930s had very different policies from those of the 1880s.[35] Thus the theoretical status of the argument linking the party of the President to strike activity is far from clear. Similar points apply to the role of the proportion of seats in Congress held by Democrats.

Despite the attempts of Snyder and Shorter and Tilly to apply one type of 'political' model to the United States, it is necessary to approach the question of politics from a different angle. Instead of concentrating on a supposed political orientation among workers (measured by unsatisfactory indices), one should examine the role of the government and its decisions on when to intervene in labour disputes. As will be shown in later chapters, there is very little evidence that, in those strikes which had government involvement, the strikers had any specific political aims. It is preferable to start with the government itself and its definition of what sort of situation required its intervention.

Conclusions

Although economic circumstances strongly influenced strike activity, their impact was not consistent; the link between strikes and the business cycle was only a very general one. Moreover, the effect of immediate conditions was limited, and it was necessary to introduce the peak and trough measures to capture, in the regression models, the broad effects of business conditions; even these measures did not exert a consistent impact on strike activity.

The findings of Chapter 2, that strike activity has not been 'withering away', are confirmed here. There was no general tendency for the

---

34. See below, Chapter 5.
35. Note also the sharp regional differences in the meaning of voting for one party or the other.

time variable to have an inverse association with strike activity; nor was there a tendency for activity to decline in the period during which institutionalized relations were established. But there is some suggestion that the determinants of strike activity changed. The change was not of the kind envisaged by Snyder, but occurred among the variables which make up the economic model. As noted above, this change suggests that there were systematic differences between 'early' and 'modern' responses of strike activity to economic conditions. But there was no simple contrast between these extremes, since an intervening position was also identified. Thus, the arguments for a shift in the pattern of strikes as industrialization advances receive some support; but the findings of the regression analysis will have to be considered against those of the following chapters before any firm conclusions can be reached.

The 'early-modern' contrast implies two very simple ideal types of worker response to complex social changes. The consideration of three sub-periods instead of two has indicated that at least three ideal types must be distinguished. This is clearly no more than a provisional extension of the early-modern contrast, and several other ideal types could readily be suggested. As will be seen in the following chapter, conceptualizations of workers' responses to early industrialization have also been very limited. One must avoid the danger of drawing simple pictures of workers' reactions to industrial changes on the basis of contrasts between the amounts of strike activity in different periods.

Similarly, over-simple views of the impact of unionization on strike activity are inadequate. As noted in Chapter 2, the theory of the institutionalization of conflict expects unionization to encourage strikes before unions have become accommodated in the system and to discourage them subsequently. The dating of this shift is not uniform, some writers suggesting that unions will from their earliest days reduce strike activity and others seeing this tendency as coming with the growth of collective bargaining. But the correlational analysis showed no pattern which fits these views, and the regression models showed that the influence of union density on strikes, compared with that of economic factors, has been slight. Although unions have achieved a 'proprietorship' of the strike, they have not affected the amount of protest.

Shorter and Tilly see the union as a necessary force mediating between economic changes and strike activity. At its most general, there is little to quarrel with in this argument; it is obvious that structural changes have to be interpreted by workers before they can 'cause' strikes, and detailed studies have shown how union organization influences these interpretive processes. However, even at this level of generality, it is doubtful whether union density is a suitable proxy for organization more generally. More importantly here, Shorter and Tilly test their arguments on time series data, seeking to show that union density was a key variable explaining strike trends. However, such a test could at best show an association between the two phenomena. Even in a path model formulation it could not demonstrate the necessary role of density. Similar points relate to the selection of political variables and the links between them and strikes. Thus, even if Snyder's approach were successful, one could not conclude that, in non-institutionalized settings, strikes are necessarily used as means of exerting political pressure.

The evidence of the present chapter suggests, on empirical as well as on methodological grounds, that a 'political' interpretation of American strikes cannot be advanced for any period since 1881. The findings on 'strike waves' presented in Chapter 2, and the more general failure of American strikes to change 'shape', similarly suggest that a political account is unsatisfactory. Snyder suggests that one aspect of institutionalized bargaining is the acceptance of labour as a body with legitimate interests in the political sphere. But several writers suggest that, on the contrary, American unions have not achieved the same level of acceptance as their European counterparts and that it is not possible for them to attain their ends through political means.[36] Thus, collective bargaining remains the centre of attention; it is here that many aspects of the employment relationship, which elsewhere are dealt with at the political level, are defined. This, combined with the continuing intransigence of employers in their dealings with unions, may well provide the outlines of the explanation of the unique character of American strike activity. These matters are considered in Chapter 7.

---

36. E. M. Kassalow, *Trade Unions and Industrial Relations* (New York: Random House, 1969), esp. pp. 132–46; D. C. Bok and J. T. Dunlop, *Labor and the American Community* (New York: Simon and Schuster, 1970), pp. 208–14; A. Sturmthal, *Comparative Labor Movements* (Belmont, Calif.: Wadsworth, 1972), pp. 51–2.

4
Strikes and Industrialization, 1881–1905

Many writers stress the importance of industrialization for patterns of strike activity, but two types of account can be identified. One suggests that strikes became more 'sophisticated' as workers learnt to deal with the challenges of industry: as unions grew, they used strikes as part of planned campaigns, and suppressed spontaneous and undirected protests.[1] The other argues that the rise of mass production methods, and the consequent changes in the division of labour, increased the power of capitalists to such an extent that strikes were repressed, with the few protests that did occur being defeated.[2] These two concepts of sophistication and repression provide points of departure for the consideration of patterns of activity which, while very complex, had features which were consistent with one account or the other.

As noted in Chapter 1, Shorter and Tilly, with their stress on the strategic use of the strike, stress sophistication and in particular the role of union organization in the mobilization of protest. But they also identify several types of response to industrialization and do not posit a uniform trend in a particular direction. The present account follows this tradition of identifying distinct forms of response, but also suggests that American strike patterns were even more complex than a small number of patterns can indicate. In general, strikes came to reflect the problems of skilled workers as they faced a challenge to their craft autonomy from technical and organizational changes in industry. The precise form of the response, however, varied markedly between industries and occupational groups.

1. P. N. Stearns, 'Measuring the Evolution of Strike Movements', *International Review of Social History*, XIX, pp. 1–27 (1974).
2. J. R. Commons, 'Class Conflict', *Labor and Administration* (New York: Macmillan, 1913), chap. 6, esp. pp. 71–5.

The Overall Pattern of Strike Activity

As is well known, urban growth in the final quarter of the nineteenth century was rapid and industry became increasingly concentrated in large-scale enterprises.[3] The organization of industry was also changing, with the development of the corporate form of ownership and the 'trust'. In particular, between 1880 and 1920 there were radical changes in the managerial control systems of large factories; these had obvious implications for the control of work by skilled men.[4] It is not surprising that several observers felt that the factory system and the division of labour 'have gradually reduced once free artisans to a new serfdom'[5] and that industrial conflict was inevitable. Aspects of the wider society which have been seen as influences on conflict include poverty, insecurity of employment and a decline in opportunities for social mobility.[6] But discontent does not always lead to protest.[7] The prevalence of rural values,[8] a pride in the industrial achievements of America, a feeling that discontents would be only temporary or a belief that protests would be bound to fail could all reduce workers' willingness to strike. Great care must therefore be taken in examining the patterns of protest which emerged.

3. See R. Higgs, *The Transformation of the American Economy, 1865–1914* New York: Wiley, 1971), E. C. Kirkland, *Industry Comes of Age* (New York: Rinehart and Winston, 1961); J. G. Williamson, *Late Nineteenth Century American Development* (Cambridge: Cambridge University Press, 1974).
4. D. Nelson, *Managers and Workers: Origins of the New Factory System in the United States, 1880–1920* (Madison: University of Wisconsin Press, 1975). On corporate growth, see R. L. Nelson, *The Merger Movement in American Industry, 1895–1956* (Princeton: Princeton University Press, 1959).
5. The Senate Committee on Labor-Capital Relations of 1885, quoted in C. K. Yearley, *Britons in American Labor* (Baltimore: John Hopkins University Press, 1957), p. 16.
6. J. A. Garraty, *The New Commonwealth, 1877–90* (New York: Harper and Row, 1968), pp. 136–41. The work of Thernstrom casts severe doubt on the view that the coming of industry reduced opportunities for social mobility, but the belief that mobility was declining may have been important. See S. Thernstrom, *Poverty and Progress* (Cambridge, Mass.: Harvard University Press, 1964); idem, *The Other Bostonians* (Cambridge, Mass.: Harvard University Press, 1973).
7. Garraty, op. cit., p. 156; S. Aronowitz, *False Promises* (New York: McGraw-Hill, 1973), pp. 52–3.
8. When large numbers of workers were new to industry, such values would be very important. See especially H. G. Gutman, 'Work, Culture and Society in Industrializing America, 1815–1919', *American Historical Review*, LXXVIII, pp. 531–88 (1973), esp. pp. 561, 577.

Strike Trends and Industrial Growth

The most direct way of investigating the impact of industrialization on strike activity is to use a measure of it in a regression model. Table 4.1 reports the results of using the proportion of the total work force industrialized as an independent variable for the period 1881–1910; any effect of industrialization should be most apparent in this period, when the shift away from agriculture was particularly rapid.[9] Although a positive influence was exerted on strike frequency, this effect was not statistically significant. Despite the obvious simplicity of this model, one cannot conclude that industrialization affected strike activity. The table also shows that union organization had a positive and significant effect on strike frequency; at least in this early period, unionization and strikes went together.

The second two equations of Table 4.1 consider the effect of immigration on strikes. Immigration reached its peak in the period 1881–1910 and was often cited as a factor which reduced the power of labour, because it provided employers with a body of men who were prepared to break strikes.[10] Thus, immigration's effect on the labour supply, and its role in splitting the work force into competing racial groups might be expected to depress strike frequency. Results not reported here[11] indicate that the total amount of immigration did not have a significant effect on strikes, and the total has therefore been disaggregated. Since most immigrants from Britain were skilled men and immigrants from the south and east of Europe largely unskilled, British immigration can be taken as a very rough proxy for the number of skilled men entering the country, and Italian and Russian immigration as a proxy for the entry of the unskilled. The results show that immigration from Britain was significantly related to strike frequency, whereas that from the other two countries was not. Similar results emerge when a direct measure of unskilled immigration, the number of men who said they were 'laborers' or had 'no occupation', is used in-

9. According to Williamson, whose estimates are used here, the industrial work force was 52 per cent of the total in 1881 and 69 per cent in 1910: see Williamson, op. cit., p. 295.
10. See G. Rosenblum, *Immigrant Workers* (New York: Basic Books, 1973), p. 131; G. Korman, *Industrialization, Immigration and Americanizers* (Madison: State Historical Society of Wisconsin, 1967), p. 51; J. Higham, *Strangers in the Land* (New Brunswick: Rutgers University Press, 1955), pp. 45–6.
11. P. K. Edwards, 'Strikes in the United States, 1881–1972' (D.Phil. thesis, University of Oxford, 1977), table 5–2.

TABLE 4.1

REGRESSION RESULTS, 1881–1910

Dependent Variables	Independent Variables						R^2	D–W
	Trough	Peak	T	Ind./C	Brit. Immig.	Ital. and Russian Immig.		
N/E	Neg 1%	Neg NS	Pos 5%	Pos NS			0.52	1.66
N/E	Neg 1%		Pos NS		Neg 5%	Pos NS	0.59	1.74
% Won	Pos 5%		Neg 5%		Neg NS	Pos NS	0.57	1.71

NOTE

% Won = percentage of strikes with result favourable to workers.

Ind = number of workers in industrial establishments, and

C = total civilian employment, i.e. Ind./C is the proportion of the total work force industrialized.

Brit. immig = number of immigrants from England, Scotland and Wales.

Ital. and Russian immig = number from Italy and Russia.

Other variables are as defined in Chapter 3.

stead.[12] In view of the obvious weaknesses of the immigration variable, any conclusion must be tentative: but it appears that immigration which affected the position of skilled men, and not the great mass of general immigration, had an impact on strikes.

Table 4.1 also reports the results of predicting the proportion of strikes won, rather than strike frequency. It will be seen that union membership had an inverse effect on the success rate. This is contrary to all assertions that unionization will make strikes more successful, a point which will be taken up further below. The negative coefficient of the trough variable contrasts with the positive one in the equation predicting strike frequency. It appears that a deep recession tended to re-

12. See ibid. The effect of immigration remains even when the time variable and the level of real wages are included in the equation. In view of possible problems of multicollinearity (see note 24 to Chapter 3 p. 70 above) the zero-order correlations for the independent variables of Table 4.1 are given below:

	Trough	*T*	*Brit. immig.*
T	0.11		
Brit. immig.	−0.06	0.02	
Ital. and Russ. immig.	−0.05	0.92	−0.01

duce the number of strikes, but to increase the chance of success. But this more sparing use of the strike, leading to a high rate of success, cannot be explained by increased union control of strikes.

Strike 'Sophistication'

Attention must now be given to the view that strike patterns, as distinct from the level of activity, altered during industrialization. Stearns has recently suggested several ways of distinguishing between pre-industrial and modern protests.[13] The former are not formally organized and are backward-looking, whereas the latter are forward-looking, involve the demand for new rights rather than the preservation of old ones and are large-scale activities which are timed to occur in booms rather than recessions. Other measures of 'sophistication' include the number of companies affected by strikes (since striking in more than one company shows organizational ability and the grasping of abstract issues), the regional spread of activity and the level of worker involvement. As workers learn to concentrate on well-planned efforts, strike frequency will fall, but, says Stearns, frequent striking is more sophisticated than not striking at all.

Stearns is less certain about the value of the success rate, duration, and violence of strikes as indices because they depend in part on the employer and because violence is hard to measure. However, the strike necessarily depends on the employer as well as the workers; and all the other indices of activity are as likely as these three to be affected by the employer. Elsewhere Stearns uses success as an index of sophistication: in four European countries in 1890—1914 disputes over job conditions 'were comparatively unsophisticated; and relatedly such strikes tended to decrease with time' whereas strikes 'for a reduction of hours were consistently among the most highly sophisticated, as measured by their large average size and their generally good success rate'.[14] Stearns does not make systematic use of all the measures he derives in his theoretical discussion, possibly because the data do not exist for his four countries. But most of his indices can be used in relation to the American data.

Chapter 2 has already shown that there was a marked rise in the proportion of strikes ordered by unions between 1881 and 1905, and Chapter 3 that there was a significant link between economic activity

---

13. Stearns, op. cit.
14. P. N. Stearns, *Lives of Labour* (London: Croom Helm, 1975), pp. 304, 310. The four countries are Belgium, Britain, France and Germany.

and strike frequency. On two dimensions, strikes were already 'sophisticated'. But the failure of union density to be consistently related to strike activity suggests the need for caution when using the level of organization as an index of sophistication. Furthermore, organization in strikes did not necessarily depend on the union. As Gutman has convincingly shown,[15] the new corporations were not totally dominant in society; in a number of cases they were successfully resisted by the more traditional entrepreneurs and commercial groups, who were prepared to assist workers in their fight against giant corporations. The victory of these firms came only slowly and in the face of opposition which was often severe. A corollary of this is that the workers could rely to some extent on 'unorganized' assistance from the community, so that they did not need union help. On the other hand, union involvement did not necessarily mean that a strike was 'sophisticated'. Hence, involvement is an ambiguous measure of sophistication.

The trends of five measures of the strike movement are shown in Table 4.2. No data are available for the whole of the period 1881–1905 on the number of companies or establishments affected by individual strikes, but it is possible to calculate the mean number of establishments per strike; this is given in the first column. Official figures include data on the number of employees in struck plants and it is thus possible to calculate the ratio of strikers to employees before the strike; following Shorter and Tilly,[16] this is called the plant participation ratio. If strikes were being repressed, this ratio should decline because workers would fear employers' reprisals if they joined the strike. The ratio of the number of *workers involved* to employees before the strike shows the trend in the effectiveness of strikes; the greater the proportion of a plant's workers who are affected by a strike, the greater will be the power of the strikers. The fourth column of the table shows how many establishments which had strikes were forced to cease operations; it is another index of strike effectiveness. Finally, the mean size of struck plants is given; it is calculated by dividing the number of employees in struck plants by the number of establishments affected.

15. H. G. Gutman, 'Class, Status and Community Power in Nineteenth Century American Cities: Paterson, N. J., a Case Study', *The Age of Industrialism in America,* ed. F. C. Jaher (New York: Free Press, 1968), pp. 263–87, idem, 'An Ironworkers' Strike in the Ohio Valley, 1873–74', *Ohio Historical Quarterly,* LXVIII, pp. 353–70 (1959); idem, 'Two Lockouts in Pennsylvania, 1873–74', *Pennsylvania Magazine of History and Biography,* LXXXIII, pp. 307–26 (1959).
16. E. Shorter and C. Tilly, *Strikes in France, 1830–1968* (Cambridge: Cambridge University Press, 1974), p. 59.

TABLE 4.2

INDICES OF 'STRIKE SOPHISTICATION', 1881–1905

	No. of Estabs per Strike	Strikers as % Employees Before Strike	Workers Involved as % Employees Before Strike	% Estabs Closed by Strike	Mean Size Struck Estabs
1881	6.16	60.0	76.5	55.8	57.9
1882	4.51	64.4	82.0	54.1	90.4
1883	5.68	73.0	86.7	63.4	68.2
1884	5.61	68.2	83.3	61.2	72.8
1885	3.55	55.1	81.6	72.2	128
1886	7.35	65.8	79.9	59.5	66.0
1887	5.24	50.3	66.7	61.8	83.6
1888	3.90	32.2	44.9	53.5	98.5
1889	3.53	46.7	56.2	61.8	118
1890	5.14	48.4	59.3	56.5	64.6
1891	4.85	48.8	62.1	57.2	61.3
1892	4.61	35.4	43.9	65.6	87.1
1893	3.53	37.5	51.9	64.1	114
1894	6.46	49.9	64.5	69.1	118
1895	5.85	52.7	71.8	86.0	77.2
1896	5.17	48.0	63.5	83.3	71.1
1897	7.80	60.9	74.3	83.4	64.6
1898	3.62	49.0	66.8	76.7	99.2
1899	6.33	39.1	52.3	66.7	71.0
1900	6.27	44.7	56.9	63.1	86.7
1901	3.77	37.8	51.6	42.1	96.2
1902	4.80	44.8	53.1	54.3	83.9
1903	6.45	42.4	51.8	56.9	64.6
1904	5.17	44.6	60.8	58.0	75.4
1905	4.37	37.5	46.5	49.3	68.1

There was no overall trend in the number of establishments per strike, but there was a fall in the plant participation ratio, matched by a decline in worker involvement as a percentage of employment in the struck plants. The latter two indices moved very closely together, which indicates that there was no change in the extent to which strikers caused other men to be laid off. For every hundred strikers there were typically between twenty and thirty other workers laid off. The proportion of plants closed by strikes rose until the end of the 1890s and then fell to levels similar to those of the early 1880s. Finally, the mean size of struck establishments fluctuated considerably but showed no clear trend. Plants which had strikes were much larger than the average; there were about ten workers per plant overall whereas the mean size of struck plants varied between 58 and 118 workers.[17] In view of the large number of small workshops, this difference is not very surprising, but the concentration of strikes in the large plants is still notable. Even if the very small establishments were to be left out, the difference between the strike-affected plants and the rest would remain.

Thus no clear trend towards 'sophistication' emerges. The fall in the plant participation ratio suggests that strikes were becoming less and not more solidaristic, and there is no evidence for an increased effectiveness of stoppages in terms of the number of establishments involved per strike or the proportion of struck plants which had to be closed. The stress on the sophistication of strikes and the transformation from 'pre-industrial' forms of protest covers only one side of the picture. As Stearns himself argues, strikes in the years before the first world war were transitional between the pre-modern and modern types. And, as Shorter and Tilly suggest, strikes will reflect the protests of the skilled men against the changes forced on them by industrialization as well as the secular movement to 'modern' forms;[18] 'backward looking' strikes can be expected when traditional patterns of work are threatened. Further, Commons has argued that the repressive power of the corporation was such that, although there were structural reasons for discontent, overt expression of dissatisfaction could be prevented.[19] Thus, there are two sorts of reason why a growth in the sophistication of strikes need not have occurred.

The decline in the plant participation ratio is consistent with the exercise of power by the corporations, but it also fits the view that the strike was being taken over by skilled men. If the strike is appropriated by the skilled, the size of stoppages and the participation rate will fall as disputes become concentrated on the demands of a limited part of the work force. The lack of suitable employment data makes it impossible to assess directly the relative strike-proneness of different groups, but the indirect evidence is consistent with the view that strikes reflec-

---

17. For data on plant size from 1860 to 1910, see E. L. Bogart and G. M. Thompson, *Readings in the Economic History of the United States* (New York: Longman's, Green and Co., 1916), pp. 740–41, 745. The figure of ten workers per establishment refers to all plants; when 'hand and neighborhood' industries are excluded, a figure of 23 workers per establishment is obtained for 1900.
18. Stearns, 'Measuring the Evolution of Strike Movements', op. cit., p. 7; Shorter and Tilly, op. cit., pp. 196–235.
19. Commons, loc. cit.

TABLE 4.3

ISSUES IN STRIKES, 1881–1905

	1881–85	1886–90	1891–95	1896–1900	1901–05
	% of Strikes with Given Issue				
Wage increase	42.6	30.4	27.8	30.1	25.4
Against wage decrease	21.2	11.8	16.5	9.9	4.0
Other wage	5.6	6.7	5.9	9.8	9.9
Hours	2.2	7.7	4.0	2.9	5.2
Hours, and other	1.4	3.6	2.7	5.5	5.7
Union recognition and rules, and other	7.8	14.0	15.4	19.3	29.1
Employment of certain persons, and other	6.5	8.5	8.5	8.8	8.3
Other	12.7	17.3	19.1	13.7	12.4
Total	100.0	99.9	99.9	100.0	100.0
	% of Workers Involved in Strikes with Given Issue				
Wage increase	42.1	28.0	33.6	20.5	14.9
Against wage decrease	20.2	11.6	16.5	6.6	3.8
Other wage	12.5	12.9	8.3	18.1	19.1
Hours	3.5	10.5	3.5	1.5	5.7
Hours, and other	5.7	9.8	6.6	7.4	13.1
Union recognition and rules, and other	4.5	8.5	9.6	16.5	24.0
Employment of certain persons, and other	2.9	5.7	4.5	4.3	6.5
Other	8.5	13.3	17.4	25.0	12.9
Total	99.9	100.0	100.0	99.9	100.0

NOTE
'And other' means that the principal issue was combined with other issues.

ted the problems of skilled men.[20] Such an interpretation does not conflict with a stress on 'repression': the skilled were in the strongest position to fight back, and also had most to lose by giving way to the employers. Even if the view that skilled men struck most frequently is rejected, they may still have been the leaders of those strikes in which skilled and unskilled participated. In other words, the dissatisfactions of the skilled men were the rallying point for the strikes of other workers.

20. A constant mean size of strikes despite the growth of industrial plants, a fall in the plant participation ratio, a rise in union involvement and the continued importance of strikes on working conditions issues all support this contention.

The differences between the strikes of the skilled and unskilled will be considered in detail below, but the overall importance of strikes over working conditions and job control may be examined here: such issues were, of course, of particular importance to skilled men. The trends of the issues in strikes are shown in Table 4.3, which uses a more detailed set of categories than that employed in Chapter 2. The category 'other' is of particular interest since it includes such 'miscellaneous' matters as the method and time of payment and work discipline, rules and conditions. The rise and subsequent decline of strikes on these issues is consistent with the view that the skilled men were protesting in the 1880s and early '90s against changes in job conditions but that, by the turn of the century, they realized the hopelessness of this. The fall in wage strikes and the concomitant increase in union recognition strikes also fits this interpretation; union strikes include not only 'aggressive' demands for recognition but also 'defensive' strikes against employer attempts to remove the union or alter its rules and practices and hiring policies.

Stearns suggests that strikes against wage cuts are the least sophisticated, followed by disputes over personal matters and defensive strikes over conditions; strikes for wage increases and cuts in hours are genuinely aggressive.[21] He gives no means of differentiating between offensive and defensive types of stoppage on work conditions, but the other categories are clear enough. Strikes against wage cuts fell markedly in importance, but those over the employment of certain persons constituted a more or less constant proportion of the total, while 'wage increase' strikes also fell. Thus, again, there was no unambiguous tendency for strikes to become more or less sophisticated.

The issue is illuminated further by Table 4.4 where the size and results of strikes on different issues are indicated. The whole list of 28 categories is used since, in constructing the table from which the data are taken, the Commissioner of Labor included a strike due to two or more causes under each category for which it was relevant; thus a strike for a wage increase and hours decrease appears under the headings 'wage increase and other' and 'hours decrease and other'. The discrepancy in the figure between 'pure' wage or hours strikes and those in which these issues are combined with others is thus due to the inclusion of a great many additional strikes in the categories with more than one issue. It will be recalled that Stearns argues that hours strikes in Europe were among the most sophisticated, in terms of their size and result, and work conditions stoppages among the least sophisticated. In America,

21. Stearns, 'Measuring the Evolution of Strike Movements', op. cit. p. 24.

TABLE 4.4

SIZE AND RESULTS OF STRIKES BY DETAILED CAUSE, 1881–1905

	Total No. Estabs Affected	Mean Size	% Estabs where strike was	
			Won	Lost
For wage increase	60359	187	50.0	31.4
Wage increase and other	44700	427	46.9	30.0
Against wage reduction	10536	211	34.9	52.3
Wage reduction and other	2884	324	67.4	26.4
All hours	53408	345	52.0	30.4
For hours reduction	17747	217	50.7	39.2
Hours reduction and other	33721	473	52.4	25.7
Against hours increase	817	331	50.1	37.1
Hours increase and other	1123	396	61.5	32.3
Union recognition and rules	18614	88.1	55.5	42.9
Recog. and rules and other	20000	480	38.7	36.8
Employment of certain persons	4139	107	24.8	73.5
Certain persons and other	1037	330	29.0	52.6
Employees out of regular occupation	559	92.4	50.1	47.8
Out of regular occupation and other	191	156	33.0	7.3
Overtime work and pay	574	96.1	50.7	41.8
Overtime work etc and other	3605	297	60.3	17.9
Method and time of pay	953	202	39.6	57.2
Method and time of pay and other	2170	1200	55.4	17.0
Saturday part holiday	266	75.0	43.6	54.9
Saturday holiday and other	4774	419	52.2	24.4
Docking, fines and charges	449	137	48.6	43.0
Docking etc and other	725	2140	22.1	18.5
All work conditions and rules	7626	179	47.2	38.7
Work conditions and rules	3089	122	41.6	54.4
Work conditions etc and other	4537	370	51.0	27.9
Sympathy	6361	193	20.7	76.5
Sympathy and other	521	594	11.1	83.3
Other not elsewhere included	3391	120	60.8	32.7
Other n.e.i. and other	1922	390	43.9	29.9
All strikes	199982	183	46.5	38.7

NOTE

'And other' means that the given issue was combined with other issues; e.g. there were strikes in 6361 establishments where sympathy was the sole issue and strikes in 521 establishments where sympathy was one of several issues.

hours strikes were among the largest but their rate of success was only a little greater than average. Strikes over work conditions were of about average 'sophistication' when all stoppages involving this issue are considered, but disputes solely over job conditions were smaller, and rather less successful, than average. As Table A.11 shows, there is no strong evidence to support the view that strikes over conditions would decline, in absolute or relative terms.

It is doubtful whether the size of strikes is a very useful index of sophistication. Strikes over such matters of general appeal as a wage increase are likely to be larger than those over more limited types of demand. And, as Table 4.4 shows, strikes restricted to a specific issue were smaller than those in which many issues were involved. In many cases the difference was extremely marked. However, it does not follow that the bringing together of many issues in a strike makes it more sophisticated, although it certainly increases its mass appeal. A comparison of strikes limited to specific issues shows that the differences in size between them were not very great. Much the largest were those against an increase in hours; and the success rate here was quite high, in contrast to Stearns's view that defensive hours strikes are among the least sophisticated. In other words, one dimension of sophistication, the issue in dispute, was unrelated to two other dimensions, the size of the strike and its result. Other strikes limited to a specific issue were of a remarkably similar size although, in line with the view that strikes over work conditions and discipline will be restricted to craft groups, such stoppages were among the smallest. Union recognition disputes were even smaller, strengthening the view that at this time recognition demands were largely limited to the skilled men.

The data on results indicate, in line with the findings of Chapter 2, that sympathy strikes had a very low success rate; and when other issues are added to 'sympathy' the success rate was even lower. But in many other cases 'pure' strikes were less successful than those in which numerous issues were involved. This is particularly notable with strikes against wage reductions, where the addition of other issues raised the proportion of successful strikes from 35 per cent to 67 per cent. Since a similar, though less marked, pattern occurred with strikes against increases in hours, it seems that purely defensive strikes tended to be defeated, whereas those which were not limited to one key battle against employer attempts to alter wages or hours were more likely to succeed.

Stearns suggests that in Europe:

The strike movement as a whole confirms the notion of an increasingly

instrumental view of work, in which *full pleasure* in work was abandoned as unobtainable ... and better conditions off the job were
sought in compensation.[22]

What 'full pleasure' might be is not made clear, nor does Stearns show
that pre-industrial workers were able to obtain such total satisfaction in
their work. More directly, the American evidence does not support his
contentions: wage strikes declined in importance and disputes related
to work conditions remained significant. Strikes did not become shorter
or less frequent, suggesting that workers did not resign themselves to
industrial conditions in order to concentrate on other things. And there
was no marked move from being 'backward-looking' to being 'forward-
looking'.

Thus, the various measures of strike sophistication were often not
closely related, and small strikes over matters of work conditions and
discipline were not necessarily 'unsophisticated'. As well as the lack of a
strong link between industrialization and the amount of strike activity,
there was no association between industrial growth and the sophistication of strikes. Although industrialization may have exerted broad
effects on strikes, such as encouraging large strikes for wage demands,
struggles for job control continued. With these two tendencies co-
existing, the overall pattern of strikes showed no clear trend towards
increasing or decreasing sophistication.

The Industrial Distribution of Strike Activity

This section shows that the findings relating to trends of activity are
confirmed by cross-sectional analysis. If industrialization affects the
form of worker protests, differences should emerge between the 'advanced' and more traditional industries. However, only very broad
differences are apparent: in some sectors, the attitudes of employers
and the government were independent influences, and in others strikes
reflected craft workers' protests. The effects of industrial advance were
counteracted by several other factors.

There are, of course, difficulties in comparing whole industries, since
some parts of an industry may be more advanced than others. But
broad differences between whole sectors should be clear enough for any
effect of technical advance to be apparent in the strike figures. Apart
from these general problems with the definition of an industry, there is

22. Stearns, *Lives of Labour,* op. cit., p. 310, emphasis added.

TABLE 4.5

STOPPAGES AND TOTAL EMPLOYMENT BY INDUSTRY, 1881–1905

	Percentage of Total Accounted for by Each Industry			
	Strikes	Strikers	Estabs Affected by Strikes	Total Employment
Boot and shoe	3.0	1.3	0.9	1.2
Brewing	0.5	0.2	0.5	0.3
Building	26.0	13.6	38.5	11.7
Clothing	7.2	9.9	12.6	3.5
Coal	9.7	30.8	9.7	4.5
Cooperage	0.9	0.4	0.6	0.2
Food	1.9	2.2	4.2	1.8
Machinery	4.9	3.4	2.7	3.1
Metals: tin and steel	2.9	4.1	1.3	2.0
stove and furnace	0.9	0.3	0.3	n.a.
other	2.6	1.2	2.5	1.3
Printing and publishing	2.9	0.7	1.7	1.3
Stone, clay and glass	4.7	3.1	3.2	1.9
Textiles	4.3	4.4	1.3	3.6
Tobacco	4.9	3.6	4.1	1.0
Transport: railroad	1.4	1.8	0.4	7.3
other	2.0	2.3	1.4	7.5
Transport equipment	2.5	2.1	1.5	2.6
All above industries	83.2	86.7	87.2	54.7
All industries	100	100	100	100

NOTE
Employment figures are for 1900. The revised industrial categories of 1906 are used; these will be referred to as the 1906 classification in contrast to the earlier one, called the 1886 classification.

the difficulty that the Commissioner of Labor worked with one industrial classification in his first three reports but then felt the need to adopt a revised scheme:

In making a new classification the object has been to bring together in groups or classes, as nearly as practicable, those establishments and industries in which the employees and employers, respectively, have a common interest and consequently are likely to act together.[23]

23. U.S. Commissioner of Labor, *Twenty-first Annual Report, 1906* (Washington, D.C.: Government Printing Office, 1907), p. 111.

In general, it has proved possible to allow for changes in definition between the Commissioner's reports, but in some cases comparable data are not available. The classification adopted in 1906 was much more detailed than the earlier one and will therefore be used here. But data for the new categories were given only for the periods 1901–05 and 1881–1900 so that, when we consider trends within industries in the next section, the broader categories employed up to 1900 will have to be used.

Overall Patterns

The proportions of the total number of strikers, strikers and establishments accounted for by each of 18 major industry groups are given in Table 4.5. The industrial classification used here is designed for two purposes: to be comparable with the information in Chapters 5 and 6 (e.g. the stone, clay, and glass category), and to illuminate important aspects of the strike movement in the period 1881–1905 (e.g. co-operage).

The table shows the absolute importance of each industry in the total; that is, it shows where the 'strike problem' was concentrated. Similar tables in later chapters will indicate how the distribution of strike activity has changed.

It is notable that the building industry had already achieved a dominant position, accounting for a quarter of all strikes and over a third of all establishments which were affected by strikes; thus the number of establishments per strike was greater than the average, whereas the mean size of stoppages was less than average. The other major contributors to strike activity were coal and clothing. The former accounted for 30 per cent of all strikes and had stoppages which were about three times larger than average. The industries in the table, together with other manufacturing sectors not specifically mentioned, accounted for virtually all the strike activity recorded; strikes in agriculture were rare and stoppages in administrative and governmental occupations had not yet made an appearance.

'Sophistication' of Strikes, by Industry

With this as background the dimensions of 'strike sophistication' by industry may be investigated. Table 4.6 gives the issues in strikes; Table 4.7 reports eight measures of strike activity; and Table 4.8 shows the level of union involvement and the effect of the presence of a union on the rate of success. The only measures in Table 4.7 which have not been encountered at the aggregate level are 'establishment involvement' and 'mean duration'. The former gives the total number of struck plants as a

TABLE 4.6

STRIKE ISSUES BY INDUSTRY: PERCENT OF ESTABLISHMENTS IN WHICH STRIKES WERE FOR GIVEN ISSUE, 1881–1900

	Wage Increase	Wage Decrease	Other Wage[a]	Hours	Other
Boot and shoe	34.4	12.1	7.7	0.4	45.4
Brewing	7.7	0.5	36.5	18.1	37.1
Building	25.5	2.2	23.2	15.8	33.3
Clothing	17.9	4.9	44.9	8.7	23.6
Coal	41.0	22.6	4.6	0.3	31.4
Cooperage	73.5	13.5	2.8	0.2	10.0
Food	7.3	1.6	14.0	43.3	33.8
Machinery	17.6	5.9	30.8	21.6	24.1
Metals (all)	35.7	11.5	11.2	15.8	25.9
Printing & publishing	37.2	4.6	10.0	10.8	37.2
Stone, clay & glass	28.5	5.8	13.3	17.8	34.7
Textiles	42.2	19.5	4.1	1.8	32.4
Tobacco	38.1	9.6	4.0	28.5	19.8
Transport (all)	54.4	5.2	6.7	2.1	31.7
Transport equipment	22.0	10.8	2.2	48.5	16.4
All industries	28.7	7.2	20.2	14.4	29.6

NOTE
a. Includes wages combined with other issues.
Table based on 1886 classification.

percentage of the number of plants in the industry in 1900; the lack of annual data on the number of establishments prevents the use of this index in time-series analysis, but it gives a useful indication of the differences between industries in the spread of strikes. Shorter and Tilly remark that the proportion of all establishments on strike has been ignored in North American writings;[24] the use of the 'establishment involvement' index helps to remedy this. 'Mean duration' represents simply the Commissioner's figures on 'aggregate duration' divided by the number of strikes; this does not measure the actual length of stoppages because the Commissioner's data refer to establishments, but it is useful in comparing industries. In the later discussion, 'duration per establishment' is used to supplement this index.

There are some strike patterns which can clearly be related to the 'traditional-advanced' scale. Thus in the 'traditional' cooperage industry strikes were small and short and fought mainly over economic demands;

24. Shorter and Tilly, op. cit., p. 59.

TABLE 4.7

STRIKE INDICES BY INDUSTRY, 1881–1905

	Estabs per Strike	Estab. Involvement	Mean Duration	Mean Size
Boot and shoe	1.62	82.9	35.6	110
Brewing	5.83	36.2	110	130
Building	8.15	n.a.	201	116
Clothing	9.05	51.9	140	272
Coal	4.97	n.a.	262	588
Cooperage	3.28	51.7	74.9	79.3
Food	10.8	16.2	130	235
Machinery	2.64	47.5	118	131
Metals: tin and steel	2.10	17.7	71.6	259
stove and furnace	1.49	n.a.	29.0	72.8
other	5.24	10.6	244	93.5
Printing & publishing	3.23	15.5	104	47.4
Stone, clay & glass	3.72	39.9	128	136
Textiles	1.48	16.7	42.0	209
Tobacco	3.98	51.2	112	148
Transport: railroad	1.34	n.a.	10.8	243
other	5.74	n.a.	140	222
Transport equipment	3.16	26.6	112	157
All industries	5.19	38.8	161	195

	ST/B	ST/W	% Won	% Lost
Boot and shoe	32.0	63.8	39.8	49.7
Brewing	32.6	93.4	32.2	41.7
Building	75.2	85.7	49.6	34.6
Clothing	60.8	80.6	71.7	21.0
Coal	76.0	81.3	22.0	49.3
Cooperage	58.3	93.4	61.8	30.9
Food	27.3	83.5	55.7	39.3
Machinery	22.8	75.5	37.0	47.2
Metals: tin and steel	31.1	58.8	36.4	48.5
stove and furnace	32.4	56.9	36.5	53.3
other	30.2	74.5	54.3	38.0
Printing & publishing	22.8	71.5	40.9	48.0
Stone, clay & glass	49.6	68.3	41.0	40.8
Textiles	30.6	64.2	21.6	66.1
Tobacco	65.2	83.6	50.9	43.0
Transport: railroad	13.0	56.5	22.2	66.7
other	54.1	80.9	29.9	52.8
Transport equipment	20.1	74.9	26.6	45.6
All industries	46.9	78.5	46.5	38.6

NOTE

ST = number of strikers.

B = number of employees before strike.

Estab. involvement gives number of establishments affected by strikes as a % of the total number of establishments in the industry in 1900.

TABLE 4.8

TRADE UNION INVOLVEMENT IN STRIKES, BY INDUSTRY, 1881–1905

	% of Strikes ordered by Union	% of Strikes Ordered by Union which were		% of Strikes not Ordered by Union which were	
		Won	Lost	Won	Lost
Boot and shoe	71.4	39.7	49.2	30.9	62.6
Brewing	90.4	32.2	34.9	44.4	55.6
Building	92.4	52.5	29.9	50.9	40.0
Clothing	85.2	72.8	19.9	47.1	46.5
Coal	54.8	20.2	48.2	31.8	57.4
Cooperage	71.2	62.4	28.7	63.3	34.1
Food	81.3	56.5	39.3	61.0	36.2
Machinery	69.0	38.8	44.3	27.0	62.8
Metals: tin and steel	38.1	40.3	42.6	29.0	60.5
stove & furnace	77.6	39.0	49.8	27.7	60.2
other	88.8	70.0	20.7	24.5	67.4
Printing & publishing	86.7	45.1	45.1	23.6	73.6
Stone, clay and glass	66.0	41.7	48.9	15.5	77.0
Textiles	24.5	18.0	68.9	24.9	63.7
Tobacco	74.5	50.0	44.5	57.4	32.2
Transport: railroad	39.1	13.7	75.8	30.1	58.0
other	54.8	47.4	25.1	23.2	67.0
Transport equipment	58.7	28.5	45.5	29.1	60.0
All industries	69.0	49.5	34.6	33.9	56.4

they were more successful than average and the ratio of strikers to workers involved was high. This pattern fits the case of craft workers who did not need to strike over matters of job control and who were well organized. Indeed, their strength was such that the presence of a union did not increase the rate of success of strikes. The high 'strikers to workers involved' ratio (ST/W) shows that the strikes were solidaristic, in that nearly all the workers who were affected by the strike were actively supporting it. The plant participation ratio (ST/B) was only slightly higher than average, indicating that stoppages were limited to a small part of the work force. At the other end of the scale, strikes in machinery were relatively large and long, were less concerned with wages and less successful. The presence of a union made a difference to the success rate and there was a lack of solidarity among workers in the same plant, indicated by the low plant participation ratio.

The interpretation of the plant participation ratio is complicated, however, by the fact that it relates only to those plants where a strike occurred. But in traditional industries, where craft workers were a high proportion of the total, the ratio should be high; the cases of cooperage and building bear this out. Where the division of labour had replaced craft skills, the ratio should be low; the machinery, metals and boot and shoe industries fit this pattern.

It may seem that tobacco and clothing, both with high ratios, do not fit this explanation, for the former has been seen as a case where craft skills were being eroded and the latter as a centre for unskilled immigrant workers. But, to anticipate a later argument, strikes in tobacco reflected the protests of skilled men against machinery so that disputes would be concentrated in those shops where craft methods were still employed. Although the unskilled were important in the industry as a whole, the plants where strikes occurred were dominated by the skilled and thus the plant participation ratio was high. The apparent anomaly of clothing is removed when it is remembered that workers here were not unskilled in the same sense as workers in heavy industry; they may not have served formal apprenticeships, but they had a set of skills which had to be learnt.[25] Thus two hypotheses receive support: that skilled men dominated strikes and that plant solidarity was affected by how advanced the industry was, although in a manner different from standard expectations.

The effect of technical advance is shown further in the comparison between 'tin and steel' and 'other metals'. The latter sector included industries such as cutlery and hardware and the blacksmith craft, and was thus more 'traditional' than tin and steel: as Table 4.9 shows, the mean size of plant in 'other metals' was one-sixth of that in tin and steel. Strikes in 'other metals' were smaller and longer than those in steel, and the rate of success was greater; and, although the plant participation ratio was about the same, the number of strikers, in relation to the number of workers involved, was greater. The differences in union involvement are particularly notable. The proportion of strikes by a union was much higher in other metals than in tin and steel and the effect of the union on the rate of success more marked. In tin and steel twice as many non-union strikes were lost as were won, and the presence of a union brought the proportions to near equality; but in 'other metals' a ratio of lost to won strikes, when no union was involved, of three to one was reversed, when a union was present, with successful strikes outnumbering the unsuccessful by 3½ to one. Thus, striking in the more 'advanced' sector of the metals industry was less

25. See, for example, W. Herberg, 'Jewish Labor Movement in the United States: Early Years to World War I', *Industrial and Labor Relations Review*, V, pp. 501–23 (1952), at pp. 504–06.

TABLE 4.9

**SIZE OF ALL PLANTS AND SIZE OF STRUCK PLANTS,
MANUFACTURING INDUSTRY, c. 1900**

	Wage Earners per Estab. 1900	Employees per Struck Plant, 1901–05	Size Struck Plants to Size All Plants[a]
Boot and shoe	6.84	321	46.9
Boot and shoe excl. custom and repair shops	73.2	321	4.4
Brewing	15.6	96.4	6.2
Clothing	7.08	111	15.7
Cooperage	10.7	80.2	7.5
Food	5.29	127	24.0
Machinery	39.3	214	5.4
Metals: Tin and steel	20.4	357	17.5
Other	3.50	57.9	16.5
Printing & publishing	7.83	66.9	8.5
Stone, clay & glass	15.4	101	6.6
Tobacco	9.31	54.3	5.8
Transport equipment	32.4	219	6.8
All industries	10.4	75.9	7.3

NOTE
a. i.e. no. of employees per struck plant divided by number of wage earners per establishment.

'sophisticated' than was that in the more traditional sectors.

Some reservations are called for, however. In comparisons of the size of strikes, the size of establishments must be taken into account. In general, it is preferable to use the size of strikes uncorrected for employment when an index of spread of industrial conflict is required, since size measures how many men are prepared to strike together. This is an absolute and not a relative measure.[26] But some account must be taken of the size of plants when cross-sectional comparisons are being made; other things being equal, large plants will enable large strikes to occur. Strikes in tin and steel were larger than those in 'other metals' by a factor of 2.8 but the mean plant was six times bigger; size differences were thus less impressive. But while the correction for establishment size weakens one account of the effect of being 'advanced' it strengthens another. The view that protests will be large and brief in the advanced

26. See below, Appendix C, pp. 317–18.

sectors, because the division of labour reduced the power of the workers while at the same time making them more discontented, is weakened; but an explanation stressing the role of the skilled workers is strengthened. If their protests are central to the strike movement, the size of strikes in the advanced sectors will not match the size of establishments in them because the strikes will be limited to the skilled men, who form a relatively small part of the total work force.

A second reservation concerns the data on establishment involvement. No clear pattern emerges here, with machinery and cooperage having a high proportion of their plants affected by strikes and all the metals industries and printing and publishing having low proportions affected. Inter-plant solidarity (as distinct from intra-plant solidarity reflected in the plant participation ratio) is very variable; it would be interesting to be able to compare non-manufacturing industries, but data on the number of establishments are not available here. The number of establishments per strike also measures the spread of strikes between plants and here a clearer picture emerges. Industries dominated by factory production, such as tin and steel, machinery, textiles, and boots and shoes, had a low spread of stoppages between plants; building, clothing and food had high levels. But the meaning of this is far from obvious since in cases where there were many small establishments close to each other strikes could easily spread beyond one workshop or site; a dispute in clothing more easily spreads to neighbouring shops than does one in a factory to another separate, and distant, establishment.

Rates of Strike Activity

The third and most important reservation concerns the data on levels of strike activity. These are given in Table 4.10; as far as possible, they have been calculated on a standard basis, but the figures are not totally reliable; there are differences in the definition of employment, and a lack of complete consistency between the industrial classifications used in the strike statistics and those used for the employment data. Broad comparisons between industry groups are possible, however. The figures for the number of strikers per thousand employees do not show any close association with the state of technical advance. Apart from coal, the highest and lowest levels were recorded by less advanced industries: tobacco and printing and publishing. Similarly, there was considerable variation among the more 'advanced' industries. Although the data in earlier tables are consistent with the view that workers in such sectors as tin and steel restricted their striking because of the loss of their power, involvement in strikes was greater here than in 'other metals'.

The pattern that emerges when strike frequency is considered is only slightly clearer. Frequency was lower in tin and steel and machinery than in other metals, and was also low in transportation equipment and textiles. But the tendency for frequency to decline with the extent of technical advance in an industry was not universal. Food, which had a low mean plant size, and was similar to the traditional industries in such things as the number of establishments per strike, had a low level of activity. The general tendency for the more advanced industries to cluster around the low frequency pole suggests that skilled men were restricting their use of the strike here. The lack of any such relationship for the number of strikers per employee suggests that, when a strike occurred, it was a large stoppage, involving the unskilled as well as the skilled. This may seem to be inconsistent with the low plant participation ratio in the advanced sector, but the strikes had a large absolute size, while involving only a small proportion of the workers in any one plant. They were large protests but not 'mass' ones since few workers in each plant were engaged and their spread across plants was low.

Patterns in Key Industries

Strike activity was high in sectors not usually associated with labour militancy, as Table 4.10 shows. For example, the tobacco industry was second only to coal in the number of strikers per employee and had the highest level of strike frequency. Tables 4.6 to 4.8 show that tobacco had a high proportion of strikes for wage increases and high ratios of plant participation and establishment involvement. Strikes were large, when the small size of plants in the industry has been taken into consideration, and disputes were quite long. But the most notable feature of the industry's strike pattern was the greater rate of success for non-union than for union-led strikes. Of non-union stoppages, 57 per cent were won, compared to a success rate of 50 per cent in union-led ones; in all industries the respective figures were 34 per cent and 50 per cent.

As noted in the discussion of tobacco in Chapter 2, the industry was undergoing technical and organizational change at the end of the nineteenth century. Its strike pattern fits the model of an attempt by the skilled craftsmen to resist these encroachments. Their union was one of the first to be re-organized on 'business' principles, under the guidance of Strasser and Gompers.[27] The low rate of success of union-led strikes

27. J. R. Commons *et al., History of Labour in the United States,* Vol. I (New York: Macmillan, 1918), pp. 307–09.

TABLE 4.10

**NUMBER OF STRIKES AND STRIKERS PER EMPLOYEE, BY INDUSTRY,
1881–1905**

	Number of Strikes per Million Employees	Number of Strikers per Thousand Employees
Boot and shoe	323	35.5
Brewing	184	24.0
Building	295	34.2
Clothing	278	75.7
Coal	333	196
Cooperage	566	44.9
Food	143	33.7
Machinery	264	34.6
Metals: tin and steel	200	51.6
other	298	27.9
Printing & publishing	347	16.5
Stone, clay and glass	402	54.8
Textiles	153	32.1
Tobacco	678	100
Transport equipment	159	24.9
All industries	383	74.7

NOTE

Figures calculated on basis of employment at four base years (1880, 1886, 1893, 1900) corresponding to years at the start of each of the four periods covered by the Commissioner of Labor. Writing E for employment, with a suffix for each base year, the sum used in the denominator of the indices is:

$$(6 \times E_{1880}) + (7.5 \times E_{1886}) + (6.5 \times E_{1893}) + (5 \times E_{1900}).$$

The figures are thus comparable to those in later tables relating to each of the sub-periods of 6, 7½, 6½ and 5 years.

is consistent with an attempt by the organized men to use their union to defend themselves against mechanization, while economic strikes could still be waged successfully.[28] Gompers's changing attitudes to strikes illustrate this experience. In 1894 he argued that strikes were a result of the existing social and industrial system and his early writing was consistently militant and acknowledged the importance of the Marxist analysis of the class struggle. But he later came to believe that striking against the machine was futile and that unions should seek to

28. On the policy of the Cigar Makers and other unions regarding technical change, see H. Ober, *Trade-union Policy and Technological Change* (Philadelphia: Works Progress Administration, National Resources Project Report No. L-8, 1940).

accommodate themselves with the employers; thus he did not feel that the growth of the corporations was a threat to the unions and refused to see legislation as a means to curb corporate power.[29] Despite the success of the Cigar Makers' Union in gaining control over strikes, the evidence of Table 4.8 shows that the usual arguments about the influence of the union on strikes need not hold. Spontaneous striking was criticized for leading to defeats and the loss of members; union control was said to increase the success rate. Gompers argued that it was not necessarily wise to strike even against a wage cut, suggesting instead that the organization of the union should be maintained and that lost ground could be made up later.[30] But in his own industry union control did not lead to the results claimed for it, even though the union was particularly strong in the claims it made for itself.[31]

The stove and furnace industry is included here so that the importance of technical advance can be explored further. Like the steel industry, which will be discussed in more detail below, this industry had a strong national union relatively early and it was one of the first in which a system of trade agreements was established. But during the latter part of the nineteenth century, the position of the skilled men was eroded and finally destroyed. Although the standardization of production was one reason for this, the industry was noted for the organization of its employers and their determination to defeat the union.[32] Thus the comparison with the strike patterns of the rest of the metals industries will bring out the role of employer policy in determin-

---

29. B. Mandel, *Samuel Gompers* (Yellow Springs: Antioch Press, 1963), pp. 68, 215, 223–5; P. Taft, 'Organized Labor and Technical Change: A Backward Look', *Adjusting to Technological Change*, ed. G. G. Somers, E. L. Cushman and N. Weinberg (New York: Harper and Row, 1963), pp. 27–43 at p. 31. See also L. Ulman, *The Rise of the National Trade Union* (Cambridge, Mass.: Harvard University Press, 1955), pp. 441–6.

30. Mandel, op. cit., pp. 22–40. See also S. Gompers, *Seventy Years of Life and Labour* Vol. 1 (London: Hurst and Blackett, 1925), chaps 6 and 8.

31. A similar pattern of union strikes being less successful than non-union ones occurred in the brewing industry. Since strike frequency and worker involvement were lower than in tobacco, the lack of success in union strikes in tobacco cannot be explained by the high rate of conflict in the industry. Similarly, the Brewery Workers' Union had an industrial structure, so that the craft structure of the Cigar Makers does not seem to explain the low rate of success of union strikes. See J. H. M. Laslett, *Labor and the Left* (New York: Basic Books, 1970), pp. 9–45.

32. Commons *et al.*, op. cit., Vol. II, pp. 5–7, 48–53, 480–1; C. A. Madison, *American Labor Leaders* (2nd edn; New York: Frederick Ungar, 1962), pp. 23–32; C. E. Bonnett, *Employers' Associations in the United States* (New York: Macmillan, 1922), chaps. 2–4.

ing the character of the strike movement. Strikes were even shorter than in tin and steel and the number of establishments per strike was very low. Despite a higher rate of union involvement in strikes the overall rate of success was very similar to that in tin and steel; and, as Table 4.8 shows, the effect of union involvement was virtually identical. The lack of separate data for employment or the number of establishments in the stove industry prevents us from considering establishment involvement or the overall level of activity, but the available information points to a marked similarity with tin and steel. Thus the activity of employers may be an important independent factor in the strike movement.

This emphasis is confirmed when the two non-manufacturing industries of coal and railroads are considered. In neither of these were the technical conditions of operations being altered very significantly, but in both there are suggestions that the power of the employers was considerable. The miners engaged in large and long, although not particularly frequent, battles in which the plant participation rate was high. But the overall success rate was very low and union-led strikes were less successful than non-union ones. The proportion of 'defensive' strikes against wage cuts was higher than elsewhere. Again, it appears that the union was being used to protect the position of the workers against employers' attacks, although here the focus was on wage cuts rather than changes in work arrangements. This can be explained, of course, by the economic structure of the industry. Coal, as a primary product, has always faced an unstable level of market demand and has had constant problems of over-production; since labour cost was a large part of the total, pressure on the wage rate was the only way in which the employer could hope to maintain his profits. Hence strikes over wage cuts were a regular feature of depressions.[33] Although competition was intense in the product market, parts of the industry were coming under the control of cartels. This was particularly the case in the important anthracite fields of Pennsylvania, where the railroads were gaining control of large parts of the reserves to supplement their domination of the transportation of coal to consumers in the Eastern cities. The power of

33. On economic conditions in the industry, see W. H. Hamilton and H. R. Wright, *The Case of Bituminous Coal* (London: Allen and Unwin, 1925). On miners' struggles to 1905 see A. E. Suffern, *The American Coal Miners' Struggle for Industrial Status* (London: Allen and Unwin, 1926), pp. 11–90; M. Coleman, *Men and Coal* (New York: Farrar and Rinehart, 1943), pp. 31–74; W. G. Broehl, *The Molly Maguires* (Cambridge, Mass.: Harvard University Press, 1964); R. J. Cornell, *The Anthracite Coal Strike of 1902* (Washington, D.C.: Catholic University of America Press, 1957).

the corporations can reasonably be used to explain the lack of success of miners' strikes, despite the size and length of their stoppages.[34]

Railroad strikes were notable for their extreme brevity and the very low plant participation ratio and rate of success. Despite the long history of unions in the industry, the level of union involvement in strikes was low and, as in coal, union-led strikes were less successful than non-union ones. This pattern can be explained by the established position which the skilled men's unions (the 'operating Brotherhoods') held in the industry. As will be seen later, these unions struck rarely, and most strikes were accounted for by the less skilled men; these disputes fit the pattern of brief, large and unorganized protests, but they were not 'mass' protests since the plant participation ratio and number of establishments per strike are low. However, there were also very large outbreaks of protest, such as the 'Gould strikes' of 1886 and the Pullman strike of 1894, and before them the great upheavals of 1877.[35] These strikes typically involved a union and were lost; hence the lower rate of success for union-led than for non-union strikes.

Railroad managements often operated closely together and, particularly in the Pullman strike, individual companies left the running of their side of affairs to the General Managers' Association, based on Chicago. This strike is also notable for the involvement of the government in labour affairs. Although such involvement was not new and although the weapon of the court injunction against the strikers had been employed before, direct intervention by the government on the side of the companies was a novel feature of the strike.[36] The government does not seem to have had any clear policy of labour relations which it wished to pursue; rather, it reacted to a situation which was defined as a threat to the social order as a whole. The strikers do not seem to have had any overtly 'political' aims; as suggested at the end of

34. Kolko has argued that corporations were less powerful around the turn of the century than has often been supposed. It is true that the railroad, steel and oil trusts did not totally dominate the economy, but the concern here is their power in relation to their workers, which was very great, and not with other aspects of their power. See G. Kolko, *The Triumph of Conservatism* (Chicago: Quadrangle Paperbacks edn, 1967), esp. pp. 2–54.

35. See, respectively, R. A. Allen, *The Great Southwest Strike* (Austin: University of Texas Press, 1942); A. Lindsey, *The Pullman Strike* (Chicago: University of Chicago Press, 1942); R. V. Bruce, *1877: Year of Violence* (Indianapolis: Bobbs-Merrill, 1959).

36. D. L. McMurry, 'The Legal Ancestry of the Pullman Strike Injunctions', *Industrial and Labor Relations Review*, XIV, pp. 235–56 (1961). See also E. Berman, *Labor Disputes and the President of the United States* (New York: Columbia University Press, 1924), pp. 13–35; S. Yellen, *American Labor Struggles* (New York: S. A. Russell, 1956), pp. 101–35.

the previous chapter, government involvement in strikes should be explained in terms of the aims of the government itself. Here, a militant union, the American Railway Union, was seen as threatening the country's welfare by blocking the only long-distance form of transport available. The prevention of the passage of the Federal mails was seized on by the companies as a reason for governmental involvement; when this came the combined power of companies and courts proved far too great for the union.

Thus, the state of technical advance of an industry helps to explain its strike record. However, the pattern revealed in Tables 4.6 to 4.10 is far from totally consistent with the view that technical advance will determine the nature of workers' response. Aspects of particular industries' patterns do not fit this view, and there were inter-industry differences which cannot be explained by it. The power of employers and the government may have been important independent factors. But equally significant were attempts by skilled men to defend themselves against technical change; the failure of unions to counteract forces tending to make strikes unsuccessful suggests that men were using their unions for support in their most bitter struggles.

Trends Within Key Industries

The two previous sections have shown that, over time at the aggregate level and between industries, the level of industrial advance did not determine the pattern of strike activity. The present section considers changes in strike patterns *within* particular industries to test at a more detailed level the view that patterns will change as industries become more advanced. Again, no clear effect of industrialization is apparent, nor is there strong evidence to suggest that increasing corporate power in certain sectors led to the repression of protest.

Since the aim is to make detailed comparisons of industries where technical or other changes occurred, the building and transport equipment sectors are dropped and the glass industry, where particularly significant changes occurred, considered by itself. 'Public ways and works' is added so that we may compare an industry where unskilled work was predominant with those in which craftsmen were important. It is unfortunate that data on the sub-sectors of the metals and transport industries are not available for the first three sub-periods considered (1881–86, 1887–94 and 1894–1900); comparison will be limited to the periods before and after 1900 (see Table 4.12). Table 4.11 gives strike indices by industry for each of the four sub-periods (the above three plus 1901–05).

In the 'traditional' industry of cooperage, establishment involvement fell, as did the solidarity of strikes, as measured by the plant participation ratio and the number of plants per strike. Although strikes became longer, worker involvement and the rate of success fell. If these trends were observed in an industry undergoing technical change or 'trustification', it would no doubt be argued that they were due to these technical and organizational changes. Their occurrence in cooperage is a reminder that other forces were at work.

In the metals industry as a whole the number of strikers per employee fell at the end of the nineteenth century and then increased; the data on its sub-sectors suggest that this rise was concentrated in the 'other' section, but there is no evidence for a decline in the strike rate in tin and steel. Even after the defeats of the previous twenty years, steel workers at the start of the twentieth century maintained their strike activity at the levels of the earlier struggles. Although establishment involvement and the number of establishments per strike rose in the industry as a whole and in its constituent parts, the plant participation ratio fell, as did the rate of success of strikes. The fall in the participation rate was most marked in the stove and furnace sector, while the success rate fell most in 'other metals'. If technical change were the dominant force, the changes would be greatest in tin and steel, but Table 4.12 shows that there was no very great shift in the strike pattern here. Not only was the level of activity maintained, but the success rate did not fall very sharply and there was even an increase in the duration of strikes.

It will be recalled that Commons argued that the corporations in the trustified industries were able to repress overt protest in their plants. But the steel industry, which is the prime example of such a case, does not bear this out. Strikes were defeated and the union weakened; corporate power seems to have been a factor in this. But strikes were still held and their characteristics did not change a great deal. There are dangers, of course, in the limited comparisons possible; it is conceivable that strikes after 1905 exhibited a changed pattern. Qualitative evidence for the period certainly suggests that the workers were repressed and that the occasional protests were short, spontaneous and generally unsuccessful.[37] But such evidence is clearly weighted towards the well-

---

37. J. A. Fitch, *The Steel Workers* (New York: Russell Sage Foundation, 1910), pp. 139–46, 207–20; D. Brody, *Steelworkers in America: the Non-union Era* (Cambridge, Mass.: Harvard University Press, 1960), pp. 127–79; R. Hessen, 'The Bethlehem Steel Strike of 1910', *Labor History*, XV, pp. 3–18 (1974); J. A. Garraty, 'The U.S. Steel Corporation versus Labor: The Early Years', *Labor History*, I, pp. 3–38 (1960).

TABLE 4.11

STRIKE INDICES, BY INDUSTRY, FOR SUB-PERIODS* 1881–1905

	No. Estabs per Strike		Establishment Involvement				Duration per Strike		Duration per Establishment			
	(2)*	(4)*	(1)*	(2)*	(3)*	(4)*	(2)*	(4)*	(1)*	(2)*	(3)*	(4)*
Boot and shoe	1.51	1.36	4.30	3.67	1.77	2.90	34.5	21.7	34.5	22.8	22.1	16.0
Clothing	3.23	3.60	2.79	1.42	5.50	1.37	80.8	95.1	19.6	25.0	12.9	26.4
Coal	8.25	3.32	n.a.	n.a.	n.a.	n.a.	422	180	46.2	51.2	51.1	54.3
Cooperage	3.16	2.24	2.50	1.24	0.81	1.82	110	69.0	9.8	34.7	31.3	30.8
Glass	2.01	2.39	9.54	7.28	5.98	11.1	100	113	85.8	49.8	26.4	47.5
Machinery	1.60	2.97	0.59	0.46	1.43	5.37	67.1	136	29.9	41.9	33.3	45.7
Metals: all	2.33	4.84	0.69	0.61	0.40	1.08	53.1	339	28.9	22.8	28.7	70.0
Printing and publishing	1.95	5.36	1.05	0.75	0.79	1.60	56.3	104	27.3	28.9	20.3	19.3
Textiles	1.27	1.95	1.03	1.82	1.48	1.14	26.5	81.9	25.1	20.9	25.3	42.1
Tobacco	3.75	4.01	8.30	3.39	0.91	1.79	97.4	229	15.7	25.9	37.9	57.0
Transport: all	2.20	8.68	n.a.	n.a.	n.a.	n.a.	30.7	71.4	19.0	14.0	15.9	26.6
Public ways and works	1.85	1.90	n.a.	n.a.	n.a.	n.a.	19.2	38.0	5.2	10.4	8.4	20.0
All industries	4.64	5.00	1.61	2.15	1.96	2.83	134	166	23.6	28.9	33.4	33.2

	% Establishments where Strikes Won				% Establishments where Strikes Lost				Plant Participation Ratio (ST/B)			
	(1)*	(2)*	(3)*	(4)*	(1)*	(2)*	(3)*	(4)*	(1)*	(2)*	(3)*	(4)*
Boot and shoe	52.7	36.1	29.0	38.1	35.7	54.5	63.2	47.7	33.0	34.2	29.9	18.3
Clothing	39.3	61.6	81.9	61.3	34.5	31.3	13.0	34.8	57.8	52.9	70.2	54.6
Coal	29.1	17.3	22.7	24.1	69.2	57.6	36.7	44.1	81.9	81.9	75.5	69.0
Cooperage	72.1	54.4	51.9	53.8	15.6	44.2	43.5	40.0	85.3	78.7	57.8	39.1
Glass	37.2	34.1	43.5	37.7	58.7	59.4	48.8	57.1	40.9	36.7	31.6	35.4

Machinery	38.6	31.3	61.1	31.4	48.8	58.6	28.9	48.2	60.3	18.2	22.2	22.2
Metals: all	52.8	43.3	35.3	31.2	37.8	48.1	52.7	61.0	43.7	28.9	22.2	26.8
Printing and publishing	44.8	32.3	49.8	40.4	52.6	58.4	40.3	46.4	44.8	28.2	26.0	28.3
Textiles	33.7	25.5	17.4	17.2	58.9	63.3	63.9	73.0	61.8	22.1	30.6	36.6
Tobacco	35.9	53.8	52.9	79.8	57.7	39.5	38.8	16.4	63.9	65.6	59.8	62.4
Transport: all	70.8	23.1	34.2	18.0	25.6	60.9	49.4	41.4	74.8	18.1	33.3	35.8
Public ways and works	29.7	43.4	43.1	18.5	46.4	42.8	47.5	73.8	62.1	56.3	54.5	47.8
All industries	44.9	41.3	60.4	40.0	42.0	46.5	24.7	40.9	64.3	43.7	49.5	41.9

	Strikers per Strike (ST/N)		Strikers as % Total Workers Involved (ST/W)				Strikes per Million Employees (N/E)		Strikers per Thousand Employees (ST/E)			
	(2)*	(4)*	(1)*	(2)*	(3)*	(4)*	(2)*	(4)*	(1)*	(2)*	(3)*	(4)*
Boot and shoe	97.1	77.0	61.9	65.5	59.9	69.4	466	292	60.3	45.3	25.5	22.5
Clothing	83.9	225	78.5	79.0	83.2	78.9	380	371	56.0	31.9	122	83.4
Coal	937	532	85.3	84.2	82.8	74.6	257	293	134	241	215	208
Cooperage	63.4	70.1	99.2	93.7	84.8	89.7	520	760	90.8	33.0	19.0	53.3
Glass	156	141	50.4	44.6	47.8	47.1	344	620	81.4	53.5	41.1	87.3
Machinery	87.5	142	83.1	78.2	62.5	77.0	88	439	30.6	7.7	16.5	62.1
Metals: all	146	152	62.9	68.4	60.6	67.6	351	327	88.8	51.2	37.0	49.6
Printing and publishing	38.3	72.9	96.3	73.6	75.4	76.7	391	380	9.7	15.0	13.4	27.7
Textiles	130	310	47.7	52.3	59.5	82.1	186	162	20.6	24.1	37.5	50.2
Tobacco	125	147	84.5	86.7	73.3	88.7	831	480	251	104	56.1	70.7
Transport: all	272	116	92.1	64.6	91.5	62.2	n.a.	n.a.	n.a.	n.a.	n.a.	n.a.
Public ways and works	144	260	91.7	84.9	86.2	85.2	n.a.	n.a.	n.a.	n.a.	n.a.	n.a.
All industries	184	159	85.3	77.2	75.0	79.5	400	547	72.0	73.3	66.4	86.9

NOTE
*Sub-periods: (1) 1881–86 (2) 1887–94 (3) 1894–1900 (4) 1901–05.

TABLE 4.12

STRIKE INDICES, METALS AND TRANSPORT INDUSTRIES, 1881–1905

	No. Estabs per Strike		Estab. Involvement		Duration per Strike		Duration per Estab.		% Estabs where Strikes Won	
	(1)–(3)*	(4)*	(1)–(3)*	(4)*	(1)–(3)*	(4)*	(1)–(3)*	(4)*	(1)–(3)*	(4)*
Tin and steel	1.88	2.66	0.86	1.24	63.8	92.0	34.0	34.6	38.4	32.6
Stove and furnace	1.53	1.39	n.a.	n.a.	26.1	36.2	17.1	26.0	37.6	43.6
Other metal	3.88	7.82	0.34	0.99	31.2	649	10.1	83.0	65.7	33.6
Railroad	1.35	1.31	n.a.	n.a.	4.8	10.8	3.5	8.2	23.6	16.4
Other transport	3.73	3.04	n.a.	n.a.	153	87.3	41.1	28.7	67.9	18.2

	% Estabs where Strikes Lost		Plant Participation (ST/B)		Strikers per Strike (ST/N)		Strikes per Million (N/E)		Strikers per Thousand (ST/E)	
	(1)–(3)*	(4)*	(1)–(3)*	(4)*	(1)–(3)*	(4)*	(1)–(3)*	(4)*	(1)–(3)*	(4)*
Tin and steel	44.8	55.3	33.3	26.2	265	243	195	217	51.7	52.6
Stove and furnace	53.2	47.0	39.8	16.5	85.6	41.0	n.a.	n.a.	n.a.	n.a.
Other metal	28.5	53.4	30.3	30.0	88.4	103	266	387	23.5	40.0
Railroad	64.0	77.6	11.8	46.6	266	149	n.a.	n.a.	n.a.	n.a.
Other transport	25.6	37.3	58.6	33.0	304	107	n.a.	n.a.	n.a.	n.a.

NOTE
*Sub-periods: (1)–(3) 1881–1900 (4) 1901–05.

known struggles and need not be representative of the period as a whole; and as has been seen, some views derived from qualitative data, such as that business unionism in industries like tobacco helped to increase the rate of success of strikes, are unwarranted. More importantly, the quantitative data for 1881–1905 indicate that any process of corporate domination was a lengthy one in which the workers did not give way easily.[38]

In tobacco, strike activity fell from the very high levels of the early 1880s, but increased in the twentieth century. The duration and size of stoppages rose, but the most notable change was the marked rise in the rate of success; in the first of our four periods 36 per cent of strikes were won and in the fourth the proportion was 79 per cent. The proponents of business unionism would use this increase to support their case, particularly since in the 1880s the Knights of Labor had a considerable hold on the industry; but it is possible that the type of strike being undertaken was changing. After the defeats of the 1870s and 1880s on the issue of mechanization, strikes may have been fought over economic matters, so that an increased rate of success was to be expected. Of course, business unionists could argue that they were instrumental in the shift of strike issues, but this does not cope with the problem that the move to these issues was based on acceptance of a basic defeat over job control This defeat may have been inevitable and the resistance to machinery futile, but it is rather odd to argue that business unions improved the material conditions of their members when they were based on a refusal to challenge management on certain central issues; a rise in the rate of success of strikes cannot simply be equated with a rise in worker power. Nevertheless, the tobacco industry illustrates one means of coming to terms with mechanization after the initial battle against the machine was over.

The battle was lost in tobacco, but this was not universal. Thus in his classic study of the reaction of workers to the machine Barnett argued that printers were able to come to terms successfully because machinery in their industry did not abolish the need for craft skills.[39] The low level of strike activity in printing and publishing suggests that there was

38. Similarly, in machinery, corporate power based on technical change has been seen as significant, but changes in strike patterns do not support the inferences which may be drawn from this. See, for example, D. Nelson, 'The New Factory System and the Unions: The National Cash Register Company Dispute of 1901', *Labor History*, XV, pp. 163–78 (1974).
39. G. E. Barnett, *Chapters on Machinery and Labor* (Cambridge, Mass.: Harvard University Press, 1926), pp. 3–29. See also idem, *The Printers* (Princeton: Princeton University Press, 1909).

little need for the men to strike to defend themselves, but the data on strike issues (Table 4.6) do not show the concentration on economic matters which would be expected if there was no need to strike over matters of job control. In an industry of small plants, the mean size of stoppages was naturally low, but both the plant participation ratio and the ratio of strikers to workers involved fell, suggesting a decline in the craft solidarity of the industry; and plant participation was not at a particularly high level, indicating that the degree of solidarity may have been less than is often thought. Similarly, the rate of success was no greater than average; overall, the view of printing as an industry where the workers were uniquely successful in defending their position is in need of considerable modification.

In the coal industry, there was a rise in the success rate of strikes, but no other strong trends which would support the view that strike sophistication was increasing. Similarly, there is no evidence for a rise in corporate repression, and, indeed, the years between 1897 and 1902 were notable for the rise of the United Mine Workers and the establishment of collective bargaining.[40] In the non-railroad part of the transport industry, on the other hand, strikes became shorter, smaller, less solidaristic and even less successful; this fall in sophistication is consistent with a rise in the power of employers. On the railroads, the large and very short protests of 1881–1900 gave way, at the start of the twentieth century, to rather longer and more solidaristic disputes. After the defeats at the end of the nineteenth century, workers altered the pattern of their strikes, but remained unable to increase the rate of their success. Despite the rise in the duration of transport strikes, stoppage remained very short compared with those in other industries. In later years, transport strikes have been settled very rapidly because of their immediate impact on consumers;[41] the ability of employers and the government, backed by the public, to prevent long stoppages has had a long history.

In public ways and works construction, strikes were even shorter

40. See K. A. Kerr, 'Labor-management Co-operation: An 1897 Case', *Pennsylvania Magazine of History and Biography*, IC, pp. 45–71 (1975); R. H. Wiebe, 'The Anthracite Strike of 1902: A Record of Confusion', *Mississippi Valley Historical Review*, XLVIII, pp. 229–51 (1961); W. E. Fisher, 'Bituminous Coal' and 'Anthracite', *How Collective Bargaining Works* (New York: Twentieth Century Fund, 1942), pp. 229–79 and 280–317.

41. J. J. McGinley, *Labor Relations in the New York Rapid Transit Systems, 1904–44* (New York: King's Crown Press, 1949), esp. pp. 331–62; N. W. Chamberlain and J. M. Schilling, *The Impact of Strikes* (New York: Harper and Bros, 1954), pp. 142–86. Cf. J. J. Kaufman, *Collective Bargaining in the Railroad Industry* (New York: King's Crown Press, 1954).

than in transport. Since stoppages were also large and unsuccessful, this industry fits the argument that early industrialization will lead to brief and unorganized strikes. But it is notable that this pattern was limited to an industry dominated by unskilled work. Such a response was not common in other industries.

It is not surprising that the 'classic' response to industry was limited to sectors where unskilled work was paramount. Industry did not arrive suddenly or create a work force which was totally unaccustomed to such things as the rational planning of work. Although workers were familiar with industry, they did not accept it unquestioningly. Not only did they strike to protect their conditions but they often engaged in lengthy struggles; strikes represented a movement of protest and not the spontaneous outburst of discontent. Despite technical and organizational changes, and repression from employers, strike activity in certain key industries did not 'wither away'.

Occupational Patterns of Strike Activity

This section considers the direct evidence on the strike patterns of skilled and unskilled men. The data come from the first two of the Commissioner of Labor's strike reports, which included detailed information on every 'cessation' recorded. The evidence on the occupation of strikers has been used to build up tables of the strike patterns of particular crafts in eight key industries. As far as possible, these tables are comparable with those presented earlier, but the lack of information on employment by occupation and industry makes analysis of the overall rates of strike activity of different occupations impossible.

Shorter and Tilly suggest that three forms of reaction to industry can be identified.[42] First, there will be the craft groups which have met the challenge successfully. Their strikes will concentrate on economic demands because workers do not need to fight over matters of job control; strikes will be organized by unions, enabling workers to hold out for a long time. Second, there will be the craft groups which have failed to meet the challenge of industry. Their strikes, too, will be long and highly organized, but will be bitter fights over job control and not straightforward economic disputes. Finally, workers in the newer industries will have strikes which are poorly organized and short, for their solidarity will be short-lived; since these workers experience no loss of traditional rights, the strikes will focus on economic demands.

42. Shorter and Tilly, op. cit., pp. 217–19.

TABLE 4.13

'CESSATIONS' BY OCCUPATION, METALS AND METAL GOODS INDUSTRY, 1881–94

	Number	% with Given Issue			% Ordered by Union	% Won[a]	Mean Duration	Mean Size	ST/B
		Wage & Hour	Conditions	Union					
a. 1881–86									
Moulders and puddlers	268	76.1	11.2	12.7	48.3	44.1	34.3	71.6	22.3
Smiths	87	86.2	6.9	6.9	81.4	71.8	9.4	26.9	34.4
Screwmakers, nailers etc.	69	78.3	14.5	7.2	39.1	43.8	45.0	48.9	18.2
Helpers and labourers	47	91.5	8.5	0	21.7	37.2	10.6	60.9	11.2
Others	22	81.8	18.2	0	18.2	61.9	9.1	200	32.0
Employees	262	83.2	9.9	6.9	67.6	36.1	34.3	295	74.6
All	755	81.1	10.6	8.3	55.3	44.8	30.2	145	43.0
b. 1887–94									
Moulders	225	48.0	27.6	24.4	80.0	23.3	29.4	63.8	10.4
Puddlers	63	60.3	17.5	22.2	47.6	15.0	50.2	84.6	12.1
Smiths	45	73.3	15.6	11.1	73.3	47.4	3.8	81.3	41.2
Screwmakers etc.	56	62.5	25.0	12.5	48.2	35.3	29.1	56.5	18.7
Helpers and labourers	24	70.8	29.2	0	4.2	8.7	4.9	50.5	5.2
Tin and sheet workers	25	48.0	8.0	44.0	92.0	60.9	20.6	28.0	12.1
Others	79	72.2	25.3	2.5	32.9	13.7	24.0	73.3	11.9
Employees	163	52.1	19.6	28.2	54.6	30.3	40.7	416	77.9
All	680	56.6	22.8	20.6	60.0	26.4	30.5	150	27.5

NOTE
a. Number of strikes won as percentage total won and lost.

It is surprising that Shorter and Tilly use only three indices (organization, issues and duration) to distinguish between their three patterns. A fuller set of indices will be used here. Table 4.13 gives the relevant information for the metals industries; the data for the other industries are collected in Table A.12. The indices used in these tables are familiar, but a preliminary point must be made about the classification of strike issues. Since the present interest is in economic as against other issues a very broad division into three types is used. The 'wage and hour' group includes all strikes which can be seen as being of an economic nature and includes disputes over the method of payment and demands for more holidays. 'Conditions' includes all matters of job control, work conditions, discipline and the like; and 'union' covers such things as sympathy strikes and expressions of solidarity with workers elsewhere as well as such things as demands for union recognition and protests against the sacking of union men.

At the beginning of Table A.12 the total figures for all eight industry groups are given, to provide a basis for comparison in discussing particular cases. Between 1881–86 and 1887–94 there was a notable overall shift in strike patterns, with a decline in economic disputes and a rise in strikes over conditions and union matters; and strikes became less successful, less solidaristic and rather shorter. Thus in the occupations and industries considered here there was a general fall in the 'sophistication' of striking.

Metals and Glass Industries
As Table 4.13 shows, a similar pattern emerged in the metals industry as a whole. The shift is particularly clear among the moulders and puddlers, who were the craft workers central to the industry. The moulders had long had a strong union and had achieved a considerable degree of job control, but they were weakened by the changing organization of the industry and the growth of the employers' power. The evidence here clearly indicates that the pattern of their striking altered; and it is reasonable to attribute this to changes in the power of the occupation over the work place. But the comparison with other industries is instructive. The printing trades are usually seen as having coped successfully with the machine, but Table A.12b shows that the compositors were less successful in their strikes between 1881–86 and 1887–94 and that the issues in dispute moved away from economic matters. Table A.12c indicates that the moulders in machinery did not follow their counterparts in metals; although their strikes became less successful, the issues involved changed little and the mean length of strikes increased.

Thus there is no simple link between the threat to the position of an occupation and its pattern of protest. Not only were the changes between the two periods similar for moulders and compositors, but the levels of the various indices were alike; thus in 1887—94 the ratio of successes to failures for compositors was 27 per cent and for moulders in the metals industries 23 per cent. Differences between craft groups are brought out further in comparisons within the glass industry (Table A.12d). Until the 1890s, the window glass workers held a dominant position in their section of the industry; the crafts in the green glass section held a somewhat less powerful position; and the flint and pressed glass workers were in much the weakest position and were not recognized as skilled men by the labour aristrocracy of the rest of the industry.[43] The strikes of the window glass workers completely fit the pattern of the successful reaction to industry; they were long, successful and concentrated on economic demands. Similarly, the flint glass blowers represent the unsuccessful response. But, while bottle glass blowers fit the 'successful' pattern, green glass blowers, who should also fit this pattern, in fact matched the flint glass workers in terms of the issues in their strikes and their rate of success; and a low mean duration of stoppages placed them nearer to the 'unskilled' pattern of brief protests. Thus again the tripartite model does not wholly describe the situation. The need to distinguish between the sections of the industry exemplifies the problems of dealing with an industry as a whole and the great complexity of responses to industry by apparently similar groups.

Boots and Shoes; and Textiles

Table A.12e gives data for the boot and shoe industry. This is particularly important because the 'mechanical revolution' occurred relatively early here: one can thus compare the strike patterns of workers in a mechanized industry with those of men in industries like glass where traditional methods were still important.[44] In fact, the differences were not very great. There was the contrast between 1881—86 and 1887—94 (in terms of the issues, success and duration of strikes) which has been noted for other industries; and there was no great difference in the levels of the various indicators. The most notable feature of strikes in the boot and shoe industry was the marked decline in their mean duration from 35 to 16 days. It is impossible to say whether this represents

43. P. Davis, *The Development of the American Glass Industry* (Cambridge, Mass.: Harvard University Press, 1949), pp. 126—65; M. Derber, 'Glass', *How Collective Bargaining Works*, op. cit., pp. 682—743 at pp. 694—5.
44. See B. Stern, 'Labor Productivity in the Boot and Shoe Industry', *Monthly Labor Review*, XLVIII, pp. 271—92 (1939), esp. pp. 271—4; I. Yellowitz, 'Skilled Workers and Mechanization: The Lasters in the 1890s', *Labor History*, XV, pp. 197—213 (1977).

a secular change towards 'modern' forms of protest, but the association between a mechanized industry and short strikes is important.

This association is also shown in part f of the table, relating to the textile industries, in which the growth of factory methods preceded that in boots and shoes. Here strikes were consistently shorter than in the metals, machinery and glass industries and they were also much larger. The size of strikes may have been due, in part, to the size of plants in the industry, but the plant participation ratio was (at least for 1881–86) quite low; this thus countered the effect of plant size. The other very marked feature of strikes in textiles was the very low proportion with union involvement. In view of the constant difficulties unions have experienced here this is not surprising and there may be an association between the lack of unions and the brevity of the strikes. This, combined with their size, suggests that strikes here may have been typical of 'early' factory protests (unorganized, short and large), but the rate of success was not very different from that in other industries and the plant participation ratio did not show a tendency for strikes to have been plant-wide protests.[45] And the strikes were heavily concentrated among the weavers, whereas mass protests would involve more groups of workers; in other words, strikes of 'employees' would be particularly significant.

According to Lahne, the spinners in particular were suffering the effects of technical change in the 1880s; they might be expected to have followed the 'unsuccessful response' pattern.[46] However, their strikes were more concentrated on economic demands than those of other groups in the industry and were no less successful; and since they were shorter than average they cannot be seen as long and bitter struggles. The smallness and apparent infrequency of spinners' strikes, together with the low plant participation ratio, suggest that the spinners could not mount an effective challenge to the employers either through their own strength or through the support of other workers. Their response was to strike rarely and on issues where they had some chance of success. Thus one response to technical change is withdrawal from a battle which cannot be won. While some craft groups may engage in the bitter fights for job control described by Shorter and Tilly, others realize that such action is not possible for them and give way relatively passively. The 'unsuccessful craft response' has two forms: that described

---

45. See also the data on the textiles industry in Tables 4.5 to 4.10.
46. H. J. Lahne, *The Cotton Mill Worker in the Twentieth Century* (New York: Farrar and Rinehart, 1944), pp. 175–9. See also M. A. McLaurin, *Paternalism and Protest* (Westport: Greenwood Publishing, 1971), pp. 13–14.

by Shorter and Tilly and a relatively passive acceptance of the inevitable.

Railroads; and Public Ways and Works

The final two parts of Table A.12 consider two non-manufacturing industries. In the railroad industry, the strikes of engineers and firemen reflected the powerful position of these workers. Strikes were shorter than those in the rest of the industry, and the plant participation ratio was lower; union organization was high and rate of success greater than elsewhere. This evidence, combined with the apparent rarity of engineers' strikes, suggests that these men needed only short and infrequent strikes to achieve their ends and that they acted independently of other workers in the industry. But the issues in their strikes were not, as one might expect, heavily concentrated on economic demands; indeed, the proportion of 'wage and hours' strikes was rather lower than elsewhere. Although the success rate was higher than in the rest of the railroad industry, its absolute level was not very high. It may be that, for these workers, the strike was a last resort and that they were generally able to defend themselves by other means; but there is no evidence that, when they did use industrial action, they were particularly successful.

The Pullman strike of 1894, as one of the most important labour disputes at the end of the nineteenth century, warrants consideration in its own right. Fifty separate 'cessations' connected with the strike were recorded and, since the stated aim of the strike was support for the employees of the Pullman company, they have all been placed in the 'union' category which includes, it will be recalled, sympathy strikes. Although the Pullman cessations were longer and larger than other transport strikes, the plant participation ratio was low. This may have been one reason for their failure; although the strike is often seen as a mass battle between a militant union and the employers and government, only 13 per cent of employees in establishments in which strikes were called responded to the appeal.

Finally, in Table A.12h, data are presented for the public ways and works industry. These are of interest in showing in extreme form the characteristics of the strikes of unskilled men in an industry with no craft tradition. Disputes were very heavily concentrated on economic demands and had little union involvement; and they were large and short, with a high participation ratio. Thus they fit the 'mass protest' model for all their aspects except for the rate of success, which was not very different from that in other industries; the success rate is a very poor discriminator between types of strike within as well as between industries. This may be due in part to the technical weaknesses of the index[47], but the lack of any clear differences between occupational groups is still remarkable. 'Laborers' in public works construction were about as successful in their striking as a number of skilled groups in other industries.

For 1887—94, it is possible to separate the strikes of street pavers from the 'other' category. These stoppages were similar to those of the 'unsuccessful craft response' despite the lack of anything in this industry which could be described as a craft tradition. This pattern of protest need not stem from the disruption of long-established craft practices and seems to have occurred among a number of different groups. The pattern of teamsters' strikes is also significant. Although a strong union had not emerged by the 1880s and 1890s, and the proportion of strikes 'ordered' was low, drivers of teams had already established themselves; their strikes were very brief and highly successful and were largely of an economic nature. The sources of power of these workers are clear: the control of a key part of the distribution system and the fragmentation of the ownership of teams. The notable thing is the use of this power before the arrival of a strong union.[48]

General Patterns of Response
Some more general points about Table A.12 must now be considered. Nearly all industries include data on strikes by 'employees'. The main interest in them concerns their position as strikes in which 'class consciousness' is most likely to have been apparent; that is, workers of different trades united in their striking. As one would expect, these strikes were larger than those limited to individual trades and the plant participation ratio was generally much higher. But there was little difference from other stoppages on the other dimensions. There was no tendency for strikes by 'employees' to be concentrated on non-economic demands; or, to put this the other way round, disputes over work conditions were not particularly likely to lead to strikes in which different trades united. This goes against the view that workers were particularly likely to strike together when 'fundamental' issues of job control are involved. There was only a slight tendency for strikes by 'employees' to have a greater duration and degree of union involvement than other stoppages.

In all industries the strikes of labourers, helpers, and the like were similar, with a low level of union involvement, a concentration on

---

47. See below, Appendix B, pp. 300—01.
48. On early teamster power see R. D. Leiter, *The Teamsters' Union* (New York: Bookman Associates, 1957), pp. 22—5.

economic matters and a low mean duration. There was also a tendency, in the industries where these workers were employed together with skilled men, for the plant participation ratio to be low. This suggests that the protests of the unskilled men occurred in isolation from the struggles of other workers. But, in cases where the unskilled dominated operations, the participation rate was high; this is shown by the figures for public works construction but even more notably in the data for longshoremen given in Table A.12g. The participation ratio was 98 per cent in 1881—86 and 75 per cent in 1887—94, giving an average of 91 per cent. Thus, like miners, dockers had established a high level of solidarity at least as early as the 1880s.

In addition to these two main patterns of 'unskilled' strikes, several types of action by skilled men can be identified. Although differences have been noted in, for example, the mean duration of strikes by various occupations, the similarities are more important. The shift in strike patterns between 1881—86 and 1887—94 was common to all sectors, the rate of success of strikes varied little and there was a general focus on economic demands. Thus it has not proved possible to apply the simple dichotomy between types of craft reaction to industrialization. Occupations with different degrees of success in defending their position had similar strike patterns, and there is evidence that at least two types of 'unsuccessful response' existed: fighting against changes or accepting them passively. Similarly, a group which coped successfully with the challenge did not necessarily have a strike pattern reflecting this; the fact of having to engage in a strike may have meant that the group had been unable to defend some aspect of its position, whereas in general it could meet the challenge without a strike. Even a group which held an apparently secure position could not be sure that this could be maintained intact. In 1890 the position of the window glass workers seemed safe, but within a few years technical changes had been introduced and the power of their union destroyed. In the first two decades of the twentieth century similar changes occurred in the rest of the glass industry as a mass production system replaced a craft one.[49]

Although a tripartite model of craft adaptation is unsatisfactory as it stands, it is true that strike activity was concentrated among skilled workers. As Shorter and Tilly put it, the contemporary expectation that strikes would be concentrated in the modern industries, where the division of labour had been taken furthest, is not correct. Craft workers

49. Davis, op. cit., pp. 173—240; Barnett, *Chapters on Machinery and Labor,* op. cit., pp. 67—115; 'The Passing of the National Window Glass Workers', *Monthly Labor Review,* XXIX, pp. 773—88 (1929).

showed the greatest solidarity, had the most to lose, and were the group best organized to engage in a struggle with employers. Although no employment data exist with which to assess the extent that the skilled were more strike-prone than other workers, in absolute terms they dominated the strike movement; and they cannot have formed such a large proportion of the work force that they were less prone to strike than unskilled men. Craft workers had the leadership and resources to conduct strikes, and were under the greatest pressure from employers. Not only were their work conditions threatened, but their unions were being challenged since employers saw unions as a source of resistance to their own domination. The steel industry is a good illustration of this general point.

The Case of Steel

The history of labour in steel is well known and only a brief outline concentrating on the current issues of interest is needed here.[50] In the 1860s and 1870s the Iron Molders' Union was one of the strongest in the country and, by exerting control over the skilled crafts, was able to make itself an important force. But it and its successor, the Amalgamated Association of Iron, Steel and Tin Workers (formed by a merger of the iron unions in 1876), faced a growing challenge from the employers. Initially competition was intense and cost-cutting the order of the day; hence pressure was put on wages and efficiency. The new steel plants were large and complex and the Amalgamated was faced with a struggle to maintain the practices it had established in the older and more traditional iron foundries.[51]

The union had been of use to the iron industry in reducing competition, but, as Brody argues, only total submission would have suited the steel companies.[52] The union was a barrier to full cost reduction and was tolerated in the 1880s because it could not easily be removed. But in 1892 the Carnegie company destroyed it in the famous Homestead strike. In 1889 the Amalgamated had reached agreement with the com-

---

50. See in particular Brody, op. cit., H. B. Davis, *Labor and Steel* (London: Martin Lawrence, 1933).
51. P. Temin, *Iron and Steel in Nineteenth Century America* (Cambridge, Mass.: M.I.T. Press, 1964), pp. 154–93; K. Warren, *The American Steel Industry, 1850–1970* (Oxford: Clarendon Press, 1973), pp. 121–42.
52. This paragraph relies on Brody, op. cit., pp. 50–75; L. Wolff, *Lockout* (New York: Harper and Row, 1965); A. Benhamou-Hirtz, *Les Relations collectives dans la siderurgie Americaine* (Paris: Armand Colin, 1966), pp. 1–18.

pany on a new sliding scale and the union was to be recognized, but in 1892 the company demanded a reduction in the scale, which was refused. It then declared that the plant would henceforth operate on a non-union basis; in winning the strike (or lockout) it succeeded in this aim. The Amalgamated retained its strength in a number of areas, especially the tin-making section of the industry, but several defeats in the early twentieth century, particularly in the strikes of 1901 and 1909, effectively destroyed its remaining power.

The crucial early defeats came before the establishment of the United States Steel Corporation in 1901. The employers' interest in defeating the union was greatest when competition was the most severe and when cost-cutting was most essential for survival. Thus, the defeat of the union was not simply a result of the growth of trusts in the industry. Even when U.S. Steel was established it did not dominate the industry to the extent that might be imagined.[53] It still had to tread carefully in its anti-union campaign and employed welfare schemes to forestall unionization. On the product market front, the Steel Corporation failed to stabilize the industry and, in the first twenty years of its operations, actually lost some of its share of the market to competitors. The famous 'Gary dinners' failed to achieve any covert price-fixing in the industry.[54]

Nevertheless, says Brody, it was the power of the corporation, rather than technical change, which defeated the Amalgamated. But the power was not at first absolute and did not stem from the corporation's domination of the product market. The power was used to split the workers by means of such things as pension and stock-ownership schemes which were designed to appeal mainly to the skilled men. Care was needed even in dealing with the demoralized Amalgamated with its out-dated policy of craft exclusiveness.[55] The importance of corporate power has been stated in 'radical' form by Stone, who starts with the view that 'in the nineteenth century, work in the steel industry was controlled by the skilled workers. Skilled workers decided how the work was done and how much was produced.'[56] Stone goes on to argue

53. Kolko, op. cit., pp. 30–8; A. Berglund, *The United States Steel Corporation* (New York: Columbia University Press, 1907), esp. pp. 95–6.
54. W. Adams, 'The Steel Industry', *The Structure of American Industry*, ed. W. Adams (New York: Macmillan, 1950), pp. 145–96.
55. Brody, op. cit., pp. 73, 78–95; see also refs in note 37 above.
56. K. Stone, 'The Origins of Job Structures in the Steel Industry', *Radical America*, VII, no. 6, pp. 19–65 (1973), at p. 19. See also S. A. Marglin, 'What Do Bosses Do? The Origins and Functions of Hierarchy in Capitalist Production', *The Division of Labour*, ed. A. Gorz (Brighton: Harvester Press, 1976), pp. 13–54.

that technical developments in the period after 1860 did not replace men with machines; to do this, the owners needed unilateral control of operations. The Homestead victory gave them this control so that in the 1890s unprecedented changes were undertaken in which the need for skilled men was reduced; and they were replaced by semi-skilled machine operators who lacked any general craft knowledge of steelmaking.

This argument has been taken a step further by Wachtel.[57] He argues that this early homogenization of the working class was superseded by a renewed differentiation as the competitive phase of capitalism gave way to the monopoly form. The destruction of job control in steel in the 1890s led to a system of stratification within the working class which has existed unaltered to the present. As Palmer notes,[58] there is the danger of exaggerating the extent to which skill dilution flowed direct from the wishes of the capitalists rather than from technical advances. There is also the difficulty of obtaining adequate evidence to support the contentions made; for example, it is hard to show convincingly that the wishes of the capitalists were the dominant factor.

However, it has been shown that capitalists had an interest in destroying the craft system and that the effect of the changes at the end of the nineteenth century was to increase their power. Technical changes were clearly necessary before the new system of domination could be imposed, but they did not in themselves determine the re-organization of the social division of labour which they permitted. One need not accept the whole of the radical case, that production could be effectively arranged by the men themselves and that the capitalist could have been rendered redundant, to accept that a re-division of labour was carried out. Rational planning methods were introduced and labour came increasingly to be treated as a 'factor of production' rather than as an integral partner in the production process. But there is the danger of romanticizing the past in stressing the role of the independent skilled man before the changes of the 1890s: changes were made despite the opposition of the workers and the capitalists clearly already had a considerable amount of power, and were prepared to use it. Emphasis must be placed on structural conditions rather than on the wishes of particular capitalists like Carnegie. The workers had retained a craft system based on the iron industry in the new conditions of steel and were

57. H. M. Wachtel, 'Class Consciousness and Stratification in the Labor Process', *Review of Radical Political Economics*, VI, no. 1, pp. 1–31 (1974), esp. p. 11.
58. B. Palmer, 'Class, Conception and Conflict: The Thrust for Efficiency, Managerial Views of Labor and Working Class Rebellion, 1903–22', *Review of Radical Political Economics*, VII, no. 2, pp. 31–49 (1975), at pp. 31–2.

naturally unclear about how to alter it to meet new needs and yet defend their power over the work place. Technical change gave the employers the chance to use the power over their plants which had remained latent when craft methods were important. Thus it is not surprising that they were able to move the division of labour in the direction they wanted; they did not simply impose their desires since they had no clear aim in mind, as far as any final position is concerned. They reacted to conditions, but had a clearer idea than did the workers of how to react to, and control, technical developments.[59]

Thus technical changes and employer power were both important for the changes in the division of labour that occurred. It is now possible to understand more fully the strike patterns revealed in Table 4.13. For example, in 1887—94 tin and sheet metal workers remained relatively successful in their strikes whereas other skilled groups were already moving towards a pattern of 'unsuccessful response'. The Amalgamated Association managed to retain control of the tin and sheet mills later than the rest of the industry, but the defeat here came in 1901. The table gives a snap-shot view of part of the process whereby the skilled trades were destroyed and replaced by semi-skilled workers.

The strike pattern which followed the victory of the corporations must be briefly noted. Not surprisingly, the main feature of the first three decades of the twentieth century was the prevention of protest, partly through welfare schemes and partly through direct repression. In this period there were only two strikes involving 10,000 or more workers,[60] in 1901 and the 'great strike' of 1919, compared with eight in the period 1933—41 and 25 in 1946—60. The strikes generally took the form of mass protests, which were rapidly quelled and which did not generally achieve permanent gains.[61] The exception was the 1919

59. In an interesting comparison of the American and British steel industries, Holt has suggested that union weakness and divisions within the working class cannot be used to explain the defeat in America, since similar forces were at work in Britain. Although the inadequate strategy of the Amalgamated Association was a contributory factor, the key was the greater hostility of American employers to trade unions, a view which is clearly consistent with that advanced here. See J. Holt, 'Trade Unionism in the British and U.S. Steel Industries, 1888—1912: A Comparative Study', *Labor History*, XVIII, pp. 5—35 (1977).

60. *Work Stoppages: Basic Steel Industry, 1901—60* (Washington, D.C.: Bureau of Labor Statistics Report No. 206, 1961).

61. There were several more significant disputes, notably the strikes at McKee's Rock in 1909 and the Bethlehem steel works in 1916. These were long and bitter struggles, so that one cannot assume that protests by unorganized workers were necessarily short and ineffective; some writers even see these disputes as forerunners of the breakthrough to unionization in the 1930s. It

stoppage which involved 365,000 workers and lasted 3½ months. It occurred after an organizing drive of the A.F.L. unions with an interest in the steel industry, but can be seen as a 'mass' protest since many workers who were not union members responded to the strike call and many of these were unskilled men in whom the A.F.L. unions showed little interest. The strike was defeated and the open shop system maintained.[62]

Thus, in one key industry there was a long process of the destruction of craft skills; there was no sudden confrontation with technical change in all trades at once. And the challenge faced by successive groups of workers was not that of 'industrialization' since the iron industry had employed the factory system and a complex division of labour since at least 1860.[63] The challenge was the development of new forms of capitalist production; this was met with varying degrees of success but with ultimate defeat by the skilled craft groups of the industry. The legacy of this will be considered in the next two chapters.

The Sources of Diversity

This chapter has shown that industrialization exerted certain broad effects on the strike movement. At the national level there was a decline in the effectiveness of strikes and, between industries, differences appeared which could be related to the position of an industry on the 'traditional-advanced' scale. But this scale is only a very rough one: although measures of technical advance were consistently inversely related to strike activity, the relationship was not particularly strong. Trends within industries over time did not point to any clear developments in the direction of 'sophistication' or 'repression'. Occupational differences revealed a pattern far more complex than that suggested by Shorter and Tilly's tripartite model. And in the steel industry there was

---

is the rarity of strikes, and not their brevity, which is crucial; they were temporary eruptions within the general pattern of corporate domination. See H. B. Davis, op. cit., pp. 139–92, 238–41; Benhamou-Hirtz, op. cit., pp. 27–45; M. Dubofsky, *We Shall Be All* (Chicago: Quadrangle Books, 1969), pp. 199–209.

62. D. Brody, *Labor in Crisis* (Philadelphia: J. B. Lippincott, 1965); M. H. Vorse, *Men and Steel* (London: Labour Publishing, 1922); *Report on the Steel Strike of 1919* (Interchurch World Movement; New York: Harcourt, Brace and Howe, 1920).

63. See D. J. Walkowitz, 'Statistics and the Writing of Workingclass Culture: A Statistical Portrait of Iron Workers in Troy, N.Y., 1860–80' *Labor History*, XV, pp. 416–60 (1974).

a close interaction between technical changes and developments in the ownership of the means of production; the most notable fact was the length of time which the destruction of craft unionism took and the need for the corporations to tread carefully.[64]

Using more detailed and qualitative evidence, Gutman and other writers have shown that the picture of inevitable corporate domination was misleading; in several cases strikes were won against all the odds.[65] Pre-existing social structures were able to exert a considerable influence against 'industrialization'; or, more precisely, existing capitalist and middle-class groups were able to resist the corporate form of capitalism which they found to be as opposed to their interests as the workers found it to be opposed to theirs.[66] Nationally, the Populist movement was at the peak of its success with its campaign against 'monopoly'; as Pollack has shown, this was not a 'backward-looking' attempt to restore some golden age but a self-consciously reformist and 'forward-looking' movement.[67] These local and national movements reflected popular uncertainty about economic developments. In some cases they gave direct aid to workers in their struggles, but they also point to a more general antipathy to the corporations. In this environment, it is not surprising that the strike movement did not reveal a monolithic pattern of response by the workers.

A second source of diversity external to industry related to variations in the rate at which industrialization and urbanization proceeded. These gross changes naturally occurred at different times and in different ways. Their precise impact varied according to a wide range of factors which cannot be considered in detail here, but, as far as the

64. Data not included here indicate that different regions of the country which had been industrialized for similar lengths of time had very different strike records. Sufficiently detailed information is not available to assess whether these differences were due to differences in industrial structure, but it is possible to reject the strong argument that industrialization had certain definite effects. See Edwards op. cit., pp. 263–7 and tables 5–21 to 5–23.
65. See Gutman's papers cited in notes 8 and 15 above; B. K. Shelton; 'The Grain Shovellers' Strike of 1899', *Labor History,* IX, pp. 210–38 (1968); I. M. Marcus, 'Labor Discontent in Tioga County, Pa., 1865–1905: The Gutman Thesis, a Test Case', *Labor History,* XIV, pp. 414–22 (1973).
66. As Thompson points out in another context, there is the danger of seeing early forms of social structure as simply 'pre-industrial' and of ignoring the many variations on the theme of the transition to industrialism; and the shift in society was not to an abstract industrialism but to a particular form of industrial capitalism. See E. P. Thompson, 'Time, Work-discipline and Industrial Capitalism', *Past and Present,* XXXVIII, pp. 56–97 (1967), at p. 80.
67. N. Pollack, *The Populist Response to Industrial America* (Cambridge, Mass.: Harvard University Press, 1962).

workers were concerned, different areas represented very different environments.[68] In a country as large as the United States, such diversity was to be expected; the complexity of strike patterns here, compared to the clearer changes observed by Stearns and Shorter and Tilly, may be due to the size of America when compared with the smaller and more homogeneous European countries. As well as internal developments, America was affected by the wave of immigration from Europe. Immigration as a whole was not related to the strike movement, although there was a suggestion that the influx of skilled men was important. There are insufficient data on the number of immigrants, and their skill level, in individual industries to assess in detail the impact of immigration at a more disaggregated level. But there must have been differences. Thus, a contrast was drawn above between heavy industry, where an influx of unskilled labourers weakened craft modes of control, and the clothing trade, where immigrants had some skills to offer and where union organization was established. In other words, the nature of immigration was an important source of diversity.

Within particular industries there were important technical and managerial differences. Thus, as the consideration of printing showed, the linotype machine did not destroy the workers' power because its successful operation was found to depend on skills which only the printers could provide. Elsewhere, inventions which were similar breakthroughs in the technical sense had a much more profound effect on skill requirements. 'Technical advance' was far from being a homogeneous category. Managerial attitudes varied from outright hostility to the unions, through paternalism to reluctant acceptance of the workers' right to organization. Although not too much weight should be placed on the pious pronouncements of men like Carnegie, who declared that in principle men had the right to organize but who in practice did everything they could to prevent the exercise of this right, differences of approach were clear.[69] These were reflected in the formation of the National Association of Manufacturers in 1895 and the National Civic Federation in 1900. The former took a 'hard line' and argued on traditional *laisser faire* lines that the owner of a business had the right

68. See above, note 64. For a detailed study of one area, see Korman, op. cit. (see above, note 10).
69. See Wolff, op. cit., esp. pp. 62, 180; M. Derber, *The American Idea of Industrial Democracy, 1865–1965* (Urbana: University of Illinois Press, 1970), pp. 62–8; and the two statements by the chairman of U.S. Steel, E. H. Gary, reprinted in part in C. E. Warne (ed.), *The Steel Strike of 1919* (Boston: D. C. Heath, 1963), pp. 27–40.

to decide how it should be run, without any outside interference.[70] The latter was far more conciliatory and attempted to help the more conservative unions, as long as they kept to a moderate course.[71] It has been suggested that the N.C.F.'s policy was the more effective in disarming the labour movement.[72] This may well be true, but differences in the frequency and bitterness of strikes against employers adopting one or other of the two approaches would be expected.

Finally, there were divisions within the labour movement. Although the A.F.L. form of business unionism was being firmly established after 1890, important areas of opposition remained. Apart from the legacy of the Knights of Labor, there was a powerful Socialist presence in several unions. In addition to operating within the A.F.L., radical unionism was present outside; as well as the growth of the American Railway Union, there were several other important developments, which culminated in the establishment of the Industrial Workers of the World in 1905. Even unions with similar ideological stances were often different in approach; thus the U.M.W., was able to integrate immigrant Slav workers into its organization much more successfully than were more craft-dominated unions. But perhaps more important were differences among the workers themselves. Splits between nationality groups have long been seen as crucial in preventing the growth of a homogeneous working class; temporary unity in a strike would soon evaporate. Skill differences to some extent cross-cut national ones but, since native whites and immigrants from northern Europe held most of the skilled jobs, also re-inforced them. As we have seen in the case of steel, employers attempted to exploit these differences through such things as welfare plans which benefited mainly the skilled men.

Clearly, much more could be said on all these sources of diversity; but the mention of them indicates the great range of conditions through which the experience of industrialization was mediated. Since this experience occurred at different times for different groups, as industry advanced into new areas and as new immigrants entered industry in the long-industrialized regions, a very diverse pattern of response could be

70. A. K. Steigerwalt, *The National Association of Manufacturers, 1895–1914*, (Ann Arbor: Bureau of Business Research, University of Michigan, 1964).

71. M. Green, *The National Civic Federation and the American Labor Movement, 1900–25* (Washington, D.C.: Catholic University of American Press, 1956); cf. J. Zerzan, 'Understanding the Anti-radicalism of the National Civic Federation', *International Review of Social History*, XIX, pp. 194–210 (1974).

72. J. Weinstein, *The Corporate Ideal in the Liberal State, 1900–18* (Boston: Beacon Press, 1968).

expected. The challenges of industrialization did not exert automatic effects, and neither was there a uniformity of response from different groups of workers.

It is unfortunate that the strike data do not permit a detailed examination of responses to industry after 1905 for, as Chapter 2 showed, activity was at very high levels in the years before the first world war, and the period immediately after the war was identified as the only possible watershed between 'early' and 'modern' protests. Although this chapter has stressed the diversity of response to industrialization and the difficulty of encompassing this diversity within a few simple patterns, one must not forget the crucial changes which occurred in the organization of production in the final quarter of the nineteenth century.[73] The destruction of the craft system and the introduction of a new form of the division of labour continued in the twentieth century, and patterns of strike activity probably altered as a result. The decline of immigration before the first world war and the rapid growth of unions during the war may also have contributed to the 'modernization' of strikes. However, there was no immediate breakthrough to modern forms of strike activity. During the 1920s corporate domination was re-established in the mass production industries on the basis of a mixture of paternalism and direct repression. It was not until the 1930s that a system of collective bargaining emerged.

73. See D. Montgomery, 'Workers' Control of Machine Production in the Nineteenth Century', *Labor History*, XVII, pp. 485–509 (1976), for an extensive review of these changes and their effects. See esp. pp. 506–07: strikes in the early twentieth century were different from earlier stoppages because union officials sought to control their members and to ally the 'friendly' employers, and because new forms of industrial management undermined craft autonomy. Although having certain differences of emphasis, Montgomery's account of the struggles of craft groups is broadly similar to the conclusions drawn here from the analysis of strike trends.

5

The Years of Institutionalization, 1933–1946

Introduction

During the period covered by this chapter, a set of formal institutions for the regulation of industrial relations was established. It is thus reasonable to call the period the 'years of institutionalization'. This does not mean that a 'mature' system had developed by 1946, or that the trend towards institutionalization was an inevitable or irreversible progression. But the institutional developments of the period are of central importance to the study of strike trends. Thus it was explicitly argued in the preamble to the National Labor Relations Act of 1935 that collective bargaining was the best means to reduce the level of industrial conflict in general and of strikes in particular.[1] Moreover, government action was crucial in the establishment of industrial relations institutions; in terms of the discussion of Chapter 1 political factors may have to be given explicit consideration in explaining changes in strike patterns.

The main focus, then, is the development of strikes during the process of institutionalization. Considerable attention will have to be given to the details of this process, and in particular to the causes of it. The view that is taken of the dramatic developments of the 1930s has profound implications for the interpretation of strike trends, during

---

1. For discussion of the New Deal labour legislation, see I. Bernstein, *The New Deal Collective Bargaining Policy* (Berkeley and Los Angeles: University of California Press, 1950); R. W. Fleming, 'The Significance of the Wagner Act', *Labor and the New Deal,* ed. M. Derber and E. Young (Madison: University of Wisconsin Press, 1957), pp. 121–55; R. C. Cortner, *The Wagner Act Cases* (Knoxville: University of Tennessee Press, 1964).

this period and subsequently. This point can be illustrated by reference to two broad interpretations of events during the New Deal period.

The standard 'liberal' view of the New Deal in general is that the government was favourably disposed towards the workers and that genuine aid to union organization was given;[2] although in several respects the Administration was ambivalent towards unions, and although in the National Recovery Administration (N.R.A.) period little real help was forthcoming, government encouragement was crucial for the unions' success.[3] It is true that workers had to fight to win their new rights, which were not granted by an enlightened government or employers,[4] but the political atmosphere was crucially important. This approach stresses the importance of the C.I.O. in building on workers' discontents and in establishing stable organizations which could not only make concrete gains from the employers but also defend these gains against later attacks.[5]

According to 'radicals', on the other hand, the approach underplays the importance of rank and file militancy and sees the strikes of the early New Deal merely as mass eruptions which paved the way for the bureaucratic unionism of the C.I.O.[6] But, it is argued, this militancy explains the resurgence of a dormant union movement, and must, therefore, be given central importance. But the rank and file movement did not continue to grow. Two reasons are given for this. The 'class collaboration' view is that the C.I.O. leaders held a 'corporate ideology' and were, in practice, not very different from the leaders of the A.F.L.; they sought to use the militancy to gain union contracts and establish themselves in power, and therefore channeled it into 'safe' forms of

2. See R. R. R. Brooks, *When Labor Organizes* (New Haven: Yale University Press, 1937), p. 53; P. Ross, *The Government as a Source of Union Power* (Providence: Brown University Press, 1965), pp. 51–132.
3. On the weakness of government aid to the unions under the N.R.A., see W. E. Leuchtenburg, *Franklin D. Roosevelt and the New Deal, 1932–40* (New York: Harper and Row, 1963), pp. 108–09, A. M. Schlesinger, *The Age of Roosevelt*, Vol. II of *The Coming of the New Deal* (London: Heinemann, 1960), pp. 142–4.
4. D. Brody, 'Labor and the Great Depression: The Interpretive Prospects', *Labor History*, XIII, pp. 231–44 (1972), at p. 235; P. Taft, 'The Philosophy of the American Labor Movement', *Labor in a Changing America*, ed. W. Haber (New York: Basic Books, 1966), pp. 133–42, at p. 137.
5. The two standard histories taking this line are: W. Galenson, *The C.I.O. Challenge to the A.F.L.* (Cambridge, Mass.: Harvard University Press, 1960); I. Bernstein, *Turbulent Years* (Boston: Houghton Mifflin, 1970).
6. J. Green, 'Working Class Militancy in the Depression', *Radical America*, VI, no. 6, pp. 1–35 (1972), at pp. 3–13.

expression.[7] The 'hegemony' line is that the workers were unable, because of the domination exerted by the system, to understand the extent of their own power or to develop programmes to put their vague demands for job control into practice.[8]

In order to choose between these interpretations, much detailed research is required. We cannot as yet say whether the collective bargaining contract was a burden for the workers or whether it was, as Brody claims, the aim of most strikes.[9] But the approaches have a great deal in common. They agree that there was an important strike wave in 1933–34 and that this was more dominated by the rank and file than was that of 1937.[10] They both stress the need of the workers to fight for recognition and the lack of real support during the early New Deal. The liberals do not deny the significance of the sit-down strikes of 1936–37 or the control of the workers by the union leaders; indeed, Brody has suggested that in stressing this control the radicals are merely stating the obvious.[11] And, more generally, it would be agreed that the reform impetus of the government was strictly limited and that the Administration was acting in the liberal tradition of its predecessors.[12]

In particular, there is a broad agreement on the effects of developments under the New Deal. Whatever the causes of the pattern of accommodation which began to be established at the end of the 1930s, its effect was to control the more 'spontaneous' protests of the rank

7. See in particular, S. Lens, *Left, Right and Center* (Hinsdale: Henry Regnery, 1949), pp. 287, 294–6; A. Preis, *Labor's Giant Step* (New York: Pathfinder Press, 1972), pp. 46–50, 85, 187; S. Lynd, 'Introduction', *American Labor Radicalism*, ed. S. Lynd (New York: Wiley, 1973), pp. 4–5.
8. J. Brecher, *The Sit-down Strikes of the 1930s* (Cambridge, Mass.: Root and Branch Pamphlet no. 4, n.d.).
9. D. Brody, review essay on *Rank and File: Personal Histories by Working Class Organizers*, ed. A. and S. Lynd, *Labor History*, XVI, pp. 117–26 (1975), at p. 125.
10. Brody, 'Labor and the Great Depression', op. cit., p. 242. For discussion of strike waves in general, see above pp. 28–9. As Table A.4 shows, both 1933 and 1934 qualify as years of strike waves in the technical sense.
11. Brody, review essay, op. cit., p. 121.
12. For 'liberal' views of this, see Leuchtenburg, op. cit., pp. 107–09, 163–5; R. Hofstadter, *The American Political Tradition* (London: Jonathan Cape, 1962), pp. 332–8. Cf. the 'radical' view in B. J. Bernstein, 'The New Deal: The Conservative Achievements of Liberal Reform', *Towards a New Past*, ed. B. J. Bernstein (New York: Pantheon Books, 1968), pp. 263–88. See also J. S. Auerbach, 'New Deal, Old Deal or Raw Deal: Some Thoughts on New Left Historiography', *Journal of Southern History*, XXXV, pp. 18–30 (1969).

and file and to strengthen the position of the union leaders. These tendencies were further encouraged by the events of the second world war. Thus, in analysing the strike movement, it is possible to accept that rank and file discontents were at the root of the militancy which was characteristic of the period and examine in this light the differences between 1933—34 and 1937, and such things as the sit-down strikes of 1936—37. Similarly, the process of institutionalization may be seen in terms of the effects of a growing control of the rank and file by the union leadership. In broader terms, the dispute between 'liberals' and 'radicals' can be seen as an illustration of the problems of imposing a general concept such as 'modernization' on a complex social movement.

Overall Levels of Strike Activity

To assess the movement of strike activity as closely as possible, data on an annual basis will be used in this section, beginning with 1927 rather than 1933 so that activity during the New Deal period can be compared with earlier trends. There are two key questions about the strike activity. The first concerns the effects of the government's policy of encouraging collective bargaining; and the second relates to the relative importance of union leaderships and the rank and file in the strike movement, and to the process of interaction between leaders and led.

Aggregate Trends
As Table 5.1 shows, there was a great increase in strike activity, on all three indices of frequency, worker involvement, and volume, after 1933. Matters of union organization and recognition became increasingly important (see above Table 2.5, p. 37). These developments obviously reflect a change in government policy on union organization, but, since this change occurred in the midst of many other changes, the effects of government policy are hard to separate from other factors. There was certainly no simple relationship between the degree of government encouragement to unions and the level of strike activity. Thus, the legislative climate was more favourable to the unions after 1937 than it had been before, since the constitutionality of the Wagner Act was now established: although the government had formally endorsed the policy of encouraging collective bargaining since 1933, it was not until 1937 that effective legal protection was given to the unions. But strike activity was not markedly higher after 1937 than it had been before.

The stated aim of the Wagner Act was to reduce strike activity, but

TABLE 5.1

ANNUAL STRIKE INDICES, 1927–46

	W/N	D/W	N/E	W/E	D/E	Mean Duration	Estabs per Strike
1927	467	79.5	23.8	11.1	0.883	26.5	4.14
1928	520	40.2	20.3	10.6	0.425	27.6	4.49
1929	313	18.5	29.7	9.3	0.173	22.6	4.13
1930	287	18.1	21.9	6.3	0.114	22.3	4.06
1931	422	20.2	30.7	13.0	0.261	18.8	3.75
1932	385	32.4	35.9	13.8	0.449	19.6	3.77
1933	689	14.4	72.1	49.7	0.718	16.9	3.92
1934	790	13.4	72.2	57.1	0.762	19.5	4.00
1935	555	13.8	75.1	41.7	0.577	23.8	3.74
1936	363	17.6	75.4	27.4	0.483	23.3	3.42
1937	393	15.3	154	60.7	0.926	20.3	3.40
1938	248	13.3	95.9	23.8	0.317	23.6	3.32
1939	448	15.2	86.2	38.6	0.588	23.4	3.32
1940	230	11.6	78.1	18.0	0.209	20.9	2.64
1941	551	9.8	119	65.3	0.637	18.3	2.76
1942	283	5.0	74.6	21.1	0.105	11.7	2.63
1943	528	6.8	89.1	47.1	0.321	5.0	1.76
1944	427	4.1	119	51.0	0.210	5.6	1.82
1945	730	11.0	119	86.7	0.951	9.9	2.01
1946	923	25.2	121	111	2.81	24.2	2.99

NOTE

W/N, D/W and D/E are all simple numbers i.e. they are, respectively, the number of workers involved per strike, the number of days lost per worker involved and the number of days lost per employee. N/E is the number of strikes per million employees. W/E is the number of workers involved per thousand employees. Mean duration is in days.

'Estabs per strike' is estimated from data on the frequency distribution of strikes by number of establishments affected. It is assumed that the mid-point of the 'eleven establishments and over' category is twenty.

The effect of different estimates of the mid-point is shown below, for 1940.

Mid-point:	15	20	30
Estimated estabs per strike:	2.37	2.64	3.18

Since the effect is not very great, the series in the table indicate trends adequately, i.e. any change in the position of the mid-point will not affect the data very seriously.

this was clearly not achieved in the short term. The marked decline at the end of the period under consideration was associated, of course, with America's entry into the second world war, and not with the operation of the Act. But the war is important for the light it throws on government policy. The Administration had a clear interest in maintaining production and thus sought to achieve the unions' support for the war effort. It did this by bringing union leaders into the planning of the war; for example, in 1940 the National Defense Advisory Commission was set up with Sidney Hillman of the Clothing Workers as its labour director and labour members were included on the National War Labor Board.[13] As well as seeking union co-operation, the government used direct pressure against strikes that were seen as threats to the war, and in several cases struck plants were seized; in some, troops were used to prevent strikes.[14] As Table 5.1 shows, this 'carrot and stick' policy had a considerable degree of success; although the Administration was defeated by the miners in 1943, in general it secured a high degree of compliance with its demands for no strikes and rigid wage control.

Unions and Strikes

To turn to the second question, the role of unions and their members, there was of course a positive association between union membership and strike activity during the 1930s, but the causal importance of the former for the latter is less clear. Strike activity began to rise rapidly from 1930 and this seems to have preceded the rise in union density. A common pattern in the early thirties was for strikes to break out among unorganized groups, with a union taking this as a cue for an organizing drive. Table 5.2 shows that, until 1933, a high proportion of strikes had no union involvement. Peterson suggests that many strikers 'had once belonged to trade-unions but the locals had disintegrated during the depression. The workers, however, were accustomed to collective action and the strike weapon.'[15] Nevertheless, a willingness to strike even without the support of a union indicates the extent of workers' discontents. And many workers in the mass-production industries, who lacked a union tradition, began to strike. Their willingness to strike preceded their unionization, and they were often dissatisfied with their leaders.[16]

---

13. M. Josephson, *Sidney Hillman* (New York: Doubleday, 1952), p. 481 (on Hillman's later activities, see chaps 21 and 22); J. Seidman, *American Labor from Defense to Reconstruction* (Chicago: University of Chicago Press, 1953), pp. 55–69, 81–4.
14. Preis, op. cit., pp. 112–19; Seidman, op. cit., p. 48; H. Pelling, *American Labor* (Chicago: University of Chicago Press, 1960), pp. 172–6.
15. F. Peterson, *Strikes in the United States, 1880–1936* (Washington, D.C.: U.S. Department of Labor Bulletin no. 651, 1938), pp. 54–5.
16. S. Fine, *The Automobile under the Blue Eagle* (Ann Arbor: University of Michigan Press, 1963), pp. 142–227, 274–83, 377–400; R. R. R. Brooks,

TABLE 5.2

STRIKES BY UNION INVOLVEMENT, 1927–46

	% of Strikes with		% of Workers Involved in Strikes with	
	Union Involvement	No Organization	Union Involvement	No Organization
1927	90.3	9.7	97.1	2.9
1928	89.8	10.2	97.1	2.9
1929	84.3	15.7	86.8	13.1
1930	85.8	14.3	91.6	8.5
1931	82.5	17.5	93.2	6.8
1932	84.7	15.3	91.6	8.5
1933	79.1	20.9	92.9	7.1
1934	93.5	6.5	98.2	1.8
1935	92.0	8.0	97.1	2.9
1936	91.5	8.5	95.4	4.6
1937	93.7	6.3	97.8	2.1
1938	97.3	2.7	98.4	1.6
1939	98.1	1.9	99.1	1.0
1940	98.1	1.8	98.9	1.1
1941	96.9	3.0	99.0	0.9
1942	95.3	4.7	98.1	1.9
1943	92.8	7.2	98.4	1.6
1944	95.8	4.2	98.8	1.2
1945	97.2	2.8	99.6	0.4
1946	98.1	1.9	99.7	0.3

The decline in 'no organization' strikes from 1934 suggests that the unions re-established their control over stoppages. But it must be remembered that a rise in union density was almost bound to increase recorded union involvement because B.L.S. data report not whether a strike was ordered by a union but whether the strikers were union members. Even if the strikers were not union members at the start of a stoppage, subsequent union involvement would qualify the strike for inclusion under the 'union' category. Thus the hypothesis that rank and

As Steel Goes (New Haven: Yale University Press, 1940), pp. 46–89; C. R. Daugherty, M. G. de Chazeau and S. S. Stratton, *The Economics of the Iron and Steel Industry* (New York: McGraw-Hill, 1937), pp. 932–43; R. McKenney, *Industrial Valley* (New York: Harcourt, Brace and Co., 1939), pp. 93–207; D. Brody, *The Butcher Workmen* (Cambridge, Mass.: Harvard University Press, 1964), pp. 154–66. See also M. Goldbloom *et al.*, *Strikes under the New Deal* (New York: League for Industrial Democracy, n.d.), esp. pp. 36–40.

TABLE 5.3

SIT-DOWN STRIKES, 1936–39

	Number	% of All Strikes	Number of Workers Involved (000s)	% of All Workers Involved
1936	48	2.2	88	11.2
1937	477	10.1	398	21.4
1938	52	1.9	29	4.2
1939	6	0.2	3	0.3

SOURCES
Monthly Labor Review, XLVIII, p. 1130 (1939); L, p. 1105 (1940).

file militancy was important throughout the New Deal period cannot be rejected.

The Sit-Down Strikes and Rank and File Protest during the War
A spectacular expression of rank and file protest came in the sit-down strikes of 1936–37. Since these stoppages were often short and did not result in the workers leaving the plant, they are particularly likely to have escaped inclusion in the official figures. But the B.L.S. was able to produce data on them, counting as a sit-down a strike in which the workers stayed in the plant for at least a day after stopping work; that is, the rule that a stoppage must last at least one day to be counted was maintained.[17] Table 5.3 shows the incidence of recorded sit-downs for 1936–39. In 1936 and 1937 they accounted for large numbers of strikes, and many others were not counted. It is notable that sit-downs accounted for a greater proportion of workers involved than of strikes; thus, they were larger than average. This is surprising in view of the difficulties of organizing plant occupations and indicates their 'mass' nature.

Although union organization was the main issue in the sit-downs of 1936, in 1937 and 1938 organization matters were less important than they were in other strikes; specific grievances over work conditions came to have a relatively high significance. The rate of success was not

17. 'Work Stoppages in 1936', *Monthly Labor Review*, XLIV, pp. 1229–40 (1936), at p. 1234.

very different from that of strikes in general.[18] The proportion of sit-downs without union involvement was slightly higher than average, but very few seem to have had formal authorization from the union hierarchy.[19]

The sit-down movement as a whole was short-lived and represented the end of the 'spontaneous' actions of the rank and file which had been going on since the early '30s. In several cases, notably in rubber and autos, it was a sit-down which led the way for union recognition, but such stoppages were not popular with the union leaders or the government and measures were soon introduced to control them.[20] But they were large plant-based actions and were quite successful: the sit-downs were not minor exceptions to the growth of bureaucratic unionism but were important in a continuing rank and file movement.

Shop-floor protests achieved renewed significance during the second world war. Although wartime strikes were very short, worker involvement did not decline despite the 'no-strike' policy of the unions. Both this index and strike volume fell in 1942, the first full year of the war, but subsequently increased. The strike wave of 1946 was not so much a sudden explosion as the culmination of trends which had been apparent during the war. Table 5.2 shows that union involvement in strikes fell, despite a rise in union density. This evidence, combined with more qualitative findings,[21] suggests that there was a considerable amount of

18. Ibid.; 'Number of Sit-down Strikes in 1937', *Monthly Labor Review*, XLVII, pp. 359–62 (1938), at p. 361; 'Work Stoppages in 1938', *Monthly Labor Review*, XLVIII, pp. 1125–41 (1939), at p. 1130. Cf. Preis, op. cit., p. 64, where it is said that the sit-downs were rarely defeated.

19. See refs in note 16 above. The proportion of the sit-downs of 1936 and 1937 accounted for by each type of union was as follows:

A.F.L.	20.6%	No Organization	10.7%
C.I.O.	59.9	Rival Unions	3.1
Other	5.7	Total	100.0

20. They were made illegal in the Fansteel decision of 1939: see Bernstein, *Turbulent Years*, op. cit., p. 678. Union leaders' attitudes are reflected in the remark by J. L. Lewis, the C.I.O. President: 'A C.I.O. contract is adequate protection for any employer against sit-downs, lie-downs, or any other kind of strike' (quoted in Galenson, op. cit., p. 145). On local government attitudes, see J. W. Howard, 'Frank Murphy and the Sit-down Strikes of 1937', *Labor History*, I, pp. 103–40 (1960).

21. J. R. Sperry, 'Rebellion within the Ranks: Pennsylvania Anthracite, John L. Lewis and the Coal Strikes of 1943', *Pennsylvania History*, XL, pp. 293–312 (1973); A. M. Winkler, 'The Philadelphia Transit Strike of 1944', *Mississippi Valley Historical Review*, LIX, pp. 73–89 (1972); I. Howe and B. J. Widick, *The U.A.W. and Walter Reuther* (New York: Random House, 1949), pp. 107–25; E. Jennings, 'Wildcat: The Wartime Strike Wave in

rank and file protest. Union leaders and the government were able to ensure that strikes were short and their economic impact minimized, but they could not prevent disputes from developing into stoppages. Wartime conditions, however, meant that the rank and file movement was limited to the shop level. As the final column of Table 5.1 shows, the mean number of establishments affected by strikes continued the fall which had begun about 1934.

Bureaucratization

Thus, rank and file action was important throughout the 1930s but a continuing movement was not established. The year 1934 was a turning point of many strike indices and also seems to have been central in the development of rank and file protests. Several important strikes were defeated and threats of stoppages elsewhere de-fused. The upsurge of discontent was met with determined employer resistance, and government assistance to unions proved to be of a less concrete kind than had been hoped. The optimism of the early '30s disappeared and a reaction set in against the N.R.A.[22]

On the other side of the picture, there was a growth of union control of strikes. The foundation of national C.I.O. unions took power away from the rank and file: the policy of seeking formal recognition from employers through the channel of collective bargaining fitted into the new national policy of giving the employer a duty to bargain with representatives of their employees' 'own choosing'. The C.I.O. did not represent a departure from the model of business unionism and was led

---

Auto', *Radical America*, IX, nos. 4–5, pp. 77–112 (1975). See also pp. 161–2 below.

22. A national textile strike was defeated and a general strike in San Francisco, in support of demands by longshoremen, petered out. Strike threats in steel and autos did not materialize. Labour attitudes are represented by T. Brown, President of the Mine, Mill and Smelter Workers: 'the only thing the N.R.A. did was to solidify industry into one common mass with one purpose to disfranchise labor' (quoted in V. H. Jensen, *Nonferrous Metals Industrial Unionism, 1932–54* (New York: Cornell University Press, 1954), p. 13). For other aspects of N.R.A. codes, see S. Fine, 'President Roosevelt and the Automobile Code', *Mississippi Valley Historical Review*, XLV, pp. 23–50 (1958); J. P. Johnson, 'Drafting the N.R.A. Code of Fair Competition for the Bituminous Coal Industry', *Journal of American History*, LIII, pp. 521–41 (1966). Each code was to include the rights of organization laid down in the N.I.R.A., but the auto firms were able to exclude their industry from two important provisions, and companies elsewhere ignored the Act's requirements.

by men who believed in this model.[23] It grew up only after government labour policy had been formulated and could probably have done little to alter the fundamentals of the policy, even if it had wanted to.[24] Thus it is not surprising that collective bargaining under government supervision became the accepted approach. Given the advantages in terms of wages and security which the C.I.O. could offer, as well as the memory of failures in the early 1930s and the lack of a clear alternative, even workers who had doubts about unionization 'from the top down' were prepared to go along with the C.I.O.[25] As will be seen below, the control of strikes which the C.I.O. unions developed did not come easily or immediately. In the unions of auto and rubber workers, the rank and file retained an important voice, but elsewhere, as in meat packing, bureaucratic unionism was established with relative ease.

During the Defense and war periods, bureaucratic tendencies were strengthened. The unions largely acceded to the government's requests for co-operation, and found themselves involved in a large number of boards whose activities they were unable to control.[26] Increasing governmental involvement in disputes is shown in trends in the methods of settlement of strikes. During the Defense period, the proportion of strikes settled by direct agreement between employers and unions fell and the number settled by government officials and boards increased. During the country's active involvement in the war, these trends continued further; at its peak in 1943 the proportion of strikes settled by governmental intervention was 70 per cent, and these strikes included 82 per cent of all workers involved.[27]

23. See, for example, L. L. Cary, 'Institutionalized Conservatism in the Early C.I.O.', *Labor History*, XIII, pp. 475–504 (1972).
24. Cf. Galenson, op. cit., p. 608, where it is argued that there was no chance of the C.I.O. helping to establish a third political party.
25. See L. de Caux, *Labor Radical* (Boston: Beacon Press, 1970), pp. 237–47.
26. P. A. C. Koistinen, 'Mobilizing the World War II Economy: Labor and the Industrial-military Alliance', *Pacific Historical Review*, XLII, pp. 443–78 (1973); B. Stein, 'Labor's Role in Government Agencies during World War II', *Journal of Economic History*, XVII, pp. 389–408 (1957). See also J. Green, 'Fighting on Two Fronts: Working-Class Militancy in the 1940s', *Radical America*, IX, nos. 4–5, pp. 7–47 (1975), for a discussion of the reasons why workers' militancy did not develop into a national challenge to the growth of bureaucracy.
27. Figures on the method of settlement of strikes between 1935 and 1946 are given in the annual reports on strikes in the *Monthly Labor Review*. They are reported in P. K. Edwards, 'Strikes in the United States, 1881–1972' (D.Phil. thesis, University of Oxford, 1977), table A–17. A rise in the proportion of representation cases handled by the N.L.R.B. suggests that representation was increasingly a matter of bureaucratic procedure. See Edwards, op. cit., table A–18, which derives figures from Department of Labor, *Handbook of*

Unions were similarly constrained in other matters. On wages, the famous 'Little Steel' formula strictly limited the gains available. And, on union security, 'maintenance-of-membership' agreements prevented unions from strengthening their position. Under these agreements a worker who had become a union member was obliged to remain in membership during the life of the labour-management contracts of which they were part. Although protecting unions from hostile employers, the agreements limited their ability to expand their influence and increased the separation between leaders and led.[28]

As Weir puts it, the way in which collective bargaining was institutionalized at the start of the war meant that the process was conducted on the worst possible terms for labour.[29] The decline in the militancy of the union leaders was cemented through an alliance between government, business and labour which in fact gave labour little power:

Only when the employers recognized that they no longer had the needed legitimacy to act as the full disciplinarians of the people in their employ, and that the union leadership could be used as a substitute disciplinary force, were they willing to join in building the institution of collective bargaining.

Although the unions were able to establish themselves during the war, collective bargaining was carried out largely on the terms of the government and employers.

The broadest contribution of New Deal developments to the strike movement came in the establishment of formal procedures for dealing with industrial conflict. As will be seen below, strike activity had been very low in several industries in the 1920s; this is usually associated with the strength of employers. The New Deal policy prevented such a situation from arising again[30] and helped to determine the form which the institutionalization of conflict would take. For example, formal government involvement has been a feature of industrial relations since the 1930s. Institutionalization was not the result of a growth of 'reason'

Labor Statistics, 1968, Bulletin no. 1600 (Washington, D.C.: Government Printing Office, 1968), pp. 318–9.

28. Seidman, op. cit., pp. 94–105, 109–29; Preis, op. cit., pp. 154–67; Lens, op. cit., pp. 341–52.

29. S. Weir, 'Class Forces in the 1970s', *Radical America,* VI, no. 3, pp. 31–77 (1972), at pp. 42–3 (following quote from p. 44). See also T. R. Brooks, *Toil and Trouble* (New York: Delacorte Press, 1964), p. 204.

30. Several writers stress the liberating aspect of strikes in the 1930s, for example Brecher, op. cit., p. 2; de Caux, op. cit., p. 229.

or the immediate recognition by employers of the advantages they could gain from working with business unions. 'Liberals' as well as 'radicals' stress that the initial impetus to a change in governmental policy came from the strikes of the early '30s, in which rank and file discontent was an important element. They give the reminder that 'power and interest can be issues of deadly conflict even in a system in which men agree on fundamentals.'[31] Although the C.I.O. accepted the business union model, this did not prevent it from being engaged in serious conflicts with employers. But the basis of these conflicts was the discontent of the rank and file.

This section has shown how strikes developed in this crucial period. Government policy, although important, reflected the pressures of rank and file unrest. Employers took time to be convinced of the value of recognizing unions. And unions did not necessarily set out to frustrate rank and file desires. The interaction of government, the employers and the unions created a formalized bargaining system in which 'spontaneous' expressions of discontent were channeled. The war years were crucial in this development, and did not represent a marked shift from the patterns which had been established in the 1930s.

The Parameters of Conflict

General Influences

At the most general level, Galenson has argued that the 'turning point for labor' came in 1937[32] and has suggested elsewhere that between 1936 and 1941 'the average duration of strikes tended to be inverse to their number'.[33] Correlational analysis gives some support to the latter statement, although the shortness of the period means that the relationship is not statistically significant.[34] When this is compared with the inverse link between frequency and duration for the years 1940–72

31. Brody, 'Labor and the Great Depression', op. cit., p. 236.
32. W. Galenson, '1937: The Turning Point for American Labor' University of California at Berkeley Institute of Industrial Relations, Reprint no. 120 (University of California, 1959).
33. Galenson, *The C.I.O. Challenge*, op. cit., p. 601.
34. The correlation matrix for four strike variables for 1936–41 is:

	N/E	W/E	W/N
W/E	0.83		
W/N	0.40	0.84	
Duration	-0.59	-0.71	-0.49

TABLE 5.4

REGRESSION RESULTS, SELECTED PERIODS: DEPENDENT VARIABLE,
NUMBER OF STRIKES (N)

	Equation (1)				Equation (2)			
	Indep. Variables				Indep. Variables			
	U	Time	R^2	D–W	H/P	Time	R^2	D–W
1916–27	Neg	Neg	0.87	2.04	Neg	Neg	0.85	1.75
	NS	1%			NS	1%		
1928–39	Neg	Pos	0.65	2.18	Pos	Neg	0.68	2.19
	NS	1%			NS	NS		
1940–51	Neg	Pos	0.19	2.01	Pos	Neg	0.43	2.30
	NS	NS			5%	5%		
1952–63	Neg	Neg	0.66	2.11	Neg	Pos	0.58	2.67
	5%	NS			NS	NS		

NOTE
Variables are as defined in Chapter 3; i.e. U is the number unemployed and H/P
the level of real hourly wages. Since relatively short periods of time are under consideration, N and U may be used without correcting for the size of the labour force.

and the lack of association between these indices in earlier years (see
Table 3.1 p. 56), it seems that the late New Deal period marked some
sort of turning point for strikes: features of the strike movement of the
postwar period began to be apparent during the late 1930s.

However, evidence such as this is of course far from sufficient to
sustain a wider claim that the parameters of conflict were changing.
Such a claim is naturally difficult to test very rigorously, since the
period in question is too short for detailed statistical analysis. Moreover, when political and economic parameters are being considered
there is a further problem. The 'party of the President' variable, which
was introduced in Chapter 3 as one index of political factors, changes,
at most, once every four years. And throughout the period under consideration it was of course constant. As a result, it would not be useful
to apply the general models of the determinants of strike activity
developed in Chapter 3 to the period 1933–45.

Instead, particular aspects of a simple economic model may be considered. As noted in Chapter 3, the overall association between variables

For six years, the 5 per cent significance levels for the one- and two-tailed
tests are, respectively. 0.73 and 0.81; thus only the correlations between frequency and worker involvement and between worker involvement and size
are significantly different from zero.

such as the unemployment rate and strike frequency was very weak, but relationship became stronger when shorter periods of time were considered. Thus, it is possible to take fairly short periods of time and compare the operation of a given model. If the overall explanatory power of the model alters or if the signs of the coefficients of the independent variables change in a systematic manner, the parameters of conflict may be said to have changed.[35]

The results for two very simple models are given in Table 5.4. As with the indices of the political climate, the measures of business cycle peaks and troughs might not give meaningful results for the New Deal period considered in isolation, because of the overwhelming effect of the Great Depression. In any event, as argued in Chapter 3, the straightforward index of the level of unemployment should be usable for relatively short periods. Hence, one model uses unemployment and a time trend as independent variables. Because of the short time periods under consideration, it would be unwise to use more variables in the same model, and hence a second model employs the real wage rate and the time trend as independents. As Table 5.4 shows, for neither model was the New Deal period markedly different from periods before or after it. In most cases, the two models performed satisfactorily in terms of the amount of variance explained. There were exceptions to this which might repay further study. But these exceptions do not display any pattern consistent with a shift in the parameters of conflict. Moreover, the direction of the influence of economic factors on strike frequency did not alter.

It might be suggested that these results would not hold if other periods or models were considered. It is true that the findings reported in Table 5.4 are very limited, and not too much weight should be placed on them. But, as well as having some importance on their own, they are consistent with the fuller analysis of Chapter 3. Moreover, other results for different periods and models not reported in detail here[36] support the general argument that, during the 1930s as much as at other times, strike activity was related to economic conditions.

This is not to deny, of course, that a more qualitative change was taking place. As noted above, there were many crucial developments during the 1930s, which might qualify the period as a 'turning point'. But despite these momentous changes the patterning of strike activity remained largely unaltered.

35. This need not, of course, indicate a more general change of a kind which only a more complete model could assess; the change would merely be with respect to the variables considered in this particular model.
36. See Edwards, op. cit., table 6–4.

Role of the Employer

The position of the employer has not yet been given systematic attention. However, the attitude of employers is as important as that of unions and workers in determining whether a strike will occur. From the 1930s, data are available which permit the economic position of employers to be related to strike activity. The results reported here relate to the period 1927–41, and the analysis is extended into the postwar period in Chapter 6. As well as being of interest in its own right, this consideration of the employers' position during and after the 1930s will provide a further test of the view that the parameters of conflict altered with the New Deal.

The results of the 'employer well-being' model are given in Table 5.5. Three independent variables are used. The productivity variable reflects the rate at which economic efficiency was increasing; a slow rate of increase would be expected to be associated with a firm line by employers, with the result that the productivity variable would be inversely related to strike activity.[37] Similarly, a low rate of profit should lead to employer militancy: profits and strike activity would be inversely associated. With the third variable, the rate of change of wholesale prices, a rapid rate of increase should increase employer prosperity, so that the variable should also be inversely linked to the level of strike activity.

It might be argued that employers have little influence over the initial decision to call a strike, but that they can affect the duration and severity of disputes by making concessions or holding firm. Thus, as well as strike frequency, the number of striker-days per employee (D/E) and two measures of strike duration (D/W and mean duration) are used as dependent variables.[38]

The first part of Table 5.5 reports the results of predicting strike activity from the three independent variables. Strike frequency was explained most satisfactorily, and there were moderate levels of association with the measures of duration. For frequency, only the sign of the profits variable was as predicted and the coefficient was not significant. The significant positive coefficients of the other variables suggest that factors other than employer prosperity were at work. The higher the level of productivity and the rate of change of prices, the more strikes

37. The level of the productivity index, and not its rate of change, is used to measure the general progress of productivity; the interest is the effect of the state of productive efficiency on employers' attitudes, and not the year-to-year changes in productivity growth.
38. See Appendix C, pp. 316–7, below for the distinction between D/W and the length of the 'average strike' as measures of duration.

TABLE 5.5

REGRESSION RESULTS: EMPLOYER WELL-BEING MODEL, 1927–41

Dependent variable	Independent Variables					R^2	D–W
	Prod	Profits	Ch.P	Peak	Trough		
N/E	Pos	Neg	Pos			0.63	1.67
	1%	NS	5%				
D/E	Neg	Neg	Pos			0.19	1.62
	NS	NS	5%				
D/W	Neg	Pos	Neg			0.30	1.23
	5%	NS	NS				
Mean duration	Neg	Pos	Neg			0.32	1.79
	NS	1%	NS				
N/E	Neg	Pos	Pos	Pos	Pos	0.82	1.97
	NS	NS	NS	1%	5%		
D/E	Neg	Pos	Pos	Pos	Pos	0.18	1.79
	NS	NS	NS	NS	NS		
D/W	Neg	Pos	Neg	Neg	Neg	0.15	1.21
	NS	NS	NS	NS	NS		
Mean duration	Neg	Pos	Neg	Neg	Neg	0.16	1.77
	NS	NS	NS	NS	NS		

NOTE
Prod is an index of labour productivity; Profits is the rate of return (book values) after tax; Ch.P is the proportionate change in the Wholesale Price Index.

there were. In other words, strikes, as has been seen in Chapter 3, were commonest in prosperous times, for reasons not directly connected with the well-being of employers. It is thus particularly interesting that, for the measures of strike duration, the direction of operation of all three independent variables was opposite to that for strike frequency. Employer well-being seems to have had an effect on the length of strikes which was separate from more general economic influences. The positive coefficient for the profit rate is a puzzle, for it suggests that strikes were longest when employers were most prosperous. A plausible *ex post* explanation is that a high rate of profit indicates that employers have large funds with which to resist a strike; when they are well off they are willing to 'take a strike' because they have the resources to support a long struggle.

The second part of Table 5.5 reports the results of adding the peak and trough variables to the employer well-being model. Thus the influence of general economic factors may be compared with that of indices specifically related to the employer. In line with the argument of the preceding paragraph, only the peak and trough measures were significantly related to strike frequency; an R^2 of 0.82 was obtained, compared with one of 0.63 when only the measures of employer well-being were used. The position of the employer was not important for the number of strikes called, when compared with other influences. For the measures of duration, the addition of the peak and trough variables reduced the overall R^2 and no coefficient was significant. Moreover, the coefficients of the 'peak' and 'trough' variables were negative, whereas in predicting strike frequency they were positive.

Thus, as might be expected from general considerations and from the analysis of Chapter 3, the frequency and duration of strikes were related to economic conditions in different ways. Only frequency was satisfactorily explained by the models of Table 5.5, which suggests that it is the timing of strikes, and not their impact in terms of days lost or mean duration, which is influenced by economic conditions. When considered in combination with the peak and trough measures, the well-being of employers did not contribute significantly to the explanation of frequency or duration. The general implications of this will be considered in Chapter 6, when the model has been extended to the postwar period.

In general, strike frequency continued to be related to economic conditions. Although, as argued above, the growth of mass unionism and collective bargaining greatly affected the nature and significance of strikes, the timing of strike action was as strongly related as at other times to the general economic climate.

The Industrial Distribution of Activity

One of the most notable features of strikes under the New Deal was the upsurge of activity in the mass-production industries. This section investigates the industrial distribution of activity, compared with that in 1881—1905, and then concentrates on the auto and rubber industries as key examples of the 'breakthrough' to a 'modern' pattern of strikes. The steel industry is used to illustrate an alternative means by which the breakthrough was achieved.

The Overall Pattern
The distribution of each of the three main measures of strike activity by industry is given in Table 5.6. The industries listed first are, as far as possible, the same as those considered in Chapter 4; four other sectors of interest are added at the end of the table. Comparison with Table 4.5 reveals that building and coal became less dominant, but that

TABLE 5.6

PROPORTION OF ALL STOPPAGES AND OF EMPLOYMENT ACCOUNTED FOR BY EACH INDUSTRY, 1927–40

	Per Cent of			Employment as % Total
	N	W	D	
Boot and shoe	1.9	2.2	2.2	1.3
Building	12.4	5.8	5.2	4.0
Clothing	13.1	12.1	8.3	3.2
Coal	4.2	21.1	31.3	2.9
Food	5.3	2.6	2.2	3.5
Machinery: non-electrical	2.6	1.9	2.0	2.5
electrical	0.8	0.6	0.7	1.2
Metals: basic steel	0.6	2.2	2.2	2.3
other iron and steel	2.8	3.7	2.1	2.2
other	1.6	1.1	1.2	1.1
Printing and publishing	1.2	0.2	0.3	1.3
Stone, clay and glass	1.8	1.1	1.4	1.2
Textiles	7.0	9.9	12.1	4.5
Tobacco	0.5	0.5	0.5	0.4
Transport: railroad	0.1	0.1	—	3.6
other	7.0	6.3	5.3	5.8
Transport equipment: locos, cars and ships	0.5	0.8	1.1	1.6
other	1.6	6.9	4.5	1.3
All above industries	64.8	79.2	82.7	43.9
Chemicals	1.0	1.1	0.7	1.3
Lumber	6.1	3.3	4.4	1.8
Rubber	0.8	1.9	0.9	0.5
Domestic and personal service	5.7	3.5	2.8	7.2
Trade	7.9	3.0	2.2	21.6
All above industries	86.4	92.0	93.7	76.3
All industries	100	100	100	100

NOTE
Figures for employment are for 1940 and based on estimates of total employment; thus they are not comparable with the data in Tables 5.7 and 5.8, which are generally based on employment of production workers only.

this was not balanced by an increase in the major manufacturing sectors. The machinery, metals and transportation equipment industries, for example, did not increase their share of strikes. The most marked shift was into the 'tertiary' industries, with services and trade accounting for one-eighth of all strikes and the 'other transport' sector considerably increasing its share. The shift was less marked for worker involvement, but still apparent. In very broad terms, the strike move-

TABLE 5.7

NUMBER OF STRIKES PER MILLION EMPLOYEES (N/E), BY INDUSTRY, 1927–41

	1927–29	1930–33	1934–37	1938–40
Boot and shoe	118	120	199	101
Building	122	169	206	253[a]
Clothing	192	318	479	490
Coal	103	145	148	138[a]
Food	29	64	188	182
Machinery: non-electrical	16	34	148	127
electrical	7	12	135	93
Metals: basic steel	5	21	47	34
other iron and steel	30	67	162	116
other metal	17	51	244	165
Printing and publishing	27	55	99	78
Stone, clay and glass	22	66	213	178
Textiles	72	112	183	86
Tobacco	19	90	138	80
Transport: all	6	12	77	76[a]
railroad	0.8	0.2	2	—
Transport equip: locos,				
cars, ships	15	49	182	85
other	14	26	141	85
Chemicals	16	14	106	126
Rubber	18	49	228	177
Trade	3	5	39	44
All industries	25	39	96	96[a]

NOTE
a. Figures are for 1938–41.

ment seems to have followed the growth of the economy and the expansion of service industries.

As Tables 5.7 and 5.8 show, the level of strike activity in the tertiary industries, represented by 'trade', was much lower than that in other industries. These tables also indicate the areas where the 'strike explosion' of the 1930s was concentrated. Although activity in industries with a long union tradition, such as building, coal and clothing, increased, it did so much more slowly than the rise in mass production industries. In nearly all of these, very marked increases occurred; at the end of the 1920s, strike activity here was, in general, lower than the average but, by the end of the '30s, it was closer to the average and, in several cases, well above it. For example, in the 'other transport equipment' sector, which consists very largely of the automobile and aircraft

TABLE 5.8

NUMBER OF WORKERS INVOLVED PER THOUSAND EMPLOYEES (W/E), BY INDUSTRY, 1927–41

	1927–29	1930–33	1934–37	1938–40
Boot and shoe	52.3	94.5	89.0	28.6
Building	26.3	34.8	38.7	70.3[a]
Clothing	56.2	276	193	77.8
Coal	200	212	386	632[a]
Food	2.7	17.6	38.7	39.6
Machinery: non-electrical	1.2	6.5	56.0	36.7
electrical	2.0	6.1	50.5	21.2
Metals: basic steel	1.4	23.3	101	27.2
other iron and steel	3.9	12.2	38.5	25.8
other metals	4.5	13.3	71.7	40.5
Printing and publishing	2.3	2.7	5.6	12.3
Stone, clay and glass	5.4	11.7	70.6	35.6
Textiles	24.3	61.8	150	28.9
Tobacco	4.9	63.1	45.2	45.1
Transport: all	2.4	4.3	33.6	21.5[a]
railroad	1.5	—	0.4	0.1
Transport equip: locos,				
cars, ships	8.6	19.8	167	44.5
other	3.0	27.3	267	175
Chemicals	2.8	2.0	28.4	35.4
Rubber	6.4	19.7	90.0	117
Trade	1.0	1.8	6.2	5.5
All industries	10.3	19.7	46.7	37.6[a]

NOTE
a. Figures are for 1938–41.

industries, worker involvement rose from less than one-third of the average in 1927–29 to over four times the average in 1938–40.

The contrast is made even clearer when the data on strike activity for 1916–26 are considered. Only the number of strikes in each industry was recorded, and the industrial classification used was unspecific and not readily comparable with that employed later. For those industries for which adequate employment data are available, figures of strike frequency are given in Table A.13. There were very few strikes in mass production industries: many were not even mentioned in the classification and, in those which were mentioned, strike frequency was very low. Stoppages were concentrated in building, clothing, coal and 'other metals'. As the breakdown of Table 5.6 into sub-periods (Table A.14) shows, the domination of strikes by building and coal continued

TABLE 5.9

SIZE OF STRIKES AND DAYS LOST PER WORKER, BY INDUSTRY,
1927–40

	W/N	D/W
Boot and shoe	500	18.5
Building	200	16.1
Clothing	394	12.5
Coal	2160	26.9
Food	214	15.0
Machinery: non-electrical	313	19.0
electrical	320	21.9
Metals: basic steel	1522	18.5
other iron and steel	571	10.4
other metals	274	20.1
Printing and publishing	84	21.1
Stone, clay and glass	262	22.5
Textiles	607	22.2
Tobacco	483	17.9
Transport: railroad	583	7.5
other	385	15.3
Transport equip: locos, cars, ships	740	23.2
other	1805	12.0
Chemicals	468	11.4
Rubber	971	9.1
Trade	160	13.4
All industries	427	18.2

until 1930–33, but their share of total activity subsequently fell rapidly.

The data on industrial strike patterns in the '30s are much less detailed than those for 1881–1905; the available breakdowns, by size of strikes (W/N) and the number of days lost per striker (D/W), are given in Table 5.9. Some of the newly-organized industries, such as steel, rubber and autos and aircraft, were marked by large and relatively short disputes. In the last two of these, overall levels of activity were very much above average. In steel, strike frequency remained low; only in 1934–37 was worker involvement much above average.

Rubber and Automobile Industries

Since the rubber and auto industries were noted for their high level of rank and file militancy, it seems that strikes here can be seen as 'mass protests'. This is not to say that they were 'backward looking' or unplanned; but they were based on the demands of the rank and file. In both industries, new unions emerged and were led by men who had risen from the ranks, in contrast to many other C.I.O. unions where the leaders were from existing national unions, particularly the Mine Workers.[39]

In the case of autos, Mitchell has argued that 'the *characteristic* achievement of the C.I.O. was in organizing the auto industry, which stood as the *model* of mass production, and employed almost entirely semi-skilled and unskilled workers, most of these drawn from small towns and rural districts.'[40] But the industry's strike experience was very different from that in several other newly-organized sectors. For example, in chemicals strike activity was at about average levels and, although the strikes were short, they were also quite small. In electrical engineering, strikes were long and small, with frequency and worker involvement at about average levels; in non-electrical machinery there was a very similar pattern. The form of unionism which developed in autos was very different from that elsewhere, with organization 'from above' being rejected in favour of a union led by men from within the industry; the United Auto Workers developed into the prime example of so-called 'social' unionism, in contrast to the more usual 'business' unionism.[41] Rank and file action remained central to the strikes of the industry later than was the case elsewhere; the peak of this was the sit-down strike at General Motors in 1936–37, which led to union recognition here and paved the way for recognition in the rest of the industry.[42]

The rubber industry was similar to autos in many respects other than the pattern of strike activity. Sit-downs were important; indeed, the rubber workers were among the first to make systematic use of this

39. On autos, see Fine, *The Automobile under the Blue Eagle,* op. cit.; and, for example, S. Fine, 'The Toledo Chevrolet Strike of 1935', *Ohio Historical Quarterly,* LXVII, pp. 326–56 (1958). See also Galenson, *The C.I.O. Challenge,* op. cit., pp. 123–84; Bernstein, *Turbulent Years,* op. cit., pp. 96–8, 220–29, 499–516. On rubber see McKenney, op. cit.; Galenson, *The C.I.O. Challenge,* pp. 266–82; A. W. Jones, *Life, Liberty and Property* (Philadelphia: J. B. Lippincott, 1941), pp. 83–138.

40. B. Mitchell, *Depression Decade* (New York: Holt, Rinehart and Winston, 1964), p. 295, emphasis added.

41. Howe and Widick, op, cit., pp. 47–82; J. Skeels, 'The Background of U.A.W. Factionalism', *Labor History,* II pp. 158–81 (1961); J. R. Prickett, 'Communists and the Automobile Industry in Detroit before 1935', *Michigan History,* LVII, pp. 185–208 (1973).

42. S. Fine, *Sit-down: The General Motors Strike of 1936–37* (Ann Arbor: University of Michigan Press, 1969); H. Kraus, *The Many and the Few* (Los Angeles: Plantin Press, 1947).

weapon.[43] Organization from above was rejected and mass action stressed. These similarities of worker action are the more notable when the parallels in the structures of the rubber and auto industries are considered. Both were concentrated in particular cities: respectively, Akron (Ohio) and Detroit. Both used mass production methods and had grown up with virtually no threat of unionization. In 1935 a government committee listed the discontents of the auto workers:

Labor unrest exists to a degree higher than warranted by the depression. The unrest flows from insecurity, low annual earnings, inequitable hiring and rehiring methods, espionage, speedup and displacement of workers at an extremely early age.[44]

These problems were, by and large, shared by the rubber workers. Their industry relied heavily on autos for a market for its products and thus the instability of the demand for automobiles affected their earnings and security. The rubber industry was well-known for the speed-up of operations and for sacking men who became too old to tolerate the high pressure of work which was characteristic of the rubber factories.[45]

In view of all these similarities, it is interesting that the strike experience of the rubber industry was not only similar to that of autos but was very different from that elsewhere. Perhaps particular stress should be placed on insecurity and the speed-up. For autos, Fine argues that these things were more important than the monotony of mass production work;[46] as other studies have shown, this feature of the technology of auto production is a less important cause of unrest than is often thought.[47] And the level of earnings in autos was higher than it was in other industries;[48] it was the high variability of earnings which was the characteristic feature of rubber and autos. Insecure employ-

---

43. McKenney, op. cit., pp. 56–68; Jones, op. cit., p. 99; M. H. Vorse, *Labor's New Millions* (New York: Modern Age Books, 1938), pp. 7–10.

44. This was the so-called Henderson Committee (quoted in Kraus, op. cit., p. 12).

45. McKenney, op. cit., p. 166; Jones, op. cit., pp. 137–8.

46. Fine, *Sit-down*, pp. 55–60.

47. H. A. Turner, G. Clack and G. Roberts, *Labour Relations in the Motor Industry* (London: Allen and Unwin, 1967), pp. 169, 329–33; J. H. Goldthorpe, et al., *The Affluent Worker: Industrial Attitudes and Behaviour* (Cambridge: Cambridge University Press, 1968), esp. pp. 180–83. Assembly line work is not as dominant in the industry as is often thought: see C. R. Walker and R. H. Guest, *The Man on the Assembly Line* (Cambridge, Mass.: Harvard University Press, 1952), pp. 38–65.

48. 'Wage Structure of the Motor-vehicle Industry, Part I', *Monthly Labor Review*, LIV, pp. 279–304 (1942), at pp. 279, 291.

ment, the speed-up and inequitable hiring were, of course, not a new feature of these industries in the thirties and they are thus not a sufficient explanation of the outbreak of unrest here. But they distinguish them from other industries and help to explain their relatively high strike-proneness, within the context of the depression and governmental encouragement to organization.

The process of unionization had implications for the form of institutionalization which emerged. The following chapter will consider the results of this in the post-war period, but, even before the start of the war, the U.A.W. was becoming more similar to other unions. Factionalism was declining and the distance between the workers and their leaders growing. During the war, the no-strike pledge was closely adhered to,[49] but the pattern of strike activity did not necessarily reflect the extent of the union leaders' co-operation with the government. Four indices of strike activity for the three full years of war, 1942–44, are given in Table 5.10. Strike activity in motor vehicles was not only greater than the national average but was considerably higher than that in comparable sectors.[50] It is notable that the strikes were small and 'short' (i.e. they had a low D/W ratio), suggesting that they were 'unorganized' protests. The contrast with aircraft is interesting since this was, of course, one of the key war industries. Here strikes were very large, but infrequent and short, suggesting that they were occasional mass protests. Whether the low level of strike activity was due to the aircraft workers' commitment to the war or to the repression of their dissatisfactions is impossible to say, but the contrast with the auto workers, who were to a large extent organized by the same union, is significant.

The Steel Industry
The steel industry illustrates a very different mode of institutionalization from that of autos and rubber. Here, a national union was created 'from above' and the crucial breakthrough, the recognition of the Steel Workers' Organizing Committee (S.W.O.C.) by U.S. Steel, achieved

---

49. By 1941, the aircraft and rubber industries had union agreements which, like those in most other industries, banned strikes during the term of the contract: see 'Strike Restrictions in Union Agreements', *Monthly Labor Review*, LII, pp. 546–64 (1941), at pp. 549, 560–61.

50. The separation of the motor vehicle and aircraft industries is possible for this period; before the war the aircraft sector was relatively insignificant in the strike movement and this, plus the lack of adequate employment data before 1942, means that little would be gained by separating it from motor vehicles before the war.

TABLE 5.10

STRIKE INDICES, SELECTED INDUSTRIES, 1942–44

	N/E	W/E	W/N	D/W
Building	123	18.5	116	6.14
Clothing	147	33.5	227	4.63
Coal	543	349	642	11.6
Food	149	29.1	195	3.23
Machinery: non-electrical	179	68.8	384	3.00
electrical	91	42.9	474	2.93
Metals: basic steel[a]	400	173	433	3.23
all iron and steel	389	160	413	2.72
Textiles	153	55.6	363	6.11
Transportation	77	15.8	204	4.08
Transport equip: all	120	142	118	2.77
motor vehicles[a]	268	404	151	3.13
aircraft[a]	79	118	1488	2.12
Chemicals	130	39.3	303	3.66
Rubber	322	260	811	2.82
All industries: 1942–44	95	40.0	423	5.35
1943–44	104	49.0	470	5.42

NOTE
a. 1943–44 only.

without a strike. As noted in Chapter 4, craft unionism was destroyed by the early twentieth century and, despite several important strikes, particularly that of 1919, the companies were able to maintain their domination. Throughout the 1920s they faced little opposition from the workers, but in the early thirties several local unions were established and strike activity began to increase. This is naturally seen as more than a response to the improvement of business conditions since strikes were previously concentrated in the late rather than the early stages of recovery; unrest had accumulated, and conditions under the N.R.A. provided some outlet for this. Strikes were seen as a protest against the system of repression which the companies had built up, and as a plea for independence for the workers.[51]

In these early years, organization seems to have been based on the rank and file. Several insurgent groups entered the Amalgamated Association, which retained a slight presence in the industry, and attempted to revitalize it. From 1933 to 1935, organization 'from below' became more important, but was never able to achieve a significant breakthrough. In particular, a strike threat in 1934 did not materialize and

51. Daugherty, de Chazeau and Stratton, op. cit., pp. 187–98, 932–77.

by 1935 the union stood more or less where it had two years pre-viously.[52] With the arrival of the S.W.O.C. in 1936, the situation changed dramatically: professional organizers entered the mill towns in a carefully planned drive, manned and financed largely by the U.M.W. The agreement with U.S. Steel was negotiated by Lewis, the president of the C.I.O. as well as of the U.M.W., and presented as a *fait accompli*. But this 'from the top' method was not completely successful: the S.W.O.C. received a severe setback in the Little Steel strike of 1937 and did not organize this part of the industry until 1941.

It is not possible to consider here the questions of whether the failure of the 1933—35 movement was 'inevitable' and whether the S.W.O.C. 'sold out' on its members by concentrating on material gains and a union contract.[53] Steel illustrates one road to an institutiona-lized system. The standard view of institutionalization sees a period of hostility and aggression giving way to more harmonious relations. But U.S. Steel, despite its position as a leader of the anti-union movement, recognized the union without a fight. Relations before the recognition cannot be characterized as entirely hostile: the growth of 'reason' did not begin after the signing of the first contract but was central to the decision to sign in the first place. The differences between U.S. Steel and the Little Steel companies show that, even within one industry, there were marked differences in the process of institutionalization. And, as the earlier militancy showed, directions of unionism other than that examplified by the S.W.O.C. were possible. This militancy, together with the great differences between steel and industries such as autos and rubber, indicates that institutionalization was not inevitable and that it took many forms.

Other Industries

Strikes were not, of course, restricted to the mass production indus-tries. Tables 5.6 to 5.9 show that many sectors not noted for a high level of militancy in the thirties, such as clothing and tobacco, had high

52. See S. Lynd, 'The Possibility of Radicalism in the Early 1930s: The Case of Steel', *Radical America*, VI, no. 6, pp. 37—64 (1972).
53. Many reasons have been suggested for the failure of the earlier rank and file movement and for the capitulation of U.S. Steel, in view of the company's long history of opposition to unionism. See Galenson, *The C.I.O. Challenge*, pp. 91—5; Bernstein, *Turbulent Years*, pp. 467—9; D. Brody, *Labor in Crisis* (Philadelphia: J. B. Lippincott, 1965), pp. 180—83. One obvious reason for the company's decision was the belief that unionism was inevit-able: the company thus sought to accommodate the union on terms most beneficial to itself. It is unlikely that this belief would have been held in the absence of a background of militancy in the industry.

rates of strike activity. Even where the unions were re-established fairly quickly, as in clothing[54] and building, activity was high, suggesting that the strike movement represented a general protest against conditions induced by the Depression. But on the railways activity 'withered away' to become negligible by the end of the decade. As Kaufman has pointed out, this was partly due to the depressed state of the industry, in contrast to the generally improving situation elsewhere. But it was also associated with the long history of collective bargaining and the established position of the unions.[55] In one industry, at least, the institutions of collective bargaining insulated the workers from the protests going on elsewhere.

The most notable feature of wartime strikes (Table 5.10) is the very high level of activity in the coal industry. Although coal was as important as aircraft to the war effort, miners were able to challenge successfully the government's attempts to maintain production. Coal strikes, and in particular the national stoppage of 1943, were the main focus of public attention and the impetus to the passing of strong anti-strike measures, notably the Smith—Connally Act. But they are of interest here for the light they throw on the expression of protest during the war. Only the miners were able to hold strikes which were anything like as long as peacetime stoppages. Other workers were prevented from holding more than protest strikes. This could be explained in terms of the miners' traditions of independence and their isolation from community pressures, or of the particular problems of wages and conditions which they faced. The former set of causes is the more important here, for it suggests that miners were not open to the pressures which were applied to other workers. There is no reason to suppose that their high strike-proneness was due to a lack of 'patriotism'. The implication is that strikes would have been much more serious elsewhere in the absence of considerable efforts by the government and union leaders to prevent stoppages.

The cases of the mass production industries considered in this sec-

----

54. Like the U.M.W., the clothing unions grew rapidly during the early New Deal. In two months in 1933, the U.M.W. added 300,000 members, the International Ladies' Garment Workers Union 100,000 and the Amalgamated Clothing Workers 50,000: T. R. Brooks, op. cit., p. 163.

55. J. J. Kaufman, *Collective Bargaining in the Railroad Industry* (New York: King's Crown Press, 1954), pp. 78—80. See also Galenson, *The C.I.O. Challenge,* op. cit., p. 579: the gains of the railroad workers were made with a minimal amount of strife, but subsequent events showed that the 'millenium had not yet arrived for railroad industrial relations. . . Maturity in trade union organization and collective bargaining relationships constitute no certain guarantee of industrial peace.'

tion, and of the other industries mentioned more briefly, indicate the variety of forms which the institutionalization process took. Thus Lewis, who was one of the labour leaders most committed to business unionism, was prepared to lead the miners in wartime strikes. But Reuther, despite his background in the militant United Auto Workers, backed the war effort.[56] In clothing the unions regained their position of influence, but strike activity remained high, whereas on the railroads the established position of the unions was associated with low levels of activity. The auto industry's strike record was not 'characteristic' of that in newly-organized sectors; the industry may have been crucial in achieving the key breakthroughs, but it was significant precisely because of this leading, and not 'typical', role. Certain common factors were present, however. In the mass production industries, rank and file action provided the basis of later developments, although the precise form of these varied. The 'breakthrough' of the thirties ensured that domination by the employer was eliminated. But, at the same time, the operation of union leaderships within the context of governmental involvement in labour relations meant that, even in the auto industry, institutionalized bargaining developed.

Aspects of the Geographical Distribution of Strikes

The present and previous chapters have given prime emphasis to the distribution of strike activity by industry. The main justification for this, apart from the substantive interest of charting developments in particular industrial sectors, is that one industry is fairly readily distinguished from another in terms of bargaining arrangements, union structure, market conditions, and so on. The same cannot be said of other means of disaggregating strike figures. But two particular aspects of the geographical distribution of activity warrant attention. Since the data relating to them are available in the most convenient form for the period examined in the present chapter, they will be considered here.

Industrial and Geographical Influences
Although industries can be distinguished on various criteria, it remains possible that a given industry has a high strike rate not because of its own characteristics but because its constituent factories tend to be

---

56. See, for example, W. P. Reuther, 'Labor's Place in the War Pattern', an essay of 1942 reprinted in M. Dubofsky (ed.), *American Labor since the New Deal* (Chicago: Quadrangle Books, 1971), pp. 132–41.

located in areas with a high strike-proneness.[57] And, as argued at the end of Chapter 4, the diversity of strike experience in the late nineteenth century may be partly due to the great regional differences of the United States.

These points may be investigated by taking the number of strikes to occur in each industry in each state and applying a model which compares the influence of the 'industry' and 'state' effects. To restrict the number of empty cells in the matrix, the analysis is restricted to 10 industry groups and states which had at least 25 strikes in any one year; the period of analysis is 1927–36.[58] For each industry in each state, the number of strikes was divided by the number of employees to obtain a measure of strike frequency. The model used[59] begins by predicting the figure in each cell of the matrix from the overall mean; this is the standard against which the other estimates must perform. Separate predictions are then made using the industry mean and the state mean in turn, followed by the combined 'industry and state' model.

The chief finding from the sample of 24 states was that even the final interaction model did not reduce the deviance of the estimating errors to any marked extent (Table 5.11). The information on each cell of the 'industry and state' matrix was then examined to see if any particular combination contributed a large part of the total deviance. The most convenient way to eliminate these 'exceptional' cases was to remove five states from the sample. For the remaining 19 states, more satisfactory results were obtained: the 'industry' effect was larger than the 'state' effect, but the difference between the 'industry' and 'industry and state' models indicates that the interaction between the two effects was also important.

These results support the greater attention given here (and of course by other writers) to industrial than to regional differences in activity. The very great differences between the 'industry only' and 'state only' models suggest that the greater importance of industry effects may not be limited to the period considered here. However, this finding relates

57. For an interesting study of regional effects, see B. J. Gordon, 'A Classification of Regional and Sectoral Dispute Patterns in Australian Industry, 1945–64', *Journal of Industrial Relations*, X, pp. 233–42 (1968).

58. This is the definition employed in the source of the data: see Peterson, op. cit., table 35. Similarly, 1927–36 is the period used in the discussion below of the strike-proneness of different cities: Peterson, op. cit., table 33.

59. The GLIM (General Linear Interactive Modelling) programme was used. I am very grateful to Clive Payne of the Nuffield College Research Services Unit for making this programme available and for help in the setting up and analysis of the model.

TABLE 5.11

RESULTS FOR 'INDUSTRY AND STATE' MODEL, 1927–36

	24 States			19 States		
	Sum of Squares	d.f.	Mean Square	MS as % MS in Mean Only Model	Sum of Squares	d.f.	Mean Square	MS as % MS in Mean Only Model
Mean Only	16.50×10^7	232	7.11×10^5	100	10.68×10^4	185	5.77×10^2	100
Industry Only	11.81×10^7	223	5.30×10^5	74.5	4.40×10^4	176	2.50×10^2	43.3
State Only	14.66×10^7	209	7.01×10^5	98.6	9.56×10^4	167	5.73×10^2	99.2
Industry and State	9.89×10^7	200	4.94×10^5	69.5	3.21×10^4	158	2.03×10^2	35.2

NOTE
Mean Only refers to the model in which each cell frequency is predicted from the grand mean alone.
Industry Only refers to the model where frequencies for any industry in each state are predicted from the mean of that industry, and so on.

only to the effects of being in a particular industry or state on the strike rate of a given cell in the matrix. It does not mean that there were no overall differences in the strike rates of particular states. Geographical differences were present, but were accounted for more by the distribution of the strike-prone industries than by the characteristics of particular localities. But even the 'industry and state' model was not very successful in explaining the strike rate of the cells in the matrix. In other words, particular combinations of industries and states had strike rates which cannot be explained by the model. One possibility is that it was individual cities, and not whole states, which were crucial.

Strikes and Urbanization

As noted in Chapter 1, Shorter and Tilly argue that the effects of industrialization were not limited to changes in technology and the size of plants. Equally important in France was the associated development of the growth of cities and, in particular, the concentration of strike activity in the area around Paris. But it was necessary to separate urban growth from the effects of size *per se*.[60] The fastest growing French cities had the lowest strike rates. Shorter and Tilly thus argued that being in a large city, and not the 'shock' of experiencing industrial life for the first time, made workers militant. Not only were workers more willing to strike, but there were obvious organizational advantages of being in large centres.

For the United States, data on the strike rates of cities are not available for the late nineteenth century, but the argument about the effects of city size is a general one and may be assessed using data for 1927–36. Moreover, as noted above, some writers see the influx of labour into the new industries as one source of the upsurge of strike activity in the 1930s. Analysis of the strike rates of cities helps to assess this more specific argument.

The data relate to the number of strikes occurring in cities which had ten or more strikes in any year. The requirement that a city must have at least ten strikes in any year leads to a severely truncated sample: one is considering not the whole range of positions on strike-proneness but only one end of the distribution. Even if all cities which had any strikes were included, there would still be the problem of whether strike-free cities should be included. However, Stern, in a study of 243 Standard Metropolitan Statistical Areas in the period 1968–70, has

---

60. E. Shorter and C. Tilly, *Strikes in France, 1830–1968* (Cambridge: Cambridge University Press, 1974), chap. 10.

concluded that strike-prone cities can be treated as a distinct population:[61] by dividing his sample into 'high-conflict' and 'low-conflict' groups, he found that there were separate clusters on variables such as city size and degree of union organization. If this conclusion holds for 1927–36, it is valid to treat the strike-prone cities as a separate population.

Adequate data exist on 41 of the 44 'strike-prone' cities; the results of the analysis are given in Table 5.12. According to Shorter and Tilly, strike frequency will be associated directly with city size and inversely with the growth rate of cities. Two measures of the rate of growth are used here: one, spanning 1900–30, reflects long-term influences and one, covering 1920–30, measures more short-term factors. Two other measures are included, the proportions of a city's population composed of negroes and foreign-born whites; the former reflects the racial heterogeneity of, and the latter the importance of immigrants in, the city's work force. As expected, the two measures of the rate of growth were inversely associated with strike frequency, but city size also had a negative coefficient. But none of the five variables attained a significant level of association with strike frequency.

To investigate the links with strikes more fully, the cities were split into two overlapping groups, composed of the 21 smallest and 21 largest cities. For the former, city size was significantly related to strike activity, but for the latter no independent variable was significant. It appears that, up to a certain size of city, a higher population restrained strike activity, but that, beyond that point, it ceased to have any impact. In neither group did the rate of growth of cities explain differences in their strike rates. The change in the importance of city size may in part reflect the truncated nature of the sample. One would expect very small communities to have few strikes so that, as city size rises from very low levels, there is a direct link with strike activity. But in the middle ranges of size further growth will discourage strikes, perhaps because cities of a certain size are dominated by one company or because of some 'industry effect'. Beyond this size range, all cities are more or less equally strike-prone.

These results must be compared with those of Stern. Stern divided his 'high-conflict' group into two and called the sub-groups the 'moderate-conflict' and 'high-conflict' cities. The former of these had a lower mean size than the latter, which is consistent with the finding here that city size affected strike frequency only within a limited range

61. R. N. Stern, 'Intermetropolitan Patterns of Strike Activity', *Industrial and Labor Relations Review*, XXIX, pp. 218–35 (1976), at pp. 219, 221.

TABLE 5.12

RESULTS OF REGRESSION EQUATIONS, 41 CITIES, 1927–36

Dependent Variable	Independent Variables					R^2	F
	Pop 1930	Ch.Pop 1920–30	Ch.Pop 1900–30	% F.B. White	% Negro		
N/Pop	Neg	Neg	Neg	Pos	Neg	0.26	2.51
	NS	NS	NS	NS	NS		5%
N/Pop (21 smallest cities)	Neg	Neg	Neg			0.51	5.95
	1%	NS	NS				1%
N/Pop (21 largest cities)	Pos	Neg	Pos			0.13	0.88
	NS	NS	NS				NS

NOTE

Pop = population of each city.

Ch.Pop = proportionate change in population.

% F.B. White = percentage of population in 1930 who were white and born abroad.

% Negro = percentage of population in 1930 who were negroes.

of size. Stern's findings demonstrate a curvilinear relationship between size and strike frequency which is supported by the results here. In his regression analysis, Stern achieved an R^2 of 0.59 which, in view of the number of independent variables employed, is not notably better than the model of Table 5.12. It is interesting that Stern's variable measuring the industry-mix of cities did not have a significant effect, which implies that the strike-proneness of cities is determined more by their other characteristics. Stern included measures of union density and plant size as independent variables, but it is questionable whether these can be taken as indices of the characteristics of cities. Plant size, in particular, seems to be a characteristic of industries and not cities. Thus, although the industry-mix measure was not associated with strike activity, this result may not hold in a different explanatory model.

However, Stern's approach helps to correct an over-emphasis on the industrial distribution of strikes. The results reported in Table 5.12 relate to a much simpler model but show that the view of Shorter and Tilly on the effects of urbanization does not fit the American case. It is argued that the concentration of workers in large plants and cities encouraged strikes. It was argued in Chapter 4 that plant size does not help to explain inter-industry differences;[62] the present section shows that city size did not exert a consistent effect and that, when it did, the direction of the effect was opposite to that predicted by Shorter and Tilly. Moreover, cross-sectional analysis can show only whether large cities were proportionately more strike-prone than small ones and whether those which had grown fastest were highly strike-prone. It cannot relate changes in a city's strike rate to changes in its size.

The results here give no support to the view that mass immigration was a major cause of strike activity. As Table 5.12 shows, the proportion of a city's population who were black or born abroad did not affect its strike propensity. But internal migration from the south and rural areas has also been stressed, for example in explaining the high strike rate in the auto industry.[63] Similar arguments have been advanced in relation to the rubber industry.[64] Detailed data, giving strike rates by industry and city, which would enable this proposition to be tested are not available, but more qualitative findings can be assessed. For autos, Harris states that immigration into the cities of four states during the 1920s meant that, by 1930, 47 per cent of the work force was from rural areas.[65] Evidence for the rural and southern origins of auto workers also exists for the 1950s.[66] For rubber, Jones says that one-third of Akron's population came from the south and border

62. See above, pp. 103–7. See also Edwards, op. cit., tables 6–12 and 6–13 for inter-industry regression analyses showing an *inverse* link between mean plant size and strike frequency. This does not, of course, mean that small plants were the most strike-prone; indeed, there is evidence to the contrary (see above Table 5.4). But the fact that industries characterized by small plants tended to be relatively highly strike-prone suggests that there was no automatic link between plant size and strike activity.
63. See the quotation from Mitchell, cited in note 40 above, and M. Handman, 'Changing Ideologies in the American Labor Movement', *American Journal of Sociology*, XLIII, pp. 525–38 (1938), at pp. 529–31.
64. 'Rubber Workers: Sit Downs, Short Days and Caution', *Business Week*, 11 April 1953, reprinted in J. Barbash (ed.), *Unions and Union Leadership* (New York: Harper and Bros, 1959), pp. 130–38.
65. H. Harris, *American Labor* (New Haven: Yale University Press, 1939), p. 272. See also Howe and Widick, op. cit., pp. 6–11; Fine, *The Automobile under the Blue Eagle*, op. cit., p. 12.
66. A. Kornhauser, H. L. Sheppard and A. J. Mayer, *When Labor Votes* (New York: University Books, 1956), pp. 24, 26. Cf. J. C. Leggett, *Class, Race and Labor* (New York: Oxford University Press, 1968). Although Leggett stresses the role of the 'uprooted' in the development of class consciousness, he does not mention immigration in his list of the causes of unrest in the thirties and, in his own study, excludes the southern-born from his sample (pp. 48, 174–8).

regions.[67] But it also seems that the steel industry had a high proportion of its workers who were migrants, although its strike pattern was different from that in autos and rubber.[68]

The argument about immigration needs to be carefully specified. It is a variant of the view that workers who are 'new to industry' will react against their conditions through overt protest; but instead of concentrating on the effects of industry on a population which was wholly unaccustomed to industry, or on immigrants from other countries, it focuses on migrants from rural areas within the United States. These people, it is said, will experience their migration as a 'shock' and will have to adjust to industry; while they are doing this, they will exhibit discontent which will be manifested in absenteeism, a high quit rate and strikes. The strikes will not have any clear direction, but will be spontaneous, unorganized and short. As this argument stands, it is hard to test with the sort of data being used here, but some light can be thrown on it. It is obvious that rural origins are not sufficient to explain levels of strike activity among a group of workers. Many other factors were at work in the 1930s; and evidence for the steel industry for earlier decades indicates that workers were being recruited from the south without any great protests being apparent.[69] It is true that the solidarity of the 1919 strike was partly due to the discontents of the unskilled men who were new to industry. But the argument being considered here is that strikes are an immediate response to the shock of industry, rather than being delayed for an indefinite period. It is possible that the discontents of 'new' workers will contribute to strikes when they occur, but the immediate causes of the strikes must be sought elsewhere.

Much of the 'militant migrants' argument is based on the supposition that moving to industry will make workers dissatisfied. Although the breakdown of old cultural ties and the imposition of new routines are likely to induce discontent, it is also possible that new workers will tolerate industry because they simply want to earn as much as they can and are not interested in improving conditions of work. Since they are unorganized and not accustomed to industry, they may fall under managerial domination; cultural values of obedience to authority may contribute to this.[70] Numerous firms certainly thought that rural

67. Jones, op. cit., p. 66; an explicit comparison is made with the Michigan auto cities. Cf. rather different figures in McKenney, op. cit., p. xv.
68. Daugherty, de Chazeau and Stratton, op. cit., p. 126.
69. H. B. Davis, *Labor and Steel* (London: Martin Lawrence, 1933), pp. 28–9.
70. See, for example, S. Aronowitz, *False Promises* (New York: McGraw-Hill, 1973), p. 183 for the view that the most important factor in the domination of the employers after 1890 was the agrarian origin of the majority of the work force.

workers provided a tractable work force; and, independent of this, there is the fact that a heterogeneous labour force, whatever the nature of its parts, is likely to break down into factional disputes.

These are only possibilities, but they are mentioned to show that it is not self-evident that migration to industry will lead to protest, although it is likely that it will cause discontent. Evidence for an earlier period on Slavic immigrants suggests that they did not provide a tractable work force and shows that their peasant traditions of solidarity supported them during strikes,[71] but it has not been shown that these workers were more likely than others to engage in 'spontaneous protests'. For the 1930s, the question is whether southern whites had particular cultural traits which predisposed them to such protests. Contemporary writers made various assertions on this, but it would be very hard now to provide any hard evidence on these workers' attitudes.

Instead of dealing with the question in terms of some pre-determined view of the effect of migration, a more cautious approach is needed. The concentration of new migrants in some cities and industries may well have contributed to their strike record in the 1930s, but only alongside other factors. Strikes occurred in many areas not noted for their new immigrants. Rather than responding to the situation at once, it seems more likely that the new workers would have brooded on their discontents and the failure of their expectations and would thus have reacted particularly aggressively once other sources of dissatisfaction became significant. More generally, this aspect of strikes in the thirties provides a link with those of earlier years. It suggests that the newness of groups of workers to industry was a continuing theme in nineteenth and twentieth century America; as Chapter 6 shows, it did not disappear even in the post-war period. It was one of the sources of challenge to the existing system of industrial relations; new groups have had to be accommodated and the system has been unable to remain static. The final chapter will take this up at more length.

The regression analysis of this section suggested that there is no evidence that the process of becoming urban affects a population's strike activity. The presence of new immigrants may have been one source of discontent, but this did not show up in the overall regression analysis; it is likely that it was restricted to a limited number of cities in the industrial north-east, where it may have been important, but only in addition to many other factors. Immigration should be seen as one structural

71. V. R. Greene, *The Slavic Community on Strike* (Notre Dame: University of Notre Dame Press, 1968).

factor putting pressure on the existing system, rather than as a force which necessarily led to protest.

Conclusions

This chapter has shown how strike trends developed during the crucial period when the institutionalized system was established. During the early New Deal important rank and file movements grew up; in addition to those in the mass production industries which have been mentioned, there were significant upheavals in, for example, the San Francisco general strike of 1934 and the 'teamster rebellion' in Minneapolis in the same year.[72] These protests did not reflect the unfocused 'hostility' posited by the institutionalization theory but were based on very real discontents connected with control of the work place. Being concerned with the day-to-day running of operations, they were not amenable to solution through formal collective bargaining. Even during the second world war, small-scale strikes continued despite union leaders' attempts to restrain them; and, as the following chapter shows, protests based on the work place remained important in the post-war period. The wider implications of such protests are considered in Chapter 7.

However, rank and file protests came increasingly under institutional control as the New Deal progressed. Union recognition and collective agreements with employers were made the main aim; and the conservatism of C.I.O. leaders and the revival of the A.F.L.[73] illustrate the absorption of rank and file militancy by union structures. The limitation of the scope of strikes is indicated by the decline in the number of establishments affected by the 'average strike' (Table 5.1) and the rapid end of the sit-down movement.

This process had several variants, as the comparison of the rubber and auto industries with steel has shown. These mass production industries have been the centre of attention here because they illustrate the two extremes whereby the strike movement was brought under institu-

---

72. These are treated in the standard works. See also C. P. Larrowe, 'The Great Maritime Strike of '34', *Labor History*, XI, pp. 403–51 (1970) and XII, pp. 3–37 (1971); F. Dobbs, *Teamster Rebellion* (New York: Monad Press, 1972).
73. Contemporary estimates exaggerated the growth of the C.I.O.; the A.F.L. was much larger, and moved into several new areas. See Bernstein, *Turbulent Years*, op. cit., pp. 773–4; Galenson, *The C.I.O. Challenge*, op. cit., pp. 584–8; M. Derber, 'Growth and Expansion', *Labor and the New Deal*, op. cit., pp. 1–44, at pp. 14–16.

tional control. It may be possible to describe general tendencies in terms of concepts such as 'modernization' and 'institutionalization', but it is equally important to consider the detailed developments which lay behind such large-scale changes. In particular, there was a 'breakthrough' to a 'modern' form of strike activity, after the very low levels of the 1920s, but the results of this were far from certain. In the auto and steel industries the basis of the breakthrough was an upsurge of rank and file action in 1933 and 1934, but in the former such action 'from below' continued to play a more important role than it did in the latter. The final form of the strike movement was not determined by the eventual emergence of control from above but reflected a continuing process of interaction between the rank and file, union leaders, employers, and the government.

Whatever the outcome of the debate between 'liberals' and 'radicals' over the interpretation of the New Deal, it is apparent that most attention must be given to the interaction between the various parties to industrial conflict. This chapter has not sought to contribute to this debate, but has used it to illustrate how the strike movement developed during the key period of the 1930s.

This chapter has also examined some of the influences underlying general trends. Thus, the continued importance of economic conditions for strike frequency has been demonstrated, even though one might have expected, in a time of upheaval, that such influences would be less significant than at other times. And although the attitudes of employers were crucial in particular cases, measures of the prosperity of employers were not closely related to the frequency or duration of strikes. The decision to recognize a union does not seem to have stemmed directly from the employer's economic position. The change in attitude may have been influenced by economic factors, but the precise policy adopted was not determined by them: employers had considerable freedom of action to decide how to deal with the union challenge. This freedom meant that employers' actions were an important independent influence on the way strikes developed.

By 1945, the impact of wartime conditions on the developing pattern of accommodation between employers and unions had established an institutionalized system of relations. The following chapter investigates the working of this system during the post-war period.

6

The Working of the Institutionalized System, 1947–74

The second world war was followed by a large wave of strikes; more days were lost in 1946 than in any other year. But this high level of activity took place within the framework of collective bargaining. Disputes still occurred over the scope of bargaining, but the parties recognized the right of the other side to exist.[1] With the decline in strike activity in the 1950s it is not surprising that industrial relations were seen as 'mature'.[2] In the 1960s, however, there was an increase in strike activity which has been seen as part of a more general 'labor revolt': it has been argued that, although unions were able to raise wages, matters of work conditions and discipline were ignored and that the increase in strike activity reflected rank and file attempts to control the work process.[3] It will be suggested here that the extent of this revolt has been exaggerated and that the institutionalized system was not destroyed by protest from below. Indeed, union leaders tended to become more fully integrated into the Democratic Party;[4] as a result one

1. See 'The Labor Situation', *Fortune*, XXXIV, no. 5, pp. 121–6, 280–86 (1946); J. Barbash, *Labor Unions in Action* (New York: Harper and Bros, 1948), p. 134; T. R. Brooks, *Toil and Trouble* (New York: Delacorte Press, 1964), p. 211; J. Seidman, *American Labor from Defense to Reconstruction* (Chicago: University of Chicago Press, 1953), pp. 224–5, 246.
2. R. A. Lester, *As Unions Mature* (Princeton: Princeton University Press, 1958).
3. See R. Herding, *Job Control and Union Structure* (Rotterdam: Rotterdam University Press, 1972); S. Aronowitz, *False Promises* (New York: McGraw-Hill, 1973), pp. 214–50; S. Weir, 'U.S.A.: the Labor Revolt', *International Socialist Journal*, no. 20, pp. 279–96 and no. 21, pp. 465–73 (1967). Cf. J. Barbash, 'The Causes of Rank-and-File Unrest', *Trade Union Government and Collective Bargaining*, ed. J. Seidman (New York: Praeger, 1970), pp. 39–79.
4. J. D. Greenstone, *Labor in American Politics* (New York: Vintage Books, 1970); V. Vale, *Labour in American Politics* (London: Routledge and Kegan Paul, 1971), pp. 129–45; I. Richter, *Political Purpose in Trade Unions* (London: Allen and Unwin, 1973), pp. 190–217.

aspect of institutionalization, namely the separation of political from economic struggles, was strengthened.[5]

Aggregate Trends and the Militancy of the 1960s

As Table 6.1 shows, strike activity was high in the late 1940s and early 1950s, but subsequently fell rapidly. Overall trends may be somewhat misleading for, as Ross has argued, they were influenced by 'cycles of strikes' in certain industries;[6] these cycles, particularly those in the steel industry, exerted a large impact on the aggregate figures, with the result that the degree of harmony elsewhere was understated. The decline in activity was reversed in the early 1960s; as the following section shows, this was due not to an upturn in the 'cycle' in particular industries but to a widespread increase in strike-proneness. The marked differences between the 1950s and the 1960s suggest that a background cause may have been responsible. It is necessary to examine influences which affected all strikes before turning to matters specifically related to the 'labor revolt' of the 1960s. Two predictive models are employed, the first relating to the role of the employer and the second to economic influences on strike activity in the 1960s. On the former, it has been noted that a 'hard line' against unions emerged at the end of the 1950s, representing a desire to restore certain managerial prerogatives.[7] Radicals have also stressed a change in managerial attitudes, explaining it in terms of economic stagnation and a slowing of the rate of growth of productivity: capitalism was facing a crisis and it responded with a tougher line on wages and production standards.[8] One might expect, therefore, that differences in strike activity between the '50s and '60s could be explained by changes in the economic position of employers.

5. See, in particular, R. Dahrendorf, *Class and Class Conflict in Industrial Society* (London: Routledge and Kegan Paul, 1959), pp. 267–78. It is not being suggested that institutional isolation was necessary or irreversible, but that certain trends in this direction were strengthened.
6. A. M. Ross, 'The Prospects for Industrial Conflict', *Industrial Relations*, I, no. 1, pp. 57–74 (1961), esp. pp. 66–72.
7. See the symposium in *Industrial Relations*, I, no. 1, pp. 9–55 (1961); G. Strauss, 'The Shifting Power Balance in the Plant', *Industrial Relations*, I, no. 3, pp. 65–96 (1962).
8. P. M. Sweezy and H. Magdoff, *The Dynamics of U.S. Capitalism* (New York: Monthly Review Press, 1972), esp. pp. 43–50; B. Wycko, 'The Work Shortage: Class Struggle and Capital Reproduction', *Review of Radical Political Economics*, VII, no. 2, pp. 11–30 (1975), esp. pp. 12–13.

TABLE 6.1

ANNUAL STRIKE INDICES, 1947–74

	W/N	D/W	N/E	W/E	D/E	Mean Duration
1947	588	15.9	84.9	49.9	0.795	25.6
1948	574	17.4	77.0	44.1	0.768	21.8
1949	840	16.7	83.3	70.0	1.17	22.5
1950	498	16.1	107	53.3	0.858	19.2
1951	469	10.3	99.0	46.4	0.479	17.4
1952	692	16.7	105	72.5	1.21	19.6
1953	471	11.8	101	47.8	0.563	20.3
1954	441	14.8	70.7	31.2	0.461	22.5
1955	613	10.6	85.2	52.3	0.556	18.5
1956	497	17.4	73.0	36.3	0.632	18.9
1957	378	11.9	69.4	26.3	0.312	19.2
1958	558	11.6	71.8	40.1	0.465	19.7
1959	507	36.3	69.4	35.2	1.29	24.6
1960	396	14.5	61.5	24.3	0.352	23.4
1961	431	11.2	62.1	26.7	0.301	23.7
1962	340	15.1	64.7	22.0	0.333	24.6
1963	280	17.1	58.8	16.5	0.282	23.0
1964	449	14.0	62.8	28.2	0.394	22.9
1965	391	15.0	65.2	25.5	0.383	25.0
1966	445	13.0	69.0	30.7	0.398	22.2
1967	625	14.7	69.6	43.4	0.637	22.8
1968	525	18.5	74.0	38.9	0.719	24.5
1969	435	17.3	81.3	35.4	0.611	22.5
1970	578	20.1	80.9	46.8	0.940	25.0
1971	639	14.5	72.6	46.4	0.673	27.0
1972	342	15.8	68.0	23.3	0.367	24.0
1973	421	12.4	69.7	29.3	0.364	24.0
1974	457	17.3	77.5	35.5	0.613	27.1

NOTE

Indices are as defined in Table 5.1.

Role of the Employer

The results of a regression model which attempts to test the view outlined above are given in Table 6.2; the first five independent variables are the same as those employed in Table 5.5 and no further comment on them is required. The sixth variable, 'wage control', is taken from a study of strikes in the building industry;[9] it is a dummy variable, taking

9. D. B. Lipsky and S. Farber, 'The Composition of Strike Activity in the Construction Industry', *Industrial and Labor Relations Review*, XXIX, pp. 388–404 (1976).

the value of 1 in years when a government policy of wage control was in operation and zero otherwise. The model examines the period 1948–72 as a whole and then compares two over-lapping sub-periods to see whether the effects of employer well-being have changed. For the simple equation using productivity, profits and the rate of change of wholesale prices, strike frequency was predicted satisfactorily only in 1957–72, which is consistent with a change in managerial attitudes around 1960. But only the price change variable attained significance, suggesting that a general effect of inflation, and not a specifically managerial influence, may have been at work; this is taken up further below. The addition of the 'peak' and 'trough' variables improved the fit considerably for 1948–72 as a whole; as for 1927–41, these variables seem to have been more important than measures of employer well-being. In the two sub-periods, none of the 'employer' variables was significant, and the overall results were improved little by the addition of 'peak' and 'trough'. But for the first sub-period the use of the wage control dummy improved the results considerably. Thus, the expectation that strikes will be most frequent in times of economic crisis for employers is unfounded.

The final part of Table 6.2 considers the relationship between employer well-being and strike duration and volume. There was a link between well-being and mean duration, but not with the number of days lost per worker (D/W) or strike volume (D/E). For mean duration, the negative coefficient of the price change variable indicates that strikes tended to be shorter the faster the rate of inflation; taken together with the findings of Table 6.3, reported below, this suggests that stoppages were frequent and short when price inflation was rapid. The addition of the 'peak' and 'trough' measures improved the overall fit only slightly, and neither variable attained significance. The measures did not dominate the employer well-being variables as they did in the model explaining strike frequency. In other words, duration was less dependent than was frequency on general economic conditions, a finding which also held for 1927–41. However, well-being did not necessarily determine strike duration. Since the productivity variable measures the level, and not the rate of change, of productivity, it displayed an upward trend which need not have caused the similar upward trend in duration; and the lack of significance of the profits and price change variables reveals that the well-being model, as a whole, was not strongly related to strike duration. It is clear, however, that frequency and duration were, in general, related to economic conditions in opposite ways: in the equations predicting them from employer well-being and the peak and trough variables, only the profits variable had

TABLE 6.2

REGRESSION RESULTS, EMPLOYER WELL-BEING MODEL, 1948–72

Dependent Variable	Independent Variables						R^2	D–W
	Prod	Profits	Ch.P	Trough	Peak	Wage Control		
N (1948–72)	Neg 5%	Pos NS	Pos NS				0.19	0.77
N (1948–72)	Neg 5%	Pos NS	Pos NS	Pos 5%	Neg 1%		0.55	1.26
N (1948–72)	Neg 1%	Pos NS	Pos NS	Pos 5%	Neg 1%	Pos NS	0.57	1.65
N (1948–59)	Neg NS	Neg NS	Pos NS				0.11	1.54
N (1948–59)	Neg NS	Pos NS	Pos NS	Pos NS	Neg NS		0.27	1.67
N (1948–59)	Pos NS	Pos 5%	Neg NS	Pos 5%	Neg 5%	Pos 5%	0.67	2.32
N (1957–72)	Pos NS	Neg NS	Pos 1%				0.49	1.15
N (1957–72)	Pos NS	Neg NS	Pos NS	Pos NS	Neg 5%		0.57	1.50
N (1957–72)	Pos NS	Neg NS	Pos NS	Pos NS	Neg NS	Neg NS	0.58	1.51
Duration (1948–72)	Pos 1%	Pos NS	Neg 5%				0.47	1.48
Duration (1948–72)	Pos 1%	Pos NS	Neg NS	Neg NS	Pos NS		0.48	1.56
D/W (1948–72)	Pos NS	Pos NS	Neg NS				–0.10	2.25
D/W (1948–72)	Pos NS	Pos NS	Neg NS	Pos NS	Pos NS		–0.10	2.23
D/E (1948–72)	Neg NS	Pos NS	Neg NS				0.08	1.50
D/E (1948–72)	Neg NS	Pos NS	Neg NS	Pos NS	Neg NS		0.08	1.95

NOTE

Prod = index of productivity.

Profit = rate of profit (book value) after tax.

Ch.P = per cent change in wholesale prices.

Wage control = a dummy variable: see text.

Duration = mean duration of strikes, in days.

the same sign.

The results for 1957–72, taken together, indicate that there was no tendency for economic stagnation and a squeeze on profits to make firms more willing to 'take a strike'. It is interesting that Herding sees attempts to control wages through government policy as an important cause of the labour revolt.[10] Table 6.2 shows that, for strike activity as a whole, wage control was important in the 1950s and not in the 1960s. Controls were imposed during the Korean War when, as Table 6.1 shows, strike activity was high; the coefficient of the wage control variable was therefore positive. But in the 1960s the coefficient was negative, since controls were in operation when activity was relatively low.

Quarterly Data

The second predictive model uses quarterly data for 1962–72 to examine in detail the impact of price changes on strike activity. Such data have been used earlier (see Table 3.6, p. 74) to assess certain accounts of the link between strikes and economic conditions; the present discussion is a continuation of this analysis.

The results of several regression equations are given in Table 6.3. The first three use the level of unemployment and the levels and rates of change of prices and wages to explain strike frequency.[11] Although, as the first equation shows, the levels of prices and wages had significant effects on strike frequency when considered in combination with the unemployment rate, they lost significance when the variables measuring rates of change were added. Of the five variables in the third equation, only the rate of change of prices had a significant coefficient. It might be felt that this result is due to a time trend operating through the rate of change of prices. But the fourth equation shows that, when a time trend and the level and rate of change of prices were considered together, it was only the price change variable which was significant.

The overall explanatory power of these equations is low. But, as the fourth and fifth equations show, the addition of seasonal dummies does much to improve the situation. Apart from the dummies, only the time trend and rate of change of prices were significant when predicting strike frequency and worker involvement. As the final equation of the table shows, lagging the explanatory variables improved the fit slightly and enabled the unemployment rate to attain significance.

In general, the results of Table 6.3 give strong support to the view that price inflation was a source of rising strike activity in the 1960s. Trends in strike frequency were associated with price changes but not, as Chapter 3 showed, with changes in real wages; more qualitative evi-

10. Herding, op. cit., p. 298.
11. The rates of change of wages and prices and not the rate of change of real wages are considered here so that their separate effects may be assessed. For the relatively short time period considered, the number of strikes can be used without correcting for employment: see above, pp. 64–5.

TABLE 6.3

REGRESSION RESULTS FOR IMPACT OF INFLATION, 1962–72

Dependent Variable	Independent Variables						R^2	D–W
	U/E	P	H	Ch.P	Ch.H	Time		
N	Neg 1%	Pos 5%	Neg 5%				0.29	2.00
N	Pos NS			Pos 1%	Pos NS		0.36	1.98
N	Neg NS	Pos NS	Neg NS	Pos 5%	Pos NS		0.34	1.99
N		Pos NS		Pos 1%		Pos NS	0.35	2.02

	Independent Variables							
	U/E	Ch.P	Ch.H	Time	Q_1	Q_2	Q_3	
N	Neg NS	Pos 1%	Pos NS	Pos 1%	Pos 5%	Pos 1%	Pos 1%	0.87	1.76
W	Neg NS	Pos 5%	Neg NS	Pos 5%	Neg NS	Pos 1%	Pos NS	0.55	0.88

	Independent Variables							
	$(U/E)_{t-1}$	$(Ch.P)_{t-1}$	$(Ch.H)_{t-1}$	Time	Q_1	Q_2	Q_3	
N_t	Neg 5%	Pos 1%	Neg NS	Pos 1%	Pos 1%	Pos 1%	Pos 1%	0.90	2.26

NOTE
Q_1, Q_2, Q_3 are dummies for the first three quarters of the year. $t-1$ denotes lagging a variable by one quarter.

dence on this is given below. However, as was also argued in Chapter 3, the association between economic variables and strike activity is not stable. Comparison of results for the period 1952–67 with the present evidence for 1962–72 revealed that the direction of the impact of some key variables had changed. Thus, it would be dangerous to extend the present conclusion about the role of price inflation more generally. However, the importance of inflation, combined with the much weaker effects of employer well-being revealed in Table 6.2, suggests that identifiable economic factors lay behind the rise in strike activity.

The Labour Revolt

'Radicals' naturally place great weight on the trends of this period as revealing a rise in working-class militancy. Previous sections have argued that the general rise in strike activity must be seen in its economic context, but it is now necessary to concentrate on the strikes stressed by radicals: small, 'unofficial' stoppages based on immediate workplace grievances. But it is important to remember that large disputes were still a very important part of the total. As Table 2.3 showed, strikes involving at least 10,000 workers grew in significance during the 1960s. Although a greatly increased share of large strikes, similar to that observed in Britain,[12] did not occur, the rise was sufficient to show that there was no wholesale shift to small and unconstitutional stoppages. Large strikes were more important in 1970–72 than at any time during the 1930s and the proportion of workers involved in them was surpassed only in 1946–49.

On 'unofficial' strikes, no direct data exist on the extent to which stoppages were formally authorized by union hierarchies, but it is possible to estimate trends using indirect evidence. Since 1961 the B.L.S. has recorded the contract status of strikes; the three main categories are 'first agreement and union recognition', 're-negotiation of existing agreement' and 'during term of agreement'. The last includes those strikes which occurred while a contract was in force; in the great majority of cases, these were unconstitutional because most agreements include a clause banning strikes during the term of the contract. Stieber suggests that the number of strikes which occurred during the term of an agreement and lasted three days or less is an index of unofficial stoppages,[13] since these strikes are short as well as unconstitutional. Clearly, this can be no more than an index of trends because it does not measure unofficial stoppages directly; not all short and unconstitutional strikes need be unauthorized, and longer or constitutional strikes need not be authorized.

Table 6.4 shows the trend of 'unofficial' strikes from 1961 to 1974, divided into those lasting one day and those lasting two or three days. There was a slight but clear upward trend in the proportion of such strikes in the total; since the total was also increasing, the rise in absolute terms was more marked. Trends for worker involvement and days lost were less clear, but some rise occurred towards the end of the period. The coefficient of correlation between the total number of strikes and the proportion 'unofficial' was 0.69, indicating quite a strong tendency for a rise in activity to be associated with an increase in unofficial action. This contradicts the view that official and unofficial

12. See M. Silver, 'Recent British Strike Trends: A Factual Analysis', *British Journal of Industrial Relations*, XI, pp. 66–104 (1973); R. Hyman, 'Industrial Conflict and the Political Economy: Trends for the 1960s and Prospects for the '70s', *Socialist Register, 1973*, pp. 101–53.

13. J. Stieber, 'Grievance Arbitration in the United States', *Three Studies in Collective Bargaining*, Royal Commission on Trade Unions and Employers' Associations, Research Paper no. 8 (London: H.M.S.O., 1968), pp. 24–5.

TABLE 6.4

'UNOFFICIAL' STRIKES, 1961–74

| | % of All Stoppages Accounted for by Strikes which were During Course of Agreement and which Lasted | | | | | |
| | 1 Day | | | 2–3 Days | | |
	N	W	D	N	W	D
1961	7.3	5.4	0.5	9.0	5.7	1.1
1962	5.9	5.0	0.3	7.7	7.7	1.1
1963	8.2	6.3	0.4	9.4	9.8	1.2
1964	7.4	5.8	0.4	9.3	7.4	1.1
1965	7.6	5.9	0.4	8.4	6.8	1.0
1966	8.2	6.6	0.5	9.0	7.3	1.1
1967	8.7	4.8	0.3	8.5	6.3	0.9
1968	9.3	5.0	0.4	8.4	6.5	0.9
1969	9.9	8.2	0.5	8.3	8.1	0.9
1970	9.3	4.4	0.2	7.7	4.8	0.5
1971	10.4	4.8	0.3	8.3	4.5	0.6
1972	13.2	9.9	0.6	11.5	11.0	1.4
1973	13.2	10.6	0.9	10.1	8.7	1.3
1974	11.1	5.7	0.3	7.0	5.2	0.6

strikes are alternatives and that they will therefore be inversely related. Without comparable data for the 1950s, it is hard to assess the significance of the evidence of Table 6.4. But the increase in unofficial action was far from dramatic, particularly when worker involvement is considered; and the growth of such action seems to have been reversed in 1973 and 1974. At the same time, short, small and unconstitutional stoppages have accounted for between 14 and 25 per cent of the total and cannot be ignored.

The distribution of strikes by contract status is considered further in Tables 6.5 to 6.7. The first table shows that about one-sixth of all strikes were for union recognition or a first agreement. If these strikes are added to those which were 'unofficial', over one-third of all stoppages can be seen to have occurred outside union-led bargaining disputes at the end of contracts. Although such bargaining disputes accounted for most workers involved in strikes, the number of stoppages which occurred outside them shows the picture of American strikes as bargaining encounters at the end of contracts to be an exaggeration.

Strikes during the term of agreements might be expected to be small when compared with large-scale disputes over contract re-negotiation, but, as Table 6.6 shows, this was not the case. The smallest strikes were

TABLE 6.5

STRIKES BY CONTRACT STATUS, 1961–74

	% of Strikes with Given Contract Status				% of Workers Involved in Strikes with Given Contract Status			
	First Agree-ment	Re-nego-tiation	During Term	Other	First Agree-ment	Re-nego-tiation	During Term	Other
1961	15.2	45.1	32.2	1.7	2.5	70.2	26.0	0.5
1962	16.8	48.3	29.8	2.5	4.1	64.6	28.3	2.5
1963	18.1	43.4	35.8	1.9	7.0	81.7	11.1	0.2
1964	17.7	44.1	36.1	1.6	6.5	83.2	9.9	0.3
1965	17.5	45.5	34.7	1.7	7.9	80.0	11.6	0.2
1966	17.1	44.1	36.5	2.0	7.5	79.8	12.3	0.4
1967	16.0	46.9	33.9	2.7	4.8	87.6	7.3	0.3
1968	15.0	47.7	34.2	2.5	4.9	80.0	14.6	0.5
1969	14.2	48.6	34.4	2.2	5.0	59.4	34.7	0.8
1970	12.8	51.3	33.1	1.6	4.7	89.4	5.6	0.1
1971	12.7	51.0	33.4	2.0	3.7	90.5	5.5	0.2
1972	13.4	43.5	39.8	2.6	7.4	83.0	8.7	0.6
1973	12.0	52.8	33.9	1.3	3.1	66.3	30.3	0.3
1974	9.9	60.8	27.4	2.0	3.7	75.3	19.2	1.8

NOTE

Percentages in each year do not add to 100 because of the exclusion of the 'insufficient information' category; this generally accounted for less than 1% of strikes and 0.1% of workers involved.

First agreement includes union recognition strikes.

Other includes cases where there was no contract.

in the 'first agreement' category, although they might be expected to be large battles on 'fundamental' matters. As shown below, this is partly explained by the industrial distribution of first agreement strikes, but it is significant in indicating that recognition strikes were small (and probably limited to a few marginal sectors), whereas strikes during the term of contracts were not minor disturbances but were as large as strikes over the re-negotiation of contracts.

The breakdown of strikes by contract status and issue is given in Table 6.7. As would be expected, most strikes in the 'first agreement' category were over union organization and security, while those over the re-negotiation of a contract were heavily concentrated on 'wages, hours and other contractual matters'. More interesting is the tendency for strikes during the term of agreements to be focused on matters relating to the work place, with particular emphasis being given to 'job security and plant administration'. It is unfortunate that further sub-

TABLE 6.6

STRIKES BY CONTRACT STATUS AND SIZE, 1961–72

	% of Strikes in Each Size Class				% of Workers Involved in Strikes in Each Size Class			
	First Agree-ment	Re-nego-tiation	During Term	Other	First Agree-ment	Re-nego-tiation	During Term	Other
6–19 workers	32.3	10.2	14.5	31.3	3.7	0.2	0.5	2.0
20–	46.4	37.6	31.6	40.7	18.3	2.9	4.2	9.6
100–	13.2	24.0	23.4	13.3	17.2	5.7	10.0	10.9
250–	4.8	12.6	15.3	7.7	13.8	6.5	14.1	14.6
500–	1.8	7.5	8.2	4.7	10.6	7.7	14.9	17.0
1000–	1.3	6.3	6.4	2.2	18.2	18.7	33.2	20.4
5000–	0.1	0.9	0.4	0	5.3	9.1	7.3	0
10000–	0.1	0.8	0.3	0.2	12.9	49.3	15.9	25.5
All	100	100	100	100	100	100	100	100

TABLE 6.7

STRIKES BY CONTRACT STATUS AND ISSUE, 1961–72

	% of Strikes with Given Issue				% of Workers Involved in Strikes with Given Issue			
	First Agree-ment	Re-nego-tiation	During Term	Other	First Agree-ment	Re-nego-tiation	During Term	Other
Wages, hours and other contractual matters	31.1	89.6	10.8	60.6	39.1	81.2	13.7	61.1
Union organiz-ation and security	61.7	3.6	3.9	6.3	51.5	5.3	2.4	3.7
Job security, plant ad-ministration	5.1	5.1	49.9	24.6	4.5	12.4	63.5	26.6
Inter and intra union	1.5	0.2	27.7	4.4	4.3	0.3	13.5	4.1
Other work conditions	0.6	1.5	7.8	4.2	0.6	0.8	6.9	4.5
All	100	100	100	100	100	100	100	100

divisions by the duration of strikes are not available, but it is likely that strikes 'during term and lasting three days or less' were concentrated on work place matters at least as heavily as all strikes during the term of an agreement. Thus unofficial strikes fit the radical model in being rank and file actions concentrated on work place issues, but it does not follow that a 'rank and file revolt' was occurring; to assess this question, other dimensions of the revolt must be considered.

In addition to unofficial strikes, Herding lists seven elements in the 'labor revolt'.[14] These are: violations of plant discipline and absenteeism; challenges to union leaders in elections; contract rejection by the rank and file; disaffiliation from national unions; de-certifications of a union as the bargaining agent for a group of workers; de-authorization of obligatory union membership agreements; and the re-emergence of political strikes. This is an impressive list, but the elements are not of equal significance for Herding's case. Thus disaffiliation, de-certification and de-authorization can all be seen as reflecting the 'crisis of the labor movement'[15] rather than a rise in rank and file militancy. They indicate a dissatisfaction with national unions and do not necessarily imply a growth of militancy. Indeed, a desire to leave a national union may well indicate the lack of class solidarity rather than the reverse. This is apart from questions of the extent to which there has been an increase in disaffiliations and so on.

Similarly, contract rejection is only an indirect index of militancy. It indicates the extent to which proposals for a new contract made by union leaders are rejected by the members. But there is considerable disagreement as to the significance of this. Simkin[16] argues that in most cases contract rejection reflects the repudiation of the union leaders; he shows that the rate of rejection was rising from 1964 to 1967. But these figures relate, as Simkin stresses, only to cases in which Federal mediation was involved; they were thus the most difficult to solve and rejection was less significant among negotiations in general. In 62 per cent of cases, no strike followed rejection: in the majority of cases, a

14. Herding, op. cit., pp. 257–84.
15. Writers on the 'crisis' argued that unions were losing their direction and that members were leaving out of apathy and disillusionment rather than because unions were not militant enough. See A. A. Blum, 'Labor at the Crossroads', *Harvard Business Review*, XLII, no. 4, p. 6–19, 172 (1964); S. Barkin, 'A New Agenda for Labor', *Fortune*, LXII, no. 5, pp. 249–55 (1960); symposium on 'The Crisis in the Labor Movement', *Annals of the American Academy of Political and Social Science*, no. 350, pp. 1–94 (1963); P. E. Sultan, *The Disenchanted Unionist* (New York: Harper and Row, 1963).
16. W. E. Simkin, 'Refusals to Ratify Contracts', *Industrial and Labor Relations Review*, XXI, pp. 518–40 (1968), esp. pp. 520–21, 528.

tentative agreement was rejected but a subsequent one accepted. Summers[17] has pointed out that contract rejection is not as simple as it may seem. Union negotiators may pretend to agree with the employer and then urge rejection; submission of the terms to the membership is here merely a bargaining ploy to support further demands. Or demands may be submitted to the members only at the employer's insistence; here, rejection is a statement of confidence in the union leaders' refusal of the employer's offer. These and other problems make the use of the overall rate of rejection very difficult. Summers's conclusions are supported by a study by Burke and Rubin.[18] They found that rejection was less widespread than is often thought and that it was often due to a failure of communication within a union; the members are not properly informed of the conditions of an agreement and express their discontent by voting against the leadership.

Herding also emphasizes direct challenges to a union's leadership through the procedures for the election of new officers. The two most well-known instances are the unseating of the presidents of the Steel Workers' and Mine Workers' unions in 1965 and 1973. Rank and file discontent with union policy seems to have been important in this. For example, after a series of strikes in the 1950s, McDonald, the Steel Workers' leader, began a policy of active co-operation with the employers which involved relatively low wage settlements. It is not surprising that this encouraged discontent with the centralized nature of the union's bargaining which, as noted in the previous chapter, has been characteristic of it since the 1930s. But, as Edelstein and Warner point out, the unseating of an incumbent union president usually depends on the presence of a highly-placed opposition group with considerable power in the union.[19] Thus the defeat of a union's leaders need not reflect rank and file dissatisfaction.

17. C. W. Summers, 'Ratification of Agreements', *Frontiers of Collective Bargaining*, ed. J. T. Dunlop and N. W. Chamberlain (New York: Harper and Row, 1967), pp. 75–102.
18. D. R. Burke and L. Rubin, 'Is Contract Rejection a Major Collective Bargaining Problem?', *Industrial and Labor Relations Review*, XXVI, pp. 820–33 (1973), esp. pp. 826–7, 833.
19. J. D. Edelstein and M. Warner, *Comparative Union Democracy* (London: Allen and Unwin, 1975), p. 319; see pp. 319–30 for discussion of the Steel and Mine Workers' and other cases. See also J. Herling, *Right to Challenge: People and Power in the Steelworkers' Union* (New York: Harper and Row, 1972); L. Ulman, *The Government of the Steel Workers' Union* (New York: Wiley, 1962); T. O'Hanlon, 'Anarchy Threatens the Kingdom of Coal', *Fortune*, LXXXIII, no. 1, pp. 78–85 (1971); and references in note 3, above.

Herding's final two elements are the political strike and the violation of plant discipline. He cites strikes in plants producing arms for the Vietnam war after the assassination of Senator Kennedy as an example of the former; but such cases are hardly sufficient to establish that a general trend to politically-motivated action was occurring. One can point to the contrasting case of attacks on anti-war demonstrators by building workers to suggest that political involvement need not go in one direction.[20] On plant discipline, Herding notes that it is hard to analyse such aspects of the labour revolt and uses wildcat strikes as an index of the infraction of discipline. Thus attention returns to un-official disputes as an index of rank and file protest.

Although the evidence for each of Herding's factors does not demon-strate that large-scale rank and file action was occurring, taken together they suggest an increase in protest. Several other writers have pointed to an increase in unrest. For example: 'At the work place, class struggle has been as intense and serious in the U.S. setting as in any other . . . but its focus has always been local.'[21] As in the 1930s, action at the level of the work place did not become generalized. And, as Flanagan *et al.* argue, the extent of job dissatisfaction has been exaggerated and the link between feelings of discontent and protest behaviour assumed rather than demonstrated; job discontent does not provide much of the explanation for the increase in strike activity.[22] Radicals do not, of course, place much weight on job satisfaction surveys, but it is then necessary to find some other source of the revolt, and to explain why it remained a limited and disconnected movement.

It is reasonable to see the revolt as, in the first instance, a reaction to the policies of union leaders. Disputes based on the immediate work place can be resolved only in day-to-day struggles with employers and are not amenable to solution through collective bargaining. The rank and file rebellion of the 1960s can thus be attributed to union leaders' earlier concentration on formal bargaining, together with increasing managerial pressure on work standards as the 'hard line' took effect. As

20. H. Bigart, 'Hard-hats Attack Demonstrators', *American Labor since the New Deal*, ed. M. Dubofsky (Chicago: Quadrangle Books, 1971), pp. 302–6.
21. S. Rosen, 'The United States: A Time for Re-assessment', *Worker Militancy and its Consequences, 1965–75*, ed. S. Barkin (New York: Praeger, 1975), pp. 333–63, at p. 353. See also P. Henle, 'Organized Labor and the New Militants', *Monthly Labor Review*, XCII, no. 7, pp. 20–25 (1969).
22. R. J. Flanagan, G. Strauss and L. Ulman, 'Worker Discontent and Work Place Behavior', *Industrial Relations*, XIII, no. 2, pp. 101–23 (1974). For similar conclusions, see H. Wool, 'What's Wrong with Work in America? – a Review Essay', *Monthly Labor Review*, XCVI, no. 1, pp. 38–44 (1973).

Barbash says, the revolt in the early 1960s was a defensive reaction to managerial pressure, when it was realized that official union channels could not deal with work-based matters. It then adopted a more aggressive character, possibly stimulated by the rapid economic growth of the mid-sixties.[23] But as inflation developed, demands for wage increases became more important (see Table 2.5, p. 37 for the trends in strike issues). Union leaders are much more able and willing to press for wage increases than to deal with matters of job control. Hence pressure on wages led workers to operate through their union leaders; in turn, this enabled the leaders to adapt to the 'challenge from below' and disarm the potential threat to their position. Although the significance of the revolt should not be dismissed, it was a limited and partial response to work-based problems; problems connected with real wages served to restrict its development.

Two more general factors which have been cited as sources of unrest must also be mentioned. Firstly there is the 'generational conflict'. It is said that the new generation of young workers is no longer willing to submit to industrial discipline or to emulate its elders in the pursuit of material reward.[24] Young workers concentrate on intrinsically satisfying work and are prepared to forego high earnings to pursue their non-work interests. This argument can be rapidly dealt with; Herding is correct in suggesting that it is, at best, of secondary importance to the explanation of strike trends.[25] 'Generational conflict' is much too vague a concept to be useful; the evidence for its presence is not very substantial; and its applicability to industrial conflict unclear. Strikes involved workers in many different positions and cannot be seen as reflecting only or largely the discontents of the young.

More important is the possibility that technical change during the

23. Barbash, 'The Causes of Rank-and-File Unrest', op. cit., p. 53.
24. See *Work in America* (Report of a Special Task Force to the Secretary of Health, Education and Welfare; Cambridge, Mass.: M.I.T. Press, 1973), esp. pp. 43–51; B. Kreman, 'No Pride in this Dust', *The World of the Blue-Collar Worker*, ed. I. Howe (New York: Quadrangle Books, 1972), pp. 11–22. On the more general problem of 'blue-collar blues' see H. L. Sheppard and N. Q. Herrick, *Where Have All the Robots Gone?* (New York: Free Press, 1972); S. A. Levitan (ed.), *Blue-collar Workers* (New York: McGraw-Hill, 1971); J. Gooding, 'Blue-collar Blues on the Assembly Line', *Fortune*, LXXXII, no. 1, pp. 69–71, 112–17 (1970). As with job dissatisfaction, there are obvious problems with explaining strike trends by some general factor of blue-collar discontent. In particular, changes in discontent cannot explain changes in strike rates; and other processes have to be involved before individual discontent can be translated into collective action.
25. Herding, op. cit., p. 296.

fifties and sixties was putting increasing pressure on work conditions. In the early sixties, automation was widely cited as a cause of increasing industrial conflict; the challenge of automation was seen as important in the 1959 steel strike, the stoppage in New York newspapers in 1962–63, the lengthy work rules dispute on the railroads and in several other cases.[26] However, as Kennedy has suggested, automation may increase the possibility of conflict only up to a certain point, beyond which operations can be continued without the presence of production workers so that the power of the strike is much reduced.[27] He, like other writers, suggests that in sectors such as chemicals this point has already been reached. Thus there is no agreement whether, in the aggregate, automation will increase or reduce the amount of conflict.[28] It is also notable that the stress placed on automation declined during the sixties, but it can be seen as a background factor which in some cases exerted recognizable effects. Its present significance is *not* that it may have increased the potential for conflict in some industries and reduced it in others. It was one influence which helped to unsettle the relatively stable relations of the 1950s; it was a challenge to the system which brought work conditions and rules to the centre of attention and may have contributed to the rise in rank and file protests based on these aspects of day-to-day operations.

Technical change, possibly combined with a change in managerial policies, may have posed a background challenge to the institutionalized system. The direct challenge came from the rank and file, but this challenge had a limited scope; it indicated that workers were not pre-

26. See J. Stieber (ed.), *Employment Problems of Automation and Advanced Technology* (London: Macmillan, 1966); A. R. Weber, 'Collective Bargaining and the Challenge of Technological Change', *Industrial Relations: Challenges and Responses,* ed. J. H. G. Crispo (Toronto: University of Toronto Press, 1966), pp. 73–90; G. G. Somers, E. L. Cushman and N. Weinberg (ed.), *Adjusting to Technological Change* (New York: Harper and Row, 1963); C. C. Killingsworth, 'The Automation Story: Machines, Manpower and Jobs', *Jobs, Men and Machines,* ed. C. Markham (New York: Praeger, 1964), pp. 15–47. On work rules, see J. J. Kaufman, 'Logic and Meaning of Work Rules on the Railroads', and J. Stieber, 'Work Rules and Practices in Mass Production Industries', *Proceedings of the Fourteenth Annual Meeting of the Industrial Relations Research Association* (1961), pp. 378–88 and 399–412.

27. T. Kennedy, 'Freedom to Strike is in the Public Interest', *Harvard Business Review,* XLVIII, no. 4, pp. 41–57 (1970), at pp. 51–2.

28. Even in some traditionally conflict-prone industries, technical change was introduced peacefully. See, for example, P. T. Hartman, *Collective Bargaining and Productivity: The Longshore Mechanization Agreement* (Berkeley: University of California Press, 1969).

pared meekly to follow their union leaders in everything, but was not part of a self-conscious movement to establish job control. The system was able to survive because of the limited aims and extent of the challenge and because of its own resilience and ability to adapt to external pressure. The following section considers in more detail the interaction between challenge and response.

The Industrial Distribution of Activity

The distribution of strikes among selected industries for 1950–61 and 1962–72 is shown in Table 6.8. The table is roughly comparable with Tables 4.5 and 5.6 but differences of definition inevitably arise; for example, 'leather' replaces 'boots and shoes'. To facilitate comparison, the industries are listed in approximately the same order as in the other two tables; this explains the unconventional appearance of Table 6.8 with manufacturing and non-manufacturing industries not being separated. The most notable feature of the table is that the industries listed in the first part accounted for only 37 per cent of total non-agricultural employment. This was due, of course, to the expansion of the tertiary sector; services, trade and government included over half of total employment. Chapter 5 showed that strikes were important in the first two of these by the 1930s, but stoppages among government employees did not become significant until the 1960s. These workers are better described as 'public employees' since they include teachers, firemen and sanitation workers as well as government administrators. Their willingness to strike is one of the most marked recent changes in the pattern of activity. Just as the strikes in trade and services in the 1930s reflected a 'lagged response' to the growth of these sectors, so the government strikes of the sixties indicate that the strike movement was following, in a muted way, the distribution of employment in general.

Table 6.8 also shows the decline in the importance of steel strikes; there were no national stoppages in the 1960s on the scale of those of the fifties.[29] But there were no other marked changes apart from a rise in the proportions of workers involved and days lost accounted for by the transport industries.[30] This suggests that, except for the rise of

29. In the terms used by Ross, a cycle of strikes ended in the steel industry in 1959. Such shifts in strike activity cast doubt on the view that certain sectors are necessarily strike-prone. See Ross, op. cit., p. 67.

30. Much of this rise was due to increasing activity among East Coast longshoremen. See V. H. Jensen, *Strife on the Waterfront* (Ithaca: Cornell University Press, 1974). By contrast, the West Coast industry was largely peaceful.

TABLE 6.8

PROPORTION OF ALL STOPPAGES ACCOUNTED FOR BY EACH INDUSTRY, 1950–72

	1950–61 % of			Employment as % Total, 1960	1962–72 % of		
	N	W	D		N	W	D
Building	19.1	15.0	12.8	5.3	19.8	17.5	19.4
Clothing	3.6	1.5	0.9	2.3	2.0	0.8	0.7
Coal and mining	8.2	7.4	7.0	1.3	8.2	7.4	4.4
Food	4.4	3.6	2.8	3.3	4.5	3.1	2.8
Leather	1.2	0.7	0.4	0.7	0.6	0.4	0.3
Machinery:							
non-electrical	5.8	6.3	8.5	2.7	6.1	5.6	7.3
electrical	2.9	4.4	4.6	2.7	3.7	5.7	6.3
Metals:							
basic steel	2.3	10.5	19.1	1.7	2.4	2.5	2.6
other primary	3.4	3.0	3.6	0.6	2.1	2.2	3.2
fabricated	6.0	4.4	4.6	2.1	6.3	3.6	4.6
Printing and publishing	1.0	0.6	0.6	1.6	1.4	1.1	2.1
Stone, clay, glass	3.0	1.8	2.0	1.1	3.1	1.7	2.0
Textiles	1.9	1.7	2.3	1.7	0.9	0.6	0.5
Tobacco	0.1	—	—	0.2	0.1	0.2	0.2
Transport	7.2	10.7	7.4	7.4	6.1	20.5	13.2
Transport equip:							
motor vehicles	2.4	8.9	5.2	1.4	1.9	7.1	9.0
other	1.4	3.5	3.6	1.5	1.5	2.7	2.5
All above industries	73.9	84.0	85.4	37.6	70.7	83.7	81.1
Chemicals	2.2	1.3	1.5	1.5	2.7	1.4	2.4
Lumber	2.0	1.2	2.2	1.2	1.4	0.6	1.0
Rubber	2.2	4.4	2.2	0.7	1.9	1.9	2.6
Services	3.5	0.8	0.8	18.6	3.9	1.4	1.5
Trade	8.4	2.8	2.9	21.0	8.7	3.1	3.1
Government	0.6	0.3	0.1	15.4	4.5	5.5	2.5
All above industries	92.9	94.9	95.2	95.9	93.7	96.4	94.3
All industries	100	100	100	100	100	100	100

strikes in the public sector, the industrial distribution remained fairly constant; any rise in rank and file protest is not revealed in a sudden shift in the industrial distribution.

Tables 6.9 and 6.10 continue the comparison between 1950–61 and 1962–72. As the figures for 'all industries' show, strike frequency and worker involvement fell and duration rose only slightly. This indicates that, although activity was rising during the '60s, activity in this period, taken as a whole, was not very different from that in the past. The reason why the frequency and worker involvement figures do not show an increase is that the earlier period includes several years of high strike activity; 1959 was surpassed only by 1946 in the total number of days lost, and activity was high in several sectors in the early 1950s.

Strikes of Public Employees

Tables 6.9 and 6.10 confirm the rise in activity in the public sector. There were very large increases in strike frequency and worker involvement; and the size and duration of disputes both more than doubled. Since this sector was new to strikes on a large scale it is interesting that stoppages became more 'sophisticated',[31] to use the term employed in Chapter 4. A growth in sophistication is not limited to the 'modernization' of strikes during early industrialization, but can occur whenever a group of workers begins to use the strike weapon systematically.

Stieber has provided a useful survey of government employees' strike activity.[32] Between 1958 and 1970, 92 per cent of the strikes were at the local level, 7 per cent were among state employees and 1 per cent among Federal workers. In 1965–69 the distribution by occupation of strikes by workers other than teachers indicated that stoppages were concentrated among sanitation, sewage and street maintenance workers, although there were several strikes by police, fire and hospital workers. Thus the majority of stoppages were among manual workers at the local level and there is little reason to treat them as different from those in the private sector. Only the fact of working in sectors defined as 'public' marks these workers off from employees in private industry.[33]

31. That is, they became larger, longer and more frequent.
32. J. Stieber, *Public Employee Unionism* (Washington, D.C.: Brookings Institute, 1973), esp. pp. 161–71. See also S. C. White, 'Work Stoppages of Government Employees', *Monthly Labor Review*, XCII, no. 12, pp. 29–34 (1969); W. A. Wildman, 'Collective Action by Public School Teachers', *Industrial and Labor Relations Review*, XVIII, pp. 3–19 (1964); W. S. Fox and M. H. Wince, 'The Structure and Determinants of Occupational Militancy among Public School Teachers', *Industrial and Labor Relations Review*, XXX, pp. 47–58 (1976).
33. J. F. Burton, 'Can Public Employees be Given the Right to Strike?', *Proceedings of the Spring Meeting of the Industrial Relations Research Association* (1970), pp. 472–8; J. Stieber, 'Collective Bargaining in the Public Sector', *Challenges to Collective Bargaining*, ed. L. Ulman (Englewood Cliffs: Prentice-Hall, 1967), pp. 65–88.

TABLE 6.9

STRIKE INDICES, BY INDUSTRY, 1950–61

	N/E	W/E	W/N	D/W
Building	285	113	395	13.0
Clothing	138	29.8	215	8.9
Coal and mining	414	190	458	14.5
Food	162	68.1	420	11.8
Leather	151	45.0	298	9.1
Machinery: non-electrical	206	112	544	20.5
electrical	145	111	764	15.8
Metals: basic steel	132	307	2334	27.6
other primary	442	189	427	19.2
fabricated	288	107	373	15.9
Printing and publishing	76.0	21.5	283	15.4
Stone, clay, glass	276	82.5	299	16.9
Textiles	77.6	35.1	452	21.4
Tobacco	35.0	9.7	278	16.2
Transport	71.7	53.5	746	10.5
Transport equip: motor vehicles	162	292	1798	8.9
other	83.9	113	1346	15.9
Chemicals	173	50.7	293	17.1
Lumber	129	38.4	299	28.0
Rubber	417	427	1024	7.5
Services	17.3	2.1	120	15.4
Trade	31.9	5.3	166	16.0
Government	3.6	0.8	224	3.9
All industries	80.6	40.5	503	15.3

NOTE
N/E = number of strikes per million employees. W/E = number of workers involved per thousand employees. W/N = number of workers involved per strike. D/W = number of days lost per worker involved.

The reasons for the increase of activity can best be understood by first considering why there was such a low level of strikes before the 1960s. Stoppages by public employees were generally illegal and the right to join a union severely restricted. Many unions were opposed to the use of strikes, for reasons of professional status, as was the case with teachers' and nurses' unions, or because of the special position of the workers they represented (police federations and the Association of Fire Fighters). Although strikes remain widely illegal, the government's attitude has changed. At the Federal level, an order of 1962 allowed workers to organize and, locally, the recognition of collective bargaining as an appropriate means to deal with public employees became more accepted. Union attitudes also changed, with teachers' unions, in

TABLE 6.10

STRIKE INDICES, BY INDUSTRY, 1962–72

	N/E	W/E	W/N	D/W
Building	282	117	414	17.9
Clothing	77.2	14.1	183	14.5
Coal and mining	596	254	426	9.6
Food	173	56.7	328	14.6
Leather	90.7	31.5	347	10.5
Machinery: non-electrical	227	97.7	430	21.1
electrical	141	102	721	17.7
Metals: basic steel	161	78.5	486	16.6
other primary	287	143	500	23.8
fabricated	285	77.0	270	20.8
Printing and publishing	99.0	36.5	368	31.4
Stone, clay, glass	284	71.5	252	19.7
Textiles	51.2	16.3	318	13.2
Tobacco	34.0	48.0	1423	17.4
Transport	66.1	104	1576	10.4
Transport equip: motor vehicles	132	237	1788	20.6
other	67.5	89.6	838	15.0
Chemicals	205	54.6	254	26.8
Lumber	119	26.2	219	25.1
Rubber	224	103	460	22.5
Services	13.2	2.2	166	17.2
Trade	29.1	4.8	166	16.3
Government	18.1	10.5	577	7.3
All industries	70.2	33.1	471	16.2

NOTE
Indices are as defined in Table 6.9.

particular, accepting the need to use the strike to obtain their ends.[34] As one would expect, government strikes were over union recognition more often than was the case nationally and the proportion of unorganized stoppages was also high; the latter feature can be explained, as Stieber says, by the newness of union organization, the lack of contact between workers wanting to be organized and the unions, and the absence of legal protection for bargaining in many sectors.[35]

Thus during the 1960s several facilitating factors came into operation. For the manual workers these are sufficient to explain the rise in

34. See M. H. Moskow, *Teachers and Unions* (Philadelphia: University of Pennsylvania Wharton School of Finance and Commerce, 1966); J. Seidman, 'Nurses and Collective Bargaining', *Industrial and Labor Relations Review*, XXIII, pp. 335–51 (1970); and refs in notes 32 and 33, above.
35. Stieber, *Public Employee Unionism*, op. cit., p. 171.

strike activity, since there is nothing about them to set them apart from other manual groups. For non-manual employees matters are more complex. The standard 'sociological' argument about such workers is of course that aspects of their social position inhibit feelings of class solidarity and reduce the willingness to join unions and strike.[36] The details of this cannot be considered here, but it is worthwhile pointing out that it is unlikely that the social position of teachers changed so rapidly that the rise in strike activity can be accounted for. Apart from the enabling factors of changes in governmental attitudes, the rise in prices in the 1960s seems to have been important. A rash of teachers' strikes at the end of the 1940s has been related to the rapid inflation of the period[37] and it is certainly plausible that rising prices, combined with the high visibility of pay settlements in the private sector, led to dissatisfaction among teachers in the sixties.

Public employee strikes as a whole fit the institutionalization model of rising conflict in a period when bargaining rights are being sought. Time will tell whether activity will decline as bargaining becomes established, but it seems unlikely that strikes will 'wither away'. Until the 1960s they were prevented from occurring; the establishment of bargaining is likely to give them a place in a system of negotiations, whereas previously they were outside the normal procedures for supporting a demand. The strikes represented a desire to achieve bargaining rights on a par with those in private industries and cannot be seen as part of a 'revolt' by the rank and file.

The Labour Revolt

As Tables 6.9 and 6.10 show, several sectors were not marked by a revolt, in that there was no overall rise in strike activity during the 1960s. In clothing, for example, activity continued to decline; as the more detailed figures in Table A.15 show, this was not a function of the periods chosen for comparison but a long-term trend. Similar trends were apparent in textiles and rubber. By contrast, construction, mining, and transport all showed large rises in worker involvement in the

36. On white-collar unionism in America, see E. M. Kassalow, 'White-collar Unionism in the U.S.', *White-collar Trade Unions*, ed. A. Sturmthal (Urbana, University of Illinois Press, 1966), pp. 305–64; A. A. Blum *et al., White-collar Workers* (New York: Random House, 1971). For criticism of the 'sociological' view see G. S. Bain, D. Coates and V. Ellis, *Social Stratification and Trade Unionism* (London: Heinemann, 1973); cf. R. Crompton, 'Approaches to the Study of White-collar Unionism', *Sociology*, X, pp. 407–26 (1976).

37. B. Yabroff and L. M. David, 'Collective Bargaining and Work Stoppages Involving Teachers', *Monthly Labor Review*, LXXVI, pp. 475–9 (1953).

1960s; and there were less marked increases in machinery and fabricated metals. But in many cases these rises were not great compared with post-war experience as a whole.

Particular attention must, however, be given to the steel and auto industries since it is here that the rank and file revolt is said to have been concentrated. In the former, the strike pattern fits this picture, with frequency rising slightly between the 1950s and 1960s and worker involvement falling; a concomitant of this was a sharp fall in the mean size of strikes. The number of days lost per striker fell between the late fifties and early sixties and then rose again. Although the great national strikes ended, strike activity at plant level remained high. In autos, frequency and worker involvement both fell between the two decades, and the recovery during the sixties was not particularly rapid; there was no strong trend in the size of strikes and loss per striker increased. This contrasts with the expectation from the picture of rank and file revolt that strikes will be short, small, and frequent expressions of work place discontent.

TABLE 6.11

STRIKES BY CONTRACT STATUS, SELECTED INDUSTRIES, 1961–72

	% of Strikes in each Industry with Given Contract Status				% of Workers Involved in Strikes with Given Contract Status in each Industry			
	First Agreement	Re-negotiation	During Term	Other	First Agreement	Re-negotiation	During Term	Other
All manufacturing	15.4	58.4	25.4	0.8	3.6	62.8	33.4	0.2
Building	7.0	34.6	57.2	1.1	1.4	79.6	18.6	0.4
Clothing	27.4	31.3	40.3	1.0	10.5	56.6	32.4	0.5
Coal and mining	3.0	7.2	89.3	0.4	1.3	19.2	79.4	0.1
Food	17.8	59.7	21.5	1.0	4.9	64.0	30.4	0.6
Metals: primary	9.5	53.6	36.6	0.3	2.7	52.0	45.2	0.1
Printing and publishing	25.0	61.6	12.9	0.4	4.0	86.2	9.7	—
Textiles	25.4	50.2	20.3	4.0	6.1	76.1	16.7	1.1
Transport equipment	12.4	47.6	39.6	0.4	1.6	67.3	31.0	0.1
Services	38.0	46.6	10.9	4.5	18.9	69.4	10.3	1.4
Government	27.5	37.2	12.7	22.6	32.9	37.1	18.9	11.1

Tables 6.11 and 6.12 enable the matter to be considered further; they give, respectively, the distribution of strikes by contract status and issue for ten selected industries, plus 'all manufacturing', for 1961–72.[38] Of the manufacturing industries, primary metals and transport equipment were particularly prone to stoppages during the term of agreements; and they had more strikes than average over matters of job security and plant administration. They were thus prone to unofficial actions based largely on the work place. On changes over time, Herding suggests that wildcats in autos and steel have not been increasing more rapidly than strikes in general, but that these industries have remained on a plateau while the rest of industry has been catching up with them.[39] As Table A.16 shows, the number of such strikes in these two industries fell while in all manufacturing it remained constant; thus there was a 'levelling down' rather than a 'levelling up'. For worker involvement, the proportion of strikes during the term of agreements fell in these two industries but rose elsewhere.

In 1973–74, in particular, there was a marked fall in the proportion of strikes during the term of agreements in all the sectors considered in Table A.16. Moreover, as Table A.17 shows, wages and contractual matters were becoming increasingly important. Thus, as argued above in relation to aggregate data, union leaders were able to re-assert control over strikes. In the sectors where the 'labor revolt' was concentrated, as well as in industry in general, there was a revolt in the mid-1960s[40] which declined subsequently as pressure on wages became more acute. This does not mean, of course, that auto and steel workers became satisfied with their leaders. Plant-level problems remained, but were overshadowed by other matters; despite possible cynicism about their leaders, workers were prepared to work through unions when this seemed the most practical course.

The increases in the overall level of strike activity in steel and autos were not particularly marked: the sectors of 'revolt' did not lead the strike movement as a whole. By contrast, in the building industry a high and increasing level of activity led to growing public concern during the

38. For more detailed data on four sectors, broken down into four sub-periods, see Tables A.16 and A.17, pp. 277–8.
39. Herding, op. cit., pp. 281–2.
40. There is some disagreement as to the precise timing of the revolt. Herding concentrates on the 1960s as a whole, whereas Aronowitz (op. cit., pp. 214–15) focuses on the period after 1967. The various indices of revolt are not closely correlated; for example, 'unofficial' strikes were most frequent in the early 1970s whereas opposition to union leaderships was probably most common in the mid-1960s.

TABLE 6.12

STRIKE ISSUES, SELECTED INDUSTRIES, 1961–72

	% of Strikes with Given Issue						% of Workers Involved in Strikes with Given Issue					
	(1)	(2)	(3)	(4)	(5)	(6)	(1)	(2)	(3)	(4)	(5)	(6)
All manufacturing	63.9	11.7	5.3	14.9	2.8	1.5	56.3	5.8	6.1	27.4	3.0	1.4
Building	36.4	11.6	2.2	8.4	0.9	40.5	66.2	13.2	2.5	5.8	0.5	11.9
Clothing	47.8	26.3	4.7	12.2	5.9	3.1	65.4	10.0	3.1	15.0	4.5	2.0
Coal and mining	14.2	3.5	11.6	54.6	8.8	7.4	23.5	3.9	8.8	47.4	5.4	10.9
Food	63.1	11.8	5.4	15.6	1.9	2.2	59.7	5.4	7.1	21.5	1.9	4.5
Metals: primary	60.4	6.4	5.8	23.6	3.0	0.8	51.1	3.8	8.0	32.4	3.1	1.7
Printing and publishing	59.6	18.9	7.0	11.0	2.0	1.5	68.0	7.5	12.8	8.8	1.8	1.1
Textiles	57.7	20.8	2.1	14.9	3.0	1.5	62.5	13.8	1.1	19.5	2.5	0.7
Transport equipment	50.8	8.7	5.5	30.6	2.7	1.6	32.5	3.2	5.8	55.7	2.3	0.5
Services	55.5	29.3	2.5	9.1	0.9	2.7	63.0	16.7	8.2	7.7	0.5	3.8
Government	65.3	15.3	2.6	14.1	1.6	1.1	81.0	6.3	0.9	9.5	1.5	0.7

NOTE

Issues are defined as follows:

(1) Wages, hours, and other contractual matters. (4) Plant administration.
(2) Union organization and security. (5) Other working conditions.
(3) Job security. (6) Inter and intra union.

1960s. Although strikes were concentrated in the 'during term' category of contract status, this cannot be taken as indicating a protest against union leaders: the industry has had a long history of action by craft groups over matters of immediate concern. The large number of jurisdictional disputes, revealed by Table 6.12, has been a constant feature of the industry.[41] Thus, an important contributor to the rise in aggregate levels of activity did not have a significant rank and file revolt.

The Auto Industry

Finally in this section, it is necessary to consider the auto industry in more detail, to examine the characteristics of the revolt more fully than

41. W. Haber, *Industrial Relations in the Building Industry* (Cambridge, Mass.: Harvard University Press, 1930), esp. p. 152; W. Haber and H. M. Levinson, *Labor Relations and Productivity in the Building Trades* (Ann Arbor: Bureau of Industrial Relations, University of Michigan, 1956).

is possible through statistical treatment. As Chapter 5 showed, the industry was one of the centres of the militancy of the 1930s. In the strikes of the immediate post-war period, the Auto Workers' union attempted to make matters of pricing and profits subjects for collective bargaining, but failed to break General Motors' determination not to give way.[42] Harbison and Dubin argued in 1947 that this pattern of conflict was not typical of the industry as a whole and suggested that 'constructive relations' were possible.[43] They compared General Motors with the Studebaker company and sought to explain the differences in their patterns of labour relations; the stability of relations in Studebaker was attributed to mutual trust between the two sides, the sharing of information and the exclusion of outsiders from the bargaining relationship. The writers argued that the constructive relations in Studebaker can be developed elsewhere.

As an argument that labour relations are not determined by technical or other conditions of an industry, this is a valuable contribution; but its position as a case study supporting the thesis that harmony can prevail given goodwill on both sides is much less certain. As the approach of Harbison and Dubin itself makes clear, and as Macdonald has subsequently pointed out, stable relations in Studebaker depended on the company's position at the periphery of the industry.[44] It was not one of the 'pattern-setting' firms and was able to follow the agreements reached elsewhere; domestic relations could thus continue peacefully. The company was noted for its loose production standards and this further reduced the potential for conflict, particularly when compared with General Motors, which had always sought to keep control of standards. 'Constructive relations' in autos seem to be a special case which is limited to the economic periphery of the industry; industrial peace rests on the lack of serious economic conflict and thus the case cannot be given more general application.

Despite the appearance that the union has a strong position in the industry, it has been convincingly argued that on all important matters

---

42. B. R. Morris, 'Industrial Relations in the Automobile Industry', *Labor in Postwar America,* ed. C. E. Warne *et al.* (New York: Remsen Press, 1949), pp. 399–417; I. Howe and B. J. Widick, *The U.A.W. and Walter Reuther* New York: Random House, 1949), pp. 126–48.
43. F. H. Harbison and R. Dubin, *Patterns of Union-Management Relations* (Chicago: Science Research Associates, 1947), esp. pp. 11, 36, 86–90, 203–20.
44. R. M. MacDonald, *Collective Bargaining in the Automobile Industry* (New Haven: Yale University Press, 1963), pp. 259–84, 361–3.

of principle it has been forced to give way to the companies.[45] Although it has made important breakthroughs on the economic front, notably in securing Supplementary Unemployment Benefits from Ford in 1955 and from the other companies subsequently, it has been unable to wrest from management any say in the planning of operations or the control of line speed. Particularly during the 1960s, the practice grew up of reaching a national settlement on economic issues and leaving questions of work conditions to be settled locally; this frequently led to local strikes.[46] These have been seen as part of the 'labor revolt' but it is not clear how far the union in fact condoned them; it claimed that local negotiations were part of its democratic tradition.[47] Nevertheless, the union's lack of concern with local demands and its treatment of them as marginal to the main negotiations is likely to have stimulated local discontent. The union has also been criticized for an increasingly bureaucratic stance and for becoming dominated by 'business' ideology while retaining the language of its earlier days.[48]

These tendencies came together in the 1970 strike at General Motors and were combined with matters of economic security. The 'cost of living escalator' clause, which had initially been granted by General Motors in 1948, had subsequently been weakened and the union demanded the restoration of unlimited cost of living increases, as well as a general wage rise and a provision for early retirement. The strike began in September and ended in December with agreement on the first two union demands and a compromise on early retirement. But, as Serrin puts it:

The strike was a political strike, a strike not to win agreement but to win ratification. General Motors would have signed the same agreement in September if the UAW had made it known that it was prepared to

---

45. Ibid., pp. 348–50; Herding, op. cit., pp. 121, 139–40; W. Serrin, *The Company and the Union* (New York: Vintage Books, 1974), esp. pp. 20, 157–68, 308–9.
46. '*As is usual* in the auto industry negotiations, agreement on a national economic settlement without a strike did not prevent strikes on local working conditions issues', 'Labor Month in Review', *Monthly Labor Review*, LXXXIV, no. 9 (1961), emphasis added.
47. On this tradition see J. Stieber, *Governing the U.A.W.* (New York: Wiley, 1962); J. Skeels, 'The Background of U.A.W. Factionalism', *Labor History*, II, pp. 158–81 (1961).
48. Serrin, op. cit., pp. 144–8; B. J. Widick, *Labor Today* (Boston: Houghton Mifflin, 1964), pp. 181–206.

settle. But Woodcock is unsure whether the final settlement could have been ratified without a strike.[49]

An apparent victory was in fact a less clear gain than it seemed and local demands remained outside the national bargaining arena.

In 1972 came the strike at Lordstown, Ohio, which has been important for radical writers and which must therefore be considered here.[50] The plant had been custom-built and began to recruit workers in 1966, but production never reached company expectations. The strike was the culmination of several years of disputes between workers and management over the speed of operations and plant discipline, and has been seen as part of a revolt of young workers against the conditions of work in the auto plants and the imposition of rules of behaviour by management. For radicals, this and the growing dissatisfaction of black workers with the U.A.W. indicate the development of a militant spirit among auto operatives.[51] But too much weight has been placed on a few incidents of this type, and it has not been shown that the reaction against the work place has grown into a more self-conscious movement designed to gain control of the work process. Indeed, the evidence for a lack of commitment to monotonous work among the young suggests that they would be very unlikely to develop such a movement. This, plus the greater degree of flexibility of the U.A.W. compared with other unions, has meant that the union's leadership has not been subjected to direct challenges of the membership like those which occurred elsewhere.

The case of autos indicates that a significant strand of rank and file protest can exist without significantly altering the union's approach to bargaining or creating a movement of its own. One must not belittle the discontents of the workers or the extent to which a protest movement

49. Serrin, op. cit., pp. 298–9. See also B. J. Widick, 'Black City, Black Unions', *The World of the Blue-Collar Worker,* ed. Howe, op. cit., pp. 120–32, esp. p. 126.

50. Aronowitz, op. cit., pp. 21–50; B. Garson, 'A Strike for Humanism', *American Labor Radicalism,* ed. S. Lynd (New York: Wiley, 1973), pp. 203–13; K. Weller, *The Lordstown Struggle and the Crisis in Real Production* (London: Solidarity Pamphlet no. 45, n.d.). See also J. Child, 'Lordstown Revisited: Whatever Happened to Those Blue-Collar Blues?', University of Aston Management Centre Working Paper no. 104 (Birmingham: University of Aston, August 1978). Child argues that the revolt of Lordstown cannot be explained by 'blue-collar blues' and points out that, since 1973, the plant has been remarkably peaceful.

51. On black workers in Detroit, see J. A. Geschwender, *Class, Race and Worker Insurgency* (Cambridge: Cambridge University Press, 1977): the growth and decline of the League of Revolutionary Black Workers have close parallels with the development of the labour revolt in general.

grew up in the 1960s. But the evidence considered in this and the previous section suggests that the growth of protest was not as marked as radical writers imply and that the rank and file revolt was strictly limited to matters connected with the work place. The move towards economic bargaining strikes also suggests that workers were not prepared to forego wage increases to improve their work lives. Although they were prepared to repudiate their union leaders, this cannot be seen as a simple rejection of all that the national unions can offer. Radical writers such as Hyman stress the dual role of unions in providing a channel for protest and a means of controlling the protest which has been encouraged.[52] The protests of the sixties were a reaction against the latter function and did not necessarily mean that the unions' policies as a whole were being replaced by a more radical alternative.

Explaining Differences Between Industries

Industries differ on a wide variety of characteristics, such as technology, wage levels, bargaining arrangements, and trade union density. There has been a growing interest recently in the use of these variables to explain differences in strike rates.[53] For present purposes, the importance of this form of analysis lies in its relationship to the time-series analyses presented earlier. If the occurrence of strikes is related to economic conditions over time, it is naturally of interest to see whether a similar relationship holds between industries. And, in terms of the wider concerns of the present study, the distinction between 'institutionalized' and 'non-institutionalized' settings of industrial conflict needs to be considered against cross-sectional data: do industries characterized by the two settings differ in their levels of strike activity or the relationship between structural variables and strike rates?

The level of analysis which can be employed for inter-industry comparisons is highly aggregative, and there are obvious problems with interpreting the link between, say, union density and strike activity when whole industries are compared. General problems of interpreta-

52. R. Hyman, *Strikes* (London: Fontana-Collins, 1972), pp. 75–82.
53. See, for example, D. Britt and O. R. Galle, 'Structural Antecedents of the Shape of Strikes: A Comparative Analysis', *American Sociological Review*, XXXIX, pp. 642–51 (1974); J. Shorey, 'An Inter-Industry Analysis of Strike Frequency', *Economica*, XLIII, pp. 349–65 (1976); K. Holden, 'A Cross-Section Study of the Relationship between Strikes and Market Structure in the United Kingdom', *Journal of Economic Studies*, n.s. V, no. 1, pp. 37–49 (1978).

tion are considered elsewhere;[54] for present purposes it is sufficient to note that relationships can be explored in a general way, although findings at this level of aggregation must be treated with considerable caution.

Correlational Analysis

The simplest way of describing the links between strike activity and structural variables is to give the correlation coefficients between each index of activity and each structural variable. This is done in Table 6.13, for three measures of strikes across 17 industries.[55] The variables measuring the levels of wages and union density require no special comment, but the other independent variables need explanation. The profit rate and the four-firm concentration ratio reflect the economic organization of an industry; the former is a rough measure of 'employer well-being' and the latter an index of the concentration of productive capacity in a few firms. The next set of variables measures the bargaining structure of an industry. 'Strike ban %' refers to the proportion of collective agreements which include a clause banning strikes during their term; 'workers with strike ban' is the proportion of all workers under agreements who are covered by contracts including a strike ban. The next three measures reflect the coverage of contracts; 'X' is the proportion of all contracts limited to one plant; 'Y' the proportion limited to one employer but covering more than one plant; and 'Z' is the proportion covering more than one employer. Hence 'X plus Y' is the proportion limited to one employer and 'Y plus Z' the proportion covering more than one plant. The remaining variables measure the structure of an industry. Establishment size is already familiar. 'E_n/E_p' is the ratio of non-production to production workers. The former are those employees not directly concerned with productive operations; they have become important in several industries and the ratio is one index of the extent of technical advance in an industry. The final six variables are taken from a listing of industries' characteristics given by

54. P. K. Edwards, 'The Cross-Sectional Analysis of Strike Activity: Some American Evidence', Discussion Paper (Coventry: Industrial Relations Research Unit, Warwick University, June 1980).

55. Except where otherwise stated, all the results of this section relate to these 17 'two-digit' manufacturing industries for the period 1955–69. This spread of years was chosen for the discussion of collective bargaining coverage, but it is unlikely that taking a different period would significantly alter the results. The discussion is restricted to manufacturing because of the lack of comparable data on all series for non-manufacturing. The (reasonable) assumption is thus being made that manufacturing can be treated as distinct from other industries.

TABLE 6.13

CORRELATION COEFFICIENTS, 17 MANUFACTURING INDUSTRIES, 1955–69

	N/E	D/E	W/N
Wage level (H)	0.54	0.48	0.25
Union density (T/E)	0.50	0.33	0.23
Profit rate	−0.24	0.07	0.26
4-firm concentration ratio (C.R.)	0.04	0.38	0.72
Strike ban %	0.29	0.13	−0.14
Workers with strike ban	0.24	−0.24	−0.28
% workers in single-plant bargaining units: X	0.11	0.24	−0.03
% workers in one-firm, many-plant units: Y	0.45	0.68	0.65
% workers in multi-employer units: Z	−0.35	−0.62	−0.46
X plus Y	0.41	0.65	0.50
Y plus Z	0.03	−0.12	0.11
Establishment size	−0.22	0.19	0.89
E_n/E_p	−0.07	0.23	0.10
Score heavy-light	−0.47	−0.33	−0.01
Process	−0.18	0.05	0.15
Assembly	−0.19	−0.37	−0.01
Mixed process and assembly	0.42	0.37	−0.16
Rank on multiplant operations	−0.14	0.22	0.68
Rank on growth	0.42	0.66	0.27
Rank on flux	0.61	0.58	0.37

NOTE

For explanation of variables, see text. To be significantly different from zero, coefficients must attain the values shown below:

	Significance level:	5%	1%
2-tailed test		0.48	0.61
1-tailed test		0.41	0.56

Florence.[56] The 'heavy-light score' is a dummy variable with a value of 1 for industries such as primary metals dominated by 'heavy' operations, going up to 4 for light industry. Similarly the 'assembly', 'process' and 'mixed' variables are dummies reflecting the category into which most of an industry's operations fall. Finally, the last three variables give the ranking of an industry on dimensions of: the interdependence between plants; the rate of growth of output; and the variability of production.

In most cases, the expected link with strike activity is clear. Thus a high ratio of non-production to production workers might be expected to reduce activity, for reasons which include the ability of staff workers

56. P. S. Florence, *Economics and Sociology of Industry* (2nd edn; London: C. A. Watts, 1969), pp. 268–9.

to operate plants during a strike; such arguments have been advanced for the chemicals and other industries. A high ranking on the 'flux' variable indicates that an industry was prone to fluctuations in production; the resulting uncertainties might be expected to increase strike activity. And assembly-line production would be expected to be more strike-prone than that based on process operations.

The positive correlations with the 'flux' variable indicate that the expectations regarding it were fulfilled, but there was a negative association with the 'assembly' variable and no clear link with the E_n/E_p measure. The fastest growing industries had the highest strike rates, which accords with expectations since in declining industries the power of workers to wrest concessions from the employer is weakened. Similarly, it is not surprising that strikes were concentrated at the 'heavy' end of the heavy-light continuum. And the very high association between plant size and the size of strikes was also to be expected.

When variables measuring bargaining structure are considered, the important distinction seems to be between one-employer and multi-employer units. It might be thought that stoppages will be particularly frequent where bargaining is limited to single plants, since several individual disputes will occur whereas only one strike need be called where bargaining is more centralized. But both the 'X' and the 'Y plus Z' variables had lower levels of association with strike frequency than the 'X plus Y' index. No significant associations were observed between the 'strike ban' measures and strike activity, but the tendency was for stoppages to be smaller and more frequent the greater the proportion of agreements banning strikes. This is consistent with an attempt by management to deal with these small strikes by persuading the union to ban them. In other words, the presence of small and frequent strikes may have been the cause of the implementation of these agreements, but in many cases they had been in operation for a long time and had not solved the 'problem' of frequent disputes.

Of the remaining variables in Table 6.13, there was a slight but non-significant tendency for a high profit rate to be associated with large but infrequent strikes. The degree of concentration of ownership did not affect frequency but had a strong direct link with size. High levels of wages and union density seem to have encouraged strike activity, although the association was not as strong as one might have expected.

Regression Models
These correlational findings have indicated the direction and strength of the association between indices of strike activity and several independent variables considered in isolation. It is now necessary to consider

the joint impact of several variables, using regression analysis. Several combinations of variables might be employed and, in the current state of knowledge about the determinants of inter-industry differences in activity, it is hard to choose between various 'models'. The original strategy[57] was to consider several models in turn. One included measures of the technical structure of industries, another indices of bargaining coverage and a third reflected the nature of contract provisions. The analysis of separate models was designed to avoid the problem of the arbitrary selection of independent variables. Moreover, as has been observed repeatedly, there is no reason why several models cannot perform equally well. One must avoid the tendency to put forward one preferred model and suggest that it is the only one which 'explains' strike activity.

The results of the operation of the various models may be summarized briefly here. The 'technical structure' model, using such variables as establishment size, 'heavy-light score' and rankings of 'growth' and 'flux', gave moderately satisfactory results. As one might expect, there was a tendency for a high instability of operations, as measured by the 'flux' variable, to be associated with high strike frequency. Similarly, strike activity was greatest in sectors at the 'heavy' end of the 'heavy-light' dimension. The 'bargaining coverage' model also achieved only modest results. The chief finding was that, in line with the results of the correlational analysis, the proportion of contracts covering one employer (X plus Y) was the most important discriminator between industries on strike frequency; it performed better than the proportion of workers under single-plant agreements (X) and the proportion in multi-plant agreements (Y plus Z). The 'contract provisions' model indicated quite a strong tendency for the proportion of agreements banning strikes to be directly associated with strike frequency. As noted above, this is in contrast to the 'obvious' expectation that agreements banning strikes will reduce strike activity. Finally, measures of the concentration ratio and the profit rate were, in an 'employer well-being model', not significantly related to strike frequency or the number of days lost per worker involved.

Some of the most interesting results from combining aspects of these models are given in Table 6.14. Comparison of the first two equations indicates that predicting to the logarithm of strike frequency, rather than to frequency itself, considerably improves the results. Thus, a

57. P. K. Edwards, 'Strikes in the United States, 1881–1972' (D.Phil, thesis, University of Oxford, 1977), pp. 377–85 and tables 7–14 to 7–19.

TABLE 6.14

REGRESSION RESULTS, 17 INDUSTRIES (1955–69)

Dependent Variable	Independent Variables							R^2	F
	H	T/E	Strike Ban %	X	Y	Estab. Size	Heavy-light Score		
N/E	Pos	Pos	Pos			Neg		0.32	2.91
	NS	NS	NS			NS			NS
Log N/E	Pos	Pos	Pos			Neg		0.65	8.33
	NS	NS	1%			1%			1%
Log N/E		Pos		Pos		Neg	Neg	0.63	7.89
		1%		1%		5%	5%		1%
W/N				Neg	Pos	Pos		0.80	21.8
				NS	5%	1%			1%

	Independent Variables								
	H	T/E	Estab. Size	Rank Growth	Rank Flux	Ch.H			
Log N/E	Neg	Pos	Neg	Pos	Pos	Neg		0.69	6.83
	NS	NS	1%	NS	5%	5%			1%
Log D/E	Pos	Neg	Neg	Pos	Pos	Neg		0.62	5.38
	5%	NS	NS	5%	NS	5%			5%

NOTE
Ch.H is the proportionate change in wage level between 1955 and 1969.

curvilinear relationship seems to have been present.[58] The significant positive coefficient of the 'strike ban %' variable has already been noted. The negative coefficient for 'establishment size' suggests that, although strikes may be concentrated in large plants, industries characterized by large plants tended to have a low level of strike frequency.[59] The lack of significance for the wage and union density variables indicates that prosperity and the level of organization were not, as one might have expected, significant predictors of strike frequency.

58. On the use of the logarithmic transformation see, for example, K. A. Yeomans, *Applied Statistics* (Vol II of *Statistics for the Social Scientist*; Harmondsworth: Penguin, 1968), pp. 167–77.
59. For the concentration of strikes in large plants see above, p. 103. See also C. F. Eisele, 'Organization Size, Technology and Frequency of Strikes', *Industrial and Labor Relations Review,* XXVII, pp. 560–71 (1974); M. Cass, 'The Relationship between Size of Firm and Strike Activity', *Monthly Labor Review,* LXXX, pp. 1330–34 (1957); S. Cleland, *The Influence of Plant Size on Industrial Relations* (Princeton: Industrial Relations Section, Princeton University, 1955).

The third and fifth equations of the table indicate that two other models of strike frequency perform as adequately as the model of the second equation. They indicate the importance of various aspects of industries' technical structure, measured by the 'heavy-light score' and 'rank flux' variables, and confirm the relative unimportance of wages and union density. However, the fifth equation shows that the rate of change of wages (Ch.H) was important.

One may conclude that certain technical and contract provisions variables differentiated between industries' strike rates, although the levels of wages and union density did not. However, findings relating to the rate of change of wages and the flux variable suggest that a slow increase in prosperity and a high level of instability were associated with a large number of strikes per employee. This conclusion also holds when strike volume (D/E) is considered, although here a rapid rate of growth of output, and not instability, seems to have been important, and the level of wages was also significant. In other words, loss per head was highest where wages were high but the rate of increase low. It is possible that this was associated with the ability of workers in prosperous industries to hold out in long strikes, and with discontent at the slow increase of wages. But, in view of the obvious limitations of the data, such a conclusion can be no more than very tentative.

The generally high levels of R^2 in Table 6.14 indicate that the various models employed are, in conventional terms, quite 'successful' in explaining strike activity. This is particularly notable for strike volume, since in time-series analysis and other cross-sectional experiments, this variable is much more difficult to explain than frequency. The highest R^2, however, occurred in the equation predicting the size of strikes (W/N). The size of strikes was strongly influenced by establishment size; as one would expect, industries characterized by large plants had the largest strikes. The proportion of workers under single-firm, multiplant, agreements (Y) had a less marked effect; but other results, not reported here, show that the proportion under single-company agreements (X plus Y) was relatively unimportant. Establishment size seems to have been the dominating influence, with results from the contract provisions model being rather ambiguous. One might expect large strikes to occur where bargaining is most centralized, a view which is supported by the results of Table 6.14 but which conflicts with the unimportance of the X plus Y variable.

This section has shown that various models can be applied to inter-industry differences in strike activity. Combining various aspects of these models, as was done in Table 6.14, may appear to be invalid, but all one is doing is exploring various aspects of the problem and comparing the explanatory power of one set of variables with that of another. One may tentatively conclude that the levels of wages and union density were relatively unimportant in differentiating between industries' strike rates, and that technical and other variables were more significant. The wider significance of this will be considered when the effects of collective bargaining coverage have been given more detailed attention.

Strikes by Collective Bargaining Coverage

The effect of collective bargaining on strike rates is clearly of central importance to any theory which relates institutional arrangements to the incidence of industrial conflict. The proportion of workers covered by collective agreements, in industries where suitable data exist, is classified in Table 6.15. The data are for 1962, and the measures of strike activity are for the period 1955–69.

There was a clear tendency for strikes to be larger the greater the coverage of bargaining; this held in comparisons between otherwise similar industries, such as electrical and non-electrical machinery, as well as in the aggregate. One common expectation is that, although strikes may be large where collective bargaining is well-established, stoppages will be rare because bargaining institutions will be able to channel grievances into peaceful directions. But among manufacturing industries strike frequency was highest among industries with moderate bargaining coverage. Since frequency in the industries with coverage between 75 and 100 per cent was much greater than in those with 25 to 50 per cent coverage, it seems that bargaining encouraged strikes. Or, at least, a high level of bargaining coverage was a concomitant of a high rate of activity; as the case of textiles suggests, factors peculiar to an industry may militate against both strikes and a high coverage of its workers by collective agreements.

Worker involvement rose continuously with an increase in bargaining coverage, which again suggests that bargaining does not make strikes 'wither away'. Strikes were frequent, even though bargaining is said to deal with many disputes through procedures which avoid the need for a strike; and worker involvement was high, even though bargaining should help to establish democracy in industry and remove certain 'fundamental' sources of dissatisfaction.[60] The only index on which industries with a high bargaining coverage scored lower than those with less coverage was the number of days lost per striker (D/W). Since strikes were

---

60. L. Woodcock, 'U.S.A.', *Industry's Democratic Revolution*, ed. C. Levinson (London: Allen and Unwin, 1974), pp. 199–218, esp. pp. 199, 205–07.

'shorter' in this sense, one expectation is fulfilled. The difference between the manufacturing industries with high and moderate bargaining coverage would be greater if the steel industry were excluded; as has been seen, there were long national strikes in the fifties which distort the picture here. But the lack of any difference betwen the industries with moderate and low coverage suggests that the tendency to a shortening of strikes occurred only when bargaining had become widely established.

From the very limited comparisons which are possible within the non-manufacturing sector, a pattern similar to that in manufacturing is apparent; bargaining encouraged larger and more frequent strikes, but tended to make them 'shorter'. The comparison among sectors with 75−100 per cent coverage shows that non-manufacturing industries had strikes which were more frequent, but smaller and rather shorter than those in manufacturing. As noted earlier, the frequency of strikes in building and mining can be explained by the tendency for disputes over immediate work place matters to develop into stoppages. In line with this, strike frequency in transport and communication was relatively low. Thus the high frequency in non-manufacturing as a whole is partly explained by the characteristics of particular industries and not by the extent of bargaining coverage. Similarly, the low ratio of days lost to strikers in transport is, as noted in Chapters 4 and 5, a persistent feature of the industry. It might be suggested that this brevity is due to the inability of employers to depend on inventories to last out a strike. But building employers are also unable to rely on stocks, and strikes here were relatively long; and in the newspaper section of the printing and publishing industry employers are in a similar position and yet strikes, in the industry as a whole, were particularly long. As suggested in previous chapters, the brevity of transport strikes may be associated with the high level of involvement of outside parties and the belief that strikes here endanger the community much more than those in sectors where the effect on consumers is less immediate and visible.

When Table 6.15 is considered as a whole, the most notable feature is not a tendency for strike activity to be low where bargaining was widespread but the very low level of activity where bargaining was rare. This is consistent with the finding, reported earlier, that among public employees a trend over time towards an increase in the extent of bargaining was associated with a rise in strike activity. More generally, as Chapter 5 showed, strike activity was very low before the New Deal in sectors where bargaining was virtually non-existent; activity was low not only in relation to subsequent trends in these sectors, but also when compared with contemporary rates elsewhere. Thus, bargaining

TABLE 6.15

STRIKE ACTIVITY BY COLLECTIVE BARGAINING COVERAGE, BY INDUSTRY, 1955–69

% of Workers under Union Agreement		N/E	W/E	W/N	D/W
	Manufacturing Industry				
75–100	Machinery: electrical	1.43	1.11	778	16.1
	Metals: basic steel	2.05	3.06	1498	26.3
	Ordnance	0.80	0.91	1150	11.8
	Rubber	4.27	2.77	650	15.3
	Stone, clay and glass	3.23	0.98	302	19.1
	Transport equip: motor vehicles	1.85	3.38	1830	10.7
	other	1.06	1.26	1184	14.4
	All	1.88	1.84	983	16.8
50–75	Chemicals	1.98	0.53	270	21.1
	Furniture	3.12	0.60	191	17.1
	Instruments	1.21	0.44	364	19.9
	Leather	1.49	0.51	343	10.0
	Metals: primary, other than basic steel	3.10	1.32	426	24.5
	Machinery: non-electrical	2.48	1.23	497	19.5
	Paper	1.68	0.51	301	17.8
	Printing and publishing	0.90	0.34	377	27.9
	Tobacco	0.33	0.30	903	11.4
	All	2.23	0.81	365	19.5
25–50	Lumber	1.46	0.32	218	22.5
	Textiles	0.81	0.26	328	16.8
	All	1.07	0.29	267	19.4
	Non-manufacturing Industry				
75–100	Building	4.46	1.53	342	15.7
	Mining	4.81	2.01	418	13.9
	Transport & communication	0.95	0.96	1006	11.0
	All	2.65	1.27	481	13.6
Less than 50	Trade	0.47	0.07	155	15.3

NOTE
Employment is at 1960.
Figures for N/E and W/E are the totals of N and W divided by employment in this year (N/E is the number of strikes per thousand employees and W/E the number of workers involved per employee); the figures are thus not comparable to those in other tables.
The percentage of workers under union agreement is at 1962.

allowed 'unrest' to be made overt, but this was not limited to the New Deal period: as the cases of public employees and industries where bargaining is still rare suggest, the absence of bargaining means that 'unrest' cannot be expressed. But there are as yet no signs that bargaining has solved the problems which lead to unrest, since activity is still high in the sectors with a high level of bargaining coverage.

Conclusions

The analysis of industries by bargaining coverage has shown that, although there were important differences, these differences were not so great that a contrast could be drawn in terms of strike shapes. It will be recalled from Chapter 2 that, for Shorter and Tilly, 'early' or 'non-institutionalized' strikes tend to be infrequent, small, and long, whereas 'modern' strikes are frequent, large, and short. The differences between industries with high and low levels of bargaining coverage do not fit this contrast: although the size of strikes increased with the level of 'institutionalization', duration (as measured by D/W) altered little, and there was a curvilinear relationship between frequency and bargaining coverage. This is, of course, not surprising since all manufacturing industries were covered by the National Labor Relations Act and were thus influenced by institutionalization at the national level. Nor should too much be read into the evidence on bargaining coverage alone, when other measures of institutionalization might be put forward. Nevertheless, inter-industry patterns within the institutionalized system reveal important differences. Not the least of these was the marked contrast between industries with similar levels of bargaining coverage; in other words, particular industries had their own strike shapes, which overrode any simple contrast between institutionalized and non-institutionalized settings.

As the earlier discussion of regression models showed, aspects of these shapes can be explained fairly satisfactorily by a variety of structural factors. In other words, it has been possible to identify 'parameters of conflict' at the industry level. Given the very sketchy nature of data for earlier periods, it is not possible to investigate whether these parameters are different from those operating before the institutionalized system was established. However, there is some evidence to suggest that in earlier periods strikes were concentrated in 'disadvantaged' industries, where wages were low and unemployment high.[61] In 1955–69, strikes were concentrated where wages increased slowly,

61. For details, see Edwards, 'Strikes in the United States, 1881–1972', op. cit., tables 5–17 and 6–11 to 6–13.

plants were small and the uncertainty due to fluctuations in production marked. Similarly, evidence on the profit rate shows that, if anything, stoppages were concentrated where profits were low. The obvious explanation for this is that the disadvantaged industries were those where the conflict of interest between workers and employers was most clearly felt. Although, over time, strikes have been concentrated in the most prosperous periods, this activity occurred in the least prosperous sectors. It may be suggested that, within these sectors, strikes will be concentrated in the most advanced plants, where the conflict of interest will be most acute; but this suggestion cannot be taken up here.

Although substantive conclusions can be reached from analysis of a few large industry groups, one must also stress the tentative nature of such conclusions. These groups are far from homogeneous, and certain characteristics, such as establishment size, may be more suitably examined at the level of the individual plant. However, other characteristics, such as bargaining structure, relate to whole industries; and even factors such as plant size can be seen as marking some industries off from others. But great care must be taken in treating them as industry characteristics; one must not conclude from an inverse link between plant size and strike activity that large plants are the least strike-prone. Although tentative and exploratory, the inter-industry results point to certain important differences between industries which have implications for differences in their strike rates.

The Character of Strikes

Many theories which assess the modernization of a society or institution see changes in its general character as of prime importance. It has been argued that strikes since 1945 have been much more peaceful than earlier stoppages, and that the cessation of work has become a ritualized part of a bargaining game whose rules are well known to both sides.[62] And Shorter and Tilly, although eschewing theories which stress the inevitability of modernization or imply the moral superiority of 'modern' over 'early' or 'pre-industrial' institutions, see the character

---

62. R. Dubin, 'Power and Union-Management Relations', *Readings in Industrial Sociology,* ed. W. A. Faunce (New York: Appleton-Century-Crofts, 1967), pp. 465–81, esp. pp. 471–3; P. Taft, 'Violence in American Labor Disputes', *Annals of the American Academy of Political and Social Science,* no. 364, pp. 127–40 (1966), esp. p. 128; P. Taft and P. Ross, 'American Labor Violence: Its Causes, Character and Outcome', *Violence in America,* ed. H. D. Graham and T. R. Gurr (Washington: U.S. Government Printing Office, 1969), pp. 221–301.

of French strikes as one index of a shift to modern forms of activity.[63]

In the most general sense it is obvious that strikes since the second world war have differed in character from earlier disputes. Violence has largely, although not completely, disappeared;[64] the language of management has come to stress accommodation with unions rather than outright hostility to them; the significance of disputes over union recognition has declined; and so on. The differences between the outstanding strikes of the periods discussed in this and the two preceding chapters are too obvious to require special comment; the strikes in the steel industry in 1919 and 1959, at General Motors in 1936 and 1970, and in the railroad industry in 1894 and 1963 supply sufficient contrasts.[65] Moreover, several aspects of the change in strike character, particularly the decline in violence, have been attributed to the establishment of collective bargaining.[66] Whether bargaining was itself the key, or whether it merely reflected more general tendencies in society away from the violent resolution of differences, is hard to say. But at a descriptive level the differences between the periods before and after 1945 remain.

It is, however, difficult to go beyond the level of general description. This is largely due to the vagueness of the concept of the character of strikes. Certain matters which have been felt to be relevant to character, such as the role of recognition strikes, are amenable to quantitative analysis and have been considered above. But other aspects, such as the acceptance of the strike as a legitimate bargaining weapon, are less easy to measure. More importantly, it is not clear which phenomena should be included in a measure of character or how they should be combined to assess changes over a long period of time. In any event, the construction of such a measure would be a large task which cannot be attempted here. Some general comments may be made however.

As noted above, a significant proportion of strikes occurs outside the area of disputes at the end of contracts. To show that collective bargaining influences strike character would require a comparison of these strikes with those occurring at the end of contracts and showing that

63. E. Shorter and C. Tilly, *Strikes in France, 1830–1968* (Cambridge: Cambridge University Press, 1974).
64. Apart from the intra-union violence associated with the challenge to A. Boyle, president of the Mine Workers, several violent incidents connected with labour relations were reported. See, for example, 'Labor Month in Review', *Monthly Labor Review*, LXXXIII, nos. 1 and 2 (1960) and LXXXVII, no. 3 (1964); and references in note 67, below.
65. On the 1959 steel strike, see R. L. Raimon, 'Affluence, Collective Bargaining and Steel', *Labor Law Journal*, XI, pp. 979–86 (1960).
66. Taft, loc. cit.: Taft and Ross, op. cit., p. 288.

they differed in relevant respects. But even this would involve difficulties, since the model of post-war strike character seems to have derived from strikes over the renewal of contracts and there would thus be a danger of circular argument: typical strikes are defined with reference to bargaining disputes, and those which are not bargaining disputes are shown to be different. But strikes outside the 'normal' pattern are still of interest. Such notable disputes as those at the Kohler company and in the Californian agricultural industry[67] suggest that intransigent employers can still resist unionization and that the resultant strikes can be as embittered as any before the New Deal. Moreover, even in sectors where bargaining had been established, disputes such as the Lordstown strike occurred which cannot be fitted into the picture of modern strikes as unemotional bargaining encounters.

Although these points show that the picture of 'modern' strikes is not applicable to all stoppages, and thus that 'modernization' is incomplete, they do not take the argument much further. The conventional view, which stresses the role of bargaining in altering strike character, cannot explain why some employers remained unwilling to agree to bargaining or why, even where bargaining was established, strikes occurred which do not fit the picture of modern strikes. Description of certain features of strikes has been mistaken for analysis.

Although there were broad differences between the periods before and after 1945, these have not been analysed in sufficient detail to show how and why strike character changed. In any event, changes must be seen in the context of the overall pattern of activity revealed in Chapter 2. The shape of American strikes has changed little so that, whatever their other characteristics, they have remained as large and long as they ever were. The reasons for this will be taken up in the final chapter.

The Role of the Employer

Challenges to the Institutionalized System
This chapter has argued that the institutionalized system of relations in operation since 1945 has been able to adapt to the stresses placed upon

---

67. S. Petro, *The Kohler Strike* (Chicago: Henry Regnery, 1961); W. H. Uphoff, *Kohler on Strike* (Boston: Beacon Press, 1966); J. G. Dunne, *Delano: The Story of the California Grape Strike* (New York: Farrar, Strauss and Giroux, 1967); R. W. Hurd, 'Organizing the Poor—The California Grape Strike Experience', *Review of Radical Political Economics*, VI, no. 1, pp. 50–75 (1974).

it. It has not been a static structure: the pressures of inflation and a slowing of the rate of economic growth in the 1960s, combined with a 'challenge from below', have forced it out of the complacency of the 1950s. In addition to the factors considered above, a more general influence must be considered here. This is the changing nature of corporate ownership, as indicated by the growth of conglomerate firms and the multi-national character of many of the largest firms' operations.[68] American firms have had a long history of owning foreign subsidiaries, but the direct threat of this to unions at home was not very apparent until the 1960s. The growth of conglomerates, largely through mergers, became very marked at the same time.[69] Radicals argue that this has enabled employers to erode the unions' position, although they also stress that the growth of conglomerates is one more stage in the road towards the final collapse of 'monopoly capitalism'.

Craypo has studied bargaining in the conglomerate firm of Litton industries.[70] Centralized managerial control, combined with the decentralization of production and the ability of the firm to shift operations between plants, weakened the position of the unions. With one quarter of its manufacturing capacity abroad, the company was in a very strong position. Craypo argues that the cross-subsidization of operations which firms like Litton can practise invalidates the assumption of institutionalized bargaining that there is a rough balance of power between the parties. Employers are free to cut labour costs and he envisages a return to a situation similar to that which prevailed in the 1920s. Although this last statement may be too extreme, Craypo's study is important in pointing up one of the challenges to the institutionalized system which developed in the 1960s. It is not possible to say whether conglomerate operations exerted an identifiable effect on strike activity but, like automation, the growth of conglomerate firms may well have had an unsettling effect on industrial relations.

68. Conglomerate ownership is different from the level of concentration in individual industries, considered earlier. The growth of conglomerates affects concentration at the level of the whole economy, because such firms transcend industry boundaries. Conglomerate and multi-national firms are considered here, and not in earlier sections of this chapter, because their possible effects on strikes are much less direct and obvious than those of inflation and so on.

69. S. Weir, 'Class Forces in the 1970s', *Radical America*, VI, no. 3, pp. 31–77 (1972), at pp. 54–9; R. Sobel, *The Age of Giant Corporations* (Westport: Greenwood Press, 1972), pp. 196–234, Sweezy and Magdoff, op. cit., pp. 68–86, 97–100.

70. C. Craypo, 'Collective Bargaining in the Conglomerate, Multinational Firm: Litton's Shutdown of Royal Typewriter', *Industrial and Labor Relations Review*, XXIX, pp. 3–25 (1975).

An obvious response to corporate power is the development of 'coalition bargaining' by unions. According to the major study of coalition bargaining, it differs from other forms of joint bargaining in being aimed at companies which operate in several markets but bargain separately for their various operations; it is different from the multi-craft bargaining of industries such as building in not being limited to one labour market and in involving a number of industrially-organized locals, with each plant having only one local rather than several craft unions.[71] The study argues that coalition bargaining has the potential for more frequent, larger and longer strikes than would occur in its absence.[72] One might expect the centralization of bargaining to reduce strike frequency, but there are certainly good reasons to expect large and long stoppages; the mere fact that unions make the effort to work together implies that a major confrontation is envisaged.

Two of the most notable strikes of the 1960s, the national copper dispute of 1967 and the General Electric strike of 1969, occurred where coalitions of unions had been established. Both largely failed in their aim of forcing the companies to accept joint bargaining, but their length and size indicated that important struggles were being under-taken.[73] More generally, Dunlop has suggested that several other im-portant strikes in the 1960s reflected attempts to change the conditions of bargaining.[74] Thus, bargaining was not a static entity but was a pro-cess reflecting the pressures put on the institutionalized system as a whole.

The main challenge to the system as a whole, rather than to its ability to handle particular pressures such as technological change or new forms of management organization, came from the protests of the rank and file. These protests did not come up to radicals' expectations, although they indicate the limitations of a more conventional approach. Thus the General Motors strike of 1970 and the Lordstown dispute exemplify the dual nature of strikes under the institutionalized system. On the one hand, rank and file pressure was important in the 1970 strike as well as the Lordstown dispute; but, on the other, the union's pattern of accommodation with the industry survived largely unchanged

---

71. W. N. Chernish, *Coalition Bargaining* (Philadelphia: University of Pennsyl-vania Press, 1969), pp. 5–8.
72. Ibid., pp. 262–3.
73. Ibid., pp. 175–201; A. H. Raskin, 'A Kind of Economic Holy War', *Ameri-can Labor since the New Deal,* ed. Dubofsky, op. cit., pp. 245–59.
74. J. T. Dunlop, 'Structure of Collective Bargaining', *The Next Twenty-five Years of Industrial Relations,* ed. G. G. Somers (Madison: Industrial Rela-tions Research Association, 1973), pp. 10–18, esp. pp. 15–16.

and the issues on which the pressure was focused left unresolved. Similar remarks apply to the 1969 General Electric strike. There would be nothing particularly remarkable about this, were it not for the extreme views of at least some of the radical writers, who felt that the institutionalized system could be overthrown. Perhaps the vehemence of their arguments can be explained as a reaction against the complacency of the conventional approach during the 1950s and early 1960s; but this seems to have led to an over-emphasis on the radical possibilities of rank and file action and a corresponding lack of concern with its limits and the resilience of the institutionalized system.

The Employer and Strikes

As in 1927–41, indices of employers' prosperity were not closely associated with trends of strike activity. Moreover, differences between industries could not be explained by these indices. This does not mean that the role of the employer was unimportant in questions of whether a strike occurred or, after it had begun, how long it lasted. His influence was less direct than that of other factors. In a particular case, unions may take account of a firm's profit position before striking, and may decide against such action or direct their attack at firms which are felt to be most able to pay. Similarly, individual employers will no doubt take account of their stock and profits positions when deciding whether to 'take a strike'. But their decisions do not seem to have been rigidly determined by their economic position. As a result, levels of strike activity in the aggregate were more closely related to other factors.

It will be recalled that Shorter and Tilly use a model in which the position of the employer has two sorts of effect on strike activity: a direct one and an indirect one which works through the prosperity of workers and the level of labour organization.[75] The evidence of this and the previous chapter indicates that the first sort of effect has not been present in the United States; or, at least, the use of several indicators of employers' prosperity does not suggest that a strong effect on strike activity was present, although it is always possible that the use of different indices could lead to other conclusions. The indirect effect of the employer is hard to assess since, in time-series and cross-sectional analysis, the high level of association between measures of workers' and employers' prosperity makes it difficult to separate their independent effects. Moreover, cross-sectional analysis in this and the previous chapter did not suggest that the profit rate or the concentration ratio were significant in explaining differences in strike activity between

75. Shorter and Tilly, op. cit., esp. p. 103.

industries. However, the role of the employer cannot be ignored, and Chapter 5 gave examples of cases where decisions by employers were crucial in the occurrence or non-occurrence of strikes. Thus one can suggest that the employer may have had an important background effect, a point which is taken up at more length in the following chapter.

7

Conclusion: American Strike Trends Reconsidered

Strikes in the United States have always been very long and, as a result, their overall volume has been much greater than the volume of strikes elsewhere. This chapter tries to account for this in terms of the extent and intensity of the struggle for job control in America. Like other explanations of 'American exceptionalism', the interpretation advanced here is an *ex post* account and not an *ex ante* theory: it does not begin with a theory of strike patterns in capitalist societies and proceed to test the theory against the data, but attempts to explain aspects of American strike patterns which have remained obscure. The test of the present account is not that it is right while others are wrong. As argued in Chapter 1, less clear-cut criteria have to be used. The account claims to be more illuminating and satisfying than previous accounts: illuminating because it copes with aspects of American strikes which have been obscure, and satisfying because it provides a clearer link between explanatory variables and the phenomenon to be explained.

Alternative Explanations of American Exceptionalism

Political Accounts
In addition to their length and volume, the main features of American strikes which require explanation are their failure to 'wither away' after 1945 and an associated tendency for their 'shape' to exhibit a marked consistency throughout the period since 1881. Most European countries' strike patterns changed shape in the 1930s, with strikes becoming shorter and more frequent.[1] In recent years, there has been a remark-

---

1. E. Shorter and C. Tilly, 'The Shape of Strikes in France, 1830–1960', *Comparative Studies in Society and History*, XIII, pp. 60–86 (1971).

219

able growth in the number of studies attempting to explain international patterns of strikes. They differ in the number and character of distinct strike patterns which they identify and in the ease with which various countries fit the overall model. For Shorter and Tilly, for example, there are three main strike patterns, with Britain being the country which fits least well into any pattern.[2] For Korpi and Shalev, there are five patterns, and West Germany is the most recalcitrant case.[3] These and other differences[4] suggest at the outset that such broad analyses may have limited applicability to specific countries, and that more detailed consideration may be required. But, more importantly, all the analyses have two things in common: first, they agree that the United States and Canada form a single distinct pattern; second, they share a political account of strike trends. For Hibbs, strikes are one manifestation of the struggle for social power, and changes in strike activity are explained by changes in the location of the struggle: where Social Democratic and Labour parties have gained power, conflict has shifted to the political sphere and strike activity has declined.[5] Similarly, for Shorter and Tilly, strike patterns since 1945 have been influenced by the nature and extent of working-class entry to the polity.[6]

In stressing political factors, these studies attempt to show their superiority over explanations couched in terms of the industrial relations institutions of various countries. Korpi and Shalev, for example, point out that, in Sweden, the creation of institutions for the control of conflict did not lead to an immediate reduction in strike activity; this reduction came only after the accession to power of a Social Democratic government.[7] The explanation of American strike patterns is straightforward: America has lacked a Social Democratic party and

---

2. E. Shorter and C. Tilly, *Strikes in France, 1830–1968* (Cambridge: Cambridge University Press, 1974), pp. 322–9.

3. W. Korpi and M. Shalev, 'Strikes, Industrial Relations and Class Conflict in Capitalist Societies', *British Journal of Sociology*, XXX, pp. 164–87 (1979), at pp. 180–83.

4. For a critique of one account from a broadly similar 'political' perspective see M. Shalev, 'Strikes and the State: A Comment', *British Journal of Political Science*, VIII, pp. 479–92 (1978), commenting on D. A. Hibbs, 'On the Political Economy of Long-run Trends in Strike Activity', *British Journal of Political Science*, VIII, pp. 153–75 (1978).

5. Hibbs, op. cit., pp. 165–6. See also D. A. Hibbs, 'Industrial Conflict in Advanced Industrial Societies', *American Political Science Review*, LXX, pp. 1033–58 (1976).

6. Shorter and Tilly, *Strikes in France*, op. cit., p. 317.

7. Korpi and Shalev, op. cit., pp. 766–8, See also W. Korpi, *The Working Class in Welfare Capitalism: Work, Unions and Politics in Sweden* (London: Routledge and Kegan Paul, 1978).

working-class action has thus remained in the industrial sphere.

Although intuitively appealing, this approach is, as it stands, too simple to account for a given country's strike record. In the case of Sweden, for example, Korpi and Shalev dismiss explanations of the decline in strike activity which stress the role of employers' and unions' national federations or the peculiarities of the country's infrastructure.[8] But, although they make out a case for including political factors, they do not show that these alone were sufficient for the observed decline in strike rates to take place. Showing that institutional factors by themselves were unable to moderate strike rates in the period 1900–39 is not sufficient to show that political factors were the crucial influence during the very different economic environment of the years since 1945.

The absence of a Labour party in the United States is so obvious a fact that few writers in this tradition are concerned to go further by asking the question of why this absence has made American strikes unique in the post-1945 period. Shorter and Tilly do attempt to remedy this deficiency, but in doing so introduce further problems. At one point they suggest that unionization before the 1930s tended to increase strike activity in America and in France, but that, in later years, a new form of American unionism reduced strike rates.[9] According to Shorter and Tilly, the unions achieved considerable job control and ceded to the political parties the protection of workers' wider interests. As it stands, this argument contradicts a 'political' interpretation since it gives temporal and causal priority to affairs in the industrial sphere. Shorter and Tilly attempt to rescue their political interpretation by arguing that, before the New Deal, American strikes were 'as much political as economic'.[10] This is little more than assertion, however,[11] and in any event raises questions about what Shorter and Tilly regard as

8. On the economic infrastrusture, see G. K. Ingham, *Strikes and Industrial Conflict: Britain and Scandinavia* (London: Macmillan, 1974).

9. Shorter and Tilly, *Strikes in France*, op. cit., p. 193.

10. Ibid., p. 330.

11. In support of their claim, Shorter and Tilly cite: T. A. Krueger, 'American Labor Historiography, Old and New: A Review Essay', *Journal of Social History*, IV, pp. 277–85 (1971); J. H. M. Laslett, *Labor and the Left: A Study of Socialist and Radical Influences in the American Labor Movement, 1881–1924* (New York: Basic Books, 1970); and S. M. Lipset, 'Trade Unions and Social Structure', *Industrial Relations*, I, no. 1, pp. 75–89 (1961) and I, no. 2, pp. 89–110 (1962). Although works such as these help to counterbalance the view that all American unions have always concentrated solely on economic matters, they are not sufficient totally to invert such a view. It is an even further step to argue that strike action was politically motivated.

political. To support a claim that strike trends since 1945 can be explained by the absence of a Labour party, 'political' would have to mean more than 'having to do with the distribution of power'. To be consistent with the rest of Shorter and Tilly's account, the term would have to imply that strikes before the New Deal were directed at the political centre and had national political significance, a claim which it would be very hard to substantiate.[12]

At a later point, Shorter and Tilly cite the United States as an illustration of the principle that 'admission to the polity need not automatically lead to the withering away of the strike'.[13] If this is to be taken at its face value it means that America is different from other countries not because it lacked a Labour party but because the working class gained political power on different terms. This in turn raises questions about 'functional alternatives' to a Labour party which Shorter and Tilly do not attempt to solve. More generally, to imply that the European working classes have achieved genuine access to political power is to fly in the face of most serious studies of the subject.[14]

To raise the question of politics may lead to an analysis of the 'incorporation' of the working class and the interaction of political and industrial matters through such things as incomes policies.[15] Despite its 'radical' rejection of pluralism and analysis in terms of the industrial relations system, the 'political' account of strike patterns does not follow this path or develop a genuinely radical account of international differences in strike rates in terms of the contradiction of capitalist economies. By replacing one over-arching explanation for another, it

12. It is true that unions were involved in local politics to a greater extent than is often imagined. See, for example, I. Yellowitz, *Labor and the Progressive Movement in New York State, 1897–1916* (Ithaca: Cornell University Press, 1965); P. Taft, *Labor Politics American Style: The California State Federation of Labor* (Cambridge, Mass.: Harvard University Press, 1968); G. M. Fink, *Labor's Search for Political Order: The Political Behavior of the Missouri Labor Movement, 1890–1940* (Columbia: University of Missouri Press, 1973); K. L. Bryant, 'Labor in Politics: The Oklahoma State Federation of Labor during the Age of Reform', *Labor History*, XI, pp. 259–76 (1970). But this involvement has not, in general, meant that strikes have been used for directly 'political' ends. They have had political implications, but their causes must be sought elsewhere.
13. Shorter and Tilly, *Strikes in France*, op. cit., p. 330.
14. See, for example, R. Miliband, *The State in Capitalist Society* (London: Quartet Books, 1973); P. Stanworth and A. Giddens (eds), *Elites and Power in British Society* (Cambridge: Cambridge University Press, 1974).
15. See C. Crouch, *Class Conflict and the Industrial Relations Crisis* (London: Heinemann, 1977); L. Panitch, *Social Democracy and Industrial Militancy: The Labour Party, the Trade Unions and Incomes Policy, 1945–74* (Cambridge: Cambridge University Press, 1976).

remains profoundly a-historical: political conditions changed and therefore strike patterns changed.[16]

In their general approach, and in stressing the importance of the lack of a Labour party in America, these accounts follow the tradition established by Ross and Hartman.[17] Although the thesis of the withering away of the strike has been subjected to damaging criticism,[18] Ross and Hartman's account of America's exception to the thesis remains of interest. In addition to the lack of a Labour party, four key factors are identified: the relative youth of mass unionism in America; the presence of organizational rivalries; the lack of centralized bargaining; and the public acceptance of the settlement of industrial disputes by trials of economic strength.[19] The relevance of the first two of these is doubtful. Although mass unionism was established only in the 1930s, the trade union movement as a whole has had a history at least as long as that of movements in several other countries. And the writers do not explain why youth in itself contributes to a high strike rate[20] or whether, as American unions age, strike patterns can be expected to alter: how old do unions have to be before they learn not to strike? By organizational rivalries, Ross and Hartman mean the split between the A.F.L. and C.I.O., and earlier divisions between Socialist and business unions. But other labour movements have had much deeper and more persistent splits; the C.I.O. did not differ from the A.F.L. over fundamental principles, and the rift between the two organizations has been closed since 1955, without any apparent effect on strike patterns.

Ross and Hartman's fifth factor is, as it stands, little more than a re-description of the strike picture.[21] This leaves collective bargaining and

16. For a recent attempt to provide a more historically-based model of British strike trends see J. E. Cronin, *Industrial Conflict in Modern Britain* (London: Croom Helm, 1979). How far Cronin succeeds in his attempt cannot be considered here.

17. A. M. Ross and P. T. Hartman, *Changing Patterns of Industrial Conflict* (New York: Wiley, 1960).

18. J. E. T. Eldridge, *Industrial Disputes: Essays in the Sociology of Industrial Relations* (London: Routledge and Kegan Paul, 1968), pp. 23–35; Ingham, op. cit., pp. 11–23.

19. Ross and Hartman, op. cit., pp. 162–8.

20. The stress on the youth of unions is part of the writers' wider argument that organizational stability is a key influence on strike rates. But they do not explain how age is a proxy for stability, or consider the possibility of de-stabilizing influences.

21. The public acceptance of trials of economic strength may well reflect the operation of a peculiarly American set of values, but such acceptance is unlikely to have an effect on the attitudes of the parties directly involved unless it is organized and directed. Opinion is likely to be vague and diffuse,

the absence of a Labour party as explanatory variables but these, too, are not developed as fully as one might expect. On bargaining, Ross and Hartman see the decentralized nature of the American system as its key characteristic, but do not explain in detail how this affects the frequency and length of strikes.

Collective Bargaining

A more detailed analysis of the impact of collective bargaining on strikes has been provided by Clegg.[22] In an analysis of six countries, Clegg identifies several dimensions of bargaining and uses these to explain patterns of union membership, structure, and organization, as well as strikes. The two most important dimensions for present purposes are the extent of bargaining (the proportion of employees covered by collective agreements) and its level (the relative weight given to bargaining at local, regional, industrial, and national levels).

In addition to America's high strike volume, Clegg considers the moderate frequency of American strikes, their large size, and their tendency to be legal and constitutional. There is a link between size and constitutional status. As Clegg says, official and constitutional strikes tend to be large because they involve all the members of the relevant bargaining unit. Because a high proportion of American strikes are constitutional, the size of the average American strike can be expected to be greater than that of the average strike elsewhere. The official and constitutional status of American strikes remains to be explained. According to Clegg, the answer lies in the predominance of plant-level agreements in America which mean that 'an official and constitutional strike may be called in the United States ... at much less cost to the members as a whole than a strike to change the terms of most agreements (or awards) in any of the other five countries'.[23]

Clegg explains America's moderate strike frequency in terms of the country's well-established and efficient disputes procedures. Such

---

and members of the public are more likely to worry about the effects of a strike on themselves than about the rights and wrongs of the case. They are thus most likely to be mobilized on the side of employers, particularly when 'law and order' matters are involved. For a case where the public did exert an independent role, see M. Dubofsky, *When Workers Organize: New York City in the Progressive Era* (Amherst: University of Massachusetts Press, 1968), pp. 103–25, 148–50.

22. H. A. Clegg, *Trade Unionism Under Collective Bargaining: A Theory Based on Comparison of Six Countries* (Oxford: Blackwell, 1976), pp. 68–82.
23. Ibid., p. 76.

procedures can be expected to resolve disputes without the need for strikes. Although plant bargaining tends to lead to large numbers of official strikes, disputes procedures discourage unofficial stoppages. Nevertheless, the United States has more unofficial strikes than Sweden and West Germany, which have efficient disputes procedures. According to Clegg, this is because American unions are faction-ridden, and unofficial strikes are used as weapons in factional disputes.[24]

As it stands, Clegg's account would be rejected by those preferring a 'political' account of strikes, on the grounds that it does not explain why plant bargaining has been predominant in the United States. The account is more subtle than some commentators realize, however.[25] As Clegg states in his Preface, his theory is based on Flanders's attempts to develop a general theory of union growth. In this theory, the roles of employers and government are of central importance: many aspects of trade union growth and behaviour can be explained by the policies of employers and governments. For example, Clegg points to the importance of the Wagner Act in stimulating the growth of manual unions in the United States and to the influence of President Kennedy's Executive Order 10988 on public-sector unionism.[26] More generally, it is argued that statutory regulation of employment has become more important in the United States, thus narrowing the traditional gap between America and other countries in the degree of government involvement in regulating the terms of employment.[27]

Clegg does not develop these points into a critique of political accounts, but one can readily be provided. In considering employers and the government, Clegg does not take a narrowly 'institutionalist' position, but seeks to explain how they have had an influence on union behaviour. The political account tends to be more dogmatic, asserting that political factors were crucial but not working out the implications of this in detail. For example, an increase in the role of statutory regulation would be expected to reduce strike activity, because matters in dispute will be settled in the political arena. Political accounts of

24. Ibid., p. 79–80.
25. Thus, Korpi and Shalev, op. cit., p. 165, dismiss Clegg's work as exemplifying the excessively institutionalist concerns of the 'Oxford school' of British industrial relations. Clegg may be an institutionalist, but he does provide an account of the development of bargaining institutions in terms of the structures and policies of employers and governments. This account is, if anything, less narrow than that of his critics, and also more detailed in its discussion of how government policy, for example, has influenced a whole range of union practices.
26. Clegg, op. cit., pp. 14, 26.
27. Ibid., pp. 100–101.

American strike trends tend to ignore such problems. And, more generally, by playing down the role of collective bargaining they ignore the obvious fact that bargaining is, in all Western countries, the direct means of resolving disputes. The political environment has to be taken into account, but the effect of that environment on strikes is mediated through the bargaining system.

Clegg's explanation of strikes concentrates on only a few aspects of the bargaining system: the level of bargaining, disputes procedures, and the like. And it does not make explicit the influence of employers and the government. Later sections of this chapter will consider the role of the government and, more particularly, employers in strike trends, which is where the concept of job control comes in. But it is first necessary to examine the role of collective bargaining more closely.

Developing the Bargaining Account

The problem will be approached by considering in turn the three dimensions of strike volume: the frequency, size, and duration of disputes. For Clegg, American strike frequency should be lower than that in countries lacking effective disputes procedures, but higher than that in countries without factional splits in their union movements.[28] His own figures show, however, that American strike frequency is not very different from the British. Given the well-known difficulties with international comparisons of frequency, it may be argued that little can be inferred from this. However, the difficulties arise not from a fundamental difference in categories employed but from certain identifiable features of the statistics of each country. It may not be possible to quantify the extent of the incompatibility of the statistics, but it is possible to identify in what direction certain differences will operate. Two differences are of particular significance here. First, strikes lasting less than one day are excluded from the American figures but included in the British. As Table 7.1 shows, such strikes have formed about 20 per cent of the total in Britain. Putting the figures on a comparable basis would substantially reduce the difference between the two countries.

The second point about the statistics is that there is a virtually automatic tendency for strike frequency to be lower in centralized than in decentralized bargaining systems. Assuming a constant 'underlying' propensity to strike, centralized systems will tend to bring together in one distinct dispute what would, under plant bargaining, be counted as

28. Although Clegg's account of factionalism refers only to unofficial strikes, other things being equal more unofficial strikes will mean more strikes *in toto*.

several separate strikes. As Clegg says, the British strike pattern can 'be attributed to the widespread practice of two-level bargaining which has led to a decline in the influence of industry procedure agreements as well as industry agreements on pay'.[29] Given the stress on decentralized bargaining in Britain and America, it is not surprising that strike frequency is similar in the two countries. Moreover, the much lower frequency in Sweden and West Germany can be attributed to the pattern of centralized bargaining in those countries. The other two of Clegg's six countries, Australia and France, have high strike frequencies. This can be explained by the particular function of the strike in these countries: brief demonstrations are used to put pressure on negotiators, in Australia with respect to the system of arbitration of wage awards, and in France with respect to the 'political centre'.

This interpretation is consistent with Clegg's approach, although placing as much stress on bargaining level as on disputes procedures in explaining strike frequency. However, explaining America's record of unofficial strikes requires attention to factors other than disputes procedures and factionalism. America's record of unofficial strikes surpasses anything known in Sweden and West Germany. Although, as argued in Chapter 6, these strikes do not represent full-scale rank and file rebellion against union leaders, their significance is considerable. They may contain elements of factional dispute, but their main focus is on plant-based issues, particularly matters relating to working arrangements and discipline. This can be explained, in turn, by the limitations of disputes procedures on certain issues, combined with a feeling that union leaders were taking insufficient interest in detailed matters such as line speeds and manning levels.

In other words, it is necessary to go beyond disputes procedures to examine the issues those procedures are designed to resolve, and their success in doing so. More generally, unconstitutional strikes in America reflect a concern with matters of 'job control'. The wider significance of this will be taken up further below, but for present purposes it is sufficient to note that America's pattern of strike frequency seems to be most like that of Britain. This can be related not only to the level of bargaining in the two countries but also to the use of the strike to settle conflicts 'at the point of production'. Unconstitutional strikes form a considerable proportion of all strikes in America, and cannot be explained as the product of factional struggles alone.

Constitutional strikes are in the great majority, however. It is true that it is relatively easy for American unions to call such strikes, given

29. Clegg, op. cit., p. 78.

that the costs involved are comparatively small.[30] But the very fact that
they are constitutional does not in itself explain why, to turn to the
second two dimensions of strike activity, they are large and long. It will
be convenient to consider duration first. As Table 7.1 shows, strikes at
the end of contracts were much longer than those during the term of
contracts. Although this contrast cannot reflect perfectly the constitutional status of strikes, the differences are so great that it can be taken
for granted that constitutional strikes are much longer than unconstitutional ones. Moreover, comparison with Britain shows that American
strikes during the term of contracts were very similar in duration to
British strikes considered as a whole. Some British strikes are, of course,
official. Although those 'known to be official' form a very small proportion of the total, there is an unknown number which have quasi-
official approval, or would attain such approval were union leaders to
be aware of them. Similar processes occur in America, of course. But it
seems likely that, if official and quasi-official strikes were removed
from the British statistics, unofficial strikes could be shown to be
shorter than similar strikes in America.[31] In other words, the great
length of American strikes in the aggregate cannot entirely be explained
by the length of official stoppages.

Nevertheless, the main problem is the length of official strikes in
America. Although Clegg does not say so explicitly, the explanation of
this in terms of plant bargaining is that few resources are involved, with
the result that there is little pressure to reach a quick settlement. A
further reason can be found in another of Clegg's dimensions of bargaining, the scope of bargaining. As Kassalow points out, American
collective agreements cover a much wider range of subjects than their
European counterparts.[32] When a dispute arises, there is thus a great
deal at stake, and the parties are unwilling to settle quickly; a speedy
settlement might lead to a less advantageous result across the whole

30. On the other hand, financial costs to American unions may be higher than
    those incurred by British unions, because of relatively high levels of strike
    pay and other things. Clegg's cost-benefit view is certainly undeveloped at
    this point. But the present aim is simply to argue that there are good reasons,
    connected with the level of bargaining, why American strikes are constitu-
    tional.
31. It would, of course, be inappropriate to follow the definition of 'unofficial'
    strikes in America used in Chapter 6, since part of the definition requires
    such strikes to last three days or less. See above, p. 180.
32. E. M. Kassalow, *Trade Unions and Industrial Relations: An International
    Comparison* (New York: Random House, 1969), p. 136. See also D. C. Bok
    and J. T. Dunlop, *Labor and the American Community* (New York: Simon
    and Schuster, 1970), pp. 234–5; M. Derber, 'Collective Bargaining in Great
    Britain and the United States', *Quarterly Review of Economics and Business*,

TABLE 7.1

DURATION OF BRITISH AND AMERICAN STRIKES, 1969–75

	Per cent of Strikes in Each Category of Duration				
	U.K.			U.S.	
	All Strikes	Strikes lasting Over 1 Day		Strikes at Contract Renego-tiation	Strikes During Term of Contract
Under 1 day	21.9				
1– 1.99 days	16.3	20.6	1– 1.99 days	3.2	37.2
2– 5.99 days	32.3	40.8	2– 6.99 days	15.0	43.6
6–11.99 days	14.3	18.1	7–14.99 days	21.0	11.5
12–17.99 days	5.9	7.5			
18–23.99 days	3.1	3.9	15–29.99 days	23.2	4.1
24–35.99 days	3.1	3.9			
36–59.99 days	2.0	2.5	30–59.99 days	21.4	2.3
60 days and over	1.0	1.3	60–89.99 days	8.4	0.6
			90 days and over	7.9	0.7

SOURCES
For America, see Appendix D. For Britain, annual article on stoppages due to industrial disputes, in May or June issue of Department of Employment *Gazette*.

range of employment conditions than a longer battle.

This 'cost-benefit' interpretation helps to explain why American strikes are longer than European ones. But it does not show why strikes are as long as in the past. There are several reasons why strikes might be expected to have grown shorter, of which two are of particular significance. First, it has become a commonplace that strikes have ceased to be over 'fundamental' matters such as union recognition, and have focused instead on economic issues. If there is no longer argument about the rights of unions to organize and to bargain with employers, strikes should have lost the elements of large-scale warfare which distinguished them in the past; they should therefore have become shorter. Second, and associated with this, there has been a general growth of union-management accommodation. As mutual understanding between the two sides has increased, and in particular as they have learnt that the threat of a strike is a serious one, strikes should have become shorter.

VIII, no. 4, pp. 55–66 (1968), esp. p. 62; J. W. Garbarino, 'Managing Conflict in Industrial Relations: United States Experience and Current Issues in Britain', *British Journal of Industrial Relations*, VII, pp. 317–35 (1969).

It could be argued that these factors have been counteracted by an increase in the financial and other resources of the two sides: although there may be a tendency for bargaining to be more effective, when bargaining breaks down the increased resources mean that a lengthy dispute can be fought. In responding to this argument, it will be helpful to return to the question of strike frequency. Although there may be forces tending to make strikes longer, it cannot be argued that they will make strikes more frequent; indeed, increasingly effective bargaining should mean that disputes can be settled without strikes to a greater extent than in the past. The lack of any marked decline in the frequency of strikes indicates that this expectation has not been met. Thus, even if it were accepted that there may be good reasons why the duration of strikes has not been reduced, there remain other aspects of strike trends which are problematic.

On the question of duration, it would have to be shown that the resources for holding strikes have grown, and that the parties have been more willing to use them, for the argument under consideration to be accepted. It may be true that resources enable strikes to be held at relatively little cost, but the absolute costs are always considerable. Moreover, if union members are as apathetic as arguments about the decline of the labour movement suggest that they are, even fairly 'small' costs may be felt to be unacceptable. As Levitt pointed out long ago,[33] increasing financial commitments, in the form of mortgage and hire purchase payments, may mean that even small losses of income may have a severe impact. For reasons such as these, the reason for the continuing length of strikes cannot be found in the resources available to the parties.

There are, then, two questions about the length of American strikes: why they are longer than strikes in other countries, and why they have remained as long as those of the past? On the former, the level and scope of bargaining offer part of the explanation. But it remains to be shown why the parties should want to hold out for as long as they do. In other words, is the opportunity to strike at relatively little cost sufficient to account for the extraordinary length of American strikes? There are reasons for the comparative length of American strikes, but are these reasons powerful enough to account for the extent of the difference between America and other countries? It will be argued in the following section that there are other factors, connected with the desires of the parties to engage in long strikes, as distinct from their

33. T. Levitt, 'Prosperity versus Strikes', *Industrial and Labor Relations Review*, VI, pp. 220–26 (1953).

ability to do so, which are also important.

On trends over time, it has been suggested that existing accounts do not provide sufficient explanation of the failure of American strikes to become shorter. Thus, political accounts point to the continued settlement of disputes in the economic sphere. But, as noted above, Clegg points out that the gap between America and other countries in the extent of government involvement in the fixing of conditions of employment has been narrowed considerably since 1945. This has not, however, led to the expected decline in strike duration. Moreover, these accounts do not attempt to explain why political intervention has been less significant than in other countries.

These points will be considered further in the following section, but it is first necessary to return to the third dimension of strike activity: size. As with strike frequency, the comparison with Britain is particularly instructive. The size distribution of British strikes is therefore given in Table 7.2, together with the relevant American figures which were originally reported in Table 6.6. Although Clegg expects constitutional strikes in general to be large, such strikes in America were not much larger than unconstitutional stoppages. And, as with frequency, there was a marked similarity with Britain. However, this result is also like the frequency result in being something of an illusion. Other things being equal, countries with national- and industry-level bargaining will tend to have strikes which encompass the whole of the relevant work force and which are therefore larger than strikes where plant bargaining is the rule. America would then tend to have smaller strikes than a country such as Sweden, whereas Clegg's figures show that there was in fact little difference between these two countries.

Part of the explanation may lie in the limitations of figures on the size of the 'average' strike. These are derived by dividing the total number of workers involved by the total number of strikes. This procedure may mask differences in the size distribution of strikes. One would expect, for example, that in Sweden there would be a few large, official strikes, and a much larger number of small, workplace ones. There should then be two distinct clusters of small and big strikes, while in America there should be one cluster, intermediate in size between the two Swedish clusters, reflecting the predominance in America of strikes at the level of the plant. It is difficult to say how far such expectations are met in practice. In addition to the limitations of published figures on the subject, there are obvious complicating factors, such as difference in plant size between countries. In particular, figures for worker involvement in strikes typically include some of those laid off as a result of a strike (workers involved 'indirectly', to use the British ter-

TABLE 7.2

SIZE OF BRITISH STRIKES (1969–75) AND AMERICAN STRIKES, (1961–72)

No. Workers per Strike	U.K.		U.S.			
			Strikes at Contract Re-negotiation		Strikes During Term of Contract	
	Strikes	Workers Involved	Strikes	Workers Involved	Strikes	Workers Involved
Under 25[a]	14.5	0.5	10.2	0.2	14.5	0.5
25–99[a]	33.2	3.4	37.6	2.9	31.6	4.2
100–249	22.2	6.7	24.0	5.7	23.4	10.0
250–499	13.0	8.6	12.6	6.5	15.3	14.1
500–999	8.6	11.2	7.5	7.7	8.2	14.9
1000–4999	7.2	27.3	6.3	18.7	6.4	33.2
5000–9999	1.6	12.1	0.9	9.1	0.4	7.3
10000 and over	0.4	30.2	0.8	49.3	0.3	15.9

NOTE
a. These are the British size categories. Corresponding American categories are 6–19 and 20–99 workers.
SOURCE
As for Table 7.1.

minology). Different conventions for the inclusion of workers laid off will have an impact on figures of workers involved, and hence on the mean size of strikes.

The nature of collective bargaining may thus affect the size of strikes, although statistical problems make it hard to say anything very conclusive. In the case of America, the role of plant bargaining has to be given a different emphasis from that given by Clegg. It is not that plant bargaining encourages the calling of constitutional strikes, which tend, for other reasons, to be large. Rather, plant bargaining tends to restrict the size of all strikes, to such an extent that constitutional strikes are not substantially larger than unconstitutional ones.

Extensions of, and amendments to, the model of bargaining advanced by Clegg can help to account for certain aspects of America's strike pattern. It is true, as political accounts stress, that bargaining must be seen in the context of wider societal changes. To say this does not, in itself, explain American strike patterns; and to provide an explanation, aspects of bargaining have to be given explicit attention. Nevertheless, the bargaining model is not designed to account for long-term trends in strike patterns, being concerned with the impact of current structures on strike activity. The remainder of this chapter will be concerned with examining the origins of those structures. It has been argued above that the very great length of American strikes poses problems for all accounts of American exceptionalism. By placing current bargaining arrangements in their historical context, it is possible to see why strikes are so long, and why bargaining structures have come to have such a distinctive effect on strike patterns.

A more general conclusion is also indicated. Many writers have attempted to identify distinct patterns of strike activity, to which individual countries may be assigned. This procedure often leads to very unlikely groups of countries; for example, Britain and the Netherlands, and France and Japan, have been assigned to the same groups.[34] It is not surprising that explanations of observed 'patterns' become convoluted. The problem arises because of a reliance on a very limited series of indices, usually the three main components of strike activity or some transformation thereof. It has been seen above, in relation to measures of strike frequency and size, that this procedure can produce a very misleading picture unless the nature of the figures is given careful and explicit attention. Apparently similar patterns can reveal the operation of very different forces. Moreover, it is necessary to go beyond the use of simple averages; to measure the size of strikes, for example, the size distribution of stoppages can reveal more than a simple average. Similarly, additional measures may be appropriate; for example, the spread of strike activity can be considered by showing in how many strikes only one factory was affected, in how many two factories, and so on. But such remedies do not alter the basic point: the search for international patterns is unlikely to be fruitful if analysts continue to lump together countries with little in common apart from an apparent similarity of strike patterns. There is no substitute for detailed attention to the patterns of individual countries. This may not lead to a neat picture of a small number of distinct 'patterns', but is essential if the reasons for a particular country's pattern are to be revealed.

Job Control

A prominent characteristic of American strikes has been the uniformity of their shape. This suggests that one force, or combination of forces, has continued to affect strike patterns despite marked changes in indus-

34. For the former, see Hibbs, 'Industrial Conflict and Advanced Industrial Societies', op. cit., p. 1049; for the latter, Korpi and Shalev, op. cit., pp. 180—83.

trial structure, bargaining arrangements, and many other things. This force, it will be argued, is the intensity of struggles for job control. A stress on control is not intended to supplant other explanations, but it can do two things: link present strike patterns with those of the past, and explain the basis of the current bargaining system. A subsidiary aim is to show that control struggles can be detected even in strikes under the 'mature' bargaining system.

This in turn raises the question of what is meant by control struggles. Several 'radical' accounts have recently placed control in general at the centre of explanations of industrial conflict: there is an unceasing struggle at the point of production with which 'pluralist' institutions of conflict regulation are unable to cope.[35] The present account draws on this approach to some extent, but the basic aim is different. The aim is not to argue that job control *per se* has been more important in America than elsewhere, but to focus on the intensity of control struggles as a key factor in the explanation of strike patterns. In other words, it is the particular pattern of the general struggle for control which is important. As noted above, strike patterns in several European countries have been influenced by the centralization and politicization of strike action. This can be seen as one particular form of the institutionalization of the general struggle for control. In Britain and America, a different route has been taken. Here, the work place has remained the centre of attention. Not surprisingly, the strike patterns of the two countries have revealed important similarities, not simply in terms of the frequency and size of stoppages but also regarding the avoidance of 'political' strikes, the domination of strikes by individual trade unions, as distinct from national union federations, and several other points. An argument in terms of job control thus immediately sets these two countries off from most others. To distinguish between them requires consideration of the intensity of control struggles, a point which will be taken up below.

Thus it is the intensity of struggle for control which is the key variable, and not job control as such. The intensity of the struggle has, in turn, to be explained by the interests of the parties to conflict. As indicated above, employers and the government, as well as unions and workers, must be given attention. In other words, 'control' as used here is an 'intervening variable', linking the aims of the parties to strike activity.

35. See, for example, H. Braverman, *Labor and Monopoly Capital: The Degradation of Work in the Twentieth Century* (New York: Monthly Review Press, 1974); A. L. Friedman, *Industry and Labour: Class Struggle at Work and Monopoly Capitalism* (London: Macmillan, 1977).

It is not being argued that America has necessarily had more control struggles than other countries: indeed, there have been important pressures counteracting the tendency to conflict. But the struggles which have occurred have assumed a particularly extreme form, because crucial interests of the parties have been at stake. These interests have gone beyond 'economic' matters to include the basic rights of the parties. Thus, America has had a history of intense opposition to trade unions from employers. Unions have seen recognition and collective bargaining as crucial to their own development, whereas employers have defined any attempt to extend bargaining as a challenge to the 'right to manage'.

The general relevance of this description to America before the New Deal is hardly in doubt. As Chapters 4 and 5 have shown, the hostility of most employers to unions was intense and unwavering. The point may be given more relevance in a comparative setting by reference to a study by Holt of the British and American steel industries before the first world war.[36] Holt argues that various factors which have been put forward to explain the different experiences of trade unions in the two industries, such as technology, the craft exclusiveness of the American unions, and the racial heterogeneity of the American work force, are insufficient to account for the very great differences which emerged. It was the policy of American employers which was crucial, and which led to the lengthy battles of the period. In other words, even at this early stage, American employers were more hostile to unions than their European counterparts. The implications for the nature of the strikes which did occur are obvious.

Despite their problems with achieving recognition from employers, American unions were generally dominated by a belief in economic, and not political, struggles. Such an emphasis was encouraged by the nature of the American political system: the split between Federal and State levels, and the ability and willingness of the courts to declare unconstitutional legislation which was felt to hinder inter-State commerce or interfere with individual rights, made it difficult to obtain effective legislation on minimum wages or union rights. But, given the hostility of employers to any form of organization, unions naturally found that their first need was to establish themselves industrially. Political factors may have encouraged this, by making the legislative alternative less attractive than it was elsewhere, but unions' basic interests lay in establishing and, an equally important aspect in view of employers' willing-

36. J. Holt, 'Trade Unionism in the British and U.S. Steel Industries, 1888–1912: A Comparative Study', *Labor History*, XVIII, pp. 5–35 (1977).

ness to retaliate, maintaining an adequate membership.

All this helps to explain why the political sphere has remained relatively unimportant in America. Existing 'political' accounts do not explain why this contrast with Europe came about. Given the weakness of the American union movement at the start of the 1930s, there was, at least in principle, the possibility of governmental action on a scale similar to that which occurred in several European countries. It is true that one reason why this possibility was not realized was that American politicians disliked interventionism. But this dislike was encouraged by the pre-existing stress on job control, which made collective bargaining seem such an appropriate instrument for the regulation of disputes. As noted in Chapter 5, it was taken for granted in the Wagner Act that collective bargaining was the best means to reduce the level of strike activity. This is not the place to discuss why the Wagner Act took its particular form. But central to it was a concern to rectify what were felt to be fundamental injustices in the way unions and workers were treated in the work place. Managerial control was seen as excessive, and strikes were seen as protests against this industrial autocracy. The way to provide a proper balance was to encourage unions to be able to organize freely, and to insist that management bargain in good faith with a union which met with the approval of the majority of the work force.

In other areas, notably agriculture, the government was taking an interventionist approach which was, in the American context, revolutionary. That direct interventionism did not occur in industrial relations can be attributed to the importance which control over the work place had already assumed. Legislators took it for granted that collective bargaining would solve all the key industrial problems of the period. This approach was certainly in line with the wishes of trade union leaders. And, although employers opposed the new legislation, the speed with which prominent firms recognized unions suggests that many employers felt that they were not giving too much away. Collective bargaining was less of a threat for employers than direct government intervention. Management could control its operation more directly than it could governmental action. Although collective bargaining meant giving up some of the more extreme forms of managerial domination, it did not shift the locus of control away from the work place.

This account would naturally require amplification and modification before it could be accepted as an explanation of management's acceptance of collective bargaining. In particular, the extent to which the New Deal reforms were mere liberal attempts to strengthen capitalism would have to be assessed against the alternative view that 'genuine' reforms were made. But the present outline has served two purposes. First, it has placed in perspective political accounts of American strike trends. American strikes were lengthy battles before the New Deal not because they were 'as much political as economic' but because they involved crucial and fundamental battles over the control of the work place. And the terms of 'admission to the polity' for the American working class were not something which was simply imposed by the government. The terms of admission were a particular form of the institutionalization of the pre-existing struggle for control of the work place. Second, America's present bargaining structure has been placed in context. As the institutionalized expression of an intense struggle for control, the structure reflects the conflicts on which it was built. As explained above, a broad scope of collective bargaining and a pattern of plant agreements provide an opportunity for long strikes. Such a structure has not appeared by accident, but reflects the previous struggle for control.

In helping to explain the origins of the post-war system, a 'control' account has much to offer. But can it go further, and provide a more direct explanation of the length of strikes under the system? First, and most obviously, a battle over 'control issues' can be identified in some of the most significant strikes of the period. Thus, the strikes in the automobile industry in 1946 were seen by management as an attempt by the unions to gain control over certain key issues, of which details of company profits assumed the greatest significance.[37] The 1959 steel strike took on its intense form only after management sought to alter a contract clause concerned with manning arrangements.[38] Dunlop has listed several other prominent strikes of the late 1950s and early 1960s in which bargaining structure, as distinct from the 'economic' outcome of that structure, were the key issue.[39] And the lengthy strikes over 'coalition' bargaining in the electrical and copper-mining industries,

37. See I. Howe and B. J. Widick, *The U.A.W. and Walter Reuther* (New York: Random House, 1949), pp. 126–48; F. H. Harbison and R. Dubin, *Patterns of Union-Management Relations* (Chicago: Science Research Associates, 1947), pp. 46–9; W. Serrin, *The Company and the Union: The 'Civilized Relationship' of the General Motors Corporation and the United Auto Workers* (New York: Vintage Books, 1974), pp. 157–68.

38. R. Herding, *Job Control and Union Structure* (Rotterdam: Rotterdam University Press, 1972), p. 28. See also R. L. Raimon, 'Affluence, Collective Bargaining and Steel', *Labor Law Journal,* XI, pp. 979–86 (1960) for the view that management and unions had the resources to engage in a long strike and that industry-wide bargaining encouraged employers to stand firm.

39. J. T. Dunlop, 'Structure of Collective Bargaining', *The Next 25 Years of Industrial Relations,* ed. G. G. Somers (Madison: Industrial Relations Research Association, 1973), pp. 10–18.

which were discussed at the end of Chapter 6, similarly reveal disputes over bargaining structure. Second, as noted in Chapter 6, a significant number of strikes have occurred outside the area of institutionalized bargaining. Thus, it was shown in Table 6.5 that about one sixth of all strikes have been over a new agreement, or occurred in the absence of any collective agreement. These include such well-known and bitter struggles as the attempts to organize Californian agricultural workers. In a substantial proportion of strikes, direct struggles for control have remained important.

Even with 'economic' disputes, a control explanation can play a part. This is not to suggest that job control was the fundamental cause of such disputes. Not only would this be to commit several methodological and theoretical errors,[40] but it would also be very difficult to reconcile with the evidence of Chapter 2, which showed that wages and other economic matters have always dominated the manifest issues of strikes. But the well-known hostility of American employers towards unions has not been restricted to strikes specifically over recognition or bargaining structure. In other areas, the substantive demands have, of course, been important, but giving way on them could imply more than the concession of a wage increase. As Marshall was among the first to recognize, a strike is one part of a longer campaign: it may appear irrational to hold out when the difference between the parties is a few cents a week, but giving way can have greater implications in the future because of the symbolic importance of victory.[41] This point is, of course, applicable to strikes anywhere, but it takes on particular importance in America because of the country's tradition of union-management hostility. Defeat is more likely to lead to further defeats, as the victorious side attempts to push home its advantage, than it is in other countries. Thus, it is felt to be essential that even 'economic' disputes be pursued as vigorously as possible. If they are not, moderation will be interpreted as a sign of weakness and the initiative will swing to the other side.

The tendency to have long strikes is thus self-perpetuating. Once it becomes accepted that rapid concessions will be taken as a sign of weakness, both sides must take up apparently intransigent positions and prepare for a long fight. It is true that this process has taken on ele-

---

40. See P. K. Edwards, 'The "Social" Determination of Strike Activity: an Explication and Critique', *Journal of Industrial Relations*, XXI, pp. 198–216 (1979).

41. A. Marshall and M. P. Marshall, *The Economics of Industry* (London: Macmillan, 1891), p. 193; A. Marshall, *Elements of Economics of Industry* (London: Macmillan, 1907), p. 379n.

ments of ritual, with a well-known succession of stages leading to a strike, which is itself conducted in a ritualistic fashion.[42] But it does not follow that strikes have ceased to be 'real' conflicts. The whole point of rituals is that they place a predictable form on a given phenomenon. But they do not negate the reality of the phenomenon itself. Similarly, it might be suggested that growing mutual accommodation between unions and management means that there is no longer a struggle for control. But accommodation does not imply consensus. There may be agreement about certain matters which were in dispute in the past, and it is certainly true that much of the violence which used to characterize American strikes has disappeared. But, although bargaining has become institutionalized, the terms of that institutionalization have meant that conflict has not been removed. Collective bargaining has been a means to regulate the form of industrial conflict, but it has not attempted to prevent conflict from occurring: once the mechanisms of bargaining have been employed the resolution of the conflict lies in the use of sanctions.

This account has gone some way towards explaining why unions and management want to engage in long strikes, as distinct from their ability to do so. Many strikes, even under the institutionalized system of bargaining, involve matters of bargaining structure and job control. Even 'economic' disputes reflect the past, in that defeat is a more serious problem that it is elsewhere. And, once a system based on long battles has become established, it is likely to perpetuate itself. It is true that such battles have been eliminated from countries such as Sweden, where they used to be common. There is nothing inevitable in any trend, however self-reinforcing it may be. But the Swedish solution depended on a particular combination of factors, such as an interventionist government and strong national federations of employers and unions, which have been conspicuously absent in America. Moreover, the American system was institutionalized in a particular way, and to alter the system would require a greater effort than was needed to set it up in the first place. The self-sustaining tendency to long strikes is thus unlikely to be altered in the foreseeable future.

This account of American strikes has moved some way from international comparisons and from the original concept of control. It may be made more specific by returning to the contrast between Britain and America. The general struggle for control of the work place has prob-

42. R. Dubin, 'Power and Union-management Relations', *Readings in Industrial Sociology*, ed. W. A. Faunce (New York: Appleton-Century-Crofts), pp. 465–81 at p. 471.

ably been at least as important in Britain as it has in America, and cannot therefore be used to explain the great length of American strikes. As the previous discussion has suggested, it has been the intensity of specific struggles which has been important in America. The presence of a general struggle for control does not in itself explain the details of a country's strike pattern, but is mediated by various forces and, possibly, counteracted by others. Thus, strikes in America have been long because, when a dispute has led to a strike, the conflict has involved crucial interests of the parties. In particular, employers have not only been hostile to unions in general terms, but also prepared to put this hostility into practice when faced with a strike. Thus, each strike has been an intense struggle, in which control has often been an important issue. In the period since the New Deal this pattern has been reinforced by various characteristics of the bargaining system: strikes have not necessarily been directly about control issues, but the system has been built on the premise that a long strike is the only way to ensure that one's interests are properly defended, a premise which has been strengthened by other aspects of the system.

In Britain, the general struggle for control did not involve such intense and violent struggles over union recognition as it did in America. The bargaining system has reflected the general control struggle in a different way. To take a key example, which is cited by Clegg,[43] American automobile firms have placed great stress on creating and maintaining effective control systems, whereas their British counterparts have operated under fragmented systems. As Clegg says, this reflects the importance of disputes procedures and agreements in America, as against the power of work place organizations in Britain. But it also highlights the contrast between the presence of control struggles and the intensity of their manifestation.

As Turner *et al.* point out, the American auto industry has not been particularly strike-prone, whereas the British industry has a reputation (albeit a somewhat exaggerated one) for strikes.[44] But the American industry has had some very long and bitter strikes, most notably during the New Deal, in 1946, and in 1970. The British industry has had frequent, short strikes reflecting an immediate struggle for control. America's long strikes have involved intense struggles over particular issues, but the existence of effective managerial control systems has prevented a more general struggle for control. It is not surprising in

43. Clegg, op. cit., pp. 107–08.
44. H. A. Turner *et al.*, *Labour Relations in the Motor Industry* (London: Allen and Unwin, 1967), pp. 23, 298–300.

view of this that the long-established American-owned car firms in Britain, Ford and Vauxhall, have had strike patterns different from the rest of the industry. Vauxhall has, until recently, had a reputation for industrial peace unrivalled in the industry: control systems have been able to prevent overt protest. Ford has always made a point of defending managerial prerogative and, in particular, has refused to use piecework systems of payment. But its strikes have been long and often bitter battles. As in America, even wage disputes have taken on the character of intense battles.

Thus, as argued earlier in this chapter, a country's strike pattern undoubtedly reflects aspects of its collective bargaining arrangements. An explanation based on the form of job control develops this point in three main ways. First, it helps to show why the particular bargaining structure in America was established. The present discussion, together with that of Chapter 5, has provided an answer to one of the questions raised at the start of this study, namely how 'institutionalization' came about, and on what terms. Although a process of institutionalization took place, and although this served to eliminate some of the violence from American strikes, the system was based on the premise that 'conflict was normal': instead of channelling disputes into 'peaceful' directions, it made the strike itself an institution for regulating disputes, and helped to build in a tendency to long battles. Moreover, the system was unable to insulate conflict within the formal bargaining arena. As the development of unofficial strikes has shown, forces of de-institutionalization and challenge to the system are present; indeed, given the general emphasis on job control in America, such forces are bound to exist. The system has proved fairly resilient so far, but this need not continue.

The second point about the control explanation is that it provides an insight into the incentive to the parties to engage in long battles. In several strikes, even under the institutionalized system, key aspects of control are directly involved. In others, the parties have feared the consequences of defeat and this, together with the built-in need to hold long strikes to convince the other party of the seriousness of one's intentions, has helped to prevent strikes from growing shorter. Similarly, the emergence of unofficial disputes can be explained in terms of the importance of job control in a general sense, and the inability of a formal disputes procedure to cope with all the problems which arise as a result of this.

Third, attention to the form of a particular control struggle enables the interests of the parties to be considered. American strikes have been long not because of the presence of a general struggle but because strikes, when they have occurred, have been fought intensely. This can be related to the hostility of employers to unions, but that hostility may also help to explain why strike activity has not been even greater than it has. As the following section will show, American employers have not taken a simplistic approach of attacking all manifestations of worker organization. They have sought to create loyalty to themselves and to exploit divisions within the work force. Such actions have been assisted, albeit unwillingly, by trade unions' concentration on sectional and limited goals. There have, therefore, been forces at work tending to moderate strike frequency and size. But when a conflict has occurred, there has been no point in pursuing a policy of moderation. The conflict has emerged, and both sides have been committed to winning it.

The Parties to Industrial Conflict

Employers

Not only is the concept of managerial attitudes vague and difficult to handle, but there is a whole range of possible approaches to unions.[45] Nevertheless, it remains broadly true that American employers have been far more hostile to unions than have their counterparts elsewhere, and have been prepared to follow the practical implications of this hostility. This tendency can be explained, in turn, by the interaction between general societal values in America and the nature of capitalism in the country.

As Lipset has argued, the values of equality and individual achievement have been pre-eminent in America.[46] According to Lipset, such values explain aspects of union behaviour: for example, achievement leads to a stress on ends rather than means and hence corruption and racketeering are more likely in America then elsewhere. But such general societal values will also affect employers. Thus, a belief in individual achievement may reinforce hostility to unions: an employer

45. Clegg op. cit., p. 108. On variations in managerial policies see B. M. Selekman, 'Varieties of Labor Relations', *Readings in Labor Economics and Industrial Relations*, ed. J. Shister (2nd edn; Chicago: J. B. Lippincott, 1956), pp. 386–408; H. R. Northrup, 'The Case for Boulwarism', *Labor: Readings on Major Issues,* ed. R. A. Lester (New York: Random House, 1965), pp. 397–419. See also pp. 131–2, above, for the well-known differences between the National Association of Manufacturers and the National Civic Federation in the early years of the twentieth century.

46. Lipset, op. cit. Lipset's views on American unions are reprinted in S. M. Lipset, *The First New Nation: The United States in Historical and Comparative Perspective* (London: Heinemann, 1964), which contains several other papers on American values and their creation.

who believes in strictly individual achievement and in the openness of American society is unlikely to welcome collective organization among his work force. It is true, of course, that these values coincide with capitalist interests but they have some significance of their own. Thus, an employer faced with a demand for union recognition will find his opposition to the demand strengthened if he can rationalize his resistance in terms of certain fundamental beliefs, which are held not only by himself and other employers but also by the general public. Attacks on strikers for their 'un-American' behaviour are more than pure rhetoric.

The value of equality might be felt to counteract this opposition to unions. But equality has been interpreted in America to mean strict equality of treatment before the law, and the right of the individual to do as he pleases with his own property. It has not carried overtones of fraternity or solidarity. Indeed, it has meant that employers have been able to claim that they are formally equal to their employees and that, given the equally important value of individualism, collective organization among workers is unnecessary. As will be seen below, this is a view which has been endorsed by the courts.

Such abstract and general values cannot, in themselves, account for the continuing hostility of employers to unions. But their significance must not be overlooked: they helped to establish a social system which, even before the coming of industrial capitalism, stressed individual achievement and the right of a man to manage his property as he saw fit. And, even though the inconsistency of applying individualism to the labour contract while developing the cartel and the trust soon became apparent, these general social values remained important resources for employers challenged by collective organization by their workers. Indeed, these values may help to explain why capitalism in America took on an extreme form: they provided a fertile environment unhindered by pre-existing traditional obligations. Individual achievement was the aim, and there were few constraints on how this was attained in practice.

The absence of feudalism has long been seen as an important influence on the growth of the American social structure. But a further factor must also be considered. Although 'feudal' traditions imposed certain obligations on employers, they also called for loyalty and deference among employees. American employers were therefore faced with the problem of creating and maintaining their own legitimacy in a particularly stark way. Their genius lay, it has been argued, in creating 'feudal' traditions where none existed previously; in making themselves the focus of loyalty, they provided a moral basis for capitalism without which the system would have rested on the unstable ground of a pure cash nexus.[47] Values such as 'Americanism', although reflecting the country's own pre-industrial traditions to some extent, were developed and systematized to provide a focus of loyalty for workers with no traditional allegiances.

Employers' hostility to unions was not a straightforward reflection of the nature of American capitalism. It is true that the system developed in a more 'extreme' way than it did in Europe, and that, particularly in the early years, it was characterized by rapid technical change. But if the aim was simply profit, it may have been in employers' interests to recognize unions, thus reducing the threat to production from industrial disputes. Or, at least, it might not have been worth their while to oppose, and seek to destroy, the craft societies which had already established themselves. Control over the plant was important for other reasons. If employers had to create loyalty, they could not afford any threat to the process; workers had to be tied directly to the employer, and to no one else. Such an approach was naturally strengthened by a general stress on individual achievement: employers' attempts to foster loyalty interacted with, and were reinforced by, a general stress in society on individual, and not collective, goals.

The development of loyalty was associated with another need of employers. As noted in Chapter 4, there was considerable opposition to capitalism from the commercial classes and other groups, notably farmers, who were opposed to the 'corporate ideal'. An ideology stressing the role of business, the importance of profit, and so on helped to moderate opposition from groups outside the working class; and, by contrasting the Americanism of employers with the radicalism and subversive tendencies of workers, capitalists could drive a wedge between the working class and its erstwhile allies.

For all these reasons, direct control of the work place was crucial for American employers. Capitalists had to establish their legitimacy against challenge from several directions. Having done so, they could afford to take a slightly different approach. Thus, it was first necessary to disarm the potential challenge from craft trade unions but, after this had been done, it was possible to exploit the divisions within the working class. In other words, skilled workers had first to be separated from their unions and then from their less skilled fellow workers. The welfare programmes and attempts to co-operate with moderate unions of the

47. S. Aronowitz, *False Promises* (New York: McGraw-Hill, 1973), p. 183.

early years of the twentieth century were directed at the second of these aims.[48]

Thus the destruction of craft unions cannot be seen as the direct result of technical change; such change interacted with employers' desires to establish their own control of the work place. Nevertheless, technology has played a continuing role, not only in a general sense but also in relation to strike patterns. Part of the exceptionalism of American capitalism has lain in the speed and extent of technical advance; many industries have been more capital-intensive than their counterparts in Europe, a tendency which can, of course, be related to the drive for profit in America. The need to be free to introduce new modes of operation has reinforced employers' wishes to retain control over their plants. The 'right to manage' has been more than an abstract principle, and has reflected very real needs. In many cases, of course, that right has gone unchallenged, but technical change has been a significant strand running through the strike movement. It was the factor directly responsible for the destruction of craft modes of production at the end of the nineteenth century, and subsequent developments of mass production methods carried important implications for control of the work place. And, as noted in Chapter 6, the role of automation was clear in several long and important strikes in the 1950s and 1960s. The precise nature of these changes, and their impact on industrial relations, naturally differed widely. But they reveal a constant pressure from technology on industrial relations: the system of managerial control established at the end of the nineteenth century has had to be defended and modified. This has not always led to strikes, but it has placed a general pressure on the system, a point which will be taken up further below.

The value of individual achievement, the need to create loyalty, and the importance of introducing technical innovations have all contributed to employers' hostility to unions. Much more could be said on all these topics, but all that is needed here is an indication of the main forces which led to the particularly extreme views of American employers. In addition to providing some general idea of American employers' views, it has been possible to show why control of the work place was so important: the 'right to manage' was more at issue than it

48. See J. A. Garraty, 'The U.S. Steel Corporation versus Labor: The Early Years', *Labor History*, I, pp. 3–38 (1960); R. Ozanne, *A Century of Labor-Management Relations* (Madison: University of Wisconsin Press, 1967), esp. pp. 25–8, 71–95; and, for a general consideration, M. Dubofsky, *Industrialism and the American Worker, 1865–1920* (New York: Thomas Y. Crowell, 1975).

was elsewhere, and management had to obtain control in order to establish and legitimate that right.

If this explains the origins of hostility to unions, what accounts for its continuation? Tradition must play a part: once a particular pattern has been established, it tends to perpetuate itself. Moreover, the value of individual achievement has been a constant feature of American society. Thus, although total opposition to unions may be less common than it was, the idea of attaining goals through individual means remains prevalent. Factors such as technical change have also been important, which is where the extreme nature of American capitalism attains its significance. The drive for profit has been more intense than elsewhere because the values of loyalty which were created were directed in a particular direction; they did not involve the whole complex of 'pre-industrial' values, but were directed specifically at legitimating capitalism. Thus, once that process had been concluded, the drive for profit could develop, not only without hindrance but with positive support. The individual employer, whatever his own views on unionism, has feared the consequences of giving way to union demands and has followed the requirements of the system in stressing his own right to manage.

In addition to these general forces, the pattern of bargaining has developed its own momentum. As argued above, the institutionalization of bargaining during the New Deal has strengthened the tendency to plant bargaining. But, even before that, employers and unions were locked in a struggle located at work place level: employer hostility and unions' responses interacted to produce a system which was difficult to change. That the system did not change is also associated with government policy, which is considered next.

The Government

As Clegg points out, the American government has probably been more directly under the influence of business interests than has the government of any other major Western democracy.[49] This has been apparent in many respects, but has been particularly obvious in the field of labour relations. Until the Norris–LaGuardia Anti-Injunction Act of 1932, the Executive branch avoided direct involvement in labour relations. But the 'non-decision' to leave matters to the courts implied that the courts' approach was seen as essentially correct. That approach was based on an extreme doctrine of individualism, whereby such things as 'yellow-dog' contracts and injunctions against strikes were accepted as

49. Clegg, op. cit., pp. 26, 108.

legitimate expressions of individual rights.[50] The close conformity of this with managerial interests is readily apparent.

The Executive branch was prepared to take a more positive approach when strikes appeared to threaten 'public order'. But its intervention in such disputes as the Pullman strike of 1894 and the anthracite coal strike of 1902 was on a very narrow basis. Whether or not public order was seriously threatened went unquestioned, and the government was interested solely in resolving the strike and not in taking a longer-term interest in industrial relations.[51] The government did not always side with employers: in several cases of intervention in strikes employers were criticized, and various governments appointed commissions of inquiry into labour relations whose conclusions often displayed considerable sympathy with the workers. But there was no serious attempt to alter the courts' approach to labour matters, and direct intervention only when a dispute was defined as a problem of public order meant that the government tended to take a partial view of the situation.

Thus, except in a few prominent cases, government involvement could not be expected to help resolve a strike. The parties were left to fight it out between themselves. Several other countries were establishing systems of arbitration or mediation, or were at least tending towards patterns of *ad hoc* intervention. The absence of anything similar in America was a contributory factor in the length of strikes before the New Deal.

Formal peacetime intervention was not accepted until after the second world war. The Taft–Harley Act of 1947 empowered the government to order a cooling-off period in a dispute which was felt to endanger public health or safety. Although marking a new development in government policy, this approach has not been of a type which is likely to reduce the length of strikes. Indeed, the opposite may have been the case. For example, the government intervened in several disputes in the steel industry during the late 1940s and early 1950s, which led the employers and unions to expect this intervention and to lose

50. See C. O. Gregory, *Labor and the Law* (2nd edn; New York, W. W. Norton, 1958); E. E. Witte, *The Government in Labor Disputes* (New York: McGraw-Hill, 1932); W. D. Lane, *Civil War in West Virginia* (New York: B. W. Huebsch, 1921).

51. On the Pullman strike see G. G. Eggert, *Railroad Labor Disputes: The Beginnings of Federal Strike Policy* (Ann Arbor: University of Michigan Press, 1967); on the 1902 coal strike see R. H. Wiebe, 'The Anthracite Strike of 1902: A Record of Confusion', *Mississippi Valley Historical Review*, LXVIII, pp. 229–51 (1961).

interest in reaching a settlement between themselves.[52] More generally, a policy based on cooling-off periods and injunctions is unlikely to contribute to the speedy resolution of disputes. The East Coast long-shore industry, which has had regular experience of Taft—Harley injunctions, has been noted more for the great length and complexity of its disputes than for rapid settlements.

It is true that the government has had less formal means of intervention at its disposal, notably through the Federal Mediation and Conciliation Service, and that State as well as Federal government involvement may be important. But such involvement has not sought to challenge the idea that disputes are to be resolved by direct conflict between the parties immediately involved. The legacy of the Wagner Act, and the belief that collective bargaining is sufficient to resolve disputes, has meant that government involvement, of whatever form, has imposed little pressure on the parties to reach agreement.

Finally, the government's attitude to intervention in strikes and to the isolation of economic and political matters has influenced the integration of trade unions into the existing political structure. As noted above, Shorter and Tilly see labour's political involvement in terms of a breakthrough by the working class to political recognition. But the government and employers have exerted a crucial influence on the terms of which 'recognition' is granted to labour. Any breakthrough was on very limited terms, and did not challenge the basis of the system as a whole. Indeed, 'recognition' was granted largely because unions posed no serious challenge; it was not won by a working class determined to wrest political power from capitalists, but by a union movement which had already accepted the fundamentals of the system. The reasons for this must now be considered.

Workers and Unions

A major strand of American labour historiography has sought to explain why business unionism prevailed over more radical union movements and why socialism, despite its prominence at certain times, failed to establish a lasting hold on the American working class. It is not necessary to go into this argument in any detail here. All that is required is an indication of the influence of certain key characteristics of workers and unions on the American strike pattern.

As mentioned in Chapter 1, American unions have been seen as

---

52. F. H. Harbison and R. C. Spencer, 'The Politics of Collective Bargaining: The Postwar Record in Steel', *American Political Science Review*, LXVIII, pp. 705–20 (1954). See also Raimon, op. cit.

exhibiting a paradox because they are militant and strike-prone and yet politically conservative.[53] But there was nothing inconsistent in the use of militant means for the attainment of ends which socialists and others saw as unduly limited. Union leaders such as Gompers and John L. Lewis may have adopted a business union philosophy, but they pursued their aims vigorously. In other words, there was no real paradox, in that its two elements were not logically opposed. If the paradox is recognized for what it is, namely an unusual but not absurd feature of the labour movement, the reasons for its presence may be considered in terms of the framework outlined above. American unions placed relatively great stress on work place matters, because the intense hostility of the employers forced their attention in this direction and because action in the political sphere was less attractive than it was elsewhere. As Galenson points out, this lack of political interest can be explained in turn by two factors: the fact that several measures which became important political demands in Europe, notably the right to vote and free public education, already existed in America; and the lack of political class consciousness among American workers.[54]

The initial impetus towards concentration on the work place was encouraged by the success of business unions in attaining their goals. A high standard of living and a rapid rate of economic growth have been seen as important reasons for the weakness of socialism in America.[55] How far unions caused real wages to be higher than in Europe is an open question, but the fact of this relative prosperity enabled business unions to stress the solid material benefits to be gained from their own approach, compared with the less obvious and immediate gains from a more radical programme. Not surprisingly, business unions, when faced with the reforms of the New Deal, put their weight behind the establishment of collective bargaining and eschewed more overtly 'political' changes.

There is, then, nothing odd about American unions' acceptance of the wider political order combined with their militant pursuit of economic aims. Indeed, given the hostility from employers, there was a need to fight for any concessions. It is true that business unions were preferable, from an employer's point of view, to more radical challenges to managerial control of the work place, and that a significant strand of

53. See above, p. 3.
54. W. Galenson, 'Why the American Labor Movement is not Socialist', *American Review* (1961), pp. 1–19 at pp. 3, 16.
55. Ibid., pp. 8–10; W. Sombart, *Why is there no Socialism in the United States?* trans. P. M. Hocking and C. T. Husbands (London: Macmillan, 1976), pp. 62–92.

employer policy involved the 'incorporation' of moderate unions.[56] But even business unions posed some challenge: in particular, high wage demands could challenge the employer's profit position. Once a decision had been taken to oppose a claim, employers would, as argued above, be expected to pursue their case with vigour. Similarly, the union would need to demonstrate its success in material terms since, lacking traditions of working-class solidarity, it needed material success to retain the loyalty of its members.

Finally, the characteristics of the working class help to explain aspects of American strike patterns, in particular the moderate frequency and size of strikes. Divisions within the class and the attitudes of its members are of particular significance. At the end of the nineteenth century the division between skilled and unskilled workers was considerable: skilled men saw themselves as an elite and looked down on the unskilled worker. More specifically, the position of craftsmen was challenged in more obvious and direct ways by technical change than was that of semi-skilled and unskilled workers. This division on skill lines was overlaid with others, most notably those between native and immigrant, and white and black, workers. Moreover, the cleavages within the American working class may have been greater in some respects than those elsewhere; the depth of the division between black and white workers was probably unparalleled. And such divisions were exacerbated by other features of America, notably the geographical dispersion of the country's main industrial centres: the problems facing workers in Chicago, New York, and Los Angeles were different, and effective organization was hard to achieve.[57]

As noted above with respect to the steel industry, these divisions cannot in themselves account for America's unique strike record. Similar divisions, particularly those based on skill and religion, existed in other countries. But, taken together with other factors, they help to explain aspects of the strike picture. Thus, they reduced the solidarity of the working class as a whole and reduced the likelihood of large strikes mobilizing the whole of the class. 'General' strikes were limited to particular cities.[58] As well as inhibiting the size of strikes, class divisions operated more indirectly by limiting the appeal of unions

56. See, in particular, J. Weinstein, *The Corporate Ideal in the Liberal State, 1900–1918* (Boston: Beacon, 1968).
57. For the argument that American society was dominated by sectional interests, see R. H. Wiebe, *The Segmented Society: An Introduction to the Meaning of America* (New York: Oxford University Press, 1975).
58. W. H. Crook, *Communism and the General Strike* (Hamden, Conn.: Shoe String, 1960).

stressing radical goals. This in turn strengthened business unionism, with the consequences noted above. Finally, employers were, of course, aware of the divisions, and the use of immigrant and Southern workers was a well-known tactic to break up the solidarity of an area. In other words, the interaction between the nature of the working class and unions and employers strengthened the tendency towards sectionalism and economism.

The second feature of the working class concerns the attitudes of its members. The lack of class consciousness has been a well-known feature of American workers, and has been explained by such things as a belief in the openness of American society, which implies a stress on individual mobility and not collective advancement. Even if it is true that upward social mobility is no easier than in other countries, it is still possible that the ideology of mobility reduces feelings of solidarity. Whatever the truth about beliefs in mobility, it remains the case that American workers have displayed much less of a solidaristic attitude than their European counterparts. Moreover, as argued above, values of individualism and achievement led to a stress on material gains. The reasons for the predominance of these values do not need detailed consideration here. What is important is their interaction with other factors. Thus, American employers were able, given the relative prosperity of the economy, to meet some of the material aspirations of their workers. They could also use welfare programmes and the like to develop loyalty to themselves, which had the additional feature of tending to exacerbate divisions between groups of workers since it was the skilled, white, workers who gained most from them. Similarly, the stress on material ends encouraged business unionism, whose success acted as a further stimulant to material goals.

Many of these factors concerned with workers and unions imply a low level of militancy. They thus help to explain why strike frequency and size were not greater than they were. But, as argued above, when strikes did break out they were long battles. The characteristics of workers are part of the explanation of this. Solidarity across the whole of the working class may have been limited, but within particular groups it was often considerable. Once a strike had begun, solidarity was often as great as in any European strike. Moreover, there were times when the various sectors of the working class united in strike action. But such episodes tended to be short-lived, for reasons connected with the fragility of the unity, the lack of concern of unions with developing a more long-lasting and broader-based solidarity, and the ability of employers to combat even the largest and most militant stoppages.

Thus, there were in America powerful forces inhibiting the development of a socialist union movement. These contributed to the growth of business unionism and to an emphasis on material gains. But business unions often fought their strikes vigorously; their opposition to American capitalism as a whole was not so much disarmed as channelled into the economic arena. In that arena they were as 'militant' as their more radical challengers and, given their stress on strike funds and organization, particularly capable of engaging in long battles with employers.

This chapter has offered an explanation of the differences between American strikes patterns and those of other countries. It might be argued that the account advanced here should, in addition, be able to explain differences within America, particularly differences between industries. Although a 'job control' explanation has some things to offer in this direction, the task of developing it cannot be undertaken here. The explanation can be applied between countries because differences in employer policies, for example, are sufficiently dramatic and well-known for their implications for strikes to be considered. But detailed investigation would be required within particular industries before the role of employer policies in differences in strike rates could be established with any certainty. Moreover, some of the influences considered above, particularly government policy, apply to all industries; they are relevant only at the national level, and would have to be replaced by other measures at the industry level. And, as Tables 6.9 and 6.10 show, the tendency to have long strikes, which, it has been argued, is a key feature of the American pattern, was shared by virtually all industries.

The application of the present account to inter-industry differences would thus require a separate investigation. But previous chapters have established some of the main proximate influences on these differences. Such things as a high level of unionization have tended to increase strike activity. More generally, there was a tendency for industries undergoing rapid growth or subject to fluctuation in demand to have high strike rates. This was no more than a general tendency, however. As Chapter 4 showed in detail, there was a variety of responses to industrialization which certainly 'reflected' industrial change, but in different ways according to the nature of the change and the ability of workers to resist it. Although technical change has exerted a continuing effect on strike patterns, it has done so by posing a general challenge to existing institutional arrangements. It has not had identical effects everywhere.

At the start of this study, the question was posed as to how American strike patterns responded to industrial change. The growth of an industrial economy certainly meant that strikes emerged in sectors where they had previous been absent. And, after the defeat of craft workers' resistance to new forms of organization, strikes increasingly reflected economic struggles. But, since the 1880s, there has been no dramatic alteration in the amount of strike activity and, despite changes in industrial organization and institutional factors, strike activity has continued to fluctuate with economic forces. This is because America's regulatory institutions have not challenged the way that strikes have been fought. Strikes have been direct clashes between workers and employers. They have not been mere demonstrations or indirect means of exerting political pressure. They have been battles over control of the work place. Although industrial change has affected the nature of these battles, it has not altered their overall importance. As a result, American strikes have retained a unique degree of intensity, which is likely to arouse the interest of analysts for many years to come.

APPENDICES

Appendix A

TABLE A.1

STRIKE INDICES, 1881–1974

	W/N (no.)	D/N (000s)	D/W (no.)	W/T (×1000)	D/T (no.)	N/E (×1m.)	W/E (×1000)	D/E (no.)
1881–85	334			1150		58.3	19.5	
1886–89	287			580		125	35.7	
1890–93	192			822		141	27.0	
1894–97	365			1230		97.3	35.5	
1898–1901	235			588		139	32.6	
1902–05	205			319		168	34.5	
1906–08	117			179		162	19.0	
1909–11	198			254		135	26.7	
1912–15	270			336		144	38.9	
1916–18	351			437		153	53.5	
1919–22	791			463		102	80.4	
1923–26	422			153		45.1	19.0	
1927–29	381	19.8	41.8	89.1	4.22	24.7	10.3	0.489
1930–33	506	9.43	18.6	167	3.11	38.9	19.7	0.367
1934–37	485	7.18	14.8	316	4.68	96.3	46.7	0.691
1938–41	394	4.66	11.8	174	2.05	95.5	37.6	0.445
1942–45	512	3.92	7.67	185	1.42	101	51.4	0.394
1946–49	748	15.0	20.0	214	4.28	91.0	68.2	1.36
1950–53	534	7.54	14.1	174	2.45	103	55.0	0.777
1954–57	489	6.57	13.4	115	1.55	74.3	36.4	0.490
1958–61	476	9.82	19.1	109	2.08	66.1	31.5	0.602
1962–65	367	8.71	15.1	79.7	1.20	62.9	23.1	0.349
1966–69	504	9.58	16.0	134	2.14	73.6	37.2	0.594
1970–72	523	8.89	17.0	133	2.26	73.8	38.6	0.656
1973–74	453	6.84	15.1			73.6	32.4	0.489

TABLE A.2

STRIKE INDICES, 1881–1974 (1927–29 = 100)

	W/N	D/N	D/W	W/T	D/T	N/E	W/E	D/E
1881–85	87.7			1291		236	189	
1886–89	75.3			651		506	347	
1890–93	50.4			923		571	262	
1894–97	95.8			1380		394	345	
1898–1901	61.7			660		563	317	
1902–05	53.8			358		680	335	
1906–08	30.7			201		656	184	
1909–11	52.0			285		547	259	
1912–15	70.9			377		583	378	
1916–18	92.1			490		619	520	
1919–22	208			520		413	781	
1923–26	111			172		183	185	
1927–29	100	100	100	100	100	100	100	100
1930–33	133	47.6	44.5	187	73.7	158	191	75.1
1934–37	127	36.3	35.4	355	111	390	453	141
1938–41	103	23.5	28.2	195	48.6	387	365	91.0
1942–45	134	19.8	18.4	208	33.7	409	499	80.6
1946–49	196	75.8	47.8	240	101	368	622	278
1950–53	140	38.1	33.7	195	58.1	417	534	159
1954–57	128	33.2	32.1	129	36.7	301	353	100
1958–61	125	49.6	45.7	122	49.3	268	306	123
1962–65	96.3	44.0	36.1	89.5	28.4	255	224	71.4
1966–69	132	48.4	38.3	150	50.7	298	361	121
1970–72	137	44.9	40.7	149	53.6	299	375	134
1973–74	119	34.5	36.1			298	315	100

TABLE A.3a

PER CENT OF 'CESSATIONS' WITH GIVEN NUMBER OF DAYS' DURATION, 1881–94

	1	2–3	4–6	7–14	15–29	30–59	60–89	90 and over	N
1881	13.6	17.6	10.0	27.1	13.4	9.8	4.3	4.4	632
1882	12.7	16.4	10.8	21.7	12.9	13.0	4.7	7.8	591
1883	9.8	15.6	8.4	28.3	12.5	12.0	5.3	8.1	642
1884	12.2	14.0	9.5	24.2	10.8	11.0	6.7	11.6	629
1885	6.5	12.5	7.7	26.5	12.5	17.3	6.2	11.0	875

continued

TABLE A.3a *continued*

	1	2–3	4–6	7–14	15–29	30–59	60–89	90 and over	N
1886	10.7	13.6	9.4	29.0	15.8	12.3	3.6	5.6	2393
1887	12.7	21.3	15.4	23.4	11.6	9.0	3.5	3.1	1497
1888	12.0	22.7	14.5	24.4	10.5	7.7	2.8	5.4	943
1889	12.3	22.6	15.5	22.5	13.4	7.4	2.9	3.3	1034
1890	12.7	22.7	17.4	24.6	10.0	7.9	2.1	2.7	1895
1891	11.2	22.4	15.5	22.1	13.2	9.3	3.1	3.2	1779
1892	10.3	24.7	15.1	22.6	11.6	7.9	3.3	4.6	1348
1893	12.3	22.5	13.9	23.3	12.0	8.5	3.5	3.9	1375
1894	11.8	23.2	11.9	24.4	12.7	7.8	4.6	3.6	927

NOTE

N refers to number of cessations in year.

For meaning of term 'cessation' see below, Appendix B, pp. 308–9.

1894 figures for first six months only.

TABLE A.3b

PER CENT OF STRIKES WITH GIVEN NUMBER OF DAYS' DURATION, 1916–74

	under 1	1	2–3	4–6	7–14	15–31	32–62	63–93	94 and over
1916–18	4.0	9.3	16.2	15.4	23.2	16.9	8.2	2.5	4.3
1919–22	2.2	4.1	8.4	10.1	19.2	19.2	16.7	7.4	12.8
1923–25	3.4	6.8	12.7	13.4	23.1	19.7	10.5	3.8	6.7
1926		7.4	12.9	13.9	27.2	17.9	13.5	3.3	4.3
1927–29			35.1		22.7	17.2	14.5	5.0	5.6
1930–33			40.1		21.5	17.7	14.2	4.3	2.2
1934–37			36.4		22.2	18.5	14.4	4.8	3.7
1938–41			38.5		23.3	17.6	12.5	3.9	4.3
1942–45		19.4	31.0	20.1	17.1	7.8	3.4	0.8	0.5
1946–49		9.6	14.9	14.1	20.9	17.0	13.2	5.0	5.4
1950–53		12.8	17.7	15.1	21.1	15.0	10.9	3.9	3.6
1954–57		13.0	15.7	14.5	21.2	16.2	11.5	4.1	3.7
1958–61		11.3	15.6	14.1	21.0	16.0	12.3	4.5	5.3
1962–65		11.2	15.0	14.8	21.4	15.4	11.7	4.7	5.8
1966–69		12.0	14.4	14.1	20.7	16.0	12.9	5.1	5.0
1970–72		13.9	14.0	12.8	17.6	15.3	13.7	6.2	6.4
1973–74		14.5	13.0	11.3	18.0	16.8	14.8	5.4	6.2

NOTE

For 1927–41, figures under '2–3 days' are for all strikes lasting less than 7 days; further breakdowns not available.

Categories of duration apply to 1916–26. For categories for 1927 onwards, see Table A.3c.

TABLE A.3c

PER CENT OF WORKERS INVOLVED IN STRIKES WITH GIVEN NUMBER OF DAYS' DURATION, 1927–74

	1	2–3	4–6	7–14	15–29	30–59	60–89	90 and over
1927–29		26.5		14.5	18.1	9.1	3.8	28.0
1930–33		23.9		23.2	23.4	18.5	5.8	5.2
1934–37		35.8		16.9	22.0	14.7	6.4	4.3
1938–41		36.9		18.6	16.5	23.3	2.6	1.9
1942–45	11.9	28.9	20.9	17.1	15.3	5.0	0.4	0.3
1946–49	6.4	11.3	7.8	22.7	12.4	27.4	3.8	8.1
1950–53	8.6	15.3	14.4	19.8	15.0	15.3	4.8	6.7
1954–57	8.3	18.1	14.4	20.2	14.3	16.5	4.4	3.8
1958–61	7.7	11.1	11.5	18.2	21.5	14.3	3.7	12.1
1962–65	11.0	12.7	11.8	19.6	17.1	18.0	5.6	4.1
1966–69	9.1	15.7	12.0	17.9	12.9	19.9	6.9	5.5
1970–72	13.2	16.0	10.5	18.4	16.0	12.9	5.4	7.7
1973–74	9.7	10.0	12.9	22.8	17.8	18.3	4.2	4.2

NOTE
For 1927–41, figures under '2–3 days' are for all strikes lasting less than 7 days.

TABLE A.3d

PER CENT OF STRIKER-DAYS IN STRIKES WITH GIVEN NUMBER OF DAYS' DURATION, 1927–74

	1	2–3	4–6	7–14	15–29	30–59	60–89	90 and over
1927–29		1.6		2.6	5.5	6.3	5.0	79.0
1930–33		4.0		10.7	17.0	26.8	14.6	27.0
1934–37		7.3		7.9	19.7	28.7	16.3	20.1
1938–41		6.9		10.4	15.6	42.7	8.8	15.6
1942–45	1.9	9.3	7.4	18.0	37.0	18.0	5.0	3.5
1946–49	0.3	1.1	1.3	6.8	8.5	39.5	9.0	33.7
1950–53	0.6	2.0	3.2	7.6	12.2	31.2	13.7	29.6
1954–57	0.6	2.3	3.5	8.4	14.0	32.3	15.4	23.6
1958–61	0.4	1.2	2.0	6.0	13.3	17.6	8.7	50.8
1962–65	0.7	1.8	2.7	8.6	15.0	30.3	15.4	25.5
1966–69	0.6	1.8	2.5	7.3	11.2	28.8	19.0	28.8
1970–72	0.7	1.7	2.0	5.9	11.1	18.6	13.2	46.8
1973–74	0.6	1.3	2.6	9.6	16.3	31.8	12.7	25.1

NOTE
For 1927–41, figures under '2–3 days' are for all strikes lasting less than 7 days.

Appendix A

TABLE A.4

'STRIKE WAVES', 1886–1970

	Given Measure as a Percentage of its Mean Over the Previous Five Years		
	N	W	D
1886	298	346	
1887	201	161	
1900	144	161	
1901	217	146	
1903	165	156	
1910	120	223	
1912	109	206	
1913	134	176	
1916	122	206	
1919	101	371	
1933	222	402	218
1934	189	318	229
1937	276	192	187
1941	145	233	152
1944	154	152	67
1945	129	220	338
1946	120	214	663
1952	126	150	164
1967	121	196	198
1970	121	143	182

NOTE

The above list includes all years in which the figure for N or W is 150 or more. In the sense of E. Shorter and C. Tilly, *Strikes in France, 1830–1968* (Cambridge: Cambridge University Press, 1974), at pp. 106–07 a strike wave occurs when *both* figures are at least 150.

TABLE A.5

INDICES OF UNION INVOLVEMENT IN STRIKES, 1881–1972

	% of Union Members Involved in Strikes $\frac{L}{T} \times 100$	Relative Union Propensity to Strike $\frac{S}{N-S} \times \frac{E-T}{T}$	Relative Propensity for Unionists to be Involved in Strikes $\frac{L}{W-L} \times \frac{E-T}{T}$
1881–85	72.7	2140	3860
1886–90	47.2	1530	2700
1891–95	85.2	3860	8100
1896–1900	54.0	2560	5550
1901–05	28.8	2010	3790
1916–21	n.a.	2180	n.a.
1923–26	n.a.	5700	n.a.
1927–29	8.99	5950	12900
1930–33	15.0	3330	9230
1934–36	30.7	7980	23400
1937–41	15.4	7350	20800
1942–45	16.0	4590	21400
1946–49	20.3	11630	66900
1950–55	15.2	15300	66900
1959–60	9.35	23600	107000
1961–63	7.32	23400	236000
1964–66	9.86	20800	83800
1967–69	14.1	14900	64300
1970–72	14.2	13900	53500

NOTE
For the second and third columns, a figure of 100 would indicate equality between union and non-union strikes.
For derivation of indices, see notes 22 and 24 to Chapter 2, below pp. 31 and 32. 'L' is the number of workers involved in strikes ordered by unions. 'T' is the number of unionists. 'S' is the number of strikes called by a union. 'N' is the total number of strikes. 'E' is total employed. 'W' is the number of workers involved in strikes.

SOURCES
For the second and third columns, data for 1881–1921 are taken from P. H. Douglas, 'An Analysis of Strike Statistics', *Journal of the American Statistical Association*, XVIII, pp. 866–77 (1923), at pp. 875–6. All other figures are calculated from official data: see Appendix D, below.

TABLE A.6

**ESTIMATES OF UNION DENSITY: MEMBERSHIP AS % OF
NON-AGRICULTURAL WORK FORCE, 1870–1970**

	(1)	(2)	(3)	(4)
1870–72	9.1			
1880	3.8			
1890	5.0			
1900	8.4	6.1		
1904		12.3		
1910		10.2	10.0	
1916		11.2		
1920		19.5	18.9	
1930		11.5	10.7	11.6
1935			13.3	13.2
1940			21.8	26.9
1945			29.9	35.5
1950			31.2	31.5
1955			31.7	33.2
1960			28.6	31.4
1965				28.4
1970				27.4

SOURCES
Column 1: L. Ulman, *The Rise of the National Trade Union* (Cambridge, Mass.:
Harvard University Press, 1955), p. 19. Column 2: L. Troy *Trade Union Membership, 1897–1962* (New York: National Bureau of Economic Research, 1965), p. 2;
figures include Canadian members of American unions. Column 3: Troy, loc. cit.;
figures exclude Canadian members. Column 4: B.L.S. figures, see below, Appendix D, p. 323.

TABLE A.7a

**PER CENT OF STRIKES WITH GIVEN ASSOCIATION WITH A UNION,
1916–74**

I

	Connected with Union		Not Connected with Union		Organized After Strike Began		Union and Non-Union Members	
	(1)	(2)	(1)	(2)	(1)	(2)	(1)	(2)
1916–18	85.5	58.4	12.8	8.8	1.9	1.3	—	—
1919–22	94.5	70.4	4.8	3.6	0.6	0.5	—	—
1923–26	88.1	81.3	8.1	7.4	1.4	1.3	2.4	2.2

Column 1: as % strikes where association with union reported.
Column 2: as % all strikes.

TABLE A.7a *continued*

II

	A.F.L.	C.I.O.	Other Union	No Union
1927–29	68.5		19.2	12.4
1930–33	59.2		22.9	17.9
1934–36	79.5		12.7	7.8
1937–41	52.4	35.3	8.7	3.5
1942–45	39.4	38.0	18.1	4.5
1946–49	52.0	30.3	16.0	1.8
1950–55	51.5	27.2	20.0	1.1

III

	A.F.L.–C.I.O.	Other Union	Different Affiliations	No Union
1961–63	75.2	22.5	1.3	1.0
1964–66	77.2	20.3	1.4	1.2
1967–69	69.4	27.6	1.2	1.7
1970–72	60.6	36.2	1.3	1.9
1973–74	56.6	41.6	0.8	1.0

TABLE A.7b

PER CENT OF WORKERS INVOLVED IN STRIKES WITH GIVEN ASSOCIATION WITH A UNION, 1927–74

I

	A.F.L.	C.I.O.	Other Union	No Union
1927–29	73.0		20.9	6.1
1930–33	65.4		27.3	7.4
1934–36	84.7		12.5	2.8
1937–41	31.0	60.9	6.8	1.4
1942–45	22.4	48.4	28.2	1.0
1946–49	29.0	36.8	34.0	0.3
1950–55	32.6	45.3	21.8	0.3

II

	A.F.L.–C.I.O.	Other Union	Different Affiliations	No Union
1961–63	85.4	12.4	2.0	0.1
1964–66	83.7	13.1	2.9	0.3
1967–69	71.4	22.6	5.6	0.4
1970–72	59.1	31.3	9.1	0.5
1973–74	59.1	36.2	4.6	0.1

TABLE A.7c

PER CENT OF STRIKER-DAYS IN STRIKES WITH GIVEN ASSOCIATION WITH A UNION, 1927–74

I

	A.F.L.	C.I.O.	Other Union	No Union
1927–29	84.0		14.3	1.7
1930–33	74.4		22.6	3.0
1934–36	86.3		12.5	1.3
1937–41	32.7	61.3	5.4	0.7
1942–45	23.7	33.2	42.6	0.6
1946–49	23.9	49.6	26.5	0.1
1950–55	31.6	46.6	21.8	0.1

II

	A.F.L.–C.I.O.	Other Union	Different Affiliations	No Union
1961–63	87.1	8.7	4.1	—
1964–66	86.2	9.4	4.3	0.1
1967–69	72.2	13.3	14.4	0.1
1970–72	52.7	36.3	10.8	0.1
1973–74	70.1	26.1	3.7	0.1

TABLE A.7d

STRIKE-PRONENESS OF UNIONS, BY AFFILIATION

	A.F.L.	C.I.O.	Other Union
	Number of strikes per million members		
1937–41	441	564	399
1942–45	242	455	426
1946–49	252	278	307
1950–55	239	287	441
1942–45 as % of 1937–41	54.9	80.7	107.0
	Number of workers involved per hundred members		
1937–41	10.4	38.8	12.4
1942–45	6.73	28.4	32.7
1946–49	10.8	26.1	50.4
1950–55	8.12	25.6	25.8
1942–45 as % of 1937–41	64.7	73.2	264.0
	Number of striker-days per hundred members		
1937–41	143	509	129
1942–45	45.6	125	316
1946–49	179	706	790
1950–55	106	357	348
1942–45 as % of 1937–41	31.9	24.6	245.0

TABLE A.8a

PER CENT OF WORKERS INVOLVED IN STRIKES WITH GIVEN ISSUE, 1881–1974

	Wages and Hours	Wages, Hours and Union Recognition	Union Recog. and Security	Other Work con- ditions	Inter/ intra Union	Union
1881–85	84.0	1.4	5.6			9.0
1886–89	68.0	3.0	12.0			17.0
1890–93	63.5	4.2	12.5			19.8
1894–97	72.0	4.5	4.9			18.5
1898–1901	53.6	14.7	14.8			16.9
1902–05	48.5	17.0	15.8			18.6
1927–29	51.3	10.3	15.7		4.7	18.0
1930–33	50.4	22.0	14.5		3.7	9.4
1934–37	32.4	30.0	19.3		4.8	13.6
1938–41	40.5	10.1	27.3		5.5	16.4
1942–45	47.4	4.8	13.7	29.0	5.2	
1946–49	60.2	12.0	3.0	21.0	3.8	
1950–53	52.7	8.3	3.7	29.6	5.8	
1954–57	62.9	3.7	3.7	24.4	5.2	
1958–60	62.5	6.3	2.8	26.4	2.0	
1961–65	49.1		7.8	38.1	5.0	
1966–69	63.4		6.1	26.4	4.2	
1970–72	69.0		4.6	22.7	3.7	
1973–74	68.9		3.3	25.0	2.8	

TABLE A.8b

PER CENT OF STRIKER-DAYS IN STRIKES WITH GIVEN ISSUE, 1927–74

	Wages and Hours	Wages, Hours and Union Recognition	Union Recog. and Security	Other Work con- ditions	Inter/ intra Union	Union
1927–29	84.2	4.5	5.3		1.1	4.8
1930–33	51.9	25.3	14.5		2.8	5.4
1934–37	25.6	42.1	22.8		2.3	7.2
1938–41	34.9	15.0	38.6		5.3	6.2
1942–45	52.6	8.0	14.5	18.7	6.1	
1946–49	74.7	15.3	2.6	5.9	1.4	
1950–53	61.7	21.5	3.6	11.1	2.2	
1954–57	70.5	12.1	5.4	10.4	1.7	
1958–60	80.5	7.0	2.7	9.2	0.5	
1961–65	59.4		10.9	28.0	1.7	
1966–69	73.1		13.3	11.9	1.6	
1970–72	82.3		8.3	7.9	1.6	
1973–74	82.3		7.1	10.1	0.5	

TABLE A.9

SUMMARY OF INFORMATION ON KNOWN STRIKES, 1741–1880

	1741–1879		1880		Total	
	Number	%	Number	%	Number	%
Number	678	100	813	100	1491	100
Issues: Wages	472	78	617	81	1089	80
Other	133	22	145	19	278	20
Results: Won	147	26	169	35	316	30
Compromised	69	12	85	18	154	15
Lost	356	62	227	47	583	55

NOTE
Not all strikes had their issues or results recorded; the percentages given are based on the total number of strikes where the issue or result was given.

SOURCE
U.S. Commissioner of Labor, *Third Annual Report, 1887* (Washington, D.C.: Government Printing Office, 1888), pp. 1107–8.

TABLE A.10a

PER CENT OF ESTABLISHMENTS WITH GIVEN RESULT AND ISSUE, 1881–1905

Issue	Result	1881–85	1886–90	1891–95	1896–1900	1901–05
Wage increase	Won	65.9	54.9	38.8	47.8	48.8
	Comp.	7.1	10.4	16.1	29.8	21.9
	Lost	27.0	34.7	45.1	23.5	29.4
Hours	Won	47.0	43.0	62.2	73.2	38.1
	Comp.	12.6	17.3	11.9	13.4	24.5
	Lost	40.3	39.8	25.9	13.5	37.4
Union recog. and	Won	43.2	46.0	50.9	61.5	39.3
rules	Comp.	18.4	12.1	4.1	9.9	18.0
	Lost	38.4	41.9	45.0	28.6	42.7
Fines, work	Won	46.7	39.5	63.6	38.5	25.6
conditions, etc.	Comp.	0.6	14.4	2.6	39.6	37.6
	Lost	52.8	46.1	33.8	21.8	36.9

NOTE
Comp. = compromised.

TABLE A.10b

RESULT BY ISSUE FOR STRIKES AND WORKERS INVOLVED, 1927–41

Issue	Result	1927–29	1930–33	1934–37	1938–41
		% of Strikes with Given Result and Issue			
Wages and hours	Won	23.5	31.5	45.5	44.1
	Comp.	38.0	24.2	31.4	43.3
	Lost	38.5	44.4	23.2	12.7
Wages, hours and union recognition	Won	33.9	39.1	50.5	52.5
	Comp.	31.1	34.9	33.1	30.8
	Lost	35.0	26.1	16.5	16.8
Union recognition and security	Won	38.9	35.2	43.5	42.1
	Comp.	11.3	15.0	21.5	31.4
	Lost	49.8	49.8	35.0	26.6
		% of Workers Involved in Strikes with Given Result and Issue			
Wages and hours	Won	11.7	33.0	51.8	35.4
	Comp.	29.4	38.2	34.7	50.5
	Lost	58.9	28.7	13.5	14.1
Wages, hours and union recognition	Won	29.4	37.8	35.0	43.5
	Comp.	54.8	54.0	56.1	47.2
	Lost	15.8	8.1	8.9	9.2
Union recognition and security	Won	60.1	18.4	45.8	53.9
	Comp.	15.7	47.8	30.8	38.2
	Lost	24.1	33.8	23.4	8.0

NOTE
Comp. = compromised.

TABLE A.11

WORK CONDITIONS STRIKES, 1881–1905

	'Pure' Work Conditions and Rules Strikes[a]				All Work Conditions and Rules Strikes[b]			
	Strikes		Strikers		Strikes		Strikers	
	Number	As % Total	Number (000s)	As % Total	Number	As % Total	Number (000s)	As % Total
1881–85	87	3.3	13.3	2.0	106	4.0	20.0	2.9
1886–90	200	2.8	17.9	1.2	259	3.7	31.2	2.1
1891–95	160	2.2	28.7	1.9	208	2.9	52.4	3.5
1896–1900	150	2.2	22.6	1.5	205	3.0	38.5	2.6
1901–05	325	2.2	30.2	1.3	419	2.9	72.3	3.1

NOTE
a. Strikes in which work conditions and rules were the only issues.
b. All strikes in which conditions and rules were mentioned as an issue.

TABLE A.12

'CESSATIONS' IN EIGHT INDUSTRIES,[a] 1881–94

a: All Eight Industries[a]

	Number	% with Given Issue			% Ordered by Union	% Won[b]	Mean Duration	Mean Size	ST/B
		Wage & Hour	Conditions	Union					
(i) 1881–86	2032	79.2	12.8	7.9	50.4	43.6	25.5	145	43.5
(ii) 1887–94	2848	60.5	23.9	15.6	53.1	32.1	19.3	148	22.4

NOTE

a. i.e. the metals industry of Table 4.13 and the seven industries of parts a to g of this Table.
b. Throughout this Table % won refers to the percentage of strikes won and lost accounted for by the 'won' category (i.e. compromises are ignored).

TABLE A.12

b: Cessations by Occupation, Printing and Publishing Industry, 1881–94

	Number	% with Given Issue			% Ordered by Union	% Won[b]	Mean Duration	Mean Size	ST/B
		Wage & Hour	Conditions	Union					
(i) 1881–86									
Compositors	135	60.0	23.0	17.0	81.5	42.0	25.8	20.5	51.3
Other	23	95.7	0	4.3	69.6	45.4	44.0	124	47.2
All	158	65.2	19.6	15.2	79.7	42.5	28.4	35.6	49.1
(ii) 1887–94									
Compositors	204	37.3	34.3	28.4	78.9	26.8	21.1	25.9	28.4
Pressmen	38	63.2	21.1	15.8	71.1	41.7	17.1	25.9	10.7
Bookbinders	21	52.4	28.6	19.0	95.2	40.0	29.4	26.7	20.8
Other	54	51.9	33.3	14.2	77.8	29.4	20.6	68.1	33.4
All	317	43.8	32.2	24.0	78.9	30.2	21.1	33.2	25.4

TABLE A.12

c: Cessations by Occupation, Machines and Machinery Industry, 1881–94

	Number	% with Given Issue			% Ordered by Union	% Won[b]	Mean Duration	Mean Size	ST/B
		Wage & Hour	Conditions	Union					
(i) 1881–86									
Boilermakers	33	87.9	3.0	9.1	84.8	52.0	29.6	80.5	37.5
Molders	17	58.8	17.6	23.5	58.8	50.0	23.5	50.7	31.7
Other trades	21	95.2	4.8	0	81.0	44.4	23.8	10.3	4.6
Railroad shop workers	24	75.0	12.5	12.5	66.7	63.6	47.6	299	84.5
Other employees	53	90.6	5.7	3.8	69.8	26.1	17.3	147	78.6
All	148	84.5	7.4	8.1	73.0	43.3	21.3	126	56.8
(ii) 1887–94									
Boilermakers	29	58.6	31.0	10.3	58.6	37.0	24.6	162	15.9
Molders	28	53.6	28.6	17.9	92.9	29.2	43.1	41.8	20.1
Machinists	26	53.8	42.3	3.8	42.3	7.7	20.4	79.7	35.7
Other trades	37	62.2	18.9	18.9	59.5	22.6	22.4	31.7	5.0
Employees	17	64.7	11.8	23.5	47.1	68.8	13.5	269	89.3
All	137	58.4	27.0	14.6	61.3	29.8	25.6	99.9	19.7

TABLE A.12

d: Cessations by Occupation, Glass, 1881–94

	Number	% with Given Issue			% Ordered by Union	% Won[b]	Mean Duration	Mean Size	ST/B
		Wage & Hour	Conditions	Union					
1881–94									
Flint glass blowers	25	40.0	32.0	28.0	96.0	30.0	75.0	65.8	28.0
Green glass blowers	19	36.8	42.1	21.1	89.5	21.1	49.1	76.6	36.7
Bottle glass blowers	17	64.7	23.5	11.8	94.1	70.6	107	47.0	24.2
Other flint workers	25	72.0	12.0	16.0	60.0	44.0	69.4	181	31.5
Other green workers	13	76.9	15.4	7.7	15.4	25.0	20.3	127	27.3
Other bottle workers	15	73.3	26.7	0	40.0	35.7	33.3	49.6	35.9
Other skilled workers	33	51.5	33.3	15.2	60.6	37.9	55.2	113	39.4
Other unskilled workers	30	80.0	20.0	0	6.7	13.8	6.3	58.9	19.0
Other employees	26	61.5	23.1	15.4	53.8	33.3	58.3	160	65.9
Window glass workers	24	83.3	12.5	4.2	70.8	63.6	74.7	91.3	40.0
All	227	63.4	24.2	12.3	58.6	36.8	54.6	99.8	34.6

TABLE A.12

e: Cessations by Occupation, Boot and Shoe, 1881–94

	Number	% with Given Issue			% Ordered by Union	% Won[b]	Mean Duration	Mean Size	ST/B
		Wage & Hour	Conditions	Union					
(i) 1881–94									
Lasters	63	79.0	11.3	9.7	84.1	54.4	34.1	44.5	11.9
Cutters, stitchers etc	42	71.4	26.2	2.4	81.0	63.3	21.6	44.8	17.8
Employees	71	69.0	14.1	16.9	87.3	45.5	44.9	151	63.8
All	176	73.1	16.0	10.9	84.7	52.8	35.3	87.2	30.4
(ii) 1887–94									
Lasters	156	59.6	23.7	16.7	80.4	31.2	12.1	26.0	10.8
Cutters	52	67.3	13.5	19.2	73.1	48.9	16.7	30.0	11.6
Bottomers	38	50.0	31.6	18.4	76.3	51.4	18.6	66.4	20.9
Stitchers	26	73.1	11.5	15.4	57.7	57.9	17.1	58.4	20.0
Shoemakers and hand sewers	20	75.0	10.0	15.0	80.0	64.7	22.9	34.3	23.0
Other	30	70.0	16.7	13.3	70.0	39.1	7.6	25.9	11.4
Employees	62	61.3	24.2	14.5	77.4	46.3	24.9	225	74.0
All	384	62.5	21.1	16.4	76.3	41.9	16.0	65.4	25.2

TABLE A.12

f: Cessations by Occupation, Cotton, Silk and Woollen Goods, 1881–94

	Number	% with Given Issue			% Ordered by Union	% Won[b]	Mean Duration	Mean Size	ST/B
		Wage & Hour	Conditions	Union					
(i) 1881–86									
Weavers	130	74.6	23.1	2.3	11.5	33.3	21.1	85.6	23.1
Spinners	30	80.0	20.0	0	10.0	36.7	13.0	33.8	5.2
Employees	48	68.8	27.1	4.2	35.4	25.6	31.0	270	48.3
Other	31	90.3	6.5	3.2	3.2	54.8	5.8	86.8	16.6
All	239	76.2	21.3	2.5	15.1	35.4	20.1	116	25.1
(ii) 1887–94									
Weavers	242	70.2	25.6	4.1	39.3	33.2	15.9	149	24.8
Spinners	46	76.1	21.1	2.2	10.9	24.4	9.5	79.3	19.0
Mule spinners	40	22.5	77.5	0	22.5	60.5	10.3	27.0	4.7
Employees	57	71.9	22.8	5.3	31.6	27.1	21.8	339	57.1
Other	95	77.9	21.1	1.1	7.4	17.0	11.6	38.2	5.4
All	480	68.5	28.3	3.1	27.9	30.7	14.6	133	22.1

TABLE A.12

g: Cessations by Occupation, Transport, 1881–94

	Number	% with Given Issue			% Ordered by Union	% Won[b]	Mean Duration	Mean Size	ST/B
		Wage & Hour	Conditions	Union					
(i) 1881–94									
Engineers and firemen	22	45.5	18.2	36.4	68.2	42.1	4.23	212	8.57
Railroad employees (excl. Pullman strike)	24	58.3	16.7	25.0	66.7	45.5	20.3	1983	35.9
(ii) 1881–86									
Street railroad	59	74.6	15.3	10.2	72.9	68.0	9.08	861	93.7
Brakemen etc.	28	67.9	32.1	0	14.3	50.0	6.39	76.8	36.5
Yard and switch workers	40	77.5	7.5	15.0	37.5	40.0	11.2	101	80.0
Labourers etc.	85	94.1	3.5	2.4	11.8	27.5	8.53	190	47.4
Longshoremen etc.	116	90.5	1.7	7.8	17.2	48.7	4.54	143	98.0
Other	19	73.7	0	26.3	63.2	53.3	15.5	777	37.5
All	347	84.4	7.5	8.1	30.0	45.7	7.81	253	56.5
(iii) 1887–94									
Street railroad	76	61.8	35.5	2.6	57.9	37.7	6.49	204	73.3
Brakemen etc.	53	62.3	34.0	3.8	20.8	41.5	4.68	121	8.1
Yard and switch workers	92	58.7	33.7	7.6	38.0	21.3	5.03	72.5	2.9
Labourers etc.	101	74.3	13.9	11.9	24.8	34.1	8.07	186	55.8
Longshoremen etc.	53	67.9	20.8	11.3	58.5	28.3	8.70	534	75.2
Engineers and firemen	18	38.9	22.2	38.9	72.2	40.0	4.17	248	8.2
Railroad employees	12	50.0	33.3	16.7	75.0	41.7	20.0	2775	35.4
Railroad shop employees	37	67.6	21.6	10.8	54.1	31.4	28.4	193	18.7
Telegraphers	10	60.0	10.0	30.0	70.0	30.0	5.5	115	2.1
Pullman strike	50	0	0	100.0	96.0	0	13.8	717	13.2
All	502	57.6	23.5	18.9	48.4	28.5	9.4	314	17.2

TABLE A.12

h: Cessations by Occupation, Public Ways and Works Construction, 1881–94

	Number	% with Given Issue			% Ordered by Union	% Won[b]	Mean Duration	Mean Size	ST/B
		Wage & Hour	Conditions	Union					
(i) 1881–94									
Labourers	67	92.5	7.5	0	10.4	35.0	5.40	155	57.6[a]
Others	26	92.3	7.7	0	15.4	39.1	5.19	407	66.8
All	93	92.5	7.5	0	11.8	36.1	5.34	225	61.9
(ii) 1887-94									
Labourers	182	89.6	9.3	1.1	6.6	43.6	3.97	172	64.7
Teamsters	19	84.2	10.5	5.3	26.3	62.5	3.95	66.7	39.9
Pavers	19	42.1	21.1	36.8	73.7	47.4	15.1[b]	36.4	18.9
Others	17	64.7	5.9	29.4	64.7	66.7	5.76	47.1	41.1
All	237	83.5	10.1	6.3	17.7	46.9	4.99	143	59.6

NOTE
a. Excluding one exceptional case, figure is 74.9.
b. Excluding one exceptional case, figure is 3.26.

TABLE A.13

STRIKES BY INDUSTRY, 1916–26

	% of All Strikes Accounted for by Each Industry, 1916–26	Number of Strikes per Million Employees	
		1919–22	1923–26
Building	15.0	401	172
Clothing	12.3	592	547
Coal and other mining	7.7	124	115
Metals: iron and steel	1.3	47	8
other	11.4	n.a.	n.a.
Printing and publishing	3.2	610	43
Slaughtering and meat packing	1.2	314	64
Ships	1.7	636	32
Stone	1.1	367	118
Textiles	6.9	163	99
Tobacco	1.2	211	85
Transport	5.1	37	4
Lumber and wood	3.4	63	51
Leather	0.8	81	29
Paper	1.1	177	43
All above industries	73.5	161[a]	81[a]
All industries	100	102	45

NOTE
a. Excluding other metals.

TABLE A.14

PER CENT OF STRIKES ACCOUNTED FOR BY EACH INDUSTRY, 1927–40

	1927–29	1930–33	1934–37	1938–40
Boot and shoe	4.3	3.0	2.0	1.1
Building	27.9	20.5	8.6	13.2
Clothing	14.5	16.9	12.6	15.9
Coal	10.4	9.2	3.5	2.1
Food	2.9	4.7	6.4	6.6
Machinery: non-electrical	1.7	1.8	3.4	3.1
electrical	0.3	0.3	1.1	1.1
Metals: basic steel	0.3	0.7	0.8	0.6
other iron and steel	2.0	2.4	3.6	3.1
other	0.7	1.2	2.4	1.7
Printing and publishing	1.4	1.8	1.3	1.1
Stone, clay and glass	1.1	1.6	2.2	2.2
Textiles	11.6	11.7	8.1	4.1
Tobacco	0.3	1.0	0.5	0.3
Transport	3.3	4.2	9.2	9.0
Transport equip: locos, cars and ships	0.2	0.4	0.6	0.6
other	0.9	0.9	2.5	1.6
All above industries	83.7	82.2	69.0	67.4
Chemicals	0.6	0.4	1.3	1.6
Lumber	0.9	1.3	3.7	4.2
Domestic and personal service	4.1	4.0	7.2	7.0
Trade	2.7	2.7	9.6	12.6
All above industries	92.0	90.6	90.7	92.8
All industries	100	100	100	100

TABLE A.15

STRIKE INDICES, SELECTED INDUSTRIES, 1950–74

		N/E	W/E	W/N	D/W
Building	1950–53	304	145	478	12.4
	1954–57	274	104	380	11.2
	1958–61	281	92.9	331	15.9
	1962–65	298	85.1	286	13.0
	1966–69	282	118	418	19.5
	1970–72	261	154	589	19.6
	1973–74	153	124	813	16.4
Clothing	1950–53	186	29.6	159	8.7
	1954–57	124	13.3	107	11.7
	1958–61	105	46.5	443	8.2
	1962–65	89	17.5	198	9.4
	1966–69	77	13.1	171	13.4
	1970–72	63	11.2	178	26.4
	1973–74	41	40.9	1010	16.9
Coal	1950–53	623	329	528	13.6
	1954–57	344	127	369	8.5
	1958–61	231	85.8	371	28.3
	1962–65	257	99.1	386	10.7
	1966–69	499	253	507	11.9
	1970–72	1200	470	391	7.6
	1973–74	619	228	368	5.2
Motor vehicles	1950–53	157	269	1713	13.7
	1954–57	146	244	1672	4.5
	1958–61	190	381	2010	7.9
	1962–65	111	216	1947	15.5
	1966–69	150	257	1711	15.1
	1970–72	134	234	1748	34.6
	1973–74	118	172	1451	11.0
Steel	1950–53	166	288	1741	25.0
	1954–57	125	367	2937	11.9
	1958–61	153	263	2642	56.1
	1962–65	144	69.0	480	11.6
	1966–69	172	94.1	547	15.6
	1970–72	169	68.8	405	25.7
	1973–74	74	17.8	243	22.7
Textiles	1950–53	98	57.8	588	22.0
	1954–57	55	12.2	220	10.1
	1962–65	46	15.2	333	12.1
	1966–69	58	21.5	372	14.4
	1970–72	49	10.5	214	12.1
	1973–74	45	15.8	353	31.9

TABLE A.16

STRIKES BY CONTRACT STATUS: TRENDS IN SELECTED INDUSTRIES, 1961–72

		% of Strikes with Given Contract Status				% of Workers Involved in Strikes with Given Contract Status			
		First Agreement	Re-negotiation	During Term	Other	First Agreement	Re-negotiation	During Term	Other
All manufacturing	1961–64	18.0	55.6	25.6	0.8	3.8	67.4	28.6	0.3
	1965–68	16.4	55.8	27.0	0.8	3.6	63.1	33.0	0.3
	1969–72	13.0	62.3	24.0	0.7	3.6	59.9	36.5	0.1
Coal	1961–64	5.9	14.5	78.3	1.3	2.1	25.9	71.6	0.4
	1965–68	8.2	11.5	79.5	0.8	1.7	27.6	70.6	0.1
	1969–72	1.2	4.6	94.1	0.1	1.0	15.8	83.2	0.0
Primary metals	1961–64	10.4	50.1	39.5	0	1.5	51.3	47.2	0
	1965–68	10.0	50.1	39.3	0.6	3.6	47.6	48.5	0.3
	1969–72	8.4	58.8	32.5	0.2	2.9	56.5	40.5	0.1
Transport equipment	1961–64	12.4	43.8	43.3	0.5	0.8	73.8	25.3	0.1
	1965–68	11.3	46.3	42.2	0.2	1.0	61.8	37.1	0.0
	1969–72	13.2	51.1	35.3	0.5	3.0	65.3	31.6	0.1

TABLE A.17

STRIKES BY ISSUE: TRENDS IN SELECTED INDUSTRIES, 1961–72

| | | % of Strikes with Given Issue | | | | | | % of Workers Involved in Strikes with Given Issue | | | | | |
		(1)	(2)	(3)	(4)	(5)	(6)	(1)	(2)	(3)	(4)	(5)	(6)
All manufacturing	1961–64	60.2	15.1	7.8	13.3	1.9	1.7	44.0	5.5	8.7	38.9	1.5	1.4
	1965–68	62.0	11.6	5.0	17.0	2.8	1.6	59.4	4.3	6.3	25.0	3.5	1.4
	1969–72	67.9	9.5	3.7	14.5	3.3	1.2	63.1	7.2	4.0	20.8	3.6	1.3
Coal	1961–64	18.5	7.4	19.5	48.6	2.7	3.4	26.2	6.0	20.1	43.1	2.0	2.6
	1965–68	19.4	6.9	19.1	42.3	5.4	6.8	25.4	11.4	15.7	38.8	4.0	4.7
	1969–72	12.0	1.8	8.2	58.7	10.9	8.4	22.2	1.2	3.9	51.0	6.7	14.9
Primary metals	1961–64	52.0	7.7	10.5	26.8	2.5	0.5	36.6	2.0	15.0	41.4	4.0	1.0
	1965–68	60.8	6.8	3.5	24.1	3.4	1.4	48.0	7.6	4.7	35.9	3.0	0.9
	1969–72	65.9	5.1	4.6	20.8	3.0	0.6	65.1	1.9	5.3	22.2	2.6	2.9
Transport equipment	1961–64	43.4	9.1	8.4	34.3	1.9	2.9	15.8	0.9	5.2	77.2	0.3	0.6
	1965–68	49.0	8.4	5.4	33.2	3.0	1.1	42.2	2.9	8.5	41.5	4.6	0.3
	1969–72	56.9	8.8	3.8	26.6	2.7	1.2	45.0	7.0	3.4	41.7	2.3	0.7

NOTE
Issues are defined as follows:
(1) Wages, hours and other contractual matters.
(2) Union organization and security.
(3) Job security.
(4) Plant administration.
(5) Other work conditions.
(6) Inter and intra union.

FIGURE A.1

Worker Involvement in Strikes, Selected
Industries, 1881–1972

Each section of this Figure gives, for one industry-group, the number of workers involved in strikes per thousand employees. From 1927, the sub-periods employed are the same as those in Table A.1 (i.e. 1927–29, 1930–33, etc.). For 1881–1905, the sub-periods are those considered by the Commissioner of Labor (1881–86, 1887–94, 1894–1900, and 1901–05). Changes of definition within broad industry-groups are indicated in each section of the Figure. Gaps in a graph indicate an absence of data. For sources of data, see Appendix D, below, pp. 321–3.

A. IRON AND STEEL AND OTHER METAL INDUSTRIES

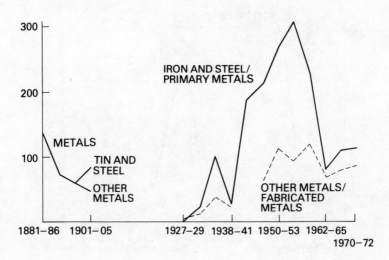

B. COAL AND MINING

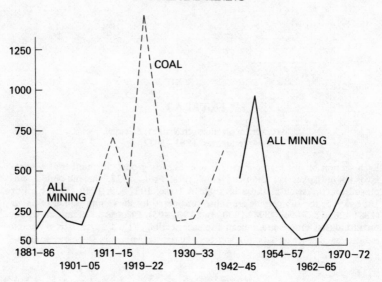

C. CLOTHING

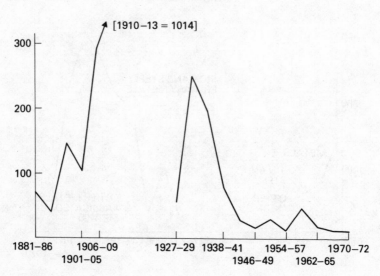

D. TEXTILES

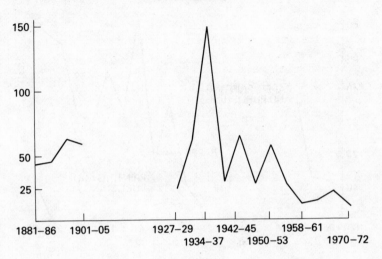

E. VEHICLES

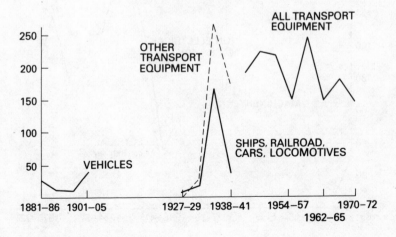

F. PAPER, PRINTING AND PUBLISHING

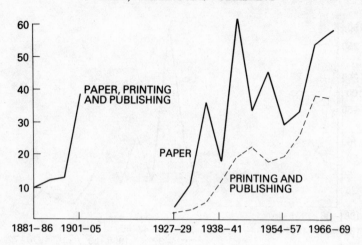

G. MACHINERY

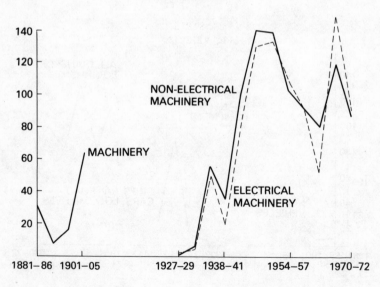

H. TOBACCO

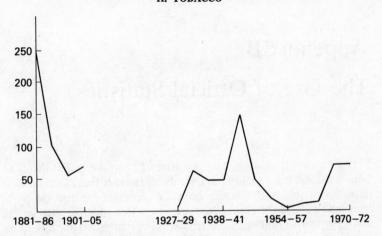

I. CONSTRUCTION

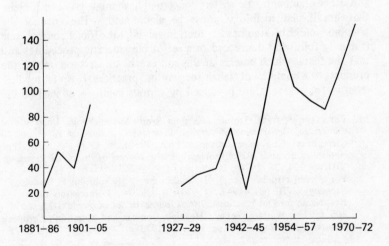

Appendix B
The Use of Official Statistics

Strike statistics have often been a matter of controversy, but there has been a tendency for analysts to state the difficulties that exist and then move on to substantive discussion without considering how the problems raised affect the conclusions reached.[1] This appendix assesses the strengths and weaknesses of American strike figures, attempting to relate these to the substantive use which may be made of the figures. But it is first necessary to consider the wider question of whether any sensible use can be made of official statistics.

1. The Phenomenological Critique

The concern here is solely with specific criticisms of the use of official data; no attempt will be made to assess whether, on the basis of these and other arguments, the writers concerned have made good their claim that 'traditional sociology' must be abandoned.[2] The core of the phenomenologists' argument is that, in relying on official sources, one is merely following the record of a set of bureaucratic procedures and that the 'data' which emerge at the end can be understood only as the products of a complex of 'taken for granted' practices. Hospital medical records, for example, are produced by various members of staff on the

1. For example, H. A. Turner, *Is Britain Really Strike Prone?*, University of Cambridge, Department of Applied Economics, Occasional Paper no. 20 (Cambridge: Cambridge University Press, 1969); W. E. J. McCarthy, 'The Nature of Britain's Strike Problem', *British Journal of Industrial Relations,* VIII, pp. 224–36 (1970).
2. For general criticisms see J. H. Goldthorpe, 'A Revolution in Sociology?' *Sociology,* VII, pp. 449–62 (1973); R. Gidlow, 'Ethnomethodology – a New Name for Old Practices', *British Journal of Sociology,* XXIII, pp. 395– 405 (1972); W. McSweeney, 'Meaning, Context and Situation', *European Journal of Sociology,* XIV, pp. 137–53 (1973).

basis of their taken-for-granted views.[3] According to this approach there is no way in which records can be produced which are independent of their context. It may seem to be obvious that statistics are the result of bureaucratic processes, but it is the implications that are drawn from this that are important: one cannot use official data because they represent a confounding of the official agencies' procedures with the 'reality' that is being measured.

A second strand of the critique points out that the nature of the 'reality' is itself problematic. Thus Douglas, in discussing Durkheim's use of statistics on suicide,[4] argues that it is the social meanings of suicide which must be given precedence and that the statistics are biased in various ways. But he does not want to argue simply that there are problems of comparability of definitions, reporting techniques and the like, for he states that a central error in the use of statistics is the assumption that actions which are fitted into the category of 'suicide' have essentially similar meanings. In other words, he is suggesting that it is in principle impossible to develop statistics on suicide that will bear any relationship to the meanings of the acts for the participants themselves.

The logic of the argument is not, of course, limited to suicide. Douglas himself extends it to all forms of moral statistics[5] and Walsh,[6] for example, takes it to cover all types of official data. These criticisms are, of course, part of a much wider attack on the methods of traditional sociology; the phenomenologist would not be satisfied with the use of data constructed by the sociologist himself, for such data would still abstract from the performances of people acting on the basis of their 'background expectancies'. For example, Churchill criticizes the use of such things as path models because they do not help in understanding how social rules are used by people, and because there is an

3. H. Garfinkel, *Studies in Ethnomethodology* (Englewood Cliffs: Prentice-Hall, 1967), pp. 11–18, 186–207. See also A. V. Cicourel, *Method and Measurement in Sociology* (New York: Free Press, 1964); A. V. Cicourel and J. I. Kitsuse, 'A Note on the Use of Official Statistics', *Social Problems*, XI, pp. 131–9 (1963).

4. J. D. Douglas, *The Social Meanings of Suicide* (Princeton: Princeton University Press, 1967), esp. p. 229.

5. J. D. Douglas, 'Understanding Everyday Life', *Understanding Everyday Life*, ed. J. D. Douglas (London: Routledge and Kegan Paul, 1971), pp. 3–44, at pp. 6–7.

6. D. Walsh, 'Varieties of Positivism', *New Directions in Sociological Theory*, by P. Filmer *et al.* (London: Collier–Macmillan, 1972), pp. 37–55, at pp. 43–53.

imposition of 'variable thinking' on the process of social interaction.[7] It is not simply that such 'positivistic' methods are incomplete; they fail to give any understanding of how people actually manage their lives.

Thus it is being argued that, since 'social facts' are the product of interaction and cannot be divorced from their contexts,[8] there is no 'true' distribution of phenomena to be observed.[9] The reliance on official categories is merely an extreme form of the positivism inherent in all attempts to construct sociological explanations that are not rooted in the affairs of 'everyday life'. Any official (or other) statistics, records, files or other documents cannot be treated as a 'resource' for sociological inquiry; rather, how they come to be created is a valid 'topic' for investigation.

In many ways, it is hard to respond to this argument, for the phenomenologist has sought to create a case that is immune to criticism; any attempt to remedy orthodox approaches will be dismissed for failing to respect the integrity of everyday life.[10] Instead of entering an arid dispute about positivism, it is more useful to focus on specific criticisms advanced by the writers in question, concentrating on strike data.

2. Strike Statistics

The fundamental point is that statistics on strikes do not suffer from the same weaknesses as those on suicide or crime. It is true that there are practical difficulties to be overcome, but it is in principle possible to conceive of adequate data on strikes. For example a frequent criticism of crime statistics is that they reflect how much effort the police make in seeking out crime; an increase in the 'rate' of juvenile crime may reflect an intensification of detective operations. Similarly the keenness with which officials search for information on strikes will affect the number recorded. But there is a crucial difference. Writers on crime and deviance have argued convincingly that there can be no 'true' rate of crime since what is defined as criminal depends on the

---

7. L. Churchill, 'Ethnomethodology and Measurement', *Social Forces*, L, pp. 182–91 (1971), esp. pp. 186–8. See also H. Blumer, *Symbolic Interactionism* (Englewood Cliffs: Prentice-Hall, 1969).

8. B. Hindess, *The Use of Official Statistics in Sociology* (London: Macmillan, 1973), pp. 28–9.

9. This seems to be the meaning of Garfinkel's term 'indexicality'.

10. D. Benson, 'A Revolution in Sociology', *Sociology*, VIII, pp. 125–9 (1974).

context in which certain acts take place; what in one context is 'hooliganism' may in another be the 'innocent letting off of steam'. In contrast the ca⁺ₒgorization of an event as a strike is not context-dependent to anything like the same extent.

Most definitions of the strike take it to be a stoppage of work by a group of employees in order to express a grievance or enforce a demand; the stoppage must also be temporary in that the men intend to return to work when the dispute has been settled.[11] While there are difficulties in establishing whether there is sufficient collective action in a given case for the event to be called a strike, the central problem relates to the intentionality aspect. Events are not counted as strikes unless there is the intent to 'express a grievance or enforce a demand'; and the criterion that the stoppage be temporary involves the intent to return to work. Thus, unlike Durkheim is his definition of suicide,[12] one cannot even try to avoid the aspect of the actors' intentions. Since intentions are context-bound, it might be argued, strike statistics, like those on suicide, are necessarily useless. However, 'expressing a grievance' is a very broad category and many events are counted as strikes even when it is not clear what particular grievance is being voiced. In other words 'for all practical purposes' an event may be counted as a strike without strong evidence on the actors' intentions.

It may appear that, in saying this, one is granting the case of the phenomenologists, for it seems that in practice the formal definition of the strike is altered in all sorts of taken-for-granted ways. But by approaching the question from a different angle, one can see that this is not really a problem. The strike is part of the employment relationship and only stoppages of work by employees are to be included; 'strikes' by master craftsmen for increases in the prices of their products have been excluded from the category because they did not involve a

11. See R. Hyman *Strikes* (London: Fontana-Collins, 1972), p. 17; A. Flanders, *Management and Unions* (London: Faber and Faber, 1970), p. 239; F. Peterson, *Strikes in the United States, 1880–1936* (Washington, D.C.: U.S. Department of Labor Bulletin no. 651, 1938), p. 3; K. G. J. C. Knowles, *Strikes: A Study in Industrial Conflict* (Oxford: Blackwell, 1952), p. 1; O. Kahn-Freund and R. Hepple, *Laws Against Strikes* (London: Fabian Society, Research series Pamphlet no. 305, 1972), p. 4; *Methods of Compiling Statistics of Industrial Disputes* (Geneva: International Labour Office, Studies and Reports Series N (Statistics) no. 10, 1926), p. 14. It is Peterson's definition which Hyman quotes, without acknowledgment.
12. E. Durkheim, *Suicide*, trans. J. A. Spaulding and G. Simpson (London: Routledge and Kegan Paul, 1952), p. 44; S. Lukes, *Emile Durkheim* (Harmondsworth: Penguin, 1975), p. 200.

dispute between an employer and his employees.[13] All sorts of problems exist as to what is defined as criminal, whether or not the person who commits 'criminal' acts sees these in the same terms as the agencies of law enforcement, and about the effect of *ad hoc* bureaucratic procedures on the statistics. The meaning of a strike in capitalist society is much less problematic. It is understood by employers and workers alike to be part of the relationship between them.[14] Although there are many types of strike and stoppages can be granted very different degrees of legitimacy, the category of a 'stoppage of work to express a grievance or enforce a demand' is broad enough to cover any dispute which one might want to count as a 'strike' and clear enough to be used without risk of ambiguity.

Several agencies have attempted to distinguish between a strike and a lock-out. The difference used to be held to rest on whether the workers or the employers are to blame for the stoppage. But this distinction has been abandoned because the side which is first to take belligerent action is not necessarily 'to blame'; and the concept of blame must obviously be used cautiously in such situations. It is useful to the parties to attach blame to their opponents, but the distinction between strikes and lock-outs is of little analytical significance. What is important is that both involve an attempt to enforce a demand or express a grievance and that they grow out of the employment relationship. In a particular case, it may be relevant to know whether a stoppage was seen as a strike or lock-out; but the similarity of form and purpose between them means that for statistical analysis they can be treated together as 'stoppages of work'.

It is true that individual strikers and employers will attach different meanings to strike action, and even that one person may change his views during the strike. But this does not affect the possibility of using strike statistics. In employing these data one is not trying to aggregate meanings, which would be invalid, but assessing the frequency with which labour-management disputes develop into stoppages of work. The meanings of the participants are not crucial in this. Or, to be more precise, the only meaning with which we are concerned is that a stoppage of work to enforce a demand or express a grievance is occurring.

13. J. R. Commons *et al.*, *History of Labour in the United States*, Vol. I (New York: Macmillan, 1918), p. 26.

14. It is notable that the most ambitious cross-national study of strike statistics restricts itself to countries with a 'free' labour market; that is, the strike is seen as an aspect of capitalist employment relations, and outwardly similar events elsewhere are not truly comparable: A. M. Ross and P. T. Hartman, *Changing Patterns of Industrial Conflict* (New York: Wiley, 1960).

Here it is reasonable to argue that there is a considerable overlap of meanings between workers and employers. There is little dispute as to whether a strike is, or is not, going on. With the enforcement of a demand, the employer will be aware of the demand and know that refusal to grant it will lead to the stoppage of work. Things are somewhat more complex with the expression of a grievance since the employer need not be aware of the grievance, which may not even be directly related to the conditions of employment; this is the case with 'political' strikes. But after the strike has begun, the grievance can be discovered. Even if there is no clear grievance, as may be the case with 'spontaneous' walk-outs, the collective and complete cessation of work will distinguish the strike from other forms of action.[15] In other words, the presence of a strike will be recognized even when the precise grievance involved is unclear; and the application of meanings is not crucial.

This is because the strike is part of the employment relationship. The employer buys his employees' labour power; the collective and complete withdrawal of this power is known as a strike. Although the intentional aspect of strikes cannot be removed from the definition, in practice it is not a problem because of the shared meanings of the participants. They may disagree over the causes of a strike, may call it by another name or may even attempt to ignore its presence. But these are practical problems. What a strike is, and what it represents, is clear: it is a collective refusal to work under the existing conditions of employment, and represents a state of overt conflict between workers and their employer.

The category of the 'strike' is not one imposed by the outside observer. An important part of the phenomenologists' case is that 'members' and observers have different means of dealing with and decoding the information with which they are presented; theoretical categories used by observers have no necessary relationship to what is going on. They are imposed on the affairs of everyday life in an *ad hoc* manner.[16] For example, it has been argued, that a category such as 'social class' should not be imposed on the world, but that people's perceptions of class, and the use of the term in everyday life, should be the focus.[17] But the strike is a category which is common in everyday

15. The 'collective and complete' nature of strikes is taken up further below; see p. 297.
16. A. V. Cicourel, *The Social Organization of Juvenile Justice* (New York: Wiley, 1968), p. 3. See also Hindess, op. cit.; Benson, op. cit.
17. See P. Hiller, 'Continuities and Variations in Everyday Conceptual Components of Class', *Sociology*, IX, pp. 255–87 (1975); E. Bott, *Family and Social Network* (2nd edn; London: Tavistock, 1971), p. 163.

life; the outside observer does not impose it on the situation in the way that concepts such as 'class' and 'crime' are imposed.

As noted above, the position of the strike in the employment relationship contributes to the creation of shared meanings among participants. It is now clear that the observer does not arbitrarily impose his own meanings on this situation. To be more precise, the fact of compiling strike statistics does not imply that meanings are being imposed. Observers (and, for that matter, 'members') may operate with different views of strikes. Some may hold that there is inherent unrest among the working class and that every strike represents an expression of class consciousness, while others may prefer to think in terms of economic gains and losses.[18] But these and other meanings are concerned with the interpretation of strike activity. The category of the strike itself is not in dispute. Disputes over the interpretation of strike action are as likely to occur in relation to a particular stoppage as to the aggregate level of activity. There is nothing in the existence of different interpretations to prevent the use of aggregate data.

It is obvious that observers and members give meaning to particular actions. There is nothing mysterious in this, although in certain cases it may lead to difficulties when statistical analysis is attempted; counting the number of 'crimes' is a case in point. But, the meaning of what a strike is, as distinct from what it signifies, is shared by participants and observers to a very large extent. In counting the number of strikes, one is not making the implicit assertion that the meaning of all strikes is identical, but merely examining how often labour-management disputes develop into overt conflicts which take the particular form of the strikes. If this is related to various independent factors, context-bound meanings are not being violated. One meaning of the strike is that it is a clearly identifiable stoppage of work, brought about by the collective action of a number of workers. There is no reason why this aspect of the strike cannot be considered in the aggregate.

Thus it is, in principle, possible to use statistics on strikes. The problems of principle encountered with the major measures of strike activity can be dealt with in terms of traditional measurement theory and its concepts of reliability and validity. In the United States and most other countries, three measures of strike activity are commonly employed:

18. J. R. Hicks, *The Theory of Wages* (London: Macmillan, 1932). See also O. Ashenfelter and G. E. Johnson, 'Bargaining Theory, Trade Unions and Industrial Strike Activity', *American Economic Review*, LIX, pp. 35–49 (1969); L. G. Reynolds, *Labor Economics and Labor Relations* (6th edn; Englewood Cliffs: Prentice-Hall, 1974), pp. 470–85.

the numbers of strikes, workers involved, and 'days lost' in stoppages.[19] These will be dealt with in turn.

Number of Strikes

It may seem that counting the number of strikes which occur is a relatively simple exercise, but the central problem is whether a stoppage that affects several factories should be counted as one strike or as several; as noted below, the U.S. officials have disagreed on this point. The approach usually adopted is to group together all the stoppages which seem to involve the same grievance or demand as one strike; but, to take one obvious case, it may not be clear whether series of stoppages in which similar or identical demands are made are indeed part of a common movement or are merely simultaneous expressions of separate grievances. It might be possible to discover how far such a series of strikes was centrally co-ordinated, but this would be difficult and often inconclusive. In that the official agencies have to follow *ad hoc* rules in deciding whether they are dealing with one strike or many, the points raised by the phenomenologists are clearly very relevant, but there is something to be said for the continued use of data on the number of strikes.

To the extent that strikes grow out of collective bargaining between employers and workers, especially where trade union involvement is important, it is usually possible to differentiate between one strike and another. Each strike will be in pursuit of a particular demand and will be called formally by union officials, so that the various stoppages that occur can clearly be seen as part of the same dispute. This is, of course, far from the whole story and where, for instance, unofficial strikes take place it may not be possible to locate them in a formal procedure. But the fact that some strikes can be so located suggests that the problems are reduced in some cases. It also suggests that there may be international differences in the extent to which figures on the number of strikes are usable; as argued in Chapter 2, in the U.S. strikes which grow out of collective bargaining disputes are a significant part of the total and therefore data on strike frequency may be more valid than they are in other countries.[20]

19. For a very useful summary of the reporting procedures and statistics used in 18 countries, see M. R. Fisher, *Measurement of Labour Disputes and their Economic Effects* (Paris: Organization for Economic Co-operation and Development, 1973), pp. 101–32, 231–4.
20. Compare France, where the rules on counting a 'conflit du travail' as one strike or several seem to have changed, possibly because it is harder than it is in the United States to place strikes within the framework of collective

Further, to point out that informal and *ad hoc* bureaucratic rules must be used is not to say that the data which emerge are necessarily unusable. If a reasonably clear set of rules can be devised, the data should be tolerably reliable. For example, it would be possible to operate with the general rule that stoppages in one plant or department should be deemed one strike unless there is evidence to suggest that separate disputes are involved; and many other rules could be devised. This will of course mean, that the number of strikes recorded will reflect bureaucratic procedures but, and this is a fundamental point, if these procedures remain fairly constant any change in the number of strikes will be a 'real' one rather than one due to the rules themselves. The data are not being used to estimate the amount of conflict present but to indicate whether there is more at one time than at another. Indeed, it is a rather meaningless question to ask how much conflict is present, since the meaning of the amount can be assessed only by comparison with other periods and places. The section on the American figures shows that recording procedures have been such that trends of activity can, in general, be compared; but comparisons of strike frequency between countries are likely to be vitiated by the use of many different classificatory rules.[21]

Worker Involvement and Days Lost

The problems with the other two dimensions of activity, worker involvement and days-lost, are much less serious. For the former, one is simply taking a count of the number of men who strike and, once a definition of what sort of activity is to be called a strike has been agreed, there are no great problems of principle involved. The difficulty comes with reconciling different estimates of how many men are on strike; in a situation of conflict it is likely that the two sides will make contrasting claims as to the effectiveness of the stoppage.[22] But there

bargaining. See M. Shalev, 'Lies, Damned Lies and Strike Statistics: The Measurement of Trends in Industrial Conflict', *The Resurgence of Class Conflict in Western Europe since 1968,* Vol. I, ed. C. Crouch and A. Pizzorno (London: Macmillan, 1978), pp. 1–19.

21. This is the conclusion of Shalev, op. cit. See also M. Silver (Shalev), 'Recent British Strike Trends: A Factual Analysis', *British Journal of Industrial Relations,* XI, pp. 66–104 (1973) at pp. 69–70.

22. For an example of this, see *Methods of Compiling Statistics of Industrial Disputes,* op. cit., p. 15: in Norway in 1919–21 workers' information indicated that 99,000 workers were involved in strikes whereas employers' estimates put the figure at 35,000.

clearly is a true number of strikers which could in principle be established accurately. A greater problem relates to the fact that not all those counted as on strike may be active supporters of the stoppage. One should certainly not infer, from the apparent solidarity of a strike, that all the strikers are behind the leaders either in the demands made or on the question of whether the strike is the appropriate means to pursue the demands. But in using strike statistics one is not trying to deal with every meaning which could be applied to particular disputes; the aggregate data record how many workers strike, and the interpretation of this is a different question.

Walsh has argued that even statistics on demographic matters are not sociologically useful, asserting, for example, that measures of the birthrate do not tell us anything about the meanings which people attach to decisions on family size.[23] But he cannot show that it is impossible to obtain valid counts of the number of births in a given period. He is merely saying that it is difficult to use such data for certain purposes. Similarly, it is possible to separate the collection of figures on worker involvement from problems of their interpretation.

The number of days-lost in a given strike is given by the product of the number of workers involved and the number of days for which a strike lasts. Thus any problems of principle, in addition to those connected with worker involvement, will relate to measuring the duration of the stoppage. The main difficulty that is likely to arise concerns strikes which are not ended by a formal settlement but in which there is a prolonged period in which the men return to work until operations are nearly normal; in some cases the final decision to call off a strike has been made years after all effective action has ceased. But even in these cases it is usually possible to make a reasonable estimate of when a strike has ended. The criterion will not be the resumption of production, since the curtailment of normal operations is not the indication that a strike is taking place; if it were, only effective strikes would be included in the figures. In the United States, a strike is considered ended when the majority of the vacancies caused by it are filled by returning strikers or new workers, or when the plant closes for good.[24] Here, as elsewhere, bureaucratic rules have to be applied, but the problems are not too serious; in very many cases formal strike settlements are reached and in others the filling of vacancies gives a reasonable measure of the ending of a strike. Thus, estimates of strike duration are usable.

23. Walsh, loc. cit.; cf. C. G. A. Bryant, 'In Defence of Sociology', *British Journal of Sociology*, XXI, pp. 95–107 (1970).
24. Peterson, op. cit. (note 11), p. 164; Fisher, op. cit., p. 56.

It may be impossible to obtain completely accurate statistics on any of the three dimensions of strike activity, but it does not follow that the data which exist are inherently unusable. The next section deals with some of the practical problems which occur, beginning by considering again each of the dimensions in turn.

3. The Usability of Strike Statistics

The Three Dimensions of Strikes

Several influences are likely to affect the data on strike frequency. Suppose that the official agency operates with the rule that stoppages in one establishment are generally to be seen as one strike. Then, if the average size of plants increases, there will be, *ceteris paribus,* a downward influence on the number of strikes recorded. Similarly, the centralization of collective bargaining and the amalgamation of trade unions are likely to reduce the number of separate bargains that are made, which in turn will tend to reduce the number of stoppages.[25] Such factors as these need to be borne in mind when long-term trends are being compared.

Other general problems relate to the completeness of the counting of strikes, in view of the possible manipulation and suppression of information, and to the effect on strike recording of different amounts of effort put into data collection.[26] It would be possible to exercise a strict control over the methods used in the collection of data to minimize the bias introduced by changing amounts of effort. As noted in the following section, the U.S. officials, like most others, have tended to alter the methods used, and this has had quite a large influence on the counting of strike frequency.

In addition to the difficulties of principle associated with deciding what is to count as one strike, the data on the number of strikes are less useful than those on worker involvement or striker-days. The practical problems are connected largely with small stoppages and it is likely that very many of these escape inclusion in the statistics, but such strikes do

25. There is some dispute over the general effect of the centralization of bargaining on strike activity, and it is possible that activity will increase if negotiations take place at the industry or national level, with local problems being ignored. All that is being said here is that the factors mentioned will exert a downward influence on strike frequency, which may be counteracted by other forces.

26. Shalev, 'Lies, Damned Lies and Strike Statistics', op. cit., pp. 4–6; Hyman, op. cit., p. 26.

not account for a high proportion of worker involvement or days lost.[27] For example, the suppression of information by managements interested in a reputation for industrial peace is quite possible in relation to small disputes, which may be defined as 'pauses for consultation' rather than as strikes; but it is the large and long stoppages which account for the great majority of worker involvement and it is very unlikely that such strikes could be kept hidden.

Thus, of the three dimensions of activity, strike frequency is the least statistically valid and reliable. However, if the recording practices of the official agencies have been reasonably consistent, it may be possible to examine trends in the number of strikes. But since the reliability of the data varies, less weight can be placed on trends here than on trends in the other dimensions. Problems of reliability also mean that breaking down the aggregate data into various series for industries or regions is likely to lead to difficulties. For example, if it is known that one industry is particularly prone to short disputes[28] or that in another management is able to suppress information, comparisons between industries will be invalid. However, it may still be possible to compare trends; thus we may be able to say that, in a given period, activity has increased more in one industry than it has in another; and, of course, comparisons of rates at one point in time may still be possible when the number of workers involved or days lost is the index.

The main practical problem relating to worker involvement is deciding where to draw the line between those directly affected by the dispute and those without direct involvement.[29] Some agencies (including the American one in 1881–1905) attempt to differentiate between strikers and those who are thrown out of work by a strike, although they are not themselves actively supporting the strike. It is clearly very hard to do this and a common solution to the problem (which has been adopted by U.S. officials since 1914) is to restrict the concern to establishments on strike. Thus all men in a struck plant who are thrown out

27. Detailed figures for the United States are given in Chapter 2; see Table A.3 in Appendix A. See also Silver, 'Recent British Strike Trends', op. cit., pp. 83–5; and P. K. Edwards, 'Strikes: Theories of their Trends and Causes; and the Application of Some Statistical Evidence' (B. Phil. thesis, University of Oxford, 1975), tables A2 and A4.

28. The car industry is often cited as an example. See H. A. Turner, G. Clack and G. Roberts, *Labour Relations in the Motor Industry* (London: Allen and Unwin, 1967), esp. pp. 52–3. On the American industry, see R. Herding, *Job Control and Union Structure* (Rotterdam: Rotterdam University Press, 1972), p. 210.

29. Knowles, op. cit., pp. 302–3. Knowles provides an excellent brief discussion of the main problems with strike statistics (pp. 299–306).

of work are counted as 'involved' whether or not they are actively supporting the strike; and all secondary idleness in other plants is ignored. This is clearly only one possible convention, but, if consistently adhered to, it makes possible the examination of trends in worker involvement: any recorded change can be attributed to 'real' forces rather than to a statistical artefact. Again, though, there may be difficulties with inter-industry comparisons. An industry which has plants in which the operations are highly inter-dependent will tend to record a higher rate of worker involvement than will one where strikes in one department do not affect work in another; and, where whole plants are dependent on each other, recorded involvement will not reflect the number of men in the non-striking plants affected by the dispute. Thus comparisons of trends rather than of rates may have to be used.

This convention of concentrating on struck plants alone has the advantage that the recorded number of workers involved is kept reasonably close to the number of strikers. After all, the aim is to measure how many men go on strike and extending the coverage to non-struck plants is likely to reduce the validity of the series. But one result of this is that the figures on days-lost will not reflect the true economic impact of the strike, since they will relate only to the loss in struck plants.[30] This, together with the fact that the striker-day index is the product of two separate measures of activity, each of which has its own problems of reliability, may suggest that this index will be the least useful of all. However, it has been suggested that the index is the most useful for international comparisons because differences of definition are less significant than they are for the other dimensions of activity.[31] And the great majority of striker-days occur in the large and long strikes; to an extent even greater than that for worker involvement, the missing of small strikes does not affect the figures much.

30. How far the number of days-lost can be used as an index of economic losses is a complex question which cannot be considered here. See Turner, *Is Britain Really Strike Prone?*, op. cit.; Fisher, op. cit., pp. 179–97. On why 'striker-days' might be a better term than 'days-lost' see Turner, Clack and Roberts, op. cit., p. 54; the two terms will be used interchangeably here.
31. See references in note 21, above; and T. G. Whittingham and B. Towers, 'The Strike Record of the United Kingdom: An Analysis', *Industrial Relations Journal*, II, no. 3, pp. 2–8 (1971).
32. C. Kerr, 'Industrial Conflict and Its Mediation', *American Journal of Sociology*, LX, pp. 230–45 (1954), at p. 232. See also H. A. Clegg, *The System of Industrial Relations in Great Britain* (Oxford: Blackwell, 1972), pp. 313–14 for the growth of forms of pressure other than the strike in Britain.

Strikes and Other Forms of 'Unrest'

A central difficulty concerns the separation of the strike from other forms of 'unrest'. As Kerr[32] and many other writers have argued, employee discontent can take the form of absenteeism, go-slows, high quit rates or a variety of other things; and it may be suggested that a focus on strikes is inadequate. Similarly, it might be said that the strike is inseparable from a continuing set of relationships and that it cannot be treated in isolation; the only way to assess some change in strike activity would be to place it in the context of the bargaining relationship.

Since it is possible to arrive at and use a reasonable definition of the strike, strikes are, by implication, separable from other forms of activity. The fact that they are collective serves to differentiate them from individual actions such as quitting. There may be borderline cases of mass resignations where a strike is illegal or illegitimate,[33] but it is usually clear that these are collective acts; to be effective they have to be organized and the presence of organizing activity will indicate that they are different from the more usual forms of quitting. Secondly, strikes involve the complete cessation of work, in contrast to go-slows which are collective but not complete. Again, there are some boundary problems, particularly when actions which do not involve a complete stoppage are called 'strikes in detail' or 'strikes on the job'.[34] Particular problems relate to cases where total stoppages occur but where the men do not leave the plant; when such sit-downs are large and long it is possible to say that a strike is going on, but when they are short it is hard to know whether they should be called strikes or go-slows. However, it seems reasonable to call any collective and complete stoppage a strike.

The strike is a fairly distinct type of event, which can be studied

33. For example, among American school teachers: see M. H. Moskow, *Teachers and Unions* (Philadelphia: University of Pennsylvania, Wharton School of Finance and Commerce, 1966), p. 97. What was reported to be the first strike by American nurses took the form of mass 'sick leave': see 'Developments in Industrial Relations', *Monthly Labor Review*, LXXXIX, p. 1131 (Oct., 1966). The Bureau of Labor Statistics, which produces American strike statistics, attempts to record all strikes, regardless of their legal status; this is particularly important in relation to stoppages by public employees, which are often illegal. See, for example, *Analysis of Work Stoppages in 1974* (U.S. Department of Labor Bulletin no. 1902, 1976). See also J. Stieber, *Public Employee Unionism* (Washington, D.C.: Brookings Institute, 1973).

34. For the use of such tactics by the Industrial Workers of the World, see J. S. Gambs, *The Decline of the I.W.W.* (New York: Russell and Russell, 1966), pp. 127–8.

separately from other forms of job action. The question then arises as to why strike patterns are of interest in their own right. One preliminary, but weak, argument is that various theories relating directly to strikes have been propounded and that it is a useful activity to test them. Similarly, strike data have been used to test more general theories, such as the hypothesis that workers who form an 'isolated mass' will be more conflict-prone than other groups.[35] More importantly, strikes are of interest because they are a-typical and breach the usual pattern of 'order' in industry.[36] If conflict is central to processes of social change,[37] the strike, as an extreme form of industrial conflict, is an important subject for study.

But this does not prove that a statistical analysis is possible. Thus it has been argued that the strike is an integral part of a set of relationships and that its causes cannot be established by examining aggregate data.[38] In other words, each strike is a unique event. But there is a danger in this approach. Having dealt with the background features of a situation, the growth of discontent and the steps in the process of negotiation,[39] it is easy to imply that a strike is more or less inevitable. Each event in the chain leading up to the strike is examined, but the strike is seen solely as the product of these events and not as a phenomenon with important similarities with other stoppages. In this study, strikes are approached from the other direction, concentrating on trends and patterns of activity and attempting to bring out the causes

35. C. Kerr and A. J. Siegel, 'The Inter-industry Propensity to Strike', *Industrial Conflict,* ed. A. Kornhauser, R. Dubin and A. M. Ross (New York: McGraw-Hill, 1954), pp. 189–212. One may also want to see if theories derived in relation to one country apply to another; see, for example, E. Shorter and C. Tilly, *Strikes in France, 1830–1968* (Cambridge: Cambridge University Press, 1974).

36. See J. S. Auerbach, 'Introduction', *American Labor: The Twentieth Century,* ed. J. S. Auerbach (Indianapolis: Bobbs-Merill, 1969), p. xxi.

37. See L. A. Coser, 'Structure and Conflict', *Approaches to the Study of Social Structure,* ed. P. M. Blau (London: Open Books, 1976), pp. 210–19.

38. See, for example, the view of Karsh: strike causes are not to be 'found alone in depersonalized charts, graphs and tables... Since a strike is first and foremost a form of human behavior acted by individuals who are the immediate participants in groups, their causes are social as much as, if not more than, economic or historical... Workers in the same objective situation will respond differently to the appeals of union organization and strike action': B. Karsh, *Diary of a Strike* (Urbana: University of Illinois Press, 1958), pp. 2, 5.

39. Good detailed studies include D. Brody, *Labor in Crisis* (Philadelphia: J. B. Lippincott, 1965); and S. Fine, *Sit-down: The General Motors Strike of 1936–37* (Ann Arbor: University of Michigan Press, 1969).

of strikes at this, aggregate, level. This approach cannot stand independently of more detailed investigations, but it can contribute to an understanding of strikes by dealing with the factors which affect the distribution of stoppages over time and space.

The strike must not be seen as an 'index of unrest'. Much effort has been spent in discussing whether strike trends measure the course of the amount of conflict in industry; in other words, the question is whether strikes are a valid and reliable index of 'general unrest'. But it is not helpful to look at strikes in this way. Activity is influenced by basic and deep-seated discontents, but is also affected by the workers' perceptions of their chances of success, the attitude of the employer and many other things. Many people, especially sociologists,[40] suggest that relating strike statistics to economic variables is unsatisfactory because it does not deal with 'fundamental' discontents. But this is misguided. There are many links in the chain from 'unrest' to strike activity, and many other chains which may be equally important. When strike activity in the aggregate is examined, the concern is with the patterns within a complex protest movement and with the causes of variations in the patterns. Of course, this does not establish the meaning of individual strikes, but it permits an analysis of the framework within which strikes take place; that is, the factors which affect the distribution of strike activity can be identified and the relative strength of different factors assessed.

Thus, strikes are separable from other forms of activity and can be analysed in their own right. They may be studied in the aggregate not because this can give us an idea about the total amount of conflict which is present, but because it leads to an understanding of the trends of activity. The view that there is a total amount of conflict which is measured by strike activity is unsound because conflict takes many forms and the notion of an 'amount' of conflict is very unclear. What is important is the trend of activity and its distribution between industries at various times. Since the strike is the most obvious and extreme form of labour-management conflict, a focus on it will reveal patterns which are of more general significance even though the view of strikes as indices of unrest is unsatisfactory. The very fact that the strike is separable from other features of industrial relations means that it cannot be expected to be an index of the character of relations in general. But an

40. See H. L. Sheppard and N. Q. Herrick, *Where Have All the Robots Gone?* (New York: Free Press, 1972), p. 3; R. Dubin, 'Attachment to Work and Union Militancy', *Industrial Relations*, XII, no. 1, pp. 51–64 (1973). Cf. D. Bell, *Work and Its Discontents* (Boston: Beacon Press, 1956), pp. 28–9.

examination of its trends can show the way in which protest activities have altered and how the 'parameters of conflict' have changed.

Other Dimensions of Strikes

In addition to the three main dimensions of strike activity, several other statistical descriptions of strikes are commonly used. There are, firstly, the various breakdowns of the data by the duration and size of stoppages and by the industries and regions in which they occur. Information on size and duration is clearly as usable as that on the main dimensions, for it involves merely classifying the statistics in the relevant ways. Some of the problems with industrial comparisons have been mentioned and, to the extent that regions do not have industrial structures identical to that of the country as a whole, these will also affect the regional breakdown. But other difficulties also exist. For one thing, it is hard to find a means of defining industries that is relevant to the task at hand; the usual definition by the type of product may not usefully distinguish between industries in terms of the production process employed or by meaningful bargaining units. Since the industrial breakdown given in the statistics is that by product, there is little that can be done about this, other than try to re-classify industries where possible. However, the trends within industry groups can be used to assess whether trends at the national level are repeated in all sectors, whether activity is becoming more or less dispersed and so on.

The data on the 'causes' and results are open to numerous and serious criticisms.[41] Attempting to classify the declared aims of strikes according to certain official categories raises all the problems of divorcing actions from their context emphasized by the phenomenologists. But most official agencies continue to provide classifications of strikes by cause, probably because it is felt that the 'issues' or the 'reasons given for striking' can be stated with a fair degree of accuracy.[42] The expressed reasons cannot be equated with the causes of strikes, partly because the strikers themselves may restrict what they say they are striking about,[43] and partly because causes at a different level of analysis can be identified. For example, a demand for increased wages may reflect dissatisfaction with many things but may be made because

41. See W. E. J. McCarthy, 'The Reasons Given for Striking', *Bulletin of the Oxford University Institute of Statistics,* XXI, pp. 17–29 (1959); Knowles, op. cit., pp. 209–12, 228–37, 240–45; Peterson, op. cit., pp. 166–9.
42. The term 'issues' in disputes is ued by the Bureau of Labor Statistics; the 'reasons given for striking' is McCarthy's.
43. Hyman, op. cit., p. 123; D. Lockwood, 'Arbitration and Industrial Conflict', *British Journal of Sociology,* VI, pp. 335–47 (1955), at p. 338.

it is more likely to be met than less conventional demands; and a desire for improved wages is clearly neither a necessary nor a sufficient cause for a strike. There are further difficulties associated with the fitting of demands which may be complex and diffuse into official categories, and it is probably impossible to develop a fully adequate set of categories. But, by taking only the broadest groupings of 'wages and hours', 'union organization' and so on, one can say something about the trends of activity. It is generally possible to determine into which of these broad categories a given strike issue falls; and, although this says nothing about the causes of strikes, an analysis of changes in the stated reasons for striking can indicate something about the changing character of strike activity.

Data on strike results suffer from as many weaknesses as those on causes. Several agencies, including the American, have ceased to publish data on results, largely because it is felt that it is hard to determine whether a strike has been won or lost. The exact terms of a return to work are often unclear and it may not be until long after the strike that some assessment can be made of 'who won'. And if the strike demands change during the stoppage it will be unclear how to categorize the result. In any case, the language of victory and defeat may not be appropriate to a wide range of strikes.[44] Such data as are available have to be used with great caution, but, again, trends may be illuminating even if it does not mean much to say that a certain proportion of strikes was won or lost.

4. Strike Data in the United States

In 1880, as part of the national census of that year, an attempt was made to record information on strikes but since this was a limited exercise of doubtful reliability no use is made of its data.[45] Between 1888 and 1907, the Commissioner of Labor produced four reports, covering the years 1881—1905 and containing a great deal of useful information. From 1906 to 1913 no national records were kept, while from 1914 to

44. Karsh, op. cit., p. 4, argues that the strike is a means of resolution of conflict as well as an expression of it. Many unionists claim that strikes are never really lost. Thus, P. J. McGuire, the leader of the Carpenters' union in America, said in 1883: 'no strike is a loss or a failure to the workers even if the point sought is not gained for the time being. If naught else, they teach the capitalists that they are expensive luxuries to be indulged in' (quoted in P. Taft, *Organized Labor in American History* (New York: Harper and Row, 1964), p. 110).

45. Peterson, op. cit., p. 2.

1926 the Bureau of Labor Statistics began to collect data on strikes, workers involved and other series. In 1927, the work was re-organized and series on striker-days and various cross-classifications of the data introduced. J. I. Griffin[46] attempted to fill the gap from 1906 to 1913 and, since the B.L.S. data for 1914 and 1915 are clearly very incomplete, his figures are also used for these two years.

The four reports of the Commissioner were published in 1888, 1896, 1901 and 1907 covering respectively the periods from 1881 to 1886, 1887 to June 1894, July 1894 to December 1900 and 1901 to 1905. Towards the end of each period, investigators examined newspapers and trade and union journals for information on strikes. Armed with this preliminary knowledge, field investigators went out to seek further details from the parties involved; they were also instructed to include information on any strike which had not been included in the initial survey. Since in some cases events were being studies which had occurred five years or more earlier, it is likely that the Commissioner's evidence is far from completely reliable; but this is counteracted to some extent by the fact that work was done in the field, in contrast to later techniques which have relied on press reports and the like and on answers to questionnaires. It is hard to know how comparable this early information is with that collected by the B.L.S. The Commissioner claimed that his method 'secured information relating to nearly every strike, if not every strike, which occurred in the United States during the period covered' and similar claims have been made for the B.L.S. methods.[47]

In 1914 a survey of printed information on strikes was made and in 1915 the method which has been followed to date was begun. From 'leads' in papers and trade journals questionnaires were sent to the interested parties requesting further information.[48] Over the years the

46. J. I. Griffin, *Strikes: A Study in Quantitative Economics* (New York: Columbia University Press, 1939), pp. 118–29.
47. U.S. Commissioner of Labor, *Third Annual Report, 1887* (Washington, D.C.: Government Printing Office, 1888), p. 10; Peterson, op. cit., p. 170; 'Strikes and Lockouts in the United States in 1916, 1917, 1918 and 1919', *Monthly Labor Review*, X, pp. 1505–24 (1920), at p. 1505.
48. Peterson, op. cit., p. 170. The response rate to the questionnaires has not always been good; in 1919 the B.L.S. reported that of 3,997 sent out only 1,392 were completed in whole or part: *Monthly Labor Review*, VIII, no. 6, p. 307 (1919). This is unlikely to affect the number of strikes recorded, since replies to questionnaires would not turn up any new disputes, but may have led to biases in the reporting of such things as the issues in disputes and the extent of union involvement. Until 1927, the 'not reported' category was quite large for some cross-classifications, but since then reporting has been much more complete.

number of 'leads' has been increased and this has had the effect of increasing the number of strikes recorded although, because the new strikes tend to be small, the number of workers involved and of days lost has been little affected. Thus, while the various claims to have covered nearly all strikes cannot be accepted fully, it seems that worker involvement and striker-days have been fairly well recorded.[49]

The Gap of 1906–15

Griffin has provided estimates of the number of strikes and workers involved and of the causes and results of disputes for the years in which the official figures do not exist or are seriously incomplete.[50] Since seven state bureaus published data for the years in question, he took the sum of the figures they provided and estimated the total for the United States by increasing this amount according to the proportion which these states' strikes held to the total in 1904–05. All the states, except Kansas, are concentrated on the eastern seaboard so that any change in the regional distribution of activity would bias Griffin's figures; similarly, these states do not have an industrial structure identical to that of the country as a whole, and, therefore, shifts of strike activity between industries would not be fully recorded. In 1904–05, the agencies in Griffin's states recorded 89 per cent of the workers involved and 45 per cent of the strikes which the Federal government recorded for these states, so that one would expect the figures for worker involvement to be the more reliable. The only other attempt to fill the statistical gap was made by Hansen,[51] who based his estimates on Canadian data and whose approach is thus much less satisfactory than Griffin's.

Griffin did not test the reliability of his data by using his estimating

---

49. Fisher, op. cit., pp. 129–30. The addition of a new source of leads in 1950 is estimated to have increased the number of strikes reported, above what it would otherwise have been, by about 5 per cent in 1950 and 10 per cent in 1951; since most of these stoppages were small, the effect on the numbers of workers involved and striker-days was about 2 per cent in 1950 and 3 per cent in 1951. See 'Work Stoppages in 1951', *Monthly Labor Review*, LXXIV, pp. 511–19 (1952), at p. 512. The size of the impact on the number of strikes recorded is somewhat disconcerting, and is a further reason to treat the figures with caution. Cf. the claim of Clague that 'most strikes, no matter how small, do get into the local papers, so the Bureau has found that the major source of information on strikes can be obtained from newspaper clippings': E. Clague, *The Bureau of Labor Statistics* (New York: Praeger, 1968), p. 142.
50. See Griffin, op. cit., pp. 118–29.
51. A. H. Hansen, 'Cycles of Strikes', *American Economic Review*, XI, pp. 616–21 (1921).

TABLE B.1

ESTIMATES OF STRIKE ACTIVITY, 1895–1918 (Annual Averages)

	Number of Strikes		Number of Workers Involved (000s)	
	Griffin	Official	Griffin	Official
1895	1188	1255	478.5	407.2
1896	679	1066	249.0	248.8
1897	948	1110	413.0	416.2
1898	855	1098	317.0	263.2
1899	1211	1838	529.6	431.9
1900	1362	1839	379.2	567.7
1901–05		2901		583.9
1906–09	2940	n.a.	386.5	n.a.
1910–13	3132	n.a.	791.5	n.a.
1914–15	3177	1399	767.0	n.a.
1916–18		3864		1355.7

NOTE
Figures for 1895–1900 in the 'Griffin' column have been calculated by Griffin's estimating procedure, with 1901–05 as base. The seven states whose data are used are: Connecticut, Kansas, Maryland, Massachusetts, New Jersey, New York and Rhode Island. The estimates are based on the Commissioner of Labor's data for these states, whereas Griffin's estimates for 1906–15 are based on the reports of each state's bureau of labour statistics, or its equivalent.

SOURCE
See Appendix D, which lists the sources of all data which are not specifically noted.

method to predict to known figures and then comparing his estimates with these figures. This problem is dealt with in Table B.1 by using estimates based on the period 1901–05 to 'predict' strike activity for each of the preceding six years; the table also compares Griffin's and official estimates for the period 1906–18. As expected, Griffin's method performs better for worker involvement than for the number of strikes; in 1896 and 1897 the fit between the predicted and actual figures for worker involvement was very close. The number of strikes was consistently under-estimated, but at least the trend of activity was indicated by the estimated figures. For 1906–15, Griffin's own figures show a notable increase in strike activity, which is consistent with qualitative evidence for these years.[52] The official figures for 1914–15 are very incomplete, but those for 1916–18 are reasonably consistent

52. See D. Montgomery, 'The "New Unionism" and the Transformation of Workers' Consciousness in America, 1909–22', *Journal of Social History,* VII, pp. 509–29 (1974); G. Adams, *Age of Industrial Violence, 1910–15*

with those for earlier and later years. Griffin's estimates are therefore used for the whole of the period 1906–15, with the qualification that the figures for the number of strikes may be substantially under-estimated.

Reliability of Early Reports

The incompleteness of the early B.L.S. reports suggests that there may be a similar problem with the Commissioner of Labor's early data. It is certainly the case that the figures for 1881–84 were lower than those for later years, but there is no way of knowing how far this was a 'real' effect and how far it was due to changing reporting reliability. Such things as the arousal of public interest in industrial conflict after the upsurge of strike activity in 1886[53] may have meant that newspaper reporting of strikes became more thorough. One possible source of bias which can be tested is the effect of the founding of state bureaus of labour statistics; it might be argued that more strikes were recorded where there was a bureau than where there was not. Table B.2 gives the strike figures for seven states, by the date of founding of their bureaus, and compares them with figures for the United States as a whole. Thus in the two years before the New York bureau was established (1881 and 1882) 2,184 establishments were recorded as being involved in strikes, whereas, in the two years after, 1,578 establishments were affected, a decline of 27.7 per cent, compared with a decline in the country as a whole of 7.6 per cent.

If the founding of bureaus affected recording, strike activity in the states concerned would increase more than, or decline less than, that in the country as a whole. The table shows that this was not the case. Although enormous increases in activity were recorded in California, this was from a very small base. For all four of the states whose bureaus were set up in 1883, the number of establishments involved fell faster than it did in the whole country, and the number of strikers rose more slowly. Thus, there is no reason to suppose that there was any signifi-cant bias in the figures from this source.

(New York: Columbia University Press, 1966); M. Dubofsky, *We Shall Be All* (Chicago: Quadrangle Books, 1969); and any standard work on labour history, for example, Taft, op. cit.

53. The year was marked by several strikes for the eight-hour day, considerable activity by the Knights of Labor, then at its peak, and the Haymarket bomb-ing in Chicago, which aroused widespread interest in labour questions.

TABLE B.2

EFFECT OF FOUNDATION OF STATE BUREAUS OF LABOUR STATISTICS ON STRIKE RECORDING

	Number of Establishments Struck			Number of Strikers (000s)		
	2 years Before	2 years After	Per cent Change	2 years Before	2 years After	Per cent Change
Founded 1883						
New York	2148	1578	–27.7	49.6	61.9	24.9
Michigan	104	132	26.9	7.99	6.94	–13.1
Wisconsin	41	23	–43.9	4.07	2.07	–49.0
California	3	49	1530	0.04	1.86	4800
Total above	2332	1782	–23.6	61.7	72.8	18.1
Total U.S.	5033	4651	–7.6	221.9	275.9	24.3
Founded 1884						
Iowa	111	93	–16.2	6.33	3.53	–44.2
Maryland	75	284	279	4.21	11.4	171
Total U.S.	4864	12145	150	243.1	558.7	130
Founded 1885						
Kansas	14	38	171	1.29	1.06	–18.2
Total U.S.	5126	16450	221	239.5	672.9	181

Changes in Recording Practices

On the details of official agencies' recording practices, there are, as has been mentioned above, difficulties with establishing the boundary between strikes and non-strikes and with recording all the small disputes that fall into the former category. In order to achieve reliable series of strikes, most agencies place limits on the size of disputes they record. In the United States since 1927, only those strikes involving at least six workers and lasting at least one full day or shift have been included; it is the latter condition which is the more important since it excludes short stoppages regardless of their size[54] and thus ignores any brief demonstration strikes that may take place. From 1914 to 1926 an attempt was made to count every stoppage. It is not known how successful this attempt was, but the published statistics show that about 3 per cent of recorded strikes lasted less than one day, suggesting that the total number of strikes recorded for this period needs to be reduced

54. Compare the practice in the United Kingdom, where strikes lasting less than a day and involving fewer than ten workers are excluded, unless more than 100 striker-days are involved in a given strike.

by about this amount to make the figures comparable with those after 1927. Unfortunately, no breakdown of duration by workers involved exists for 1914—26, but it is likely, in view of the fact that in later years the great majority of strikers were involved in long strikes, that the bias was much less than 3 per cent.

From 1881 to 1905, only strikes lasting less than one day were excluded, with no minimum on the number of workers involved. However, for the years 1901—05 some information on stoppages of less than one day was collected and reported separately from the main tables on strikes.[55] These stoppages accounted for about 4 per cent of the total number of strikes, which accords well with the above figure of 3 per cent for 1914—26, and only 1 per cent of workers involved were in these short stoppages. However, the Commissioner felt that the data were incomplete because of the insignificance of such strikes and because of the danger that people might not remember them. In an earlier report it had been argued that disturbances of less than one day's duration: 'consist mainly of cases of misunderstanding, in which there was but a few hours' cessation of work and no financial loss or assistance involved. . . They have not been considered sufficiently important to be classed as strikes.'[56] This differs from the usual view that it is in practice hard to measure short stoppages and suggests, instead, that short disputes are not serious enough to be called strikes. This view has some plausibility since a short walk-out after work has begun is likely to differ from a refusal to work one or more whole days; and the conscious act of staying away from work may require a type of decision different from that involved in stopping work in the heat of the moment. Thus strikes lasting a day or longer may be treated as a phenomenon different from strikes in general. Except for 1914—26, only strikes lasting at least one day have been recorded; the exclusion of shorter strikes has not biased the figures very much.

Some indication of the effect of the inclusion, from 1881 to 1905, of strikes by fewer than six men is given in Table B.3 (p. 309), but, before turning to this table, the nature of its construction must be considered. The first two of the Commissioner's reports included detailed information on every strike recorded, in addition to various summary tables. Each strike was entered by state, industry and year, other information recorded included the strike's duration, 'cause' and result, whether or not it was called by a trade union, the number of employees

55. U.S. Commissioner of Labor, *Twenty-first Annual Report, 1906* (Washington. D.C.: Government Printing Office, 1907), pp. 101—2.
56. U.S. Commissioner of Labor, *Tenth Annual Report, 1894* (Washington, D.C.: Government Printing Office, 1896), p. 10.

before the strike, the number of strikers and the number of workers involved.[57] It is thus possible to build up summary tables which the Commissioner did not see fit to include. Table B.3 was constructed by taking the number of workers involved (i.e. strikers plus those thrown out of work by the strike in the struck establishment) in each strike and classifying it into one of the categories shown in the table.

In his first report the Commissioner did not make the strike the unit of analysis, but asked only how many establishments were affected. It was stated that 'the exact number of strikes represented in the tables cannot be stated, nor can the exact number that may occur in any year ever be stated, though a perfect record be had of every such disturbance.'[58] This is a fundamental point, for it is being said that it is in principle impossible to determine where one strike ends and another begins; one must estimate the frequency of industrial disputes by recording the number of establishments affected. It is remarkable that in his next report devoted to strikes the Commissioner dismissed this argument: 'In the present report experience and a great amount of care have made it possible to make the strike or lockout the unit in all cases.'[59] The earlier report had said that, even with perfect information, there would be no clear way to separate one strike from another. In reporting the results of strikes, the establishment was retained as the unit of analysis (despite the claim that the strike was the unit in all cases); thus for the whole period 1881–1905 the Commissioner reported not how many strikes succeeded in their aims but in how many establishments the strikers' demands were met.

It is unfortunate that the early argument of the Commissioner was ignored, since the problems of principle with counting the number of strikes are much greater than those relating to worker involvement. Particularly suspect must be the attempt in the last three reports to re-analyse the data of the first one in order to estimate the number of strikes in 1881–86. While the post-1914 reports state the number of establishments affected, they do not break this down by industry or result.

57. The attempt to distinguish between strikers and 'workers thrown out of work as a result of the strike' was not continued by the B.L.S. Strikers were those 'who actually joined in the demand and followed their demand by a cessation of work', while those involved were the strikers plus other employees of the struck plant thrown out of work: U.S. Commissioner of Labor, *Twenty-first Annual Report,* op. cit., p. 110. The limitation of worker involvement to struck establishments has thus been a constant feature of all the official data.

58. U.S. Commissioner of Labor, *Third Annual Report,* op. cit., p. 11.

59. U.S. Commissioner of Labor, *Tenth Annual Report,* op. cit., p. 13.

TABLE B.3

'CESSATIONS' BY SIZE, 1881–94

Number of Workers Involved	1881–86		1887–94	
	Number	Per Cent	Number	Per Cent
Fewer than 6	259	4.5	854	8.1
6–19	854	14.8	2669	25.4
20–	1195	20.8	2381	22.7
50–	1083	18.8	1414	13.5
100–	1179	20.5	1530	14.6
250–	581	10.1	831	7.9
500–	347	6.0	419	4.0
1000–	169	2.9	244	2.3
2500–	53	0.9	73	0.7
5000 and over	36	0.6	75	0.7
Total	5756	99.9	10496	99.9

Even in the first strike report, there is some ambiguity since not every establishment was included in the detailed tables; in a number of cases a line of a table refers to two or more establishments. It appears, then, that some implicit means was being used to group establishments together and that the investigators had some idea that stoppages for the same end should be seen as one strike, even if they affected more than one plant. Thus the results reported in Table B.3 relate neither to strikes nor to establishments; in view of this, the events from which the data are derived are called 'cessations'. For some years, the number of these was very similar to the number of strikes reported but in others there was a marked divergence.[60]

The table indicates that, in the two periods combined, 6.8 per cent of all 'cessations' involved fewer than six workers; this figure is an approximation to the extent to which the data for 1881–1905 over-state the number of strikes, compared to the post-1927 figures. This is not to say that, even if the size distribution of strikes has remained un-

60. A comparison of the numbers of strikes and cessations for 1881–93 shows that, up to 1886, there were more cessations than strikes: some means of combining separate cessations into one strike must have been employed when the data were re-examined in an attempt to estimate the number of strikes. After 1886, the numbers were more or less equal; the slight differences which occur can be explained by errors in the recording of cessations. For details of the comparison, see P. K. Edwards, 'Strikes in the United States, 1881–1972' (D. Phil, thesis, University of Oxford, 1977), table A–25.

changed, one could estimate the 'true' number of strikes in recent years by increasing the stated number by about 7 per cent (to allow for the non-coverage of short stoppages) and a further 3 per cent (for the strikes of less than one day). It is not known how complete the Commissioner's recording of small strikes was, so one cannot take the numbers in the table as an estimate of the true number of such stoppages. The figures indicate only the extent to which the Commissioner's data are not comparable with those for later years: and since they relate to 'cessations' and not to strikes they give only an approximate indication. On the proportion of all workers involved who were in the small stoppages, one can calculate from Table B.3 that only about 0.1 per cent of the total were in strikes in which fewer than six men were involved, suggesting that the Commissioner's estimate for worker involvement is consistent with data from the B.L.S. It is not surprising that such a small proportion was involved in the very small strike since the figures used were, of course, those for the total number of men 'thrown out of work' as a result of the strike and not those for 'strikers'. Even though less than six men may have struck, it is likely that more than this number would have been affected by the dispute. A corollary of this is that the B.L.S. figures on worker involvement where six or more workers were affected are likely to be a highly reliable index to total worker involvement.

Thus, the changes in recording practice that have occurred over the years have not had a very large effect on the counting of strike activity. Further, the definitions of strikes have remained remarkably constant. For the Commissioner, 'a strike is a concerted withdrawal by a part or all of the employees of an establishment, or several establishments, to enforce a demand on the part of the employees.' For the Bureau of Labor Statistics, 'a strike is a temporary stoppage of work by a group of employees in order to express a grievance or to enforce a demand.'[61] There may be some concern that the Commissioner did not include the expression of a grievance in his formal definition of the strike, but it is clear that in practice he did not restrict himself to cases where there was an obvious demand by the employees; an examination of his four reports, and particularly of the information on individual strikes in the first two, indicates that he included such things as sympathy strikes and other stoppages lacking a clear demand by the strikers.

The Bureau has also included sympathy strikes, presumably because they can be seen as expressing a grievance and because they have some link with the strikers' own conditions of employment. Two other

61. U.S. Commissioner of Labor, *Twenty-first Annual Report*, op. cit., p. 11; Peterson, op. cit., p. 3.

potentially difficult categories are the jurisdictional strike and the political strike. It might be argued that the former is not a true strike because it is not a dispute between employees and their employer, but the Bureau argues that the employer is integral to the situation in that two groups of workers are demanding the assignment of a particular task; similarly, when the dispute is between two rival unions the Bureau argues that there must be discontent among one union's members over the conditions negotiated by the other, so that again the employer is necessarily involved.[62] It is doubtful whether this is true in all cases, but the difficulty of deciding whether the employer is sufficiently involved to call a stoppage caused by rival unionism a strike probably justifies the Bureau in including all such stoppages in its statistics. The Commissioner included strikes 'against the dismissal of a unionist' and 'against employment of members of other unions' and therefore counted as strikes stoppages resulting from disputes between unions or over the allocation of work.

The Bureau's approach to the political strike is to include it if the workers' terms and conditions of employment seem to be involved, but otherwise to exclude it. The decision is taken on a case-by-case basis so that a stoppage by public employees against some legislative action affecting their salaries would be included, whereas a refusal of longshoremen to load cargo destined for particular countries would not.[63] In other words, the attempt is made to restrict the strike statistics to work stoppages in the sense that they are directly related to conditions of work. Political strikes as they are known in some European countries are virtually unknown in the U.S. so that the problems facing the Bureau are not very great. Strikes during the second world war and the so-called 'emergency disputes' since then have certainly involved direct and powerful government intervention, but the stoppages themselves have always been concerned with the terms and conditions of employment. The decision to strike may be taken in the light of probable government action and in practice the strike may be aimed as much against the government as against the employer,[64] but it is the terms of employment which have remained the focus and the Bureau has not been faced with any important problems of classification.

There has been a continuous attempt since 1881 to record the issues

62. Peterson, op. cit., pp. 5–6.
63. Fisher, op. cit., pp. 128–9.
64. This is particularly true of railway disputes, in which the government soon came to play a significant role. See G. G. Eggert, *Railroad Labor Disputes* (Ann Arbor: University of Michigan Press, 1967); J. J. Kaufman, *Collective Bargaining in the Railroad Industry* (New York: King's Crown Press, 1954).

in dispute in strikes but a number of changes have been made in the way these were classified. The Commissioner began by giving extensive listings of the issues involved; since up to 65 groups of cause were distinguished this hid more than it revealed and made the analysis of broad trends of activity virtually impossible.[65] In later reports the data were presented in a more systematic but still far from satisfactory way. Since the B.L.S. adopted its own approach to classifying strike issues in 1914 there have been three important attempts at re-definition (in 1927, 1942 and 1960) and some minor alterations, suggesting that there is no simple answer to the problem. Thus, in analysing the long-term trends, only the broadest categories of issue can be used, although within each period of definitional consistency some further breakdowns are possible.

An examination of these attempts to classify strikes by cause reveals one point of general importance. This is that broadly similar types of dispute have been the object of attention. The official re-appraisals of the procedures have not led to any radically new classifications; for instance, that of 1960 re-ordered the data in terms of the contractual status of the strike,[66] to achieve what was felt to be a more meaningful presentation, but there is a broad similarity with the earlier methods. This supports the view that what has been defined as a strike has remained constant over the years, and also suggests that the broad categories of 'wages and hours', 'union organization' and 'working conditions' can be used for comparative purposes.

Since the presentation of information on the results of strikes has been discontinued, the figures that are available have to be used with particular caution. The statistics report whether the results were generally favourable to the workers or to the employer or whether a compromise was achieved. While these categories do not say much about the broad question of how far strikes have improved the conditions of the workers, they can be of some use; for instance, one can examine the effect of economic conditions on the rate of success and differences in the success rate of strikes in which various issues were involved.

Thus, what the official agencies count as a strike and how they go about recording stoppages have had a considerable degree of consistency. Critics of the American statistics have pointed out that short strikes are ignored and that the information is incomplete and cannot

---

65. Griffin, op. cit., p. 73. For a description of the B.L.S. procedures for all the main strike indices, see Peterson, op. cit., pp. 163–9.
66. That is, one broad division was made of all strikes which involved demands for changes in the terms of the contract between union and employer.

be reduced to statistical form.[67] The first criticism seems to imply that the amount of conflict is under-estimated in the official data and that a more complete recording would show a more 'correct' figure. This argument is valid in attacking those who argue that there are really very few strikes and that collective bargaining is 90 to 95 per cent effective (since only 5 to 10 per cent of negotiations lead to strikes).[68] There is an unknown number of small strikes, so that these sanguine estimates must be rejected. But for the analysis of trends of industrial conflict the argument is not pertinent: the interest is not in the amount of conflict but with seeing if there is more at one time than another.

5. Summary and Conclusion

The previous sections have suggested that it is possible to consider strike statistics in terms of standard measurement theory, and that the American data have sufficient reliability to be used in the analysis of trends of activity. On the first point, the difficulties which exist with all official statistics are much less severe for strikes than for some other forms of activity. The concept of the strike is part of everyday life and is not imposed by outside observers. To a very large extent, 'members' have a set of shared meanings relating to what a strike is, although this does not preclude disagreement over what a given action signifies. Strikes are a recognized part of the employment relationship and their meaning at one level is not mysterious: they involve the collective refusal to work on the existing terms. An even stronger case for the unimportance of individual meanings could be made if strikes could be defined without any element of intentionality. But, first, official agencies operate with the view that strikes intend to enforce a demand or express a grievance, so that nothing would be gained from establishing a different definition. Secondly, the intentional aspect is necessary because it stresses that strikes are conscious collective actions. But, 'for all practical purposes', this aspect of the definition raises few problems

67. S. Lens, *Left, Right and Center* (Hinsdale, Illinois: Henry Regnery, 1949), p. 355; A. M. Bing, *War-Time Strikes and Their Adjustment* (New York: E. P. Dutton, 1921), p. 291. See also H. G. Gutman, 'The Worker's Search for Power: Labor in the Gilded Age', *The Gilded Age: A Reappraisal*, ed. H. W. Morgan (New York: Syracuse University Press, 1963), pp. 38–68, at p. 46.
68. The 90 per cent figure is from *The Trade Union Situation in the United States* (Geneva: International Labour Office, 1960), p. 32. A figure of 'more than 95 per cent' is given by the editors, 'Problems and Viewpoints', *Industrial Conflict*, ed. Kornhauser, Dubin and Ross, op. cit., pp. 3–23, at p. 11.

because the 'expression of a grievance' is a very broad category; it is very unlikely that many collective work stoppages are excluded from the strike category solely because no clear grievance seems to be involved.

Turning to traditional measurement theory, several levels of validity can be distinguished. Firstly, there is the question whether the official agencies measure what they set out to measure; in the American case, this refers to the number of strikes involving at least six workers and lasting at least one day. Since small and short strikes are excluded, recording problems are kept within bounds, but the rise in the number of strikes counted when the 'leads' on strike activity are improved shows that a complete census of all stoppages is not obtained. However, counts of workers involved and days lost are more accurate. A second level of validity concerns the extent to which the strike figures cover stoppages which are excluded from the official definition. The estimates given above of the effect of excluding small and short disputes relate only to differences between the practices of different recording agencies and not to the true extent of such disputes. Several writers have studied the number of strikes in particular firms or industries and noted that this is often much greater than the number officially recorded.[69] If this is repeated throughout the economy, strike frequency is not a very close estimate of the total number of strikes; again, however, workers involved and days lost are much more fully recorded because they are concentrated in the large disputes.

The third level of validity involves the question of whether strikes can serve as an index of 'general unrest'. It is not useful to look at strikes in this way. First, 'unrest', assuming that the term can be given an unambiguous meaning, is likely to find its expression in many forms, some overt and others hidden from all but the most detailed enquiries. Secondly, strike activity reflects many things other than 'fundamental' discontent. It is preferable, therefore, to see the strike as an important form of conflict in its own right; trends of activity may reveal certain features of labour-management relations, but the focus on fundamental discontents is not helpful in doing this.

Although the validity of strike measures is open to question, their reliability can be established more firmly. In the United States, at least, recording practices have remained remarkably stable and the differences in strike definitions do not seem to have had a very great effect on the number of stoppages counted. It is not useful to ask how much conflict

69. See references in note 28 above; and, for example, J. W. Kuhn, *Bargaining in Grievance Settlement* (New York: Columbia University Press, 1961), p. 158.

there is; rather, trends and inter-industry patterns should be the focus. Thus the reliability of the indices is more important than their validity, given that some minimum level of validity is attained; the reliability of the worker involvement and days-lost measures is greater than that of strike frequency, because changes in recording practices have had a less marked effect. But trends in the number of strikes can be used since year-to-year fluctuations are unlikely to be heavily affected by the unreliability of the figures.

Appendix C

The Statistical Description of Strike Activity

Official agencies generally provide information on the number of strikes and the numbers of workers involved and days lost in them.[1] The problem has been how to combine this information in the most meaningful way. As Spielmans puts it, one seeks a way to present strike data which leads: 'to a more distinct, because more integrated, picture of the strike phenomenon than the mere "greater-or-less" comparison of the several strike figures as such.'[2] Spielmans himself proposes the use of 'strike rectangles', the sides of which measure the number of workers involved in strikes and the number of days lost per worker involved. Writing W for worker involvement and D for the number of days lost, the second dimension can be expressed as D/W and the area of the rectangle is thus, of course, W x D/W, or the total number of days lost.

There are two obvious criticisms of Spielmans's procedure. Firstly, the number of strikes is ignored. Spielmans considers that this is, in fact, an advantage since the American recording agencies will count as a single strike any stoppage covering from six to several thousand men.[3] The category of 'one strike' is therefore far from homogeneous. However, this criticism also applies to the dimension of worker involvement, which Spielmans is quite happy to use. Moreover, despite the difficulties with the number of strikes examined in Appendix B, the measure of strike frequency is of considerable theoretical interest and should not be ignored. The second criticism concerns the D/W index. As

1. For a comprehensive review of these and other indices available to various countries see M. R. Fisher, *Measurement of Labour Disputes and their Economic Effects* (Paris: Organization for Economic Co-operation and Development, 1973).
2. J. V. Spielmans, 'Strike Profiles', *Journal of Political Economy*, LII, pp. 319–39 (1944), at p. 319.
3. Ibid., p. 321.

316

Spielmans is aware, this measures not the mean duration of strikes but 'the number of days which would account for the total of man-days idle if all workers in the particular class of strikes had been idle the same length of time.'[4] In other words, the number of days lost per striker is not an unbiased measure of the duration of the mean strike. This is shown in the following hypothetical case:

	W	Duration	D
Strike A	10	10 days	100
Strike B	90	1 day	90
Total	100	11 days	190

For the sum of the two strikes, D/W is 1.9 but the mean duration is 5.5 days.

The distinction between mean duration and D/W has often been obscured. Ross and Hartman, for example, refer to D/W simply as the duration of strikes.[5] It is important to keep the distinction in mind since D/W, or 'loss per worker involved', measures the number of days for which the 'average striker' stopped work whereas the mean duration of strikes indicates the average time taken to settle individual disputes. In this study, both measures are used, and D/W employed alone only where no data on mean duration are available.

The method adopted by Forchheimer and Knowles[6] overcomes the first problem with Spielmans' approach, namely the failure to consider the number of strikes. The number of days lost in strikes can be thought of as the product of the number of strikes, their mean size and the number of days lost per striker: writing N for the number of strikes, D is identical to:

$$N \times W/N \times D/W.$$

As Knowles points out, this multiplicative relationship can be translated into an additive one by taking the logarithms of the three parts of this expression; the results can then be expressed graphically. A comparison

4. Ibid., pp. 319–20.
5. A. M. Ross and P. T. Hartman, *Changing Patterns of Industrial Conflict* New York: Wiley, 1960), p. 12.
6. K. Forchheimer, 'Some International Aspects of the Strike Movement', *Bulletin of the Oxford University Institute of Statistics*, X, pp. 9–24 (1948), at p. 10; K. G. J. C. Knowles, *Strikes: A Study in Industrial Conflict* (Oxford: Blackwell, 1952), pp. 152–3.

of the charts used by Spielmans and Knowles reveals the advantages of the new method of presentation; instead of a confusing series of rectangles which cover a great deal of space, there is a continuous graph whose components are readily identified. But the problem of relying on D/W as the measure of duration remains, and Knowles' mode of presentation is therefore not followed here.

A second problem with both approaches considered above is that they do not allow for changes in employment. They deal in terms of the absolute number of days lost in strikes, whereas for comparisons over long periods of time it is important to deflate this figure with a measure of employment. Britt and Galle have recently re-formulated Knowles's identity-statement to take account of this point.[7] Writing E for the level of employment, the number of days lost per head, D/E, is identical to:

$$ N \times \frac{W}{N \times E} \times \frac{D}{W} $$

This method is also unsatisfactory, however, since the second term measures neither the size of strikes (W/N) nor the number of workers involved per employee (W/E). At the same time, N is left unadjusted even though one would expect, other things equal, that there will be more strikes the larger the work force. It is true that one might also expect the size of strikes to rise with the size of the work force, but the argument for this is less clear-cut than that relating to the number of strikes. The size of strikes is likely to be influenced by such things as the size of plants and bargaining units, which bear no necessary relationship to total employment.[8] Thus, it is preferable to leave W/N unadjusted, since the absolute size of strikes is of considerable interest, and introduce the correction for employment into the series for strike frequency.

Thus, the most useful components of strike activity are the frequency (N/E), size (W/N), and 'duration' (D/W) of disputes. However, attention should not be restricted to these three indices since worker

7. D. Britt and O. R. Galle, 'Industrial Conflict and Unionization', *American Sociological Review*, XXXVII, pp. 46–57 (1972), at p. 48. In a footnote they assert, surprisingly, that the 'original component definition and isolation' come from an unpublished paper by Galle and P. Mariolis.
8. But note that Britt and Galle are concerned with cross-sectional and not time-series analysis, and that W/N may in this case need deflating to take account of employment. However, even here it seems more sensible to correct the number of strikes for the level of employment in a given sector.

involvement (W/E), loss per head (D/E) and mean duration may also be of interest. Thus, this study does not restrict attention to one formula but uses all six measures to chart trends in strike activity. It may appear that this path leads to Spielmans's trap of 'mere "greater-or-less" comparison', but this trap relates not so much to the precise indices employed but to the use which is made of them. It is mindless description which is to be avoided, and not the use of several different indices. If a given measure is of theoretical value, it should be used, regardless of whether it fits neatly into a pre-existing schema for the representation of dimensions of strike activity.

In the discussion of the overall 'shape' of strikes, the method of Shorter and Tilly,[9] rather than that of Knowles, is followed. As noted above, D/W is not a true measure of duration: more important is the trend in the duration of the average strike, since this indicates the speed of settlement of disputes, which is, in turn, of particular interest to the theory of the institutionalization of conflict. In addition, data on the number of days lost in strikes are not available for the period before 1927 so that, for the analysis of long-term trends, it is preferable to concentrate on mean duration.

Shorter and Tilly use the frequency and size of strikes and a measure of average duration as their key dimensions and draw boxes to represent the volume of activity, each dimension being used for one side of each box. This method is more clumsy than the graphical representation used by Knowles, but this is unavoidable if average duration is used instead of D/W, since the volume of strike activity (D/E) is no longer identical to the product of the three dimensions. However the theoretical advantages of using average duration, together with the practical point that data on D/W are unavailable before 1927, outweigh this disadvantage.

Shorter and Tilly prefer the median to the mean as a measure of average duration so that extreme values will not be given disproportionate weight; and one may add that the median has the advantage, when calculating from a frequency distribution, of being relatively unambiguous, whereas the estimate for the mean will depend on one's assumptions about how strikes are distributed over the final open-ended category (in America, 'ninety days and over'). However, the mean has the advantage of giving some sense to the volume of the box generated by the three dimensions. Since the median represents only the mid-value of the duration dimension, the volume of the box is ambiguous;

9. E. Shorter and C. Tilly, *Strikes in France, 1830–1968* (Cambridge: Cambridge University Press, 1974), pp. 51–6.

although replacing the median with the mean does not produce a simple identity-statement, it does lead to a formula which is conceptually clear, with strike volume being composed of the frequency, size and mean duration of strikes. Both the median and the mean are therefore used in drawing boxes to represent the shape of strikes.

Appendix D
Sources and Methods

The first section of this Appendix lists the sources of data not specifically acknowledged. It also indicates the methods used in estimating consistent series. It is not possible to detail every case in which two or more series have been amalgamated to create one long-run series; in general series have been linked in the conventional fashion whereby, when two series overlap, one is estimated in terms of the other on the basis of the period of overlap. The second section briefly considers more general problems concerned with the industrial classification used and the nature of employment statistics. Salient points on the regression technique employed are considered in the final section.

1. Sources of Data

This section lists the sources of all data which are not mentioned specifically in footnotes or notes to tables. Pieces of information are listed according to the order in which they appear in the text; table numbers are also used for ease of reference. The following abbreviations are used:

Hist. Stats.   U.S. Bureau of the Census, *Historical Statistics of the United States, Colonial Times to 1957* (Washington, D.C.: Government Printing Office, 1960).

Stat. Abstr.   U.S. Bureau of the Census, *Statistical Abstract of the United States* (Washington, D.C.: Government Printing Office, annual).

Annual Strike Data
1881–1905:   The following *Annual Reports* of the U.S. Commissioner of Labor (Washington, D.C.: Government Printing

Office): *Third, 1887* (1888), *Tenth, 1894* (1896), *Sixteenth, 1901* (1901) and *Twenty-first, 1905* (1907).

1906–15:   J. I. Griffin, *Strikes: A Study in Quantitative Economics* (New York: Columbia University Press, 1939), pp. 38, 43. For details of Griffin's estimating procedure, see above, Appendix B, pp. 303–5.

1916–36:   F. Peterson, *Strikes in the United States, 1880–1936* (Washington, D.C.: Department of Labor Bulletin no. 651, 1938); annual articles on 'Strikes and Lockouts' or 'Work Stoppages' in *Monthly Labor Review,* usually May or June issue.

1937–58:   Annual articles in *Monthly Labor Review;* reports in *Stat. Abstr.*

1959–74:   Department of Labor, *Analysis of Work Stoppages* (Washington, D.C.: Government Printing Office, annual). The Bulletin numbers (year of publication in brackets) are: 1278 (1960), 1302 (1961), 1339 (1962), 1381 (1963), 1420 (1964), 1460 (1965), 1525 (1966), 1573 (1968), 1611 (1969), 1646 (1970), 1687 (1971), 1727 (1972), 1777 (1973), 1813 (1974), 1877 (1975) and 1902 (1976).

Employment
1881–96:   Data in Griffin, op. cit., p. 61, on total gainful employment, multiplied by the proportion of non-agricultural employment in the total, to give estimates of non-agricultural employment. This method gives a very similar trend to that of figures given by J. G. Williamson, *Late Nineteenth Century American Development* (Cambridge: Cambridge University Press, 1974), p. 298.

1887–1920:   Calculated from figures in L. Troy, *Trade Union Membership, 1897–1962* (New York: National Bureau of Economic Research, 1965), p. 2.

1921–74:   Bureau of Labor Statistics (B.L.S.) figures, given in *Hist. Stats,* p. 73 and *Stat. Abstr.* Note that the figures relate to 'employment in non-agricultural establishments' and not to the 'non-agricultural civilian labor force'. Estimates for the former are generally somewhat higher than those for the latter.

Trade Union Membership

1881–96:   Griffin, op. cit., p. 107.

1897–1930:   Troy, loc. cit. Figures up to 1930 include Canadian members of American unions.

1931–74:   B.L.S. figures given in *Hist. Stats.* p. 73 and *Stat. Abstr.* The estimating procedure differs from Troy's (for details, see Troy, op. cit., pp. 10–11, 17), but the trends are similar.

Employment in Industry (Figure A.1 p. 279)

1881–1905:   Data on manufacturing calculated from Census of Manufactures data for 1880, 1890, and 1900, given in *Stat. Abstr., 1903,* pp. 511–26. For non-manufacturing: S. Lebergott, *Manpower in Economic Growth* (New York: McGraw-Hill, 1964), pp. 510–12. A check on the estimates for manufacturing was made using S. Fabricant, *Employment in Manufacturing, 1899–1939* (New York: National Bureau of Economic Research, 1942).

1906–26:   Coal industry: Lebergott, loc. cit. Clothing: as for 1927–72.

1927–72:   Manufacturing: biennial Census data up to 1939 (intervening years estimated by interpolation), annual data after 1939, given in *Stat. Abstr.,* various years. Non-manufacturing: data on gainfully-employed workers, given in *Hist. Stats.,* p. 73 and *Stat. Abstr.*

Strike Data by Industry (Figure A.1)

As for annual strike data, plus:

Clothing, 1906–13:   Figures for strikes in the New York industry, given in Griffin, op. cit., p. 166. National figures estimated on assumption that the percentage rise from 1901–05 was repeated nationally. This is reasonable in view of the heavy concentration of the industry in New York: as late as the 1930s, 75 per cent of the industry was located in New York State. See H. Harris, *American Labor* (New Haven: Yale University Press, 1939), p. 220.

Coal, 1906–26:   U.S. Geological Survey data, reported in *Stat. Abstr.,* especially *1921,* p. 348, *1930,* p. 715, and *1936,* p. 718. The comparability of these figures with those of the B.L.S. is hard to estimate, but inspection of the two series suggests that the effect was not substantial.

Unemployment Series
1881–99: Williamson, op. cit., p. 304, adjusted to be consistent with B.L.S. figures for later years.

1900–74: B.L.S. figures, given in *Hist. Stats.* p. 73 and *Stat. Abstr.*

Money Wage Trends
All figures are for average full-time earnings in all industries.

Annual earnings: Hist. *Stats,* pp, 91–92; *Stat. Abstr.*

Hourly earnings: 1890–1957: H. G. Lewis, *Unionism and Relative Wages in the United States* (Chicago: University of Chicago Press, 1963), pp. 75–6. 1958–74: B.L.S. figures, given in *Stat. Abstr.*

Consumer Price Index
Series with different base years have been linked to give a consistent series with 1947–49 set at 100.

1890–1926: E. W. Bakke, C. Kerr and C. W. Anrod (eds), *Unions, Management and the Public* (2nd edn; New York: Harcourt, Brace and Co., 1960), pp. 526–7.

1927–74: Hist. Stats, p. 125 and *Stat. Abstr.*

Quarterly Data, 1962–72
(Tables 3.6, p. 74, 6.3, p. 179.) All figures compiled from monthly data given in *Monthly Labor Review,* various issues. Except for contract expirations, data are given in statistical tables, because of constant revision of estimates to new 'bench-marks', several series have had to be linked to give a consistent set of observations. Data on contract expirations relate to the expiration dates specified in contracts covering 5,000 or more workers (1962–66) or 1,000 or more workers (1967–72), reported in the *Review* for December 1961–66 and January 1968–72. Contracts covering at least 5,000 workers are estimated to account for about one-third of all workers covered by a collective agreement.

Political Variables
(Table 3.9, p. 80.) *Hist. Stats,* pp. 682–3, 691 and *Stat. Abstr.*
Note that the 'per cent Democrat' variable is calculated as the proportion of the total number of seats held by Democrats and Republicans, third parties being excluded.

Industrial Employment: Immigration
(Table 4.1, p. 87.)

Industrial Employment as Per Cent of Total: Williamson, op. cit. p. 295. *Immigration: Hist. Stats*, pp. 56–7, 60–61.

Employment by Industry, 1881–1905
(Tables 4.5, p. 97, 4.10, p. 106, and 4.11, p. 112.)
For several industries, information is incomplete because not all industry divisions were identified in all Census reports. Estimates have been made by interpolation or assuming that the proportionate change in parts of an industry where data are not available was the same as in parts where figures are given.

Manufacturing: Census data, adapted for periods of strike activity as explained in note to Table 4.10.

Non-manufacturing: Labergott, loc. cit.

Indices of Employer Well-being
(Tables 5.5, p. 150, and 6.2, p. 177.)

Productivity: 1927–69: J. W. Kendrick, *Productivity Trends in the United States* (Princeton: Princeton University Press, 1961), Table A.22; idem, *Postwar Productivity Trends in the United States, 1948–69* (New York: National Bureau of Economic Research, 1973), Table A.19. 1970–72: B.L.S. figures reported in *Stat. Abstr.*, corrected to be consistent with Kendrick.

Profits: 1927–60: G. J. Stigler, *Capital and Rates of Return in Manufacturing Industries* (Princeton: Princeton University Press, 1963), errata statement p. 8. 1961–72: B.L.S. figures, reported in *Stat. Abstr.*, corrected to be consistent with Stigler. Figures relate to the rate of profit, at book value after tax.

Wholesale Prince Index: Hist. Stats, p. 116; *Stat. Abstr.*

Strike Data by Industry
(Table 5.6, p. 152, and following tables.)
As for annual strike data, plus the following B.L.S. Reports: (Washington, D.C.: Government Printing Office, various dates). *Work Stoppages: Basic Steel Industry, 1901–60*, no. 206 (1961): *Work Stoppages: Motor Vehicles and Motor Vehicle Equipment Industry, 1927–58*, no. 148 (1959); *Work Stoppages: Aircraft and Parts Industry, 1927–59*, no. 175 (1961).

Industry and State Model
(Table 5.11, p. 164.)

Strike Data: Peterson, op. cit., Table 33.

Employment Data: Department of Labor, *Employment and Earnings, States and Areas, 1939–69* (Washington D.C.: Bulletin no. 1370–7, 1970). This gives figures for 1947, which is the earliest year for which adequate data exist; some bias in estimating strike frequency for 1927–36 must result.

City Characteristics
(Table 5.12, p. 167.)
All characteristics from *Stat. Abstr. 1932.*

Industry Characteristics
(Table 6.13, p. 203, 6.14, p. 206.)

Wages, employment, number of establishments, number of union members: Stat. Abstr., figures for 1960.

Concentration ratio: H. J. Sherman, *Profits in the United States* (Ithaca: Cornell University Press, 1968), p. 85; figures for 1954.

Agreements with strike bans: calculated from Department of Labor, *Major Collective Bargaining Agreements: Arbitration Procedures* (Washington, D.C.: Bulletin no. 1425–6, 1966), pp. 7, 84.

Proportion of workers covered by agreements at plant, company or multi-plant level: Department of Labor, *Handbook of Labor Statistics, 1968* (Washington, D.C.: Bulletin no. 1600, 1968), p. 316.

Production to non-production workers: G. E. Delehanty, *Nonproduction Workers in U.S. Manufacturing* (Amsterdam: North-Holland, 1968), Table A.4.

Technology dummies and rank scores: P. S. Florence, *Economics and Sociology of Industry* (2nd edn; London: C. A. Watts, 1969), pp. 268–9.

Collective Bargaining Coverage
(Table 6.15, p. 210.)
F. Peterson, *American Labor Unions* (2nd edn; New York: Harper and Row, 1963), p. 150, figures for 1960.

2. Problems of Method

The Industrial Classification Used

Since the inter-industry analysis is concerned with broad changes in the distribution of strike activity and in the 'parameters of conflict', fairly wide industry-groups have been used. Problems of comparability over a long time preclude the use of very detailed categories. Thus, for the most recent period, analysis has not gone beyond the 'two-digit' classification of the official agencies. Although there have been some changes of definition, these have not been serious, and it has been possible to develop reasonably consistent data from 1927. As noted in Chapter 5, the attribution of strikes to industry-groups in 1916–26 was much less systematic than in later years, and the information which can be gleaned is not strictly comparable to that for the post-1927 period (see Table A.13).

The problems with the classifications used by the Commissioner of Labor are more serious, particularly since the initial method (referred to here as the '1886' classification) was replaced by a new and more detailed breakdown (the '1906' classification). Moreover, the categories used in the reporting of strikes were not always the same ones as those used in the Census of Manufactures to record employment, wages and so forth. For these reasons, and also to reduce the number of categories to manageable proportions, the Commissioner's categories have been grouped together, as shown in Table D.1. It will be seen that the industry-groups identified are broadly comparable to those used in later years.

Employment Data

As noted above, the employment data used to deflate the aggregate strike indices are for employment in non-agricultural establishments. It is conventional in international comparisons to exclude agriculture, so that figures are not distorted in countries with a large agricultural labour force. For comparability, this convention has been followed here, with the additional advantage that industry-specific strike rates can be compared directly with national rates. Figures for the period up to 1920 are only rough estimates since they are derived by indirect methods and since the original data on employment are probably far from fully accurate. They are sufficient, however, to indicate the general trend in employment, which is all that is required when a deflator of the crude strike figures is required.

For individual industries figures for the employment of production workers have been used wherever possible. The analytical reason for

TABLE D.1

INDUSTRIAL CLASSIFICATION, 1881–1905

	1886 Classification	1906 Classification
Boot and shoe	Boot and shoe	Boot and shoe
Brewing	Brewing	Brewing
Brick	Brick and tile	Brick and tile
Building	Building	Building
Clothing	Clothing	Clothing, gloves, hats and hosiery, millinery
Coal	Coal and coke	Coal and coke, mining
Cooperage	Cooperage	Cooperage
Food	Food	Bakery, canning, confectionary, flour milling, slaughtering and meat packing
Glass	Glass	Glass
Leather	Leather	Harness, leather
Lumber	Lumber	Lumber, planing mill products
Machinery	Agricultural implements, machinery	Agric. implements, gas and electric apparatus, foundry products
Metals: tin and steel		Iron and steel, tin and sheet metal
stove and furnace		Stove and furnace
other		Blacksmith, brass, cutlery, hardware, ironware and jewellery, metal goods, smelting
Printing and publishing	Printing and publishing	Lithography, printing and publishing
Public ways and works	Public ways, public works	Public ways, public works
Rubber	Rubber	Rubber
Stone and clay	Pottery and stone	Lime and cement, pottery, stone
Tobacco	Tobacco	Tobacco
Transport: Railroad		Railroad
other		Street railway, telegraphy, water transport

NOTE

In 1886, all metals industries were given together, as were all transport and communication industries.

The listing does not include every sub-category used by the Commissioner of Labor; for example, men's and women's clothing were included separately.

In 1906 the total number of categories used ran to over seventy. But the listing is sufficient to indicate how these detailed categories were combined into useful aggregates.

this is that these figures give a closer indication of the employment of manual workers than do data on total employment. Thus, comparisons between industries are less influenced than would otherwise be the case by differential levels of employment of non-manual workers. There is also the practical reason that consistent series on production workers' employment are more readily available. For non-manufacturing it is necessary to rely on the number of people gainfully employed; this tends to bias the employment figures upwards, compared with manufacturing, and thus calculations of strike rates downwards. It is hard to estimate the extent of this effect because the meaning of being a 'production' worker differs between manufacturing and non-manufacturing, which is probably why data on the number of production workers in non-manufacturing are not available in the first place. But the effect is unlikely to destroy the comparability of the figures, since the great majority of workers on non-manufacturing are employed in jobs which are directly related to production. For the period 1881–1905, data relate to the numbers of 'wage earners' in each industry; this is the closest approximation to the later series on 'production workers'.

In calculating averages of strike rates for a number of years the following method has been employed. The total number of strikes, for example, was calculated and divided by the total of the employment estimates for each years. This seems preferable to the alternative method of calculating rates for each year and then averaging these rates, since it gives a more direct and readily-understood measure.

3. Regression Techniques

The general characteristics of regression methods are well-known and need no repetition here. But they have become increasingly popular in the study of strike trends, and some indication of the link between the methods used here and in other studies is called for. The aim is to assess the general relationship between groups of independent variables and strike activity over long time spans. For reasons expounded in Chapter 3, it was not found useful to develop a rigorous 'micro' model and then 'test' it against the strike data. Thus it has not been necessary to discuss at length the most appropriate way in which a given variable might be entered into the regression equations. For example, the 'rate of change of wages' could be, and has been, measured in a wide variety of ways. The interest here is not in the most appropriate way in which a micro concept can be measured empirically (if, indeed, there is any clear means of preferring one method to another, except in terms of how 'good' the final results are), but in the general association between such things as wage changes and the level of strike activity. Variables have been entered in the simplest and most straightforward way. Although apparently 'simple-minded', this is preferable to sophisticated exercises which ignore the problem of relating 'macro' findings to 'micro' theories.

Linear techniques have generally been employed but, as indicated in the text, several linear transformations have also been applied and the results reported where they have been of interest. These transformations made little difference in the time-series analysis, but the inter-industry results suggested that various curvilinear relationships may be present. These clearly warrant further investigation.

In contrast to conventional approaches, certain unsuccessful regression results have been reported where these results go against theoretical expectations. In general, however, there are obvious dangers in relying on negative results, and most conclusions are based on experiments which meet the conventional requirements of a reasonably high R^2 and an acceptable Durbin–Watson statistic (in time-series analysis) or significant F statistic (in cross-sectional analysis). In addition, checks have been made for the existence of multicollinearity; these are reported in detail in only two cases for reasons of space.

Index of Authorities Cited

General Index